The Military in the Third World

# The Military in the Third World

GAVIN KENNEDY

DUCKWORTH

First published in 1974 by
Gerald Duckworth & Co. Ltd.
The Old Piano Factory
43 Gloucester Crescent, London NW1

© 1974 Gavin Kennedy

ISBN 07156 0734 0


Typesetting by
Specialised Offset Services Limited, Liverpool

Printed in England by
The Garden City Press Limited
Letchworth, Hertfordshire SG6 1JS

# Contents

Preface                                                              ix

Chapter One     Introduction

Chapter Two     Violence and Ideology
    1. Introduction                                                  12
    2. The Permanent Revolution                                      12
    3. The Legitimacy Thesis                                         21
    4. The Legitimacy Crisis and Military Intervention               23

Chapter Three     Violence and Governments
    1. Introduction                                                  31
    2. Violence in the Party States                                  33
    3. Violence in the Monarchical States                           40
    4. Violence in the Military States                               44
    5. Conclusion                                                    52

Chapter Four     The Role of the Military
    1. Introduction                                                  55
    2. The Role of the Military                                      55
    3. The Political Machines                                        62
    4. Political Independence                                        65

Chapter Five     Intervention in Africa
    1. Introduction                                                  69
    2. Sierra Leone                                                  70
    3. Nigeria                                                       76
    4. Ghana                                                         84
    5. Conclusions                                                   87

Chapter Six     The Military in Pakistan and Indonesia
    1. Introduction                                                  89
    2. Pakistan                                                      89
    3. Indonesia                                                     94

Chapter Seven    Arab Military Interventions
  1. Introduction                                      104
  2. Egypt                                             105
  3. The Rise of Nasserism                             106
  4. Syria and Iraq: Inter-active Intervention         112
  5. Syria                                             115
  6. Iraq                                              118

Chapter Eight    The Politics of Non-intervention
  1. Introduction                                      127
  2. Mexico                                            127
  3. Turkey                                            137
  4. Israel                                            146
  5. Conclusion                                        152

Chapter Nine    Politics and Defence Budgets
  1. Introduction                                      155
  2. Political Issues                                  156
  3. Welfare and Defence                               165
  4. Conclusion                                        172

Chapter Ten    Defence and Growth
  1. Introduction                                      175
  2. Growth and Defence                                178
  3. Per Capita Product                                180
  4. Growth of Per Capita Product                      183
  5. Conclusion                                        188

Chapter Eleven    The Economics of War: Nigeria
  1. Introduction                                      190
  2. The Nigeria-Biafra War                            190
  3. Oil                                               197
  4. Federal and State Budgets                         200
  5. The Economic Cost                                 202
  6. The Army                                          205
  7. Conclusion                                        207

Chapter Twelve    The Economics of War: Vietnam's
                  Asian Neighbours
  1. Introduction                                      208

2. Asia and Vietnam War                                    208
3. Thailand                                                219
4. Conclusion                                              225

Chapter Thirteen    The Economics of War: Israel,
                    Egypt and Pakistan
1. Introduction                                            227
2. Israel                                                  227
3. Egypt                                                   234
4. Pakistan                                                240
5. Conclusions                                             245

Chapter Fourteen    Local Arms Races
1. Introduction                                            250
2. General Situation                                       250
3. The Major Suppliers                                     254
4. The Regional Balance                                    258
5. The Middle East                                         260
6. The Indian Sub-Continent                               265
7. Africa                                                  273
8. Conclusion                                              281

Chapter Fifteen    Arms Production: The Issues
1. Introduction                                            283
2. Some Problems of Development                            285
3. Features of Military Development                        291
4. The Arms Producers                                      293
5. The Manufacturing Base                                 295
6. Conclusion                                              301

Chapter Sixteen    Arms Production: The Products
1. Introduction                                            302
2. Small Arms                                              302
3. Armour                                                  304
4. Naval Construction                                      312
5. Aircraft Production                                     318
6. Conclusion                                              325

Chapter Seventeen    Disarmament
1. Introduction                                            326

2. The World Armaments Situation 327
3. Disarmament and Development 330
4. Conclusion 335

Appendix A: *Military Interventions in the Third World 1945-1972*

Appendix B: *Political Violence in the Third World 1968-1971*

Bibliography 348
Index 362

# *Preface*

It is almost inevitable in writing about contemporary events that between completion of the manuscript and publication of the book some new events take place. There is always the risk that the new events will date the analysis, or worse, reverse its conclusions. Discussion of the military in the Third World is particularly susceptible to this; the crises that produce the military solution are themselves volatile in their outcomes, often making predictions that appear secure at the time of writing redundant within months.

Happily, at least for the author, time has inflicted little damage on this book's major themes. If anything it has confirmed them. It is particularly encouraging that so distinguished an economist as Emile Benoit, in his recent book *Defence and Growth in Developing Economies* (New York 1973), which became available in the UK after this book was written, has come to similar conclusions on the role of military spending in developing countries. Benoit characteristically confesses to his 'surprise' at the results of his detailed empirical analysis. With Benoit leading the field, I feel less of a heretic over my own approach to defence and development than I did when I began work in 1971.

The Arab-Israeli war of October 1973 has altered some aspects of this book's treatment of the balance of power in the Middle East. The analysis stood up, however, to the test of events, erring only in an over-pessimistic appraisal of the fighting fitness of the Egyptian armed forces, something this book shares with most other analyses. The essential point made in the text, that the Arabs could defeat Israel only if they prevented Israel from using its blitzkreig strategy — by holding them in combat for some weeks rather than days — was confirmed by the October war. The Arab attack caught, and kept, the Israeli forces off balance. As each day passed Israel committed more and more of its vital resources just to hold the line. If the Israeli counter-attack across the canal had failed — and evidence from the *Sunday Times* Insight report shows that the margin was wafer-thin — the war should have been a minimal, but real, victory for the Arabs. The Six Day War of 1967 was a military victory unquestionably, but it was a political defeat if the costs of the 'peace' are examined. The October war will be followed by another as inevitably as the Six Day War was a prelude to 1973 unless a political settlement is made, and made soon. As stated in the text, the real military threat to Israel, from outside, is containable for the present but will become less so as time goes by. The other military threat to Israel, from inside, in the form of a coup, is not totally excluded as a possibility, especially if concessions on territory, particularly Jerusalem, are made that threaten the perceptions of national interest and security of the Jewish population. The December election in Israel confirmed the view that the alternatives to the Israel Labour Party remained the military or the Arabs.

The worldwide campaign of terrorism by the Arab Palestinian youth proves just how intractable the problem of territory is and supports the contentions of the book regarding the real basis of violence in the Third World as a whole. Border disputes and territorial integrity, separatism and civil war remain common ingredients of the political realities of economic development. The 1973 'peace' in Vietnam has continued as a bloody civil war over rule by Hanoi or Saigon, and the ancillary wars in Cambodia, Laos and Thailand continue at more or less the same pace.

Of the military coups, the Chilean coup in September 1973 has provoked the most comment. The drift towards military intervention under President Allende's government was predictable at each stage. Only the army kept Allende from falling at several times in the year, as cabinet crises were unresolved in the political deadlocks between left and right and extreme wings in either side. In the Third World, reliance on the military to rule is a prime element leading to their intervention. The setting up of independent centres of violence, the training of armed militias as military wings of political parties, the polarisation of wide sections of the community, driving one group towards the left and the other to the right, these are the classic steps to a coup d'etat. That the debate has centred on the issue of the failure of the parliamentary road to socialism has not helped analysis of the real course of events in Chile. The current junta is unattractive and its methods of political control alien to democratic processes, but it is not unique in the Third World, nor ought it to have a monopoly of odium compared to many governments of left and right, civilian and military, that exist elsewhere.

Evidence in support of the other themes continues to accumulate. The enormous increase in the political bargaining power of the oil producers in respect to the major Western (capitalist) countries illustrates dramatically the view expressed in the text that the 'metropolitan/imperialist' powers have a declining ability to intervene in the Third World, even if they wanted to. Suez demonstrated the end of European hegemony; Vietnam that of the most powerful nation in the world. New, vigorous, independent capitalist powers are emerging in the Third World. Their forms of government, their variations in economic structure, their aspirations and their intentions will 'surprise' many, alienate others; but new thinking about old explanations and analyses is imperative if social science is to contribute anything as an explanation of the real world. In this respect Bill Warren's article, 'Imperialism and capitalist industrialisation' (*New Left Review* 81, 1973) should be studied as a contribution to the debate; it challenges the Marxist theory of neo-capitalist imperialism and suggests, as this book does from another point of view, that the traditional Marxist ideological perspectives of relationships between the First and Third World are wanting where they claim relevance, and wrong where they are specific.

Very little of this book would have been written without the active support and encouragement given to me by Professor John Vaizey. He not only directed my attention to the wider implications of my work but gave close attention to the way I wrote the ideas into a form suitable for publication. He read everything that I wrote, as I wrote it, and made many suggestions as to what I was trying to say as well as the way that I tried to say it. In many cases I took notice of these criticisms but not always, thus relieving Professor Vaizey of any responsibility for the remaining errors and misunderstandings that must continue to be my own claim to originality. His willingness to read and digest my scattered pieces over many months and to draw my attention to repeated irrelevancies, irregularities and inconsistencies, was a test of his patience. My debt to him can only be expressed by emphasising *my profound thanks*.

Dr Keith Norris kindly read through a draft and as a result of his many criticisms and suggestions he contributed in no small way to the final product. Again, not everything that he pointed out did I accept — my resistance to criticism is manifold — but a great deal was accepted and for this help I am most grateful.

Other colleagues at Brunel University, Jacqueline Cannon, Paul Bennett, David Herbert, George Krimpas, David Burningham, were from time to time subjected to discussions where I tried out ideas upon them and I am pleased to record my appreciation of their help. Dr Kabir Ahmad also was of great help in my understanding of Pakistan and Bangladesh politics and his own writings in this field were used at various points in this book. None of my colleagues, however, deserve any disapprobation for anything that appears under my name.

Professor Keith Hopkins of the Sociology Department at Brunel also read a draft and made some useful observations. Dr Caroline Hutton gave me the opportunity of participating in her Development Seminar where some of the ideas were put to her students. Their comments (mainly in disagreement) were noted and responded to in the final draft, though clearly where the disagreements were factual (the view that the military in the Third World is an arm of the American Sixth and Seventh Fleets) I could make no concessions to the facts.

Others who helped me in one way or another include Trinidad Warman, of Strathclyde University, who as my tutor in development economics in 1968-1969 sparked off my interest in the military and the development problem (though she almost certainly will not agree with my presentation of the relationship); Veena Agarwal, a research student at Brunel University, whose Ph D on Indian defence expenditures and the Five Year Plans has broken new ground in this field and with whom I have had many fruitful discussions; Anthony Baldwin, of the Law Department at Brunel University, helped in sorting through the information that appears in Appendix A; Terence Martin (Edinburgh University) assisted with Appendix B; and Fraser Cameron (Cambridge), Frank Stephen (Strathclyde), Jean Jordan (Open University), and John Cathie (Strathclyde) helped in numerous exchanges of views on individual incidents covered in the book.

The officials of the Embassies or High Commissions of Thailand, Malaysia, Singapore, India, Colombia, Venezuela, Brazil, Chile, Zambia, Sierra Leone, Portugal, Libya, Guyana, Nigeria, Ghana, Vietnam, and Indonesia were helpful in providing statistical data and other information. The Librarians and Staffs of the British Museum Reading Room, the United Nations Library, the Libraries of the Universities of Edinburgh, London and Brunel, and the National Library of Scotland, were all extremely helpful and accommodating to my inordinate requests for books, papers, articles and essays.

Finally, my thanks to my students who persevered with my wandering attention, particularly during 1971-1972; to Annemarie Maggs, the Economics Department Secretary; to Christine Stephens who typed the illegible script for inadequate recompense, and to Patricia for putting up with my absences and frustrations.

With all this help one could assume that this book could not be less than perfect; the following pages will establish just how far from perfect I managed to make it in spite of everything.

Strathclyde University
February 1974                                    Gavin Kennedy

# 1 Introduction

Nobody has yet devised a substitute for armed forces. According to Adam Smith, the first duty of the sovereign, 'that of protecting the society from the violence and invasion of other independent societies, can be performed only by means of a military force'.[1] All countries in the world today implicitly accept this proposition and have prepared themselves with varying degrees of effectiveness to carry out this first duty if circumstances make it necessary.[2] At the same time there is considerable support among politicians, and citizens, for finding some other means of resolving differences between nations. To this end international organisations, such as the United Nations, have used up considerable man-hours in searching for alternative forms of securing peace. The major powers have also paralleled these efforts in searching for an operating formula that will give each other security.[3] In the meantime the world is covered by violent challenges to the status quo, from within and between

1 Adam Smith, *An Inquiry into the Wealth of Nations*, Book V.
2 Costa Rica abolished its armed forces in 1948, but left an armed police force which carries out the function previously covered by the army. For this reason the Costa Rica exception is less exceptional. They merely re-assigned one force to do the work of another and dismantled the army and its installations — the barracks became a Museum.
3 The Strategic Arms Limitation Talks (SALT) were not aimed at general disarmament but were confined to seeking some means for the Russian and American governments to control their arms race within the context of mutual hostility and suspicions. In fact the agreement reached in 1972 leaves wide scope for the arms race to continue between them, but under agreed rules. There is much cause for scepticism as to the altruistic motivation of the two super-powers and to what extent the SALT agreements are in the interests of other countries (e.g. the emerging or potential super-powers — such as China or Europe). See E. Young, *An End to Arms Control?*, London, 1972.

countries, and, as the search for non-violent means of reconciling irreconcilable differences continues without any end in sight, the powers concerned tend to resort to the traditional means of resolution of conflict, namely, organised violence.

That part of the planet known as the Third World[4] is a violent world. All the forms of civilised savagery developed painstakingly in the European countries over many centuries are a daily occurence in some part of the Third World. The mass bombing of civilian targets in the Second World War, introduced by the Nazis and perfected by the Allies, was repeated over and over again in Vietnam by the American airforce.[5] The horrors of the religious witch-hunts of sixteenth-century Europe have their mangled replicas in too many of the developing countries for them to be mere aberration. The elimination of opposition, the jails, the persecution, the lack of compassion and the apparatus of

4 In this book the term 'Third World' is used mainly because it is a recognisable label for these countries outside Europe, North America, the Communist states, Japan and the European dominions. Thus the countries in Asia, Africa, the Middle East and Latin America are included in the 'Third World'. Other terminology, such as 'backward' countries, 'underdeveloped countries', 'developing countries', 'less developed countries' and so on, has implications which can produce objections to its use in all circumstances. 'Third World' is relatively neutral in this respect — though it still suggests a rank ordering that puts them behind the 'First World' (the West) and the 'Second World' (the Communist countries). Rather than create a new terminology which might (but might not) satisfy all the values of everybody, it is tidier to use a term recognised by the majority. In much the same way the term 'Viet Cong' has become a recognisable term, in spite of the derogatory intent of its early popularisers, for the National Liberation Front. It is part of our Western culture to turn derogatory or value-loaded terms into their opposites, e.g. the 'Desert Rats' of Tobruk and so on.

5 It would be less than fair not to draw attention to the transformation of values in the attitude of the Communists to mass bombing. In the Second World War they supported the mass bombing of German cities, and, when the atom bombs were dropped on Japan, congratulated the Americans (see *Daily Worker*, London, August 1945). Their opposition to US bombing in Vietnam is therefore related to the politics of the population upon whom the bombs are being dropped. This does not reduce criticism of mass bombing, but it does set the record straight.

repression are too widespread among the newly 'liberated' countries for them to pass unnoticed except by apologists for dictators. That this takes place against a background of desperate poverty, technical backwardness and widespread ignorance, does not make the behaviour more acceptable. The elites of these countries, irrespective of their political persuasion, are neither poverty-stricken nor ignorant.

Military government is the most common form of government in the Third World. The most common difficulties that these countries face are the structural obstacles between the will to develop and the road to development. The political structures, existent or left behind by the retreating European powers, have smashed themselves one after another against this problem. The regimes that have arisen on the wreckage of these political structures have taken several forms according to the circumstances of the country, the personalities of the leaders, the proximity to super-power interests, and the achievements, if any, of the new government.

As often as not the new regime is challenged from within. Where the new elite has shallow roots it is vulnerable to competition from other elites within the society. Where violence is a norm these challenges are bound to be violent too and the pattern of conflict is endemic. Vilfredo Pareto described social violence in terms of the perennial struggle between elites — those that are established and those that are arriving. This circulation of elites is the means by which a society is renewed; either the established elite suppresses the challenge violently or it is overthrown.[6] In some circumstances the challenge is absorbed — Britain in the industrial revolution (the aristocracy absorbed the bourgeoisie) or during the rise of the Labour Party (the bourgeoisie absorbed the proletariat).

In the Third World the challenge to the elite is as old, or new, as the states themselves; it is not a cyclic phenomenon spread over centuries, or even decades. The rise and fall of the new elites in the Third World is compressed into a period of years or, in some cases, months. Survival is a risk that is taken seriously or is settled violently. Living dangerously is a

6 V. Pareto, *The Rise and Fall of Elites: An Application of Theoretical Sociology*, Totowa, N.J., 1968.

way of life for political leaders and aspirants.

With this as the political context it is surprising that a whole literature on the problems of development has grown up which largely ignores the reality of the world that the literature is written for. Serious scholars have produced many plans for development that might as well be written for another planet for all the relevance that they have for this one. For example, a recent text-book on development economics begins with the following:

I think the importance of institutional barriers to development is often exaggerated . . . the desire for material improvement in less developed countries is very strong — certainly strong enough to counter any institutional barriers that may exist — and the evidence is not very convincing that basic institutional reform is a necessary precondition for accelerated growth. But, in any case, it is my firm belief that the economist has something positive to offer by way of analysis *unadulterated* by sociological, political and other non-economic variables. We now seem to me to be in the opposite danger of a great deal of woolly thinking about what raising living standards is all about. In the final analysis, growth must be considered as an economic process in the important practical sense that it is unlikely to proceed very far in the absence of an increase in the quality and quantity of the resources available for production. Even if we concede that the availability of the resources may depend on non-economic factors such as attitudes towards effort, saving and risk talking, and 'maximising' in general, this does not make non-economic factors prime determinants of development. Their impact is indirect. This is how economists tend to view the relation between development and institutional environment . . .[7]

It is this search for 'unadulterated' economics that leads to the myth of production functions; that there is some arrangement of economic variables that will raise output according to a mathematical law. It is a great pity that development economists did not begin with a study of the development problem from as 'adulterated' an angle as possible, instead of making a Gadarene rush to apply pure analytical models to situations which are not remotely connected to any of the assumptions needed by the models. The contribution of the social sciences to the development

7 A.P. Thirlwall, *Growth and Development*, London 1972, Preface.

process might then have been more significant than it has been up to now.

The allocation of resources is not a purely economic process, even if it is an economic problem. Confusing the two has given economics an undeserved bad name. Resources are allocated as a part of a political bargaining process. A closer look at the political processes of developing countries will contribute more to an understanding of the economic problems than the search for the point of tangency between a production possibility curve and an iso-quant.

The result of the exclusion of reality from the development economist's interests, and the concomitant exclusion of economics from the social scientist's work, has been that the study of the economic effects of political structures has fallen in between the two schools. Now this is a serious matter for social science. It means that a whole area of intervention in the development process is left unexplained. Unfortunately the majority of social scientists who work in the development field make snap judgments on the impact of the political structure on the countries concerned, which when examined do not pass even the most elementary empirical tests. For example, Thirlwall's book, quoted above, does not contain any analysis of the role of defence expenditures in development (and Thirlwall's book is one of the better in this field).

Development economists have produced a whole literature on the effects of education on development.[8] Yet this is only one item on the budgets of developing countries. Defence spending, intimately connected with the violence of the Third World, is a most neglected area of public finance. The reason is that it is taken for granted in the main that defence expenditures are wasteful of resources. That this is insufficient reason to ignore them is somehow lost in the general search for the missing elixir of self-sustained growth. Defence spending, where it is recognised as an important part of the budget, is usually regarded as a necessary evil to be minimised as much as possible so that the serious work of the analyst can be continued. The Third World is boiling with violence,

8 See J. Vaizey et al., *The Political Economy of Education*, London, 1972, for a critical approach to the literature.

institutionalised and revolutionary, and yet the organisation of resources to cope with this fact of life is a neglected subject. Just how 'unadulterated' can we get?

On the other side of the social science fence, occupied by sociologists, political analysts, historians and so on, there has been a veritable boom in studies of the Third World, especially studies of the military regimes of a wide spectrum of countries. But these have tended to be exclusively concerned with the socio-political roles of the various military groups in these countries. Some attempts have been made to delve into the economic aspects; but either the political and sociological aspects have been more interesting to the analysts, or the economic tools have been insufficiently explored, so that they tend to be limited to individual articles scattered in the professional academic journals, or to footnotes and small sections in books written for other purposes.

This book is a contribution to the discussion by the social sciences of the military in the Third World.

It divides into seventeen chapters. The violence of the Third World is examined in Chapters 2 and 3, which deal first with some ideological issues and then take up some of the factual relationships between violence and the political systems that exist in the Third World. The basic point made in these chapters is that the legitimacy crisis dominates the Third World, with a relatively faster circulation of elites than was the case in the same phase of European development. The tendency to set up military regimes is itself an expression of the fragility of the political systems in these countries.

If the allocative process is a political one then some study must be made of political processes. Military governments are not all of a kind — there are wide variations in their composition, their programmes, their histories, etc. But it is also important to understand the differences between Third World politics as a whole and Western political processes before the military can be put into perspective. In Chapter 4 the relationship between legitimacy and the use of force is looked at and also the nature of the political party in these countries. This institution has the same name as its Western progenitor, but it operates in an altogether different cultural

milieu and for subtly different purposes. Many political
parties have not got used to the idea of opposition and the
fact that the fruits of office are so important to self-esteem
encourages resistance to change in this respect.

This political tradition, left behind by the Europeans in
the 1960s, is taken up in case studies of Sierra Leone, Nigeria
and Ghana in Chapter 5. Then the role played by Colonel
Nasser in the Middle East is looked at in three studies of his
influence in Egypt, Syria and Iraq. Arab military socialism
has been a dynamic force in this region for over twenty years
and it has by no means exhausted its capability for
intervention. This theme is taken up in Chapter 6. Chapter 7
deals with military interventions in Pakistan and Indonesia.
Pakistan is a contrast to its party state neighbour, India.
Indonesia is another extraordinary country where the coup
d'état attempt of a political faction back-fired and gave
power to the army. It is not always the eventual winners who
set off the events that bring them to power (Pakistan and
Nigeria are two other examples).

The reasons for intervention are varied, and they must also
be compared with the examples of countries which have not
had interventions. Mexico is the first case considered in
Chapter 8. Here the brilliant political fight between President
Cardenas and the military is examined, showing how the
revolutionary generals were consistently out-manoeuvred by
the vigorous leadership of Cardenas until their last desperate
attempt at a come-back only exposed their isolation from the
new Mexico which they had themselves brought into existence in their youth. Turkey followed a similar path under
Kemal Ataturk, but here the position was reversed after the
Second World War. The political structure left by Ataturk
was exhausted and his heirs injected new dynamism (with
consequent tensions) at a time when the military was
rejuvenated from top to bottom by the Americans. The 1960
coup was inevitable, but the lessons from the period of
exclusion are important. Israel is in every sense a special case.
It is a vigorous democracy (for Israeli Jews) but also a
one-party state; it has a highly professional army which is
also a militia; it has a semi-permanent mobilised economy
with the military reaching all levels of the state, but the

civilian government is in full control.

In Chapters 9 and 10 the effect of the defence budgets of developing countries on the welfare allocation is looked at. The most common assumption about military spending is that it is competitive with welfare spending on education and health. This does not appear to be the case, however, and some suggestions are made as to the areas where it is more likely to be competitive, such as private consumption.[9]

Chapters 11, 12 and 13 examine the economic impact of six wars on the countries affected by them. Some of the economic gainers from the wars in the Third World were Nigeria, Vietnam's neighbours and Israel. In each case hostilities have helped to improve the economic indicators of these countries. Pakistan's and Egypt's economic losses from the wars they have been involved in are looked at. Pakistan's 1965 war was a disastrous turning point for the country which narrowed the options facing the ruling group in Western Pakistan and led to the separatist movement in the East gaining real possibilities of success. As the West wing squeezed the East to make ends meet it drove the Bengalis into resistance and eventual revolt. In Egypt the economic managers have been unsuccessful since 1952 in getting the country moving towards development. Managerial incompetence and continual purges of the already thin elite were accompanied by failures in the battlefield with Israel. On two counts the Nasserist regime failed; first, it did not lead to development on a superior scale to non-Nasserist governments (in comparison with most countries it comes off worse) and secondly, its claimed military competence was never substantiated in action (the incompetence of the previous regime was one of the alleged reasons for the Nasserist coup).

The most important military connection between the Third World and the industrialised countries is through the arms trade. The political use of weapon supplies is an obvious linkage; the support and sustenance of competing sides in the conflicts that take place is another. The big powers clearly

9 See V. Agarwal, *The Indian Development Plans and Defence Spending* (forthcoming), which contains confirmation of this hypothesis.

use their weapon supplies as counters in their diplomatic offensives, but it is important to realise that it is not the suppliers who increase the tensions (this is pure propaganda from the disarmament lobby) but the existence of tensions that enables the suppliers to exploit the demands for weapons. This is looked at in Chapter 14 where individual arms races are studied.

An alternative to importing arms, and a means to gaining political independence, is to manufacture them domestically. Less than a third of the developing countries manufacture some arms and only a handful manufacture aircraft. Chapters 15 and 16 examine this aspect of the arms business. The necessity for industrialisation, if development is to take place, is discussed and the role that arms production has in this process is considered. Arms present special problems for countries that manufacture them — for sophisticated weapons they involve high-risk capital projects — but they also present some solutions to the development problem. How to set up domestic manufacturing capacity with limited markets is one problem for growth, but the role of a government as a buyer of arms products is a way round this problem. In Chapter 16 the production of small arms, armour, naval craft and aircraft is studied in greater detail and this is linked to the accumulation of skills which have civilian uses.

The final chapter takes up the issues raised by disarmament and how this would affect the developing world. The problems of nuclear disarmament are something entirely separate from the problems faced by the developing world. The bulk of arms spending is accounted for in the developed world and therefore arrangements between the major powers on these matters may not be of direct material interest to the developing world. The hope that this might lead to greater foreign aid is discussed and dismissed. Given the level of violence in the Third World and the independence of these countries from the developed powers it is not likely that disarmament will take place in the Third World in this century. That being the case, the Third World has to face up to the necessity for defence allocations and these must be taken into account in their development plans.

The reason for using the term 'Third World' has already been explained. There are some other details that need explanation here. Several Third World countries are excluded. The island countries of the Caribbean and the Pacific are not included in any of the tables. These would add to the number of countries but not necessarily to the indicators. This decision was made before any of the research was conducted and therefore was not a post-result adjustment — there is no question of an attempt to bias the results with inconvenient figures. It was assumed that the bias produced by including these countries would not be justified given their smallness. Thus we lose Cuba from the countries studied, as well as Haiti, Dominican Republic (except for small arms production), Jamaica, Trinidad, etc. But it would have been wrong to select among these countries once a decision had been made that they were not wanted as a group.

The current (1972) colonies were also excluded, such as French and Dutch Guyana, British Honduras and Hong Kong, Portuguese Guinea, Mozambique and Angola. In the latter case guerrilla wars have been taking place, and these are of interest to the theme of this thesis, but we are concerned in the main with the independent countries of the Third World and not with those directly under European influence.[10] Both South Africa and Rhodesia have been excluded for similar reasons (along with the land-locked black states of Lesotho, Bechuanaland, etc.).

The Communist countries have not been included either, and this is explained in Chapter 2. It might be argued that with so many exclusions of interesting experiences the study is bound to be deficient. In defence there are two points to be borne in mind: first, the countries included are extremely interesting in themselves and secondly, there is a limit to which interesting and important topics — such as Portugal's African wars or Rhodesia's guerrilla and security problems — can be dealt with in one study without total surrender to generality. To consider these topics and the Communist experience would require a three-volume study rather than one.

10 See P. Kennedy, *The Economic Impact of Portugal's Colonial Wars* (forthcoming), which is a study related to Guinea, Mozambique and Angola.

Israel is included because of its relevance to the Arab countries, and Turkey as a comparison to the Latin America experience. Greece is not, because it is more a European than a Third World experience.

The four regions used in the book (except where otherwise noted) group the Third World in the following way:

*Black Africa*: All African states south of the Sahara and north of the Zambesi.

*Middle East*: All north African states, Arab states (including Sudan), Iran and Turkey.

*Asia*: All countries from Pakistan to Taiwan.

*Latin America*: All mainland countries south of Rio Grande.

The United Nations and other organisations group the countries differently. The above groupings were chosen because of a mixture of geographical and political affinities between the countries in them. There is no ideal grouping of states, and readers must judge whether different, or more, groupings would help clarify problems.

Most of the monetary information is in United States dollars. The recent devaluations and currency adjustments have made this a less stable indicator than it used to be. As most of the detail refers to the use of dollars or local currencies before 1970 this should not present too much of a problem. Few of the magnitudes involved in this book would be affected by 10 per cent changes either way. The billion is the American billion, or a thousand million.

# 2 Violence and Ideology

## 1. Introduction

In this chapter we open the discussion on the patterns of violence in the developing countries and on the theoretical explanations that are competing for attention among students of the subject. The first theory that is discussed is the theory of *permanent revolution*.[1] This is a contribution from the Trotskyist school of Marxism, and, in spite of the vulgarity of the attempts to apply it consistently to the behaviour of political forces in the Third World, it has widespread support in its various forms among 'left-wing' students and political activists.[2] An alternative theory is the *legitimacy thesis*, which is the theory most favoured by the author as an explanation of the patterns of violence and the interventions of the forces represented by the military and the insurgents in most parts of the Third World.

## 2. The permanent revolution

Long before Mao Tse Tung[3] stated his famous thesis that 'political power grows out of the barrel of a gun', a Prussian Emperor had his Guards armed with rifles upon which was engraved the warning: 'The Final Word of the Emperor'. The connection between violence and power had been learnt by the rulers and rebels over many centuries; indeed it was practised on a smaller scale by Al Capone *et al.* in Chicago in the 1920s and is practised by the 'Mafia' today. The so-called Maoist thesis is in fact a well-publicised summation of human experience.

1 L. Trotsky, *Permanent Revolution*, London, 1963.
2 T. Ali, *Pakistan: Military Rule or People's Power*, London, 1970.
3 Mao Tse Tung, *Problems of War and Strategy*, 1938; in *Selected Works*, London, 1954, vol. 2, p.228.

Political change in the Third World is a violent process. Many of the countries achieved their independent political status after violence was offered against the ruling European power. In some cases this violence was pushing against an open door as the European power concerned was willing to leave (e.g. Aden).[4] In other cases the door was (and in some cases still is) firmly shut and considerable violence was (and will be) needed to break the resolve to stay. The violence against the French in Indo-China,[5] for example, took from 1946 to 1954 to force the French to quit and this was followed by the violence of the Algerian war before De Gaulle arranged a withdrawal.[6] In Portuguese Africa there has been a series of violent conflicts for some years, though to date, the insurgency has not reached levels comparable to that in French Indo-China or Algeria.[7] Pareto's concepts of circulating elites and the role of violence,[8] applied to the French former possessions and the current Portuguese overseas territories, would explain the transfer of power in Indo-China and Algeria as being brought about by the inability of the French ruling elite to use violence effectively against insurgents (the rising elite) and, by similar reasoning, it would suggest that the Portuguese successes in this matter reflect their effective mobilisation of violence against the forces directed at their power in these countries. Because, for a number of reasons, the Black armies that are engaging the Portuguese are less skilful (and more factionalised) than those that the French had to face, the poorer and less

4 C. Cross, *The Fall of the British Empire, 1918-1968*, London, 1968, p.355.

5 E.J. Hammer, *The Struggle for Indo-China*, Stanford, 1954.

6 A. Crawley, *De Gaulle*, London, 1969, Chapter 21.

7 Views on the revolutions in Portuguese Africa differ. See: P.M. Whitaker, 'The revolution of "Portuguese" Africa', *Journal of Modern African Studies*, 8, April 1970; D.L. Wheeler, 'The Portuguese Army in Angola', *Journal of Modern African Studies*, 7, 3, October 1969; United States Army, *Area Handbook for Angola*, Washington, 1967; E. Mondlane, *The Struggle for Mozambique*, London, 1969; B. Davidson, *The Liberation of Guiné: Aspects of an African Revolution*, London, 1969. The assassinations of Mondlane (1969) and Cabral (1973) dealt serious blows to the anti-Portuguese wars.

8 Pareto, op. cit.; see also V. Pareto, *The Mind and Society: A Treatise on General Sociology*, vols 1 to 4, New York, 1963.

developed Portuguese are able to do what the powerful and rich French were unable to accomplish with all their advantages.

Whether the processes of violent change are in some way *historic* (as some believe) or merely *episodic* (as historical information on the decline and fall of elites and their empires suggest) is a central difference between the theoretical explanations of the violence of the conflicts in these and other parts of the Third World.

Since 1960 alone there have been over 200 military coup d'etats in the four regions of the Third World[9] (see Appendix A). There has also been a whole series of insurrections, guerrilla wars, civil wars and violent disturbances. There have been several large-scale military confrontations in the Middle East, India, Asia and Africa. The level of violence of the anti-colonial wars in the post-war years to 1960 has, if anything, increased after independence was gained by the majority of countries.[10] The termination, for example, of the anti-French struggle in Indo-China in 1954 and its division into four separate independent countries, Laos, Cambodia, North Vietnam and South Vietnam, was in no way a prelude to peaceful relations within and between each country. The withdrawal of the French left some fatal issues unresolved, such as the re-unification of the two Vietnams and the political complexions of the governments left in command. But these were not issues which could be resolved

9 The definition of a military coup or attempted military coup has deliberately been left vague in arriving at this total (details in the Appendix). Generally a seizure, or attempted seizure, of power by the use of regular troops or the threat of their use would be sufficient to define a coup. In the conditions of the Third World there are a number of borderline cases, where, for example, it is not clear on which side the armed forces are operating, or where the coup is attempted within the political elite and the role of the army is implicit rather than explicit.

10 See J.F. Kirkham, S.G. Levy and W.J. Crotty, *Assassination and Political Violence: A Report to the National Commission on the Causes and Prevention of Violence*, New York, 1970, Chapter 3, for a factor analysis study of the relationship between violence and socio-economic characteristics. The study found that assassination correlated highly with high levels of internal violence (guerrilla warfare) and also with high rates of socio-economic change. Both conditions are common in the Third World.

anywhere else but in the countries themselves. Hence the violence continued and intensified, dragging in the United States and the massive military power at its disposal. But it is important to recognise the 1954 withdrawal of the French as a turning point in the violent history of the region from anti-colonial struggle to internal political struggle. They were not the same wars, fought for the same reasons, but different wars. The American role in Vietnam obscures this fact for many people.[11]

The persistence of violence forms the empirical basis of such theories as the 'permanent revolution'. This is an extension of the Marxist concept of the class struggle and was originally developed by Leon Trotsky. It was put forward in the early part of this century as a conceptual model to direct the revolutionary activity of the Russian Marxists. The basic assumption of the argument was that the position of the Russian proletariat in the crisis of Russian capitalism gave it an opportunity to lead the peasantry to overthrow capitalist forms of production and establish a worker's state, rather than the contrary view that the Russian proletariat was too isolated and too weak to conduct such a strategy. Russian capitalism had first to exhaust itself (i.e. develop into a modern capitalist economy) before socialism was possible. Trotsky's view was that the proletarian state could 'leap over' the mature capitalist phase and become a bulwark of revolution against the capitalist states of the West.

The peasantry in Russia was driven to revolution against the system of capitalist property relations. The proletariat was suppressed by the Tsarist state which because it was a minor power in the capitalist world was forced to hold down its proletariat with violence because it could not 'bribe' it with the fruits of imperialist empire as in Britain. The proletariat could win the support of the peasantry by offering land to them.

The democratic revolution against Tsarist autocracy could not even be led by the Russian bourgeoisie — it was tied intimately to the landowning classes and the Tsarist state; it was also an extremely weak social class incorporating none of the vigour and revolutionary thrust of the European bour-

11 New York Times, *The Pentagon Papers*, 1971.

geoisie that had developed Europe and North America. In the class struggle between the workers and peasants and the reactionary classes in Russia the bourgeoisie would side with reaction, and their class affinities with the European bourgeoisie would express themselves in hostility even to the democratic demands of the proletariat and peasantry. Unable to press its own interests against Tsarism, hostile to the demands of the other social classes poised against Tsarism and vacillating between domestic reaction and international capitalism, the bourgeoisie was written off as a progressive social force. Thus a revolutionary socialist leadership was able to place itself at the head of the oppressed classes, and 'steal' the leadership of the democratic revolution from the bourgeoisie, and to pass over to the socialist revolution, even in a backward country.

The developing countries in the middle of the twentieth century, it is argued, are analogous to the situation in Russia at the turn of the century. The proletariat of these countries is situated at the fulcrum of the class struggle in these countries. The bourgeoisie of the former colonial world has created some identity for itself because of the racial nature of imperialism, but it is still totally unequipped to carry out the democratic tasks left behind, such as agrarian reform, socialisation of production and the continuing struggle against imperialism. The nationalist bourgeoisie arrived with too little, too late to be anything but a transmission belt for imperialist and reactionary class interests. The continuing violence of the Third World is a manifestation of the necessity of the permanent revolution operating against the worn out or aborted social formations that imperialism has placed in the way of the revolutionary parties.

In its original, Trotskyist, formulation the theory required that the democratic revolution in the backward country be led by the revolutionary proletariat, or more correctly, the vanguard party of the revolutionary proletariat, namely the Communist party.[12] Even though the proletariat was a miniscule portion of the total population (as in Russia), it is

12 For Trotsky's application of his theory to the Chinese revolution, see L. Trotsky, *Problems of the Chinese Revolution*, London, 1969 (1930).

capable of exerting a revolutionary leverage far in excess of its numbers, because it represents, in the context of Marxian theory, the only developing social formation that has a future. This was also a theoretical justification for the small Bolshevik forces exercising their monopoly of the revolutionary leadership and utilising their forces of violence against other competing groups.

Lenin, who at first disagreed with Trotsky's theory of the development of the revolution, adopted Trotsky's view immediately before the Bolshevik seizure of power in 1917. Combined with the Leninist concept of the 'withering away of the state' after the victory of socialism,[13] it gave the Bolshevik party a firm self-justification; on the one it had justified its monopoly role as the leadership of the leading social class, the proletariat, and on the other hand it justified the state terror against dissident groups, classes and individuals as a necessary prelude to the success of the revolution and the coming 'withering away' of the instruments of repression.

The problem for the theory of the permanent revolution is the experience of revolutions since it was formulated. None of them was led by a proletarian party. In China, the Maoist Communist party turned away from the urban proletariat in 1929 (after a series of disasters) towards establishing bases in the remote countryside. The revolution, when it came in 1949, was in the form of a succession of military victories against the Kuomintang armies with a minimal role played by Chinese workers in the cities. The Chinese Communist party may be represented as the Chinese proletariat only by an extreme vagueness of language; indeed the Maoist leadership had purged the party of 'Trotskyists', and anybody with 'Trotskyist' (i.e. permanent revolution) thoughts, in the mid-thirties.

In eastern Europe the 'revolutions' were carried out by the imported functionaries of the imported Communist parties, and were aided by the fortuitous presence of the Soviet army. Yugoslavia is an exception to this experience. There the Communist party was an indigenous force that gained its

13 V. Lenin, *State and Revolution* (1916).

experience in the guerrilla war against the German army of occupation. But again Tito's forces were not a revolutionary proletariat as envisaged in the theory.

In Cuba the Communist party was left behind by events when the Castroite (CIA-backed) revolution occured. It was only after the revolution and the fall-out with the United States that the leadership moved over to a socialist, and later Communist, political position. The whole of the Third World has been swept by an anti-colonial struggle, and in only two countries, China and Cuba, has the revolution passed into a Marxist camp, and neither of these countries was led by parties supporting the thesis of permanent revolution.[14]

Moreover, the Leninist thesis of the eventual withering away of the state has no empirical support whatsoever. Indeed, quite the opposite has taken place. The victory of Marxian parties does not remove succession struggles from the party. In the Soviet Union the first twelve years of the revolution were taken up by a bitter contest for power between Stalin and Trotsky and a further ten years in a struggle between Stalin and the 'Old Guard' Bolsheviks.[15] In China there has been a continuous struggle between Mao Tse Tung and various opponents, reaching its zenith in the Cultural Revolution. The struggle between factions in the European Communist states has reached such levels of fundamental discord that the Soviet army has had to be used to settle the issue. Thus, years after the victory of the

14 The only party of any significance in the Third World to support the theory of Permanent Revolution was the Lanka Samasamaja Party (LSSP) in Sri Lanka (Ceylon). But instead of the theory being put into practice, the LSSP split in 1962 and its leaders joined the 'bourgeois' government. The *Economist* (17 April 1971) summed up the result of the 1971 left-wing insurrection: 'When Trotsky's heirs do battle with Guevara's.' The divergence between experience and theory has provoked interminable splits among the Trotskyists. The outright 'revisionists' accepted Cuba, for example, as a genuine revolutionary 'workers' state', but the 'orthodox' Trotskyists analysed Castro's revolution as 'bourgeois'. Many of the Latin American Trotskyists (Argentina for example) have turned to guerrilla fighting or urban terrorism and have apparently abandoned Trotsky's strictures on the absolute necessity for *proletarian* struggle.

15 I. Deutscher, *The Prophet Armed, The Prophet Unarmed* and *The Prophet Outcast*, London 1954, 1959 and 1963.

revolution, the resources allocated to state security show no sign of withering away, and a vast apparatus has been consolidated to preserve and protect the party leadership both from internal dissension and popular revolt.

The Communist states form a separate group of states in the world. They are not party states in the conventional sense that a political party (or parties) forms the foundation for political rule according to a set of procedures inherited or developed for continuity and succession. Party states have armies and police forces but the role of these state instruments is independent of the party systems. In Communist states the party is armed: they are armed-party states rather than party states with armies. In them the army and the instruments of state security are integrated into the party and have no independent existence. They are not designed to be 'above' politics. The role of leading cadres in these forces is partly security and partly political; many of the key positions are held by party cadres chosen primarily on political grounds — the gifted professional is as suspect as a person from an 'unreliable' social class.[16]

There are differences in some of the armed party states between the relationship of the security forces and the party, representing the different experiences of the Communist states in the struggle for power. The European states came into existence without indigenous movements and their armies were created *after* the revolution. These states are modelled on the Stalinist state but the armed forces are probably less reliable than either the Soviet army or the revolutionary armies of other Communist states. The armies operate in parallel to the party apparatus and both the army and the party are subordinate to the political aims and perceptions of the Soviet leaders. They have not been engaged in action outside their own borders, with the purely nominal exception of their minor role in the 1968 invasion of Czechoslovakia, and have functions not much more complex than that of reserve frontier guards.

The revolutionary movements of China and Vietnam are

16 'Our principle is that the Party commands the gun, and the gun must never be allowed to command the Party'. Mao Tse Tung, *Problems of War and Strategy*, (1938), op. cit. p.228.

altogether different. There the army and party are a monolithic whole. While the post-Mao succession struggle will probably see a more independent political line from the Chinese Red Army this will be from the point of view of the Red Army as a militant force *within* the Chinese Communist party rather than as an extra-party force.[17] The armies of China and Vietnam have been engaged in warfare with outside forces as well as with forces within their countries. The Chinese armies have fought the Japanese (1936-45), the United Nations (1951-3) and India (1962); the Vietnamese have fought the Japanese (1942-5), the French (1945-4) and the Americans and their allies (1961-72). The Koreans also fought the United Nations in the Korean War (1950-3).

As already mentioned, this book does not include the Communist states (which are worth a study in themselves) and they are discussed here only to draw attention to the experiences of these countries. Many of the features of these experiences have been reproduced in Third World countries, and suggest continuity rather than separation. It might suit a particular ideology to see a linear process by which development proceeds from regimes less socially progressive to regimes more socially progressive, but this is a conceptual gloss over what is an essentially identical content throughout the whole experience of these countries.

Support for repressive measures in regimes that conform to a particular approved ideology, and opposition to the same measures in regimes that are not approved of, is surely of dubious merit. It does not contribute to an analysis of the political struggles of developing countries, nor to the varying social and economic impacts of these political struggles, to use selective criteria to assess political systems. The continuing violence in the Third World may be an expression of a 'permanent revolution', if that is the thesis that one wants to establish; it might just as credibly be argued that the

17 cf. J. Gittings, *The Role of the Chinese Army*, London, 1967; J.C. Cheng (ed.), *The Politics of the Red Army: A translation of the bulletins of activities of the People's Liberation Army*, California, 1966. For Vietnam, see W.S. Turley, 'Civil-military relations in North Vietnam', *Asian Survey*, 9, 12, December 1969; W.W. Whitsan (ed.), *The Military and Political Power in China in the 1970s*, New York, 1972.

continuing violence is a product of the cultural inability of the people of these countries to mediate their differences peacefully; such a thesis would conform to a racialist world view. The evidence that this study will examine is much more consistent with the legitimacy thesis than with that of permanent revolution.

### 3.   The legitimacy thesis

The number of independent states has increased since the end of the Second World War. These states face the central problem of all states, namely, to establish their legitimacy. Seymour M. Lipset defined legitimacy as the 'capacity of a political system to engender and maintain the belief that existing political institutions are the most appropriate or proper ones for society'.[18] Different states and political systems ensure their legitimacy, and by this the quiescence of their subjects, by different means.

In a parliamentary system legitimacy is inferred from the government's majority resting on the electoral mandate won in a freely contested election. In a socialist country the legitimacy of the ruling party is tied to the theory of a vanguard party representing the historic interests of the proletariat and the revered model values of socialism. In some forms of totalitarian states the alleged genius of the Leader is the legitimising force.

The extent to which a regime is secure in its legitimacy could be measured by the relative size of its internal security budgets; the stronger the sense of legitimacy that a government has in the minds of its citizens the less it will need to enforce its rule by intensive sanctions against dissidents and would-be dissidents. It is not entirely an accurate measure (nor are these budgets readily available for measurement) because a well-organised and alienated minority in a society, and particularly in the urban industrialised societies, can disrupt the process of government to such an extent that

18 S.M. Lipset, 'Some social requisites for democracy: economic development and political legitimacy', *American Political Science Review*, 53, 1, March 1959, p.86; and *Political Man: The Social Bases of Power*, New York, 1960.

extraordinary measures of security are required to enforce the will of the majority.[19] For these reasons the effectiveness of a regime may be as important as its legitimacy. Various vectors of the two forces are possible; a regime can be effective but illegitimate or ineffective and legitimate, and, of course, there can be combinations of the two qualities.[20]

Administrative incompetence can erode a regime's legitimacy which may have been earned by activity in a previous time period. For example, the enormous prestige of some of the anti-colonial leaders (Nasser, Sukarno, Nkrumah) was compromised to some extent by the general inefficiency of their adminstrations. In the latter cases this contributed to the coups against them, though the resilience of the Sukarno myth survived even when grave doubts existed as to his role in the coup of 30 September 1965 against the army.[21]

Illegitimate regimes that are ineffective have a smaller chance of survival than legitimate regimes that are effective. The legitimacy of the regime can be diluted as the people develop new ideas as to political rights and obligations and, if this coincides with gradual or dramatic evidence of a regime's ineffectiveness, it is likely to create the conditions for revolutionary disorder. The classic example of this situation is Farouk's Egypt, where the military reverses of the Egyptians in the 1948 Israeli war contributed to the questioning of the legitimacy of the regime. The Free Officers had no faith that their aspirations for Egypt could be realised by the monarchy. It is noticeable that even after the coup in 1952 the Free Officers did not eradicate the monarchy at a stroke but ruled as 'regents' for the Heir for twelve months, until the Republic was declared in June 1953. (Symbolically the coup leaders authorised a 21-gun salute for Farouk when he sailed into exile.)[22]

19 An example that illustrates this point is the special security legislation passed in the Irish Republic to deal with IRA terrorism in December 1972.

20 S.M. Lipset, 'Political sociology', in R.K. Merton, L. Broom and L.S. Cottrell, *Sociology Today: Problems and Prospects*, New York, 1959.

21 P. Polomka, *Indonesia Since Sukarno*, London, 1971, p.84.

22 E. Be'eri, *Army Officers in Arab Politics and Society*, London, 1970, p.105.

New governments face an additional problem in asserting their legitimacy — they do not have the burden of precedent working in their favour. They are untried and inexperienced. They may have aroused the expectations of the masses to a level which they cannot satisfy. The governments of the Third World (excluding Latin America) are, in the main, in charge of political structures that are little older than a decade or two. Many of them, coming to power in military coups, have cut the effective history of the political structure in their country to a handful of years. Each military coup re-starts the constitutional clock, so to speak, and makes more difficult the task of achieving legitimacy. In the older republics of Latin America, which have been prone to military intervention for many decades, the legitimacy crisis is almost institutionalised — each military coup occurs when the illegitimacy of the incumbent regime ceases to be protected by the effectiveness of its security forces.[23]

## 4.   *The legitimacy crisis and military intervention*

The search for legitimacy by governments can be measured roughly by the proneness of countries to military intervention.[24] A country that has not had a coup, or attempted coup, would be at one end of a scale of stability and a country that has had several (Syria has had 21 coups and attempted coups since 1945) would be at the other. Military intervention is a sign of elite incohesion. The ruling elite, which rests its powers on the support of the governing political party, the instruments of the executive such as the police and (in the last resort) the armed forces, the state bureaucracy, the articulated interest groups in the com-

23 I.L. Horowitz, 'The norm of legitimacy: the political sociology of Latin America', in I.L. Horowitz, J. de Castro and J. Gerassi (eds), *Latin American Radicalism: A Documentary Report on Left and Nationalist Movements*, New York, 1969.

24 See G.O. Totten, 'Models and the problems of internal legitimacy', in W.A. Beling and G.O. Totten (eds), *Developing Nations: Quest for a Model*, (Proceedings of the 45th Session of the Institute of World Affairs), New York, 1970. Totten's analysis relates the legitimacy crisis to internal factors. Military intervention can be seen as a response to these factors.

munity, and its popular base in the population at large, is vulnerable to military intervention when it is believed to have failed one, several, or all, of these forces. A disaffection felt by the popular masses may provoke rioting and disorder and give encouragement to opposition political factions both within and outside the elite. One or more interest groups could be aggrieved at a particular policy (such as farmers or the middle-class urban groups and educated unemployed).

The bureaucracy may become inefficient or corrupt and have an interest in the government pursuing policies that leave them alone with their 'clients'. If the army and police are disgruntled, either through the policies pursued by the government (which might be trying to circumvent some of the political tensions by trying to create other bases of support such as a one-party state or, at their peril, a quasi-militia force) or from a lack of faith in the government's ability to counter the growing disorders, they are the one force in the community uniquely placed to carry out an illegal operation against the government.

The army has a near monopoly of violence in the state and is trained in how to use violence. This violence may not be a match for a well-trained and armed force from an industrialised country but it is more than enough for dealing with unarmed cabinet ministers and disorderly mobs in the streets. The number of men required to carry out a coup is surprisingly small — it certainly does not need the unanimity of the armed forces, a company or a battalion may be sufficient.[25]

The armed forces are well placed then to take advantage of the difficulties of their governments and, because it does not require complete agreement within the army to take this action, coups can take place when only a section of the forces utilises the army's advantages.[26]

25 See E. Luttwak, *Coup d'Etat*, London, 1968, for an interesting study of the mechanics of a coup.

26 The criticism that the army is not as centralised a force as it is sometimes made out to be is correct as a counter to crude explanations for military intervention in developing countries. But it misses the real significance of centralism. Even a small body of disciplined men has advantages over unco-ordinated administrations and unarmed civil servants.

Party political systems have by general agreement a greater claim to legitimacy than military governments, and in the context of democratic and modern value judgments they also have a greater claim than monarchies. The value ordering implied above would probably ascribe greater legitimacy to a monarchy than a military government (excluding the views of republicans). Legitimacy rests on the capacity of the political system to persuade the citizens that it is the most appropriate system for the country (Lipset) and hereditary monarchy in this respect is likely to be more credible than that of self-appoined army leaders.

As mentioned earlier, over 200 military coups took place in the Third World between 1960 and 1972. This suggests the fragility of the legitimacy of Third World governments. Since 1945 the number of coups amounted to over 280; there were at least 42 coups in Asia, 86 in Latin America, 62 in the Middle East and 76 in sub-Saharan Africa.[27] The full list is in Appendix A. What we want to do is to see if the proneness to military coup is related to the political system of the country. The more prone a system is to coups and attempted coups the more fragile its legitimacy.[28]

First of all, the Latin American record of coups was removed from the totals because as military governments predominate in the political systems of this region it was felt that they would bias the results. This left the three other regions, the Middle East, Asia and sub-Saharan Africa. The countries were arranged into the political systems operating at the time of the coups and attempted coups (i.e. into party states, monarchies and military governments). Thus, Egypt which was a monarchy at the time of the Free Officers coup in 1952 is counted for that coup in the monarchy class but for subsequent coups and attempted coups it appears in the military government class. Togo, which was a party state at

27 These figures are approximations and may be over or under the actual figure by about 10 per cent.

28 For an earlier attempt at relating military intervention to the political systems, see F. van der Mehden and C.W. Anderson, 'Political action by the military in the developing areas', *Sociological Research*, 28, Winter 1961; and see F. van der Mehden, *Politics of Developing Nations*, Englewood Cliffs, N.J., 1964.

the time of the first coup, is classed in the party states for that coup, but for subsequent coups it is classed as a military state.[29] Guinea, which has remained a party state, is classed for all its coup attempts as a party state, and so on.[30] Summing the coup and coup attempts according to the above system produced the results in Table 1.

Table 1    Distribution of coups and attempted coups in Asia, Africa and the Middle East by political system, 1945-72

| Political system | (1) No. of countries | (2) Coups | (2) ÷ (1) |
|---|---|---|---|
| Party state | 36 | 63 | 1.75 |
| Monarchy | 12 | 24 | 2.0 |
| Military state | 27 | 109 | 4.04 |

The party states have an average of 1.75 coups per country and the monarchies slightly higher at two coups per country. The military states have an average of four coups and attempted coups per country and are more than twice as prone to further coups as the party states and monarchies. The legitimacy crisis is not resolved by military intervention; it probably exacerbates it. Once one section of the military shows the way, or there is a successful example in another country, coup making can become contagious. Even if the 21 coups that took place in Syria are removed from the military states total, the proneness to military intervention of military states is just under double that for party states.

All military governments come to power by illegal and unconstitutional means, namely the coup d'etat.[31]    Is there a relationship between per capita income and proneness to coups and attempted coups? Given that coups and attempted coups can take place in both non-military-governed and military-governed countries and that statistically they occur

29 R.W. Howe, 'Togo: four years of military rule', *African Report*, May 1967.

30 V.C. Dubois, 'The role of the army in Guinea', *African Report*, 8, 1, January 1963.

31 In those cases where the civilian authority 'invites' the army to take over this is still unconstitutional. The fact that the civilian political leadership acquiesces in the military's intervention does not make it legal.

more often in the latter, this suggests that if there is a relationship between low per capita income and military coups, then military governments are more likely in countries with lower per capita income than in countries with higher per capita income.

Hopkins showed that there was a relationship between the level of economic development (measured by per capita income) and the proneness to coups and attempted coups. (This supports work by Lipset on the economic foundations of democracy.) Hopkins' results, reproduced (in part) below, cover the years 1957-64.

Table 2  Distribution of coups and attempted coups by states of economic development, 1957-64

| Stage of development | US $ GNP per capita, 1957 | No. of countries | Coups | Per cent with coups |
|---|---|---|---|---|
| I | 45 − 64 | 12 | 9 | 75 |
| II | 70 − 105 | 18 | 10 | 55 |
| III | 108 − 239 | 31 | 13 | 42 |
| IV | 262 − 794 | 36 | 5 | 13 |
| V | 836 − 2577 | 14 | 1 | 6 |

Source:  K. Hopkins, 'Civil-military relations in developing countries', *British Journal of Sociology*, 17, 2, June 1966, p.175.

The countries in the table have been grouped according to per capita product for 1957. Then, using Finer's criteria of civil military relations and van de Meheden's tabulation of military coups, the number of countries experiencing coups in 1957-64 is taken as a percentage of the number of countries in the group.[32] The final column shows a declining incidence in the percentage of coups in each income group as per capita product increases. Countries at the lowest stage of development, under $64 per capita product, had military interventions in 75 per cent of the cases, and countries at the higher stage of development (over $836 per capita product) had military interventions in only 6 per cent of the cases. Of the 38 military coups in Hopkins' Table, 32 occured in

32 S.E. Finer, *The Man on Horseback: The Role of the Military in Politics*, London, 1962; Van der Mehden, op. cit.

countries with under $239 per capita product. His calcu-
lations involved 111 countries, which must have included
countries in southern Africa, the Caribbean and Oceania. In
this book, most of these minor countries have been excluded
for reasons given in the Introduction.

Hopkins' findings have been re-calculated for the period
1960-72 for 77 countries, according to their 1967 per capita
income. These results are set out in Table 3. Because
Hopkins' original intervals at the low income end are no
longer realistic (only three countries had per capita incomes
below $64 in 1967, for example) the first two classes have
been combined.

The tendency noted by Hopkins is confirmed. The
low-income countries have shown a marked proneness to
military intervention. Whereas 75 per cent of the lowest-
income countries experienced military intervention in the
years 1957-64, this has risen to 90 per cent for 1960-72.
There has also been an increase in the third stage (under
$239) of from 42 per cent intervention to 87 per cent
inervention. In the two higher income groups the intervention rate runs at over 50 per cent in each case whereas in
Hopkins' table it was under 14 per cent. Military intervention
has increased since 1960; of the 286 military interventions,
over 200 occured since 1960.

Excluding the smaller island countries and those land-
locked in southern Africa, which all have special characteristics (though it did not prevent an unconstitutional seizure
of power in Lesotho in 1970), military intervention is
increasingly likely in a developing country, but more likely
still in the lower-income developing countries. Of the 59
countries that had military coups, 43 of them were countries
with under $239 per capita income. However, the proneness
to military intervention is highest among the per capita
income group $105 to $239 if the actual number of coup
attempts is divided by the countries in each group. For this
group the figure is roughly four coup attempts per country,
while for the lower income group it is roughly three coup
attempts per country (it is nearly 3½ and 2 coup attempts for
the two groups above $239 per capita income respectively).

Table 3 Distribution of military intervention by stages of economic development, 1960-72

| GNP per capita | No. of countries | Interventions | Per cent interventions |
|---|---|---|---|
| Under $105 | 21 | 19 | 90 |
| $106-239 | 29 | 25 | 87 |
| $252-239 | 23 | 14 | 61 |
| Over $812 | 4 | 2 | 50 |

Source: Calculated from per capita income data in ACDA, *World Military Expenditure 1968-69*, Washington, 1969; record of military interventions from Appendix A.

A different method of testing for a relationship between military intervention and non-military intervention is simply to take the arithmetic mean income of countries that have experienced military intervention and compare it with countries that have not. Because of the varying incomes between the regional groupings (e.g. Latin America has higher per capita incomes on average) which might draw the levels upwards, each calculation is kept within each regional grouping. In each case the tendency for interventions at lower average per capita product is pronounced.

Table 4 Military intervention and average per capita product (US $ per capita, 1967; 72 countries, 1960-72)

| | Africa $ | Asia $ | Middle East $ | Latin America $ |
|---|---|---|---|---|
| No intervention | 147 | 200 | 1387 | 470 |
| Intervention | 135 | 120 | 308 | 370 |

Military intervention increased considerably in the mid-sixties in Africa (there was in fact a whole spate of military intervention in 1966, the year that Hopkins' article was published) but hardly any change occured in the minor countries that have been included in Hopkins' calculations. The Latin American countries have relatively higher per capita incomes than other Third World regions and their proneness to military interventions pulls up the tendency to coup in the middle-income range. Four countries, Bolivia, Paraguay, Honduras and Ecuador, contributed almost half of the military interventions in this continent in the 1960s. They were also the four countries on the continent with the lowest per capita income.

The tendency then is for lower-income countries to experience military intervention. The probability of a successful intervention leading to a military government depends on a number of factors. If the intervention is successful the military government is likely to allocate more to defence spending. Thus any statistical relationship that might emerge between higher military spending and low per capita product would be a consequence of the low per capita product leading to military intervention and then to higher defence spending, rather than the other route of higher defence spending leading to low per capita product.

# 3 Violence
# and Governments

## 1. Introduction

The development process in the Third World is uneven. Each country does not reach the same stage at the same time, nor do the various sectors of the economic and social structure develop in phase. Growth, development and modernisation proceed in an unbalanced way for different countries, each starting off from different previous levels and responding to different natural endowments and local pressures. The process produces strains and stresses that are articulated in different forms according to the socio-political forces and counter-forces operating in each country. The rate of change is faster than in the colonial period, for both colony and metropolitan centres, and is taking place on all fronts, economic, social, cultural, political and military.[1]

The aspiration levels of the various social groups, peasantry, proletariat, middle class, ruling elite and the dispossessed, have risen faster than their competing claims can be satisfied. The minimum tolerable levels of per capita consumption[2] press on the actually achieved levels, and the result is a continual frustration, a feeling of alienation from yesterday's liberators and widespread cynicism at the open corruption of the political elite. There is a continual struggle between competing ideologies to guide the country out of its predicament. The millennium did not arrive with the achieve-

1 See Totten, op. cit. Totten makes a fourteen-point list of reasons for the legitimacy crisis, which contributed to the next few paragraphs.

2 See D. Seers, *A Theory of Inflation and Growth in Under-developed Economies Based on the Experience of Latin America*, Oxford Economic Papers 14, 2, 1962, for an analysis of how the minimum tolerable per capita consumption is a source for social tension.

ment of independence from European rule — in some cases
the post-independence years saw a drop in real income in the
country.[3] The traditional competes with the modern, with
the result that the modern is often an uncomfortable blend
between the old and the new. In the Islamic countries this
can be seen clearly in the schizophrenic nationalism of the
new elite, searching for both an Islamic ideal of total/
community and the modern reality of the nation state.[4]
Kemal Ataturk successfuly joined the forces of the past with
the forces of the future, but Egypt, Pakistan, Indonesia,
Algeria, Libya, for example, have had some difficulties in
achieving a similar marriage and in some cases have had to
deal firmly with the extremist religious sects of the Moslem
Brotherhood who fanatically resist religious compromise.[5]

The colonial heritage left behind many unresolved national
problems, of which the Palestinian is perhaps the most
intractable, and these have called for the attention of the new
elites and some of the problems have escalated into military
confrontations.[6] The border delineations of the European
powers, in Africa and Asia, have left sources of tension which
xenophobic nationalism cannot contain. In India the communal tensions between Hindu and Moslem, which have been
prominent in three wars, have been fed by the border
troubles in Kashmir and joined by the border tensions
between India and China.[7] The issues at stake — often barren

3 For example, this happened in Egypt after 1952.

4 S.G. Hain, 'Islam and the theory of Arab nationalism', in W.Z.
Laqueur (ed.), *The Middle East in Transition; Studies in Contemporary
History*, London, 1958; Be'eri, op. cit., p. 279; W.C. Smith, *Islam in
Modern History*, Princeton, 1957.

5 See W.Z. Laqueur, *Communism and Nationalism in the Middle
East*, New York, 1956, p.24: 'Military leadership thus meant a step
forward — but only one and no more. Having forced the rulers to
resign, the new governments proved incapable of giving the country the
lead which Kemal Ataturk had given Turkey in the early 1920s.'

6 S.N. Fisher, *The Middle East: A History*, London, 1960; S.
Hadaun, *Bitter Harvest: Palestine Between 1914 and 1967*, New York,
1967; M.B. Sharif, *Strangers in Palestine*, London, 1970.

7 See C.H. Philips and M.D. Wainwright (eds), *The Partition of
India: Policies and Perspectives*, London, 1970; A. Lamb, *The
McMahon Line*, vols 1 and 2, London, 1966; N. Maxwell, *India's China
War*, London, 1970, p.116, quotes Nehru on the border issue: 'Now, it

and useless tracts of uninhabited land — have been out-weighed by the emotionalism of the competing leaderships. Even Islamic powers such as Algeria and Morocco fought in 1963 over territorial claims and counter-claims.[8]

## 2.   *Violence in the party states*

Perhaps the most serious problem in the developing countries for the political structures is that of the succession. In Western societies, based on parliamentary democracy, defeated governments leave their desks gracefully and quietly and transform into an opposition. Troops and police are not called upon to install the new government. Defeated governments in countries that are newly independent sometimes refuse to leave office. In Sierra Leone in 1967 the defeated government supported a military coup that removed the new cabinet before it had occupied the government buildings.[9] A similar incident occurred in Lesotho. In other countries where the succession is in doubt, i.e. where the return to office of the incumbents may be in doubt or where the charismatic leader is anxious about the succession, the ruling party has attempted to create a one-party state (Kenya, Tanzania, Ghana, Cameroon, Zambia, Malawi).[10]

---

is a fact whether this village or that village, or this little strip of territory is on their side or on our side . . . it does seem rather absurd for two great countries . . . immediately to rush at each other's throats to decide whether two miles of territory are on this side or on that side, and especially two miles of territory in the high mountains, where nobody lives. But where national prestige and dignity is involved, it is not the two miles of territory, it is the nation's dignity and self-respect that becomes involved.' J. Nehru, *Lok Sabha*, 4 September 1959.

8 For an account of the territorial differences between Algeria and Morocco see C. Legum and J. Drysdale, *African Contemporary Record: Annual Survey and Documents 1968-9*, London, 1969.

9 H. Fisher, 'Elections and coups in Sierra Leone, 1967', *Journal of Modern African Studies*, 7, 4, December 1969. See also Chapter 5.

10 S.E. Finer, 'The one-party regimes in Africa: a reconsideration', *Government and Opposition*, 2, 4, July-October 1967; W. Tordoff, 'Tanzania: democracy and the one-party state', *Government and Opposition*, 2, 4, July-October 1967; A. Zolberg, *Creating Political Order: The Party States in West Africa*, Chicago, 1966; G.M. Carter, *African One Party States*, New York, 1963.

Party states are states where one or more political parties form the foundation of government. The succession in a one-party state can be arranged by a change in the top leadership, but sometimes there is irregular succession in the form of a military coup. It will be useful to separate out the party states from the military states in order to illustrate the extent of political and military violence in the Third World. This violence is not confined to the states run by military governments.

*Table 1    Party states: wars and insurgency operations, 1948-72*

| *Country* | *Insurgency* | *War* |
|---|---|---|
| Malaysia | 1948-54 Communist guerrillas | 'Confrontation' Indonesia 1962-65 |
| Singapore | Communist guerrillas | Indonesia 1962-65 |
| India | Naxalite and extremist violence | Sino-Indian 1962 Indo-Pakistan 1948, 1965, 1971 |
| Sri Lanka | Left-wing rural uprising 1971 | |
| Lebanon | Civil war 1962 | Arab-Israel war 1967; Border wars 1967-72 |
| Cameroon | Insurgency 1961 | |
| Israel | Arab terrorism since 1967 | Arab-Israel wars 1948, 1956, 1967; border incider |
| Philippines | Insurgency, Huk rebellions, 1950s; Maoist rising 1972 | Troops sent to Vietnam |
| Vietnam | 1945-54; 1956-72 | Invasion of Cambodia 1970; North Vietnam invasion of Laos, Cambodia, South Vietnam 1970-74 |
| Kenya | Somali separatist insurgency, 1963-67 | |
| Tanzania | | Uganda border war 1972 |
| Guinea | Attempted 'invasion' 1971 | |

| Country | Insurgency | War |
|---------|-----------|-----|
| Chad | Regional dissidents and insurgency 1965-66 and 1968 | |
| Guyana | Separatist action south-west border area 1970 | |
| Tunisia | | Border area used by FLN in Algerian war 1958-62 |
| Malawi | Insurgency and 'invasion' 1967 | |
| Uruguay | Urban guerrillas 1970-72 | |
| Colombia | Guerrillas 1960s | |
| Zambia | Religious insurgency 1964; base for insurgency operations against Rhodesia and Mozambique. | |

In Table 1 some of the wars and major counter-insurgency operations of the countries that have party state systems are listed. Israel, although a multi-party state, has been ruled without interruption by the Labour coalition. It has been described as a 'garrison state'.[11] The necessities of defence against Arab neighbours and their allies, who declare it their aim to liquidate the Israeli state and replace it with an Arab Palestine, has meant a major role for the Israeli army.[12] It has fought three major wars, in 1948, 1956, 1967, and has been on an alert status for many years. The terrorism of various Arab organisations has produced a large internal security presence combined in a surprisingly effective way with the maintenance of democratic government and opposi-

11 H. Lasswell, 'The garrison state', *American Journal of Sociology*, 46, January 1941; with reference to Israel, see A. Perlmutter, 'The praetorian state and the praetorian army: toward a taxonomy of civil-military relations in developing polities', *Comparative Politics*, 1, 3, April 1969, and *Military and Politics in Israel: Nation-Building or Role Expansion*, London, 1969.

12 This is the situation as seen by Israel. Not all advocates of the Palestinian cause exclude a role for the Jews in the new Palestine. See D. Berindranath, *War and Peace in West Asia*, New Delhi, 1969.

tion. Israel is a prime example of the exception to the view that military preparedness and tense internal security necessities are compatible only with authoritarian forms of government.

Vietnam, since 1968, has been a party state, having been previously an open military dictatorship, but the security situation has not been accompanied by a democratic system of government. The Vietnamese government is not democratic in an Israeli sense and it has a much lower level of legitimacy, both at home and abroad. War in Vietnam has been going on since the Japanese occupation, though, as has been argued previously, it is not the *same* war. The war against the French, which ended in 1954 with the fall of Dien Bien Phu, ended the anti-colonial war, and the subsequent war, between the Communists and the South, has been a civil war. The Vietnamese war is also complicated by the associated wars in Cambodia, Laos and, to an extent, in Thailand. Proponents of the 'domino theory' (Vietnam is the first 'domino' in a line of them which when it is toppled will automatically topple the others) have fitted the facts to their schema.

The South Vietnamese army invaded Cambodia in 1970 in pursuit of the war aims of the South Vietnamese against the indigenous Viet Cong and their North Vietnamese allies.[13] This aggressive behaviour is not confined to Vietnamese armies; both the party states of India and Israel, which are democratic in ways which South Vietnam has only pretentions to being, have invaded adjacent territory, and held on to it. The Israeli occupation of Sinai, the Golan heights and the west bank of the Jordan has much more fundamental territorial aims[14] than that of the South Vietnamese in

13  M. Sayle, 'Cambodia: why Nixon went in', *Sunday Times*, London, 3 May 1970; R.W. Apple, 'A third front in Indo-China', *New Statesman*, London, 24 April 1970.

14  Israel's occupation of some parts of the captured territory is likely to be long-term. The Golan Heights in Syria have military value as a defence position. Jerusalem has strong emotional significance. Sinai, Gaza and the west bank of the Jordan river are negotiable. The South Vietnamese invasion of Cambodia was part of the on-going war against the Communist forces. There was no attempt to annexe the country. The North Vietnamese armies in Laos and Cambodia had similar intentions, fought behind the cover of indigenous forces (local People's Liberation Armies).

Cambodia, or for that matter, the North Vietnamese in Laos and Cambodia. India's dispute with Pakistan in Kashmir led to her occupying whatever parts of Kashmir she was able to hold on to in the 1948 and 1965 wars.[15] In contrast the Indian occupation of East Pakistan, now Bangladesh, in 1971, was terminated by mutual agreement with the Bangladesh authorities within a few months.[16]

The other major 'war' was the so-called 'confrontation' between Sukarno's Indonesia and the newly formed state of Malaysia during 1963-5. Sukarno was attempting to emulate his successful 'confrontation' with the Dutch in West Irian in 1963, which gave Indonesia the whole of Dutch New Guinea for a small outlay in bluster and moderate troop deployment.[17] Sukarno's campaign against Malaysia was not successful, it burdened the economy with a massive arms budget (little of which went to the army with consequent disaffection), drove Sukarno nearer to the Communists, and isolated Indonesia from other Asian countries. For Malaysia it had the opposite effect in integrating the disparate communities that made up the Malaysian Federation.

The party states have been subjected to insurgency from various sources. In Malaysia it was Communist-led but the military intervention of the British reduced it to meagre levels by 1954.[18] Further activity is being reported around the northern border region and combined operations are being undertaken by the Thailand and Malaysian governments to prevent the insurgents using either country as a refuge. A similar arrangement between the Indonesian and Malaysian armies is operating in Sarawak against dissident

15 K.M. Penikkar, *The Founding of the Kashmir State*, London, 1953; and L.J. Kavic, *India's Quest for Security: Defence Policies 1947-1965*, Berkeley and Los Angeles, 1967.

16 The Indian army took away over 90,000 Pakistani prisoners of war and was still holding these in 1973.

17 For some of the implications of the success of the anti-Dutch confrontation see the perceptive article by G.J. Pauker, 'The role of the military in Indonesia, in J.J. Johnson (ed.), *The Role of the Military in Underdeveloped Countries*, Princeton, 1962.

18 L.W. Pye, *Guerrilla Communism in Malaya: Its Social and Political Meaning*, Princeton, 1956; H. Miller, *Jungle War in Malaya: The Campaign against Communism 1948-60*, London, 1972.

Communists operating in the remote jungle areas on the border between the two countries.[19] In the Philippines the postwar 'Huk' rebellions were likewise contained, but they have recently been succeeded by new style Communist groups.[20] The reported extent of the rebellions in 1972, about 10,000 armed troops and ten times as many supporters according to official sources, was used by the Marcos government to enforce a state of martial law,[21] and establish a dictatorship, with all the hallmarks, in retrospect, of a military coup.

In India, communal violence has been a feature of the country's political life since it was founded in 1949. In the latter half of the 1960s extremist violence of an ideological type began to appear, the 'Naxalites' for example, and necessitated the use of troops and counter-insurgency policy actions.[22] Sri Lanka underwent a rural uprising led by youthful left-wing cadres in 1971. It required the use of troops and the import of modern counter-insurgency equipment to put it down.[23]

The party states, whether democratic or authoritarian, have been faced with insurgency violence, sometimes on an extensive scale but not always assisted from outside. The legitimacy crisis is not confined to regimes that have illegitimate roots. Those countries that have established forms of rule that carry the characteristics of legitimate

19 Indonesian Embassy, *Indonesian News*, London, 5 October 1972, p.11, reported the first meeting of the 'Regional Border Committee' which set up a 'Headquarters, Combined Operations Co-ordinating Command' to 'eradicate more efficiently the Communists in the border areas'.

20 E. Lachicen, *The Huks: Philippine Agrarian Society in Revolt*, New York, 1971. The Huks applied Maoist fixed-base strategy and this contributed to their defeat. The new revolutionaries have apparently learnt this lesson.

21 See *Keesing's Contemporary Archives*, November, 1972. Muslim dissidents in the south have also complicated the emergency situation.

22 See Appendix B.

23 F. Halliday, 'The Ceylonese insurrection', *New Left Review*, 69, September-October 1971; S. Arasartman, 'The Ceylonese insurrection of April 1971: some causes and consequences', *Pacific Affairs*, 45, 3, 1972. In the text Ceylon is referred to by its new (1972) official name Sri Lanka.

government, that have widespread support for and belief in their legitimate functions, and have integrated relatively successfully the administrative and political elite, are not immune to challenge to this status both within and without the country. Of the 29 party states considered here only two, Gambia and Mauritania, had not experienced military operations outside the country or counter-insurgency operations

*Table 2    Party states in the Third World, 1972*

| | | | |
|---|---|---|---|
| Malaysia | + | Zambia | + |
| Singapore | + | Sierra Leone | * |
| India | + | Gabon | * |
| Sri Lanka | + | Gambia | |
| Lebanon | +* | Philippines[1] | + |
| Mauritania | | Vietnam | +* |
| Cameroon | + | Tunisia | +* |
| Ivory Coast | * | Chad | +* |
| Niger | * | Mexico | + |
| Senegal | * | Guyana | + |
| Kenya | * | Chile[2] | + |
| Liberia | * | Costa Rica | * |
| Malawi | + | Israel | + |
| Tanzania | +* | Uruguay[3] | + |
| Guinea | +* | Pakistan[4] | +* |

Notes:  (+) indicates military activity in counter-insurgency or intra-country hostilities.
(*) indicates at least one coup or attempted coup, post-war.
1  The Marcos 'coup' in late 1972 may have permanently transformed Philippines from a party state into a dictatorship.
2  The civilian Allende government was overthrown by military coup in September, 1973.
3  The civilian government was severely compromised by illegal military actions in the summer of 1973.
4  Pakistan was under military rule from 1958 to the end of the Bangladesh war. It can be included in this table and the one for military states. How long President Bhutto's civilian regime will survive is a matter not yet determined and its inclusion as a party state is provisional.

inside between the end of the Second World War and 1972.[24] (The complete list is shown in Table 2.) This means that 93 per cent of the party states had been effected by insurgencies or wars.

### 3.    Violence in monarchical states

There is another group of states that are neither party states nor governed by military regimes. These are the monarchies and include Morocco, Iran, Jordan, Saudi Arabia, Gulf Oil States, Afghanistan and Ethiopia. The political composition of these states is mixed; Jordan, for example, is practically indistinguishable from a military-governed country: the King is totally identified with his army and personally supervises it.[25] In comparison to Egypt under Nasser, who left the army as a serving officer when he assumed supreme power,[26] King Hussein's involvement with his army is much more intimate. Yet Egypt would be described as a military state, at least under Nasser.

Morocco is somewhat different from the Jordan model. Its monarch has been introducing some form of party government into the country, but the King's relations with the army are questionable in view of the two attempted coups against his rule from within his immediate entourage[27] in a period of one year. With this in mind, and because it might have confused the issue to have included them in the category of

24 H.A. Gailey, *A History of Gambia*, London, 1964, Chapter 10, 'Political parties'; for Mauritania, see Legum and Drysdale, op. cit.

25 G.M. Haddad, *Revolutions and Military Rule in the Middle East*, vol. 2, *The Arab States*, Chapter 6, 'Jordan: the genius for survival', New York, 1971. See K.J. Newman, 'The new monarchies of the Middle East', *Journal of International Affairs*, 13, 2, 1959 for a discussion of the quasi-monarchical role of the military regimes of Egypt, Iraq and Pakistan. There are similarities between the open military regimes and the militant monarchies.

26 A. Nutting, *Nasser*, London, 1972.

27 His Chief-of-Staff and the Minister of Defence were implicated in the coups of 1971 and 1972, but were 'killed' in action. The King's personal pilot, who safely landed the damaged Royal aircraft after it was shot at by jets from the airforce, was made head of the airforce after the coup was defeated. Another coup attempt by insurrection was reported in April 1973. Many of the leaders were executed throughout 1973 and others received long prison sentences.

party state, a separate Table has been compiled (Table 3) showing the military engagements of these countries.

Table 3   Military involvements of monarchical states

| Country | Insurgency | War |
|---|---|---|
| Jordan | Palestine guerrillas 1967-72 | Arab-Israel 1948 and 1967 |
| Morocco | | Algeria, 1963 over disputed territory |
| Gulf Oil States | Numerous rebellions since 1960s | |
| Ethiopia | Eritrean separatists 1960-72 | Somalia over disputed territory 1964 |
| Saudi Arabia | | Support and refuge for Yemeni royalists |
| Iran* | Baluchistan Tribesmen across Pakistan border | Seizure of disputed islands in the Gulf |

* In 1973, Iran and Pakistan co-operated in actions directed against dissident Baluchi tribesmen living on both sides of the border.

The most serious involvement in the Table is the Jordan and Israeli wars of 1948 and 1967. In the 1956 Arab-Israeli war Jordan was not directly involved, though it felt threatened enough to ask for Iraqi military assistance. The Palestinian guerrilla organisations that were operating in Jordanian territory were a particular difficulty. The west bank of the Jordan river is Jordanian territory and is regarded by the displaced Arabs as part of Palestine.[28] The guerrilla groups, competing with each other for the leadership of the anti-Israel struggle, were less than responsible in their actions, and, frustrated with their efforts against the Israeli occupation, they turned on those Arabs whom they regard as 'soft' on Israel.

The Hussein monarchy, which has been a moderating force in the Arab-Israel conflict and has never felt at one with the

28  R. John and S. Hadaun, *The Palestinian Diary*, (2 vols.) Beirut, 1970; T. Little, 'The nature of the Palestinian resistance movement', *Asian Affairs*, 57, June 1970.

extremist republican allies of Syria, Iraq and Egypt (and even less so with the militant Libyan and Algerian republics), has sought a middle road for settlement. The guerrilla groups have also been oriented towards the ideological left, and this has worked to divide them from the Jordanian government. The outbreaks of open warfare between the Jordanian army and the guerrilla groups since 1967 have been full-scale military confrontations, but the Jordanian armour on all occasions has proved superior to the guerrilla irregulars. The guerrillas tried to force the issue between them and the government by occupying the capital, Amman, but after several days' fighting they were defeated. The guerrilla camps were vulnerable to direct attack by the Jordanians and this forced them to stand and fight against a heavier fire-power that gave the Jordanians a clear advantage.[29]

Ethiopia has also faced a substantial internal rebellion.[30] The Eritrean separatists have been fighting since 1960, though with varying levels of intensity. They have received support from the Arab countries, particularly Libya, and also from Soviet sources. The United States has a communications centre in Eritrea, but this has not been a target for the separatists, nor apparently an issue in the conflict. The border between Somalia and Ethiopia has also been a source of conflict. Somalia claims about a third of Ethiopia's territory, and also half of the French enclave of Afar and Issa on the Red Sea, on the grounds of the presence of substantial numbers of Somali tribesmen in these areas.[31] The pressure on Ethiopia broke out into a two-day border war in 1964 but

29 D. Lomax, 'A diary of the Jordan civil war', *Listener*, London, 10 October 1970; J. Bullock, 'Taming Jordan's guerrillas', *Daily Telegraph*, London, 5 March 1970.

30 J.S. Roucek, 'Ethiopia's boiling cauldron: prospects and potentials', *Contemporary Review*, May 1970; and for a pro-Ethiopian background of how Eritrea joined Ethiopia, see E.S. Pankhurst, *Ethiopia and Eritrea: The Last Phase of the Reunion Struggle, 1941-1952*, London, 1953. For a Marxist analysis see F. Halliday, 'The fighting in Eritrea', *New Left Review*, 67, May-June 1971; G. Morrison, *The Southern Sudan and Eritrea: Aspects of Wider African Problems*, London, 1971.

31 J. Drysdale, *The Somali Dispute*, London, 1964; *The Somali Peninsular: A New Light on Imperial Motives*, 1962.

the contest was indecisive (there were reports that both sides ran out of fuel). What it did do, however, was to spark off a military build-up in both countries, with the Americans supplying Ethiopia and the Russians Somalia. The problem for Ethiopia is that if it conceded the Eritrean territory, *and* the area claimed by Somalia, *and* the areas claimed by the Sudan, it would shrink to about a third of its present size. This problem has a long history; it was the 'Walwal' incident in December 1934 near Somalia's border that led to Mussolini's invasion of Ethiopia in 1936.[32]

Border problems affected Morocco, Ethiopia, Iran, Jordan, the Gulf States and Saudi Arabia in the period 1960-72. It is the common problem of the monarchies. Morocco after independence claimed large tracts of Algeria, the whole of Mauritania and part of Mali (if these claims were successful, Morocco would treble in size and double its population).[33] In five of the six cases these border disputes have led to military conflict and none of the actual disputes have been settled permanently. The Moroccans have shelved their claims for the time being, and so have the Somalis. Iran has just begun her campaign for the Gulf islands, which is seen by her neighbours as the opening moves to absorb the Gulf States themselves. The Arab-Israeli conflict is nowhere near a solution. The Yemeni disturbances, which resulted in 1972 in a unification of the two Yemeni states (Yemen Republic and South Yemen), have spilled over into border troubles with Saudi Arabia and are likely in the future to continue to be a source of difficulty for the Royalist Saudi Arabia. The Republican Yemen also has now to contain a Marxian influence following the 1972 unification[34] with South Yemen.

32 A.D. Boca, *The Ethiopian War, 1935-1941*, Chicago, 1935; G.W. Baer, *The Coming of the Italian-Ethiopian War*, Cambridge, Mass., 1967, Chapter 3.

33 Legum and Drysdale, op. cit., p.86.

34 R. Graham, 'Yemen unity: the raising of the veil', *Financial Times*, London, 15 December 1972.

### 4.   *Violence in the military states*

Thirty-five military-governed countries out of 42 listed in Table 4 have been engaged in military activity either against internal insurgency or against external armies. (see Table 5). The decision to classify a country as a military-governed country is in some cases quite arbitrary. In the Table we have included Pakistan because it was under military rule between 1958 and 1971, and during that time it fought two wars against India. Since 1971, following the defeat of the Pakistan army in the Eastern wing of the country, subsequently re-named Bangladesh, the country has had a civilian government headed by Mr Bhutto. In other cases, such as Egypt and Korea, the regime was ruled by a 'retired' leading figure whose power base remained the military. Colonel Nasser's strength lay in his balancing role between the elite groups in post-Farouk Egypt, but his mainstay was always the loyalty of the military forces. General Park of Korea retired from the army command after he sought legitimisation of his military coup in Presidential elections.[35]

In many Latin American countries the same type of formula is followed whereby the (not always) leading member of the military junta is endorsed as a 'Presidential' candidate by the other members to seek democratic endorsement of the takeover in an army-organised election. But as the military in these countries remains in a leading position within the governing elite, often providing cabinet ministers for key posts, and acts as a ghost 'second chamber' for the regime, it is more accurate to class these regimes as military in composition. The removal of the military as a force, such as in Turkey under Kemal Ataturk, or Mexico under Cardenas, is a qualitatively different process from the 'removal' of the military in Korea and Egypt, and in the 1972 political experiments in Indonesia.[36] This is not to say that

35 Se-Jin Kim, *The Politics of Military Revolutions in Korea*, Carolina, 1971.

36 See *Indonesian News*, Indonesian Embassy, London, 5 November 1972. Briefly, there has been a military-sponsored re-grouping of political parties based on religious alignments. The idea is that two parties will emerge out of these groupings to form a government and an opposition. Meanwhile the army dominates the People's Consultative Assembly in which the two groups have minority status.

leaders of Nasser's, Park's or Suharto's ability are mere puppets; far from it — it is their very charisma that holds the loyalty of the military.[37] It is their personal successes in ruling in this way that creates problems for their less charismatic successors.

*Table 4   Countries with military governments, 1970*

| | |
|---|---|
| Burma | Rwanda |
| Thailand | Somalia |
| Cambodia | Uganda |
| Taiwan | Togo |
| Yemen Republic | Upper Volta |
| South Yemen | Mali |
| Algeria | Bolivia |
| Iraq | Peru |
| Syria | Paraguay |
| Libya | Panama |
| Sudan | Nicaragua |
| Central African Republic | Honduras |
| Zaire | Guatemala |
| Congo (Brazzaville) | El Salvador |
| Burundi | Ecuador |
| Dahomey | Argentina |
| Ghana | Venezuela |
| Malagasy Republic | Brazil |
| Nigeria | Korea |
| Indonesia | Vietnam |
| Pakistan (until 1971) | Egypt |
| Chad | |

The main wars fought by military governments include the Vietnam war and the Arab-Israeli wars. These are the two major wars of the Third World. The Vietnam war has already been discussed briefly, but it should be noted here that the combatants included representative forces from Korea, Taiwan, Thailand, Philippines, Australia and New Zealand. Three of the Asian powers had military governments at the time, but Philippines was a party state. Their involvement

37 For an insight into General Park's political position see Park Chung Hee: *The Country, The Revolution and I*; *Our Nation's Path*; *Major Speeches*, Seoul, 1962 (in English).

*Table 5* *Military states — wars and counter-insurgency, 1945-72*

| Country | Insurgency | War |
| --- | --- | --- |
| Pakistan | Communal violence Pathans, Baluchi dissidents | India-Pakistan 1965 and 1971 — Bangladesh |
| Korea | | Korean war 1950-54 Vietnam 1960s |
| Indonesia | Separatist rebellions | 'Confrontation' with Dutch, 1963; Malaysia 1963-65 |
| Burma | Insurgency, Karens, Mons, Communists, KMT, Arakanese | |
| Thailand | Communists north-west region and Malaysian border | Vietnam war 1965-72 |
| Cambodia | Civil war since 1970 | Vietnam war; south Vietnamese invasion, North Vietnamese invasions. |
| Taiwan | | Mainland China since 1949; Vietnam 1960s |
| Yemen Republic | Civil war 1960-67 | South Yemen 1972 |
| South Yemen | Anti-British terrorism | Yemen Republic 1972 |
| Iraq | Kurdish revolt 1950-70 | Arab-Israel wars 1948 and 1967; Iran, Kuwait border incidents 1972-73 |
| Egypt | | Arab Israel wars 1948, 1956, 1967 |
| Syria | | Arab-Israel war 1967 |
| Algeria | Anti-government dissidents, 1967 | Morocco 1963 |
| Turkey | Urban guerrillas 1971-72 | |
| Sudan | Southern rebellion 1960-70 | |
| Libya | Aid to guerrilla movements in Africa and Middle East | Aid to Uganda 1972 |

| Country | Insurgency | War |
|---------|-----------|-----|
| Zaire | Secessionist rebellions 1961-67 | |
| Burundi | Watutsi and Bahutu tribal wars | Rwanda conflict 1963 |
| Rwanda | Watutsi and Bahutu tribal wars | Burundi conflict 1963 |
| Nigeria | Biafra civil war 1967-70 | Action in Zaire 1961 |
| Ghana | | Action in Congo 1961 |
| Somali | | Ethiopia 1965 |
| Uganda | 'Invasion' civil war 1972 | Tanzania clashes 1972 |

was relatively minor and served political purposes. The economic consequences of the Vietnam war on these countries is discussed later. The Arab-Israeli wars have been of relatively short duration. The actual fighting has lasted days rather than years and the political issues between the combatants have not been resolved in any of the military encounters. As the military preparedness has had to be maintained among all the countries concerned, and in economic terms this has given these countries the largest proportional military budgets of the Third World, it is possible to consider the entire period from the founding of the state of Israel in 1948 to the present as a continuous period of war. The Middle East is not a peaceful zone and the effects are felt in the economies of all the countries; trade and development has been distorted to take account of the hostilities between the countries. Chapter 13 will examine some of these economic effects in greater detail.

Zaire, Nigeria, Cambodia, Indonesia, Yemen and Sudan have been involved in civil wars and practically all of the Latin American countries have conducted counter-insurgency operations for some period during the 1960s.[38] Arising from

38 See R. Gott, *Guerrilla Movements in Latin America*, London, 1971; L.M. Vegas, *Guerrillas in Latin America: The Techniques of the Counter-State*, New York, 1970.

this continental problem, the Argentinians have prospects of a major breakthrough for their ailing indigenous aircraft industry with a domestically designed and produced counter-insurgency fighter.

In Yemen and Cambodia the civil wars began after the seizure of power by a military junta and were between those recently dispossessed of power, but with substantial support in the country, and prospects of assistance from abroad, and those recently taking over the country, also with support at home and abroad. The Yemeni royalists were supported by the royalist Saudi Arabians and the Yemeni Republicans were supported by the Nasserist regime in Egypt. Nasser sent up to 60,000 troops to participate in the fighting as well as part of the Egyptian airforce.[39]

In Cambodia the overthrow of Prince Sihanouk by the Lon Nol military junta had fortunate consequences for the Americans fighting in neighbouring Vietnam. It closed the ports of Cambodia to Communist war supplies and threw the whole logistical burden of the Viet Cong and North Vietnamese on to the so-called 'Ho Chi Minh' route to South Vietnam. The anti-Lon Nol forces consist of the Communist armies (North Vietnamese regular troops, Viet Cong and Khmer Rouge guerrillas) and Cambodian troops loyal to Sihanouk. There are South Vietnamese regulars and Cambodian American-trained veterans of the Vietnam war arrayed on the government side with the main Cambodian army.[40]

The Indonesian civil war was resolved after about 300,000 people were killed, most of them members of the PKI (Indonesian Communist Party).[41] The Communist coup of 30 September 1965 was foiled by the surviving army leaders, who then turned on the Communists (and encouraged others

39 For an assessment of the economic consequences of Egypt's role in Yemen see E. Kanovsky, *The Economic Impact of the Six Day War: Israel, the Occupied Territories, Egypt, Jordan*, New York, 1970.

40 D. Warner, 'Cambodia's Achilles' heel', *Daily Telegraph*, London, 21 June 1971. The civil war in Cambodia has not been resolved by September 1973, though Phnom Penh, the capital, was under severe rebel pressure.

41 Polomka,   op. cit., pp. 160-1.

to do likewise). Eventually the army leadership removed President Sukarno from office and installed a military government. (This will be dealt with in more detail in Chapter 6.)

In Nigeria the Biafran civil war had similar beginnings in an attempted coup that was foiled by surviving army leaders and loyal units. The January 1966 attempted coup was interrupted in the sense that the original leaders agreed to recognise the surviving Commander-in-Chief, General Ironsi, who assumed executive power. The rebels had liquidated the major political leaders of Nigeria in the early stages of their coup. Ironsi fell in July 1966 to another coup led by a tribal group, the northerners, who had interpreted the January coup as a tribal attack on non-Ibos. The resultant anti-Ibo purges and murders drove the Ibos into a state of paranoia. In 1967 the Ibos declared their secession from Nigeria and the Biafran war began.[42] It ended with a reported 2 million dead and a re-unified Nigeria.

In Zaire (formerly the Belgian Congo) the country was torn by a civil war between the secessionist Katanga state and the central government headed by Lumumba.[43] The military governments of Mobuta came after periods of civil unrest and secessionist campaigns. The military came to power to enforce central authority in a country which in many areas did not feel subject to government from Kinshasa.

In Sudan, the southern rebellion for independence continued through military and civilian governments and was finally settled by the granting of autonomy within the state of Sudan by the military government in 1970.[44] In both the

42 R. Luckham, *The Nigerian Military: A Sociological Analysis of Authority and Revolt, 1960-1967*, London, 1971; W. Dillon, 'Nigeria's two revolutions', *African Report*, 11, March 1966; R.L. Sklar, 'Nigeria's politics in perspective', *Government and Opposition*, 2, 4, July-October 1967; M. Perham, 'Reflections on the Nigerian civil war', *International Affairs*, 46, April 1970.

43 A.P. Merrican, *Congo: Background to Conflict*, Evanston, Ill., 1961; C. Hoskyns, *The Congo Since Indepence, January 1960-December 1961*, London, 1965: C.C. O'Brien, *To Katanga and Back*, London, 1964.

44 M.O. Beshir, *The Southern Sudan: Background to Conflict*, London, 1968; O. Albino, *The Sudan: A Southern Viewpoint*, London,

Congo and the Sudan the military regimes were not the cause of the rebellions; neither were they entirely a consequence of them. The central authority was challenged by secession and was not able to cope, but this ineffectiveness was expressed in other fields beside secession; they were ineffective right across the administrative structure. The military intervention was aimed at re-organising the whole of the government and dealing with a wide range of problems, as well as that of the rebellions.

This is in contrast to the civil war in Cambodia, and probably Nigeria as well, where the direct issue of the survival of the central government had to take precedence over other issues. The legitimacy of the central government is at stake in all cases, but there is a difference between these civil wars. In Cambodia the civil war is about which political group shall run the central government (similarly in Laos and Vietnam), while in Sudan, Pakistan, Zaire, Nigeria, Ethiopia, the issue was, or is, about whether there shall be a central government at all. Secessionist civil wars aim to break up a country; civil wars aim to change the government.

To date the only successful secessionist example is Bangladesh. This was aided by the vast geographical distance between the two wings of Pakistan and the decisive support of the Indian army.[45] Katanga (Zaire) and Biafra (Nigeria) are two examples of total failure of secession. The central government had substantial assistance from outside powers in the form of military aid (Nigeria) and military intervention (Zaire). The Bangladesh war was a local affair involving the Indian army, the West Pakistan army and the East Pakistan irregulars. Threatened intervention from China and America did not materialise.

---

1970; P. Kilner, 'Sudan: a year of revolution', *African Affairs*, 69, October 1970; A Nutting, 'A new Biafra looms behind Sudan's grass curtain', *Sunday Times*, 29 November 1970; Morrison, op. cit.

45 'How India set out to win the east', *Economist*, December, 1971; P. Hazelhurst, 'Obsession with war on the sub-continent', *The Times*, London, 25 October 1971; K.U. Ahmad, *Break-up of Pakistan: Background and Prospects of Bangladesh*, London, 1972. Ahmad makes the additional point that the success of Bangladesh separatism was an expression of the motivation of the Bengali people to overcome Pan-Islamic religious fantasies.

The Katanga and Biafra separatists had a less obvious case than Bangladesh; they were geographically adjacent to central government territory, they contained vast sources of natural wealth (copper in Katanga and oil in Biafra), which were earmarked by the central government for the purchase of development resources and also as a source of revenue, and, while the economic viability of the proposed states was not in doubt, the political and economic effects of separation on the central government states was, with as little doubt, likely to be serious.[46]

The separatist rebellions in Indonesia, a country which lends itself to disintegrative upheavals, were eventually put down by the central authorities. In spite of conditions conducive to weak central government, Indonesia has managed to produce a central government apparatus, both in the Sukarno phase and after, with sufficient cohesion to hold together the vast country, spread as it is among numerous islands.[47]

In Burma, the military socialist government is in firm control, and the numerous isolated ethnic and political rebellions have become an established feature of the country.[48] The Communist guerrillas in north-western Thailand are an inevitable counter-force to the pro-American military governments and with their counterparts along the Malaysian border will require increased attention after the end of open hostilities in Vietnam.

Iraq has had to face the Kurdish separatists since they returned from the Soviet Union in 1954. The Kurds have fought for a separate Kurdish Republic with varying degrees of intensity over the years. Their presence in Iraq and their campaign of violence against the central authority was not unhelpful to the Soviet Union's foreign policy of loosening

46 See E.W. Nafziger, 'The economic impact of the Nigerian civil war', *Journal of Modern African Studies*, 10, 2, 1972, for the importance of the Eastern Region's oil to the Nigerian economy.

47 Pauker, op. cit.; J.R. Smail, 'The military politics of North Sumatra, December 1956-October 1967', *Indonesia*, October 1968.

48 J.H. Badgley, 'Two styles of military rule: Thailand and Burma', *Government and Opposition*, 4, 1, 1969. M. Lissak, 'The military in Burma: innovations and frustrations', *Asian African Studies*, 5, 1969.

up the Baghdad Pact countries which were in alliance with America during the Cold War. The Kurdish demands for autonomy were persistent enough to continue even throughout periods when Iraqi governments were friendly to the Soviet Union. Some of these governments made truces with the Kurds, granted them limited autonomy and, without exception, went on to try a military solution to the unresolved difficulties. The problem therefore remains.[49]

Military governments are not more successful in dealing with ethnic rebellions than party governments. If the ethnic minority are persistent enough and well led, the central authority must come to terms with them. A country that includes several nations cannot have a legitimised government that ignores their felt interests. They can have a government ruling by force, and under siege, but this has economic costs that in the end produce war-weariness. Genocide may suggest itself to some beleaguered governments, and the fact that it has been tried on a modest scale by some, some of whose governments have the technology available for genocidic policies, suggests that the problem does not always produce this solution. When the ethnic problem is also complicated by ideological allegiances — for example, the Eritrean separatists have a Marxist-Leninist wing — the central government's task is not made any easier, because this invites material or diplomatic assistance from their ideological friends.

### 5.    Conclusion

Does the political system, then, have any relationship to the incidents of wars and insurgency? First, we can take the number of wars and insurrections that each political system has experienced as a percentage of the number of countries that had that political system. If we take the type of political system — party state or military government — at the time that the event occured, countries that experienced war or insurrection when they were a party state and then when they were a military state will of course appear in both divisions.

---

49 Haddad, op. cit., vol. 1, *The Northern Tier.*

*Table 6  Percentage of countries in each political group that have experienced war or insurrection since 1945 according to political status at time of event*

| Political system | War | Insurrection |
|---|---|---|
| Party (40) | 28% | 55% |
| Military (43) | 30% | 56% |

The percentages in each category are almost identical and this suggests that the percentage of countries in each political system that have *not* experienced war or insurrection is about the same. Whether the incidence of war and insurrection is the same in each group would be of interest as well because this would indicate the proneness of the political system to these forms of violence. The difficulty here is that the political system sometimes changed between violent incidents, and also it is extremely difficult to judge when, say, an insurrection is a continuing event or an isolated incident.

About a third of all countries in the Third World (i.e. on the sample used here) have been involved in wars and about half of them in insurrections. This is a significant record of major incidents of violence.

Another way that we can answer the question about the incidence of violence in the political system is to find the percentage of countries that have experienced major incidents of violence according to the political systems that existed in 1971. Thus a country that had experienced a war or insurrection as a party state and had subsequently changed its political system to a military state (e.g. Indonesia) would be included only in the military state division.

*Table 7  Percentage of countries in each political group by 1971 political status that have experienced war or insurrection since 1945*

| Political system | War | Insurrection |
|---|---|---|
| Party (29) | 26% | 45% |
| Monarchy (7) | 71% | 57% |
| Military (42) | 45% | 64% |

In Table 7 there is a much more pronounced tendency for the military states of 1971 to have experienced major violent incidents such as war or insurrection since 1945 than for the countries whose political system of party rule had survived by then. A large number of countries have changed their political system from party states, or monarchies, to military states. As Table 6 shows, the experience of major violence is evenly distributed between the political systems, and therefore if the states that have experienced major violence as party states have also gone over to military rule in any numbers this is bound to increase the apparent relationship between major violence and the military states.

This cannot imply a causal relationship between violence and military government. For example, in a similar exercise we could relate natural disasters such as earthquakes and floods to the political systems. Assuming that natural disasters are equally distributed geographically, then as the number of military governments increased over time one could be drawn to the spurious conclusion that natural disasters are related to military governments. Thus the relationship between violence and military governments may be a qualified relationship such that the violence creates conditions in which a military solution is a possibility. In that the violence is an element in the legitimacy crisis, the prevalence of military rule after ten or twenty years of wrestling with this crisis can be seen to be a consequence of the violence rather than a cause of it.

# 4 The Role of the Military

## 1. Introduction

We have already expressed the view that the legitimacy thesis is the most appropriate explanation for the military in the Third World. This chapter takes up some of the implications of this view. In later chapters we will examine in greater detail military interventions in a number of countries.

## 2. The role of the military

The legitimacy crisis in the developing world rests on the inability of any of the competing elites to sustain a political leadership for a long enough time for its concepts of public good to be supported by other elites and by the masses.[1] The conflict situation is a permanent feature of the political system;[2] it is pluralistic, involving conflicts within the governing elite (which group or family or personality is to lead), and between the traditional and the modernising, between village and city, peasant and worker, landlords and tenants, collective and individual, ethnic groups and religions, Europeans and nationals, the unemployed and the employed, buyers and sellers, administrators and subjects, and the rising and falling groups.

In a developed society the pluralistic conflicts are constrained and within limits reinforce the stability of the society; in the developing world, the pluralistic conflicts are factionalising and keep the state off-balance.

1 I.L. Horowitz, 'Political legitimacy and the institutional crisis in Latin America', *Comparative Political Studies*, 1, 1, 1968, p.45.

2 S. Andrzejewski, *Military Organisation and Society*, London, 1954, p.8.

The competing elites are inward-looking with short horizons — today's manoeuvre against opponents is more absorbing than tomorrow's — and this is prismatically reflected in the whole social structure by the acceptance of corruption. Corruption is a tax on getting things done, it raises the cost of activity.[3] It ensures that a minority re-distributes income towards themselves, by virtue of their position in the state bureaucracy, and this transforms the state into a semi-private 'taxation' system. The struggle for power in the state is also a struggle for access to this 'taxation franchise'. Illegal taxes have always been a source for sedition, and for cynicism. These are two sufficient conditions for a crisis in legitimacy, and a challenge to civil order.[4]

Civil order is preserved by the legitimacy of the regime or by the force of arms. In a developing country the armed forces (sometimes) are the only uncontaminated force in the state. Their attitude on these occasions to corruption is disdainful, a mixture of self-congratulatory piety and an outspoken bitterness regarding politicians who are thought to be practising corruption. They regard the military virtues as being unquestionably superior to civilian virtues.[5]

The military is often the most successfully Westernised of all the institutions in the developing countries.[6] Its hierarchical organisation is a carbon-copy of the Western army; its weapons are comparable, if slightly dated, and the organisational prerequisites of a Western army, which they invariably copy, flow from the technology common to both.[7] Supersonic aircraft, missiles, heavy armour, artillery and

3 See G. Myrdal, *Asian Drama: An Inquiry into the Poverty of Nations*, London, 1969, vols. 1, 2, 3. Corruption is an important phenomenon, particularly in the Third World; yet it is also one of the most neglected areas of research in social science. Myrdal makes several suggestions as to why this is so.

4 For an illuminating account of the role of the state and taxation in the early development of a society see J. Hicks, *A Theory of Economic History*, London, 1968.

5 M. Janowitz, *The Military in the Political Development of New Nations: An Essay in Comparative Analysis*, Chicago, 1964, p.58.

6 H. Daalder, *The Role of the Military in the Emerging Countries*, The Hague, 1962, p.12.

7 For the organisational imperatives of military technology see M. Janowitz, *Sociology and the Military Establishment*, New York, 1965.

logistical capacity, all require trained and skilled men, organised and disciplined: the Nation, the Flag, 'Destiny' etc., become the centralising ethos, which raises the army above the secular issues that divide civilian society.

The army can become an inculcative force for nation-hood.[8] Where it succumbs to fractionalism the result is a threatened disintegration of the nation (e.g. Nigeria). It is not necessary that this role for the military be mirrored in every country at all times, but it is a natural role for the army and, in the absence of other integrative forces, it will tend to develop to a greater or lesser extent. The foundations for such a role may be tenuous, its articulation may be mythical, but there is no doubt that the military interventions that have taken place in the Third World have been based on some local version of this concept of their role.[9]

The army in many African countries is equipped, trained and motivated for intervention.[10] The civilian government deploys the military essentially for an internal security role, but the military is able to transform its subordinate role into a dominant one. By kinship and peer-group affiliation it is aware of the prizes flowing from command of the state. By observation of the behaviour and living standards of the European it has acquired, like everybody else with ambition, an envy for living standards commensurate with its concep-tions of its special role. It can only look with paternalistic disapproval on the struggle between political factions for power, which in no way resembles party politics in a traditional Western state in the intensity and ferocity of competition and the struggles between competing social groups for a share in the resources of the country. For these reasons some of the early interventions over the pay and allowances of the army (Kenya, Uganda, Tanzania, Sierra Leone, etc.)[11] or the share of the army in the state budgets

8 S.P. Huntingdon, *The Soldier and the State*, Harvard, 1957.

9 See F. Greene, *The Military Sieze Power: Towards Understanding Coups*, Washington, 1966.

10 J.M. Lee, *African Armies and Civil Order*, London, 1969, p.89.

11 See A.A. Mabrui and D. Rothchild, 'The soldier and the state in East Africa: some theoretical conclusions on the army mutinies in 1964', *Western Political Quarterly*, 20, March 1967; W.F. Gutteridge, *The Military in African Politics*, London, 1969, Chapter 4.

(e.g. Central African Republic, Upper Volta),[12] were not articulating any particular political creed. They were merely asserting the army's place in the queue for the benefits of independence.

The army which intervenes with relatively clean hands[13] may campaign against corruption, a few offenders may be jailed, and some may even be shot, but the command of resources in 'soft' states soon leads inexorably to a diversion of resources. In an atmosphere where status and prestige are bound up with power and wealth, the scarcity of income among the pious is in conflict with the aspirations of the ambitious; either they succumb to the opportunities or they slide down the social scale.

There is another route that does not involve corruption directly, and that is to develop political ambitions exercisable on the basis of support from the corrupted within the military hierarchy. Thus rising political fortune may be a substitute for direct graft; the status of office, with the perks and privileges that this provides, may compensate for abstaining from the lower ranks' opportunities to graft. In these ways the army itself becomes as corrupted as the previous administration, but the leaders may in good conscience be able from time to time to threaten action against the corrupt as a disciplinary tool over lower ranks. The military leaders have authority over lower ranks and they can remove the 'licences' to state position at will. The lower ranks return loyalty for the 'licence'.

The military in Africa is relatively new as an independent force; its officers were commissioned almost entirely post-independence.[14] The European elites ruled through their own officer class in command of local troops. The crash programmes of the independence preparations left relatively inexperienced officers in these armies.

In the Middle East the armies had been officered by their own nationals for decades and the military tradition is more

12 D. Nelkin, 'The economic and social setting of military takeovers in Africa', *Journal of African and Asian Studies*, 2, 3-4, June 1967.
13 N.J. Miners, *The Nigerian Army, 1956-66*, London, 1971, p.105; op. cit.
14 Luckham, op. cit.

indigenous than in black Africa.[15] In Latin America the army has been a national force for all this century and has a longer experience of intervention. Until the mid-1960s it was more or less a client social force for the ruling oligarchies.[16] In Asia the two types are represented, the post-independence, and the traditional.[17]

To what extent are the military a modernising force? There is some controversy about this aspect of the military. One view sees the military as an essential factor in the process of nation building: 'The military coup is crucial for the continuation and acceleration of nation building in Asia and Africa'.[18] The military removes obstacles to modernisation rather than creates them.

The good soldier is also to some degree a modernised man. Thus it is that the armies of newly emergent countries come to play key roles in the process by which traditional ways give way to more westernised ideas and practice . . . the acculturative process tends to be focused on acquiring technical skills that are of particular value for economic development . . .[19]

This view of the army as an agency of modernisation is challenged by those who exclude the idea of independent social forces other than the bourgeoisie in the early period of industrial capitalism or the proletariat in the twentieth century. What this view boils down to is this: that the only progressive social force is the political movement which 'represents' the historical interests of the latter-day prolet-

15 D.A. Rustow, 'The military in Middle-Eastern society and politics', in S.N. Fisher (ed.), *The Military in the Middle East: Problems in Society and Government*, Ohio, 1963, p.19.

16 J.J. Johnson, *The Military and Society in Latin America*, Stanford, 1964.

17 D.N. Fryer, *Emerging South-East Asia: A Study in Growth and Stagnation*, New York, 1970; C.I.E. Kim, 'The military and political change in Asia', *Pacific Affairs*, 15, 1 and 2, 1967.

18 D.W. Chiang, 'The military and nation-building in Korea, Burma and Pakistan', *Asia Survey*, 9, 11, 1969, p.818.

19 L. Pye, *Armies in the Process of Political Modernisation*, in J.J. Johnson (ed.), op. cit., p.80: See also C.E. Welch, 'Political modernisation and the African military', in Welch, *Political Modernisation: A Reader in Comparative Political Change*, London, 1967.

ariat, that is, the Marxist revolutionaries. There is inevitably bitter disagreement among Marxists as to which of the 'Marxist' parties truly represents the proletariat's interests. If this question is indeterminate it reduces the concept of an 'historical force' in the form of a Marxist party to the level of a myth agreed upon by its exponents.

Another source of criticism of the military as a modernising force is that of the empirical critics (mainly sociologists) who contrast what is claimed for the military as a modernising force with what the military has achieved in practice. In arguments between theory and practice the latter must start favourites, because if theory has to bend reality to make it fit there is something to be said for sticking with reality.

Modernising armies, whether they intervene in politics or not, are often said to be modernising agents at large in their societies, because military investment in men and machines invariably produces positive non-military side effects . . . Such a claim may be good sales talk but it is poor social science. It might have been ignored but for endorsement by reputable social scientists . . . The double-duty enthusiasts trip over hard facts. They resort to deductive reasoning and tend to overlook the empirical evidence.[20]

Another critical view tackles the argument from a different angle:

The political intervention of the military seems to me to proceed not so much from its prior attitudes to social change but from its strategic position within the arena of social discensus, from its relatively large size, and hierarchic organisation that facilitates a cohesion which no other elite group can match . . . Nor does it seem very profitable to talk of a desire to modernise in the abstract. Such a desire may be widespread, like the desire to consume Western goods. What matters more is the order of priorities and of sacrifices. Who is going to be deprived of what in order that others should consume what goods?[21]

This approach is taken by Dorothy Nelkin:

The military, then, acted upon a social base composed of a small but strategic part of the population. In no country can the shift be regarded

20 J.C. Hurewitz, *Middle-Eastern Politics: The Military Dimension*, New York, 1970, p.430.
21 Hopkins, op. cit., p.171.

as more than a transfer of power. There were no revolutionary changes within the social structure: the support of the coups came from groups, already relatively favoured vis-à-vis the rest of society.[22]

The one common theme in these divergent views on the significance of the military contribution to modernisation is that they all recognise the strategic position that the military has in the political power balance of a developing country.

The military is not a homogeneous force.[23] The possibility of upward mobility has made the military attractive to recruits from the lower classes, and minority tribes. Upward mobility is a function of time and therefore the military at any one time will have various layers of personnel from different classes, tribes and strata spread across age and seniority of service cohorts. In Nigeria, for instance, the army had a different tribal composition at each major rank level and whether intended or not this contributed to the tribal characteristic of the 1966 coups.

In the post-independence armies the rapid promotion of officers brought to the High Command soldiers who were trained, often hurriedly, by the previous European administration, and in the case of Indonesia also by the Japanese.[24] Below them were officers recruited and trained post-independence. In some armies (Indonesia, Bangladesh, Sudan)[25] a proportion of these recruits were former irregular or guerrilla troops and this presented problems of integration and professionalisation.

In Egypt, the High Command was closely identified with the monarchy and there was a political, class, social and age gap between them and the officers who supported the Free Officers Movement.[26]

22 Nelkin, op. cit., p. 242.

23 Daalder, op. cit., p. 15.

24 Pauker, op. cit., p. 189.

25 For Indonesia, see Pauker, ibid.; for Sudan, see *Financial Times*, London, 24 November 1972.

26 'The Egyptian Officers at the time of the Palestine War were for the most part from well-to-do families, some from the wealthy and upper classes, some from the middle and lower-middle classes . . . There were no Officers who were members of Egypt's top social "aristocracy" ', Be'eri, op. cit., p. 496.

Colonels, majors and captains occupy strategic command positions within the strategic social position of the military. They are near enough both to the ranks and to the top command, and learn to appreciate their potential role in the political structures. Some senior officers have managed to read the situation accurately and have placed themselves at the head of popular army revolts to contain them (Pakistan) or been placed there by the junior officers looking for acceptable figureheads for their coup (Egypt). Where such figureheads have not appeared, the junior officers have had to act alone (Libya) and take on both the ruling oligarchy and the High Command. Where senior military figures are not available, it has sometimes led to a variation of this particular gambit, namely using senior civilian figures in the revolutionary cabinet.[27]

### 3.   *The political machines*

The format of the military intervention will depend on circumstances. Before examining these circumstances it is essential, first of all, to say something about party politics in the developing countries, particularly in Africa, which differs from party political behaviour as understood in the European industrialised countries. The party parliamentary form of government left behind by the European powers in African states rapidly ceased to resemble the model upon which it was based. The form was often there, but the original content, which was foreign, was rapidly replaced.

Political parties evolved over many decades in the United Kingdom and are able to demonstrate fairly consistent mass support, and thereby they operate on the relatively safe assumption that they speak for some part of the electorate. An indication of the stable and genuine mass base of the major parties in the post-war years was the unlikelihood of a candidate being elected without the sponsorship of the major party caucuses (though this need not continue indefinitely). Between 1945 and 1972 only a handful of candidates have

27 This was attempted in the 24 March 1971 military coup in Argentina, but the civilians declined. General Amin of Uganda had an all-civilian cabinet for some months in 1972.

been successful against major party nominees in the seats held by a major party — successful challenges have normally been made only from the other major party. British political parties articulate the interests of their supporters, whatever the personal motives of the party activists, and the need to win support by persuasion is so much taken for granted that election strategies have been exclusively based on this premise.

The hiring of thugs to terrorise opposition candidates, the intimidation of electors, the partisan intervention of the state, the illegal disqualification of the candidates, and large-scale personation of electors, are not common aspects of the electoral system. (Some of these features have of course appeared in the Northern Ireland province, but that is atypical of the United Kingdom.) The political leaders' desire for office is not carried beyond the point of legality and their ability to compromise on essential principles (however vaguely these are defined) is constrained to some extent by the party activists, but, above all, by the electorate.

African post-colonial experience does not conform to the same behaviour patterns. The political leadership emerged rapidly out of relative obscurity. Their nationalist campaigns developed rapidly. Some of the leaders were active for many years in the independence struggle (e.g. Dr Hastings Banda), but this was often from within the metropolitan country itself, where political conditions were more liberal than in the colonies, or they were active in clandestine groups isolated from the population.

The ruling European powers prepared to hand over power to the local versions of political forces that were common in the metropolitan countries, namely political parties with a mass following. Therefore competing nationalists had to produce 'mass parties' to lay claim to the succession. On the eve of independence mass parties were created that were articulating liberal values and were competitive, and these were virtues that impressed anti-colonial liberals, who saw in these the proof that these countries were mature and ready for an indigenous version of London-type parliamentary democracy.

The parties took on the same form as political parties

elsewhere. They had national leaders, local branches, conferences and rallies, symbols, platforms and, of course, promises. The content was, however, different. They were not political *parties* so much as political *machines* for getting, holding and extending political power. The distinction was not merely a difference in emphasis (Western political parties have similar aims) but, because it operated in a different cultural climate, it took on an entirely different meaning.

The distinction is that a party aggregates demands and converts them into legislative policy, whereas a political machine exists almost exclusively to stay in power. To this end its main concern is to offer rewards and bribes to anyone who can contribute to keeping it in power. Office alone is its reason for existence and with office comes the opportunity for enrichment at public expense.[28]

The road from political machines competing for the scarce fruits of office to the one-party state is a straight and well-worn road in this context.[29] Some liberal apologists who see the one-party state as a form of government 'most suitable to Africa's conditions' ('There is so much to be done that all efforts must be directed towards that end and diversionary opposition must be dispensed with until the country is developed' etc.) are only partly correct.[30]

The one-party state is a development from the special character of African post-independence parties as machines for hanging on to power.

A one-party state has been created partly because those in power cannot afford to lose its fruits and the (many) 'carpet crossers' are unable to resist accepting a share; but also because, in the absence of an extensive and skilled bureaucracy, the 'parti unique' is seen as a means of using less technically trained men to further national union, partly

28 E. Feit, 'Military coups and political development: some lessons of Ghana and Nigeria', *World Politics*, 20, 2, January 1968.

29 See S.E. Finer, 'The one-party regimes in Africa: a reconsideration'; Tordoff, op. cit.; Zolberg, op. cit.; T. Hodgkin, *African Political Parties*, London, 1961.

30 J. Hatch, 'Kaunda's one-party state', *New Statesman*, London, 29 December 1972.

by appeals to Cameroonian solidarity and partly through the distribution of benefits.[31]

The reference is to the experience of Cameroon, but it could just as well be written about Ghana, Kenya, Tanzania, Uganda, Malawi and Zambia.

## 4. Political independence

Luckham sees the development of the African political elite into the form it has taken as part of the 'contract' between the departing European power and the elite to whom the power was handed:

The colonial government handed over to the inheriting elite, the political class, the right to control the machinery of government in return for the protection of its economic interests. In practice, this meant the inheritors had the right to create and mobilise political resources without hindrance, to appropriate for themselves all patronage in government jobs and appointments, to create networks of political clientage and to use the bureaucracy and the means of coercion to maintain themselves in office, to make themselves secure in their employment and the lucrative rewards of politics. In return, the departing Nationals kept control of large-scale private economic enterprise and the profits extracted therefrom.[32]

Luckham's point can be taken without reading as much as he does into the 'contract'.

Whatever 'contract' was implicit in the transfer of power, the mutual obligations, such as they were, quickly lost importance as local autonomy gained experience and metropolitan priorities changed. For example, the demise of Empire and the Commonwealth reduced the importance of the 'colonial' lobby in the decision centres of British government. Other lobbies became more important (e.g. the 'European') and took up more time and consequently, within a short space of time, British interests in independent states were much more vulnerable than before. Even if the British government wanted (even implicitly) to enforce the

31 Robson and Lury, p. 241.
32 Luckham, op. cit., p. 207.

'contract' that Luckham suggests existed, a position was rapidly reached where it was unable to (e.g. Rhodesia, 1965 and Uganda, 1972).

Inside these countries the developing political situation also put pressure on the domestic parties to the 'contract'. The political machine which succeeded the European power may have gained its status by convincing the European power that it was acceptable as the ruling elite by virtue of tradition (that it had for example previously been dominant in the country) or by demonstration of its popularity. This selection of a succession elite, which would inevitably exclude competing elites or emerging elites, would not necessarily lead to the acquiescence of everybody in the arrangement. Indeed some resented the arrangements and set out to stake a claim to office.

Successive changes, inside the ruling elite, also contributed to the overturning of the 'contract'. The force of nationalism is pervasive; in some countries it has been called 'Africanisation', but the effects are the same; the appropriation of expatriate interests either outright or by stages.

Foreign commercial interests have in the main to accept the indigenisation measures; the prospect of 'heavy' intervention by their governments to prevent take-overs is so remote as to be discounted. The main arguments are likely to be confined to the compensation terms. The political weakness of the foreign companies in this respect and the lack of ready funds in the countries that are encouraging indigenisation do not make the 'contract' relationship a sound one. For example, Nigeria's Indigenisation Act, which comes into force in 1974, and excludes foreign commercial activity in a number of areas such as retail trade, light industry, transport and services and in activities requiring a fixed capital below £200,000, will cost up to £250 million in compensation.[33] Whether in the event the Nigerians can raise this sum, and, as important, permit the foreigners to repatriate it, is a matter of some doubt. The Ugandan solution of stripping the owners of assets and preventing them removing anything except the barest personal possessions is not necessarily the most tactful of policies, but it is

33 *West Africa*, March 1973.

evidently one that can be carried through without intervention other than from public appeals to morality.

Analysing the new political leadership of the developing world merely as some kind of client of Western business interests is increasingly at variance with experience. While considerable evidence has been accumulated of the alleged relationship between Third World economies and the industrialised economies, and much of it is critical of the relationship, the growing independence of the economic managers of these countries, their aggressive assertion of their own national interests and their general non-compliance with behaviour that would be expected from dependent partners to a dual form of exploitation, which is what is implied by the theories of neo-colonialism, suggest that the relationships that were thought to be apparent in the 1960s are not as naked, or as direct, and that new explanations are needed.[34]

The three major forces working in favour of military intervention as a solution to the legitimacy crisis are therefore: the failings of the implanted political party system in the cultural milieu of the developing countries; the strategic position of the military — a small force with leverage; and the growing realisation of the potentialities of independence among the elites, or, to put it another way, the realisation that the European powers are less committed, and less able, to intervene against governments or policies they disapprove of.

The post-independence order has in the main broken down. Where it survives it has been transformed to accommodate to forces within the country (the one-party states), but few of the one-party states have so far faced the next test: how to survive the succession from the charismatic leadership of the independence period. With these personal

34 The growing militancy of the nationalists in the Third World, and the realisation of the relative weakness of the metropolitan powers suggests that the Marxist habit of writing off the bourgeoisie in these countries as 'cowardly message carriers for international imperialism' is in need of revision. As the metropolitan powers take a greater interest in their own affairs (European Economic Community for example) there is immense scope for the Third World to flex its muscles. G. Myrdal, in *Asian Drama*, op. cit., is one of the few social scientists to have appreciated this change and to have documented its consequences.

leaderships removed (a problem facing Kenya, Malawi, Zambia and Tanzania) the question is open whether the party system will continue or whether the disintegrative forces will assert themselves as in other countries. The following chapters will go into greater detail regarding the military 'solution' and to what extent the intervention solution can be seen as a general solution or one confined to the circumstances in each country.

# 5 Intervention in Africa

## 1. Introduction

In this chapter the military interventions in three African countries are examined. The first country is Sierra Leone, which is one of the smaller countries in Africa. The intervention is of particular interest because it arose out of the refusal of one of the political parties to accept the role of opposition after a general election. The tribal divisions in the country were present as a factor but do not explain the whole of the legitimacy crisis.

The next country is Nigeria, and in contrast to Sierra Leone, where tribalism was one factor, it is the conclusion of the study of Nigeria that tribal divisions were the major, if not the sole, explanation for the collapse of the first Federation. In taking account of the realities of tribal divisions, the architects of the Federal state actually ensured that they would be dominant in subsequent years. The three major tribal areas, the North, the East and the West, were in political conflict from the beginning, as nobody could gain an outright majority.

The normal party political deficiencies of the African political system meant a stagnation of political leadership and a fractionalising of effort. In these conditions the intervention of the Nigerian army was predictable, but this intervention could not take on a unifying and nation-building form precisely because the army itself was tribalistically divided in the crucial aspect of officer ranks. Coups often involve the removal of some part of the elite; if the elite is stratified by tribe the removal of a rank inevitably means the destruction of a tribal group. Whatever the motivations of the coup makers, this is bound to have tribalistic consequences. In Nigeria it led to civil/tribal war.

The last part is a brief analysis of the 1966 Ghana coup against Nkrumah. This is looked at from the mechanics of a coup against a personal dictator. Tribal divisions played an insignificant part in Ghana's political crises since independence.

## 2.    Sierra Leone

In Sierra Leone there were two main political parties contesting for power. The social groups represented by the two parties roughly corresponded to the major tribal and regional divisions and also to class differences. The Sierra Leone People's Party (SLPP) represented the most Westernised of the elites. It was also allied with the traditional chiefs and was predominantly supported by the Mende tribe.[1] The All Peoples' Congress (APC) had a more plebeian composition, with tribal support concentrated in the Tenne, Limba and other smaller tribes. Arriving on the nationalist scene later, and less close to the European oriented elite, it had a more open class appeal. The tribal divisions can be seen in the Table 1.

*Table 1    Sierra Leone general election results, 1962 and 1967 by percentage of votes for major parties by tribal area*

| Region and tribe | 1962 | | 1967 | |
|---|---|---|---|---|
| | SLPP | APC | SLPP | APC |
| | % (seats) | % (seats) | % (seats) | % (seats) |
| South (Mende) | 38.8 (15) | 4.8 (0) | 47.5 (20) | 9.9 (1) |
| North (Tenne Limba) | 27.6 (2) | 44.8 (10) | 19.0 (0) | 79.0 (18) |
| Other | 34.2 (7) | 10.7 (4) | 36.7 (3) | 60.5 (15) |
| No. of seats | 24 | 14 | 23 | 34 |

Source:  J.R. Cartwright, 'Party competition', *Journal of Contemporary Political Science*, 1972, p.75.

The figures in brackets are the number of seats gained in each area. These should be summed vertically to get total representation in the House for each party. Most of the

1 For a history of Sierra Leone and the emergence of the SLPP see C. Fife, *Sierra Leone Inheritance*, London, 1964, Chapter 16.

independents (not shown in Table) sided with SLPP. The percentages should be summed horizontally (but note that the independent percentage votes are not included), as each percentage is the vote received by the major parties out of the total votes cast in that region.

In the 1962 election the SLPP had 31 seats (plus the independents who declared for the SLPP after the election) and the APC had 14. This 14 diminished through the defection of 4 members to the ruling SLPP in the first three years of the parliament and then by a further 5 when they were imprisoned on various charges.[2] The SLPP, led by Sir Milton Margai, was firmly in command of the country and upon his death in April 1967, his brother, Sir Albert Margai, took over. The 1967 general election took place under conditions of severe tension between the SLPP and the APC, led by Dr Siaka Stevens. The election results gave the APC 34 seats against the SLPP's total of 23, not counting the independents and paramount chiefs who may have declared later for the SLPP. Instead of Dr Stevens assuming power, a military coup intervened and civilian government was suspended.

The governing party in a manoeuvre to outflank the opposition APC only succeeded in thoroughly discrediting itself. In February 1967, the SLPP 'discovered' a 'plot' in the army to take over the government and promptly arrested some officers, including the second-in-command, Colonel Bangura. The opposition APC was publicly accused of planning a military intervention. The general election took place in March 1967, under conditions where, as a subsequent official enquiry reported, 'the whole of the government's arrangements for the 1967 election was rigged and corrupt . . . they were determined to use all means fair or foul to win and remain in office and if all failed to get Brigadier Lansana to take over'.[3] These methods included: increasing the deposits from candidates from 200 Leones to 500 Leones (from \$440 to \$1100), increasing the cost of

2 *African Research Bulletin*, vol. 4, p.929. See also J.R. Cartwright, *Politics in Sierra Leone 1947-1967*, Toronto, 1973.

3 From the official Dove-Edwin Report, quoted in Legum and Drysdale, op. cit., p.712.

election petitions, withdrawing the right of appeal in election disputes, raising the lost-deposit threshold from one tenth to one quarter of the poll, and the selection of returning officers on the basis of party affiliation. It is perhaps of no surprise then that the Prime Minister, with six colleagues, was returned 'unopposed'. In spite of the electoral disabilities the APC was declared the winner by the Governor, Sir Henry Lightfoot Boston.

The military commander, Brigadier David Lansana, announced on the radio that day that he was taking over to 'protect the constitution and maintain law and order'. This was the one act most likely to provoke a disruption of law and order. The tribal divisions had been intensified in the election in 1967. The northern regions had been swept by the APC which won all the seats and 79 per cent of the vote (see Table 1). The situation was potentially threatening, but the fact that apart from the SLPP leadership there was little support for Brigadier Lansana's action, particularly within the army itself, actually opened the door to the next phase of the crisis in which the SLPP leadership had placed Sierra Leone by supporting the coup in the first place.

On 23 March, two days after the first coup, another coup took place. Brigadier Lansana was removed and a National Reformation Council took over. Its leader, Lt. Colonel Juxon-Smith, warned 'trouble makers' in blunt terms:

Whoever it is in Sierra Leone, wherever you may be, who is planning trouble, let me warn you, in your own interest, in the interests of your family, to go back home. Regardless of your rank or status, regardless of personality, you will be immediately apprehended, you will be tried by court martial, and you will be shot by firing squad. That is what martial law means.[4]

Brigadier Juxon-Smith did not hand over power to the elected assembly but set up a Civilian Rule Committee, and used the cover of civilian participation to continue military rule.[5]

4 H. Fisher, op. cit., p. 635.
5 See D. Dalby, 'The Military takeover in Sierra Leone', *The World Today*, August 1967; R. First, *The Barrel of a Gun: Political Power in Africa and the Coup d'Etat*, London, 1972.

Like the Lansana coup the Juxon-Smith coup made the elementary error of not ensuring its base. Illegitimacy was combined with carelessness. On 18 April 1968, a group of NCOs and warrant officers, dissatisfied with a rejection of a pay claim, seized power by arresting the entire officer corps, except for those out of the country, and the National Reformation Council. The NRC was accused of being 'more corrupt and selfish than the ousted civilian regime'[6] and, to emphasise this theme, an Anti-Corruption Revolutionary Movement was set up. The elected Assembly was recalled and Dr Stevens was asked to set up a government. Learning from the past, Dr Stevens formed a coalition government from both parties. The country returned to civilian rule and has been led since by Dr Stevens.

The armed forces in Sierra Leone before the coup numbered only 1,360; even the police force was larger with 2,000. The military share of the budget was only 4.9 per cent or 1.3 per cent of GNP.[7] The third coup was caused by dissatisfaction with pay among the lower ranks. The ruling military government had neglected its most important base.

The political conflicts of the 1960s had neglected the armed forces, and it was only in the context of a stubborn fight to hold on to power that the politicians inculcated the idea of military intervention, thus immediately raising the potential status of the armed forces as a balancing power in the political structure. Once the intervention was sanctioned, events took their own course. The SLPP, presumably confident of controlling the army leaders, did not anticipate the possibility of the immediate removal of their officers and replacement by another set of leaders. But these other leaders did not apparently have much political experience or ambition and they soon exhausted their interest in power. The restored civilian government brought back to power experienced politicians (Dr Stevens had been exiled to Guinea) and the political machines settled down to an uneasy acceptance of more democratic parliamentary rules.[8]

6 Legum and Drysdale, op. cit., p. 589.
7 Hopkins, op. cit., p. 173.
8 Relations between the SLPP and the APC in 1972 were anything but cordial and sporadic outbreaks of violence between supporters was reported.

In November 1968 a State of Emergency was necessary and there were attempted coups in 1971. Dr Stevens, in a move to prevent his deposition from power by military intervention, signed an agreement with Guinea that gave him power to call upon Guinea for military assistance in the event of army mutiny or threats to internal security.[9] This insurance policy between the two governments is a response to the proneness of developing countries to military intervention and insurrection.

A government can strengthen its defences against insurrection by arrangements similar to those that Sierra Leone and Guinea have made, which echo the kind of arrangement that Francophone Africa had with Metropolitan France, and which were activated in French intervention against some military coups against pro-French governments.[10] The British also intervened at the request of the Ugandan, Kenyan, and Tanzanian governments in the 1964 army mutinies.

The extent to which French support for African governments facing rebellions can be relied upon has diminished in the past few years. General Edouard Cortadellas, former French Military Delegate and Commander-in-Chief of the Chadian armed forces, stated in 1972 that 'the French army, without doubt, would not intervene in case of elections or palace revolution'.[11] A repetition of British intervention is also unlikely. The only prospect for intervention is of the kind provided by Libya to Uganda in the 1972 'invasion', where several hundred Libyan soldiers were flown to Kampala to act as a special guard for General Amin.

The use of foreign troops to fight for a government is not a popular action among so-called independent states, and in the competitive nationalism of the Third World it is not helpful towards the building of an image of the leadership as an anti-imperialist force. Where countries have close affinities of

9 S. Stevens, *Broadcast No. 3: The Honourable Prime Minister*, undated, Sierra Leone High Commission, London, 1971.

10 The French had secret defence agreements with ten African governments and have intervened in attempted coups (e.g. Gabon 1964) but they have recently intimated that they will follow a policy of non-intervention; see *West Africa*, 15 September 1972, p. 1210.

11 *West Africa*, ibid., 'Sierra Leone: what prospect for democracy?' p. 1211.

interest and ideology, as in Sierra Leone and Guinea, mutual security pacts are possible, but they have yet to be tested.

The return to civilian rule in Sierra Leone has not, unfortunately, led to a genuine multi-party democracy. The bitterness over the SLPP role in promoting the period of military intervention continued long after Dr Stevens resumed office. The State of Emergency imposed in 1971 continued throughout 1972 in most areas. But more ominously the practice of 'unopposed' candidates in elections re-appeared.[12] This had two possible explanations; either the electorate were satisfied with the governing APC candidates and did not want to contest their re-election, or there was an element of political intimidation preventing persons from publicly challenging the regime. To argue that unopposed candidates were due to the technical incompetence of the opposition in carrying out nomination procedure is not acceptable; if there was this kind of incompetence present it would affect both parties, unless, of course, the hypothesis is that electoral incompetence is an attribute reserved exclusively for African political oppositions.

The APC leaders were also flirting with the idea of declaring Sierra Leone a one-party state, or as the government-owned *Daily Mail*, put it, a 'no-party' state.[13] The arrest of opposition SLPP leaders in 1972 and 1973 on various charges of conspiracy and instigation of violence must reduce the effectiveness of the opposition even further. A breakaway party from the APC, the United Democratic Party, was also banned in 1972.[14] Thus the APC, itself the victim of unconstitutional action, has swung full circle and must increasingly take on the all too familiar features of a party on the road to dictatorship. With a tight rein on the military and a nobbled opposition, there is nothing but fortune between Dr Stevens and absolute power.[15]

12 *West Africa*, ibid., p. 1211.

13 *West Africa*, 19 February 1973, p. 250; see also 'The Margai legacy', *West Africa*, 19 March 1973.

14 *West Africa*, 15 September 1972, p. 1211.

15 Under the SLPP government some APC members of parliament 'crossed the floor' seeing the new opportunities and dangers; reverse 'floor crossing' under the APC government was reported in *West Africa*, 5 February 1973, p. 189.

### 3.    Nigeria

The intervention of the majors in Nigeria set off a train of events that was to encompass another coup in July 1966 and a bitter secessionist war from 1967 to 1970. The January 1966 coup and the period to the end of the Biafran war was a connected and continuous period of struggle. The struggles within the military, and between the tribal groups that made up the military leadership, were not isolated but were sequential events — it was no military roulette. They were in fact struggles around the same central issues: if the civilian post-independence political system was to be replaced, and after the elimination of the political leaders by the January 1966 coup its replacement was unpostponable, what form would the military regime take and who would be represented in its upper leadership? The struggle over these issues in Nigeria was one of the bloodiest in Africa.

Nigeria is the most populous country in Africa with a population over 50 million of diverse ethnic composition.[16]

*Table 2    Ethnic composition of Nigeria*

| Group | Approximate number in millions |
|---|---|
| Hausa-Fulani | 16 |
| Ibo | 10 |
| Yoruba | 9 |
| Northern Yoruba | 1.5 |
| Kanuri, Nupe and other northern tribes | 13.8 |
| Tiv, Bamileke, Efiks and Ibibio | 2.4 |
| Ijaw | 0.7 |
| Ika, Edo and Urhobo | 2.5 |

Source:  N.J. Miners, *The Nigerian Army, 1956-66*, London 1971, p. 16; and Luckham, op. cit., Table 38, p. 208.

The details in Table 2 are only approximate and have been estimated by a crude comparison of ascribed tribal areas with

16 Gutteridge, op. cit.

estimates of the populations living in these areas. The last census was in 1963, but this was taken under circumstances that place grave doubts on its reliability, and the government, for political reasons, refrained from taking another census in case the fictions that were created in 1963 were challenged and led to new inter-regional tensions.[17] In all there are 235 ethnic groups in Nigeria, the largest being the Hausa, Fulani, Yoruba and Ibo. The Hausa and Fulani predominate in the North, the Yorubas in the West and the Ibos in the East.[18] Upon these tribal divisions, to which the first regions in the Federation corresponded, we can trace the political tensions of the post-independence period up to 1966.[19]

The Nigerian military in 1966 was differentiated from the type of army found in, say, the Middle East. In the first place it was relatively new, particularly at higher command levels. Eighty per cent of the Nigerian army combat officers had only five years, or less, experience in command by 1966. Five of the seven most senior officers (including the top three most senior) were ex-NCOs from the British-led pre-independence army. Military training of Nigerian officers did not get under way until 1958. Of the 45 officers recruited before 1958, 24 were from the ranks and 21 had received some training at military establishments overseas (Sandhurst, etc.). In the next two years (1959-60), of the 35 Nigerian entrants to the officer corps, only 13 were from the ranks and the rest were graduates, short-service intake, or Sandhurst-trained. The origins of the officer corps rapidly changed from 1960 to 1961, the year of independence; only four entrants were ex-NCOs, the rest being recruited from other sources.[20]

The pattern of recruitment was important. It telescoped into a period of a few years a similar process of change of

17 See Luckham, op. cit., pp. 212-3 for details of the controversy over the 1963 census and why it is important to the regions. In 1973 the government announced it intended to take a full census by the end of the year. *West Africa*, 5 March 1973, p. 309.

18 Central Office of Information, *Nigeria* (Fact Sheets on the Commonwealth), May 1972, p. 2.

19 For a contrary view see Sklar, op. cit., and his 'Political science and national integration: a radical approach', *Journal of Modern African Studies*, 5, 1, May 1967.

20 Luckham, op. cit., pp. 98, 240 and Appendix 1, pp. 343-6.

origin in the officer corps that was going on in the other Third World armies over a much longer period. The Arab officer corps preceded political independence (Nasser and his contemporaries had been officers for many years), but the Nigerianisation of the officer corps was a development subsequent to political independence; the only candidates available to turn into officers before independence were experienced NCOs, who were, in the nature of things, thoroughly imbued with British methods and traditions.[21] The result, as Nigerianisation spread, was that the most senior officers were separated by background, outlook and rank from their junior officers. The ranks below them were often better educated, better trained, and, most important, from the same peer groups that were susceptible to the awakening nationalism, and who were taking jobs in the expanding state bureaucracy, or becoming the new entrepreneurs, or staffing the academic centres and the political machines, and who were much less interested in a Nigeria that looked like a pale reflection of British traditions.[22]

The rapid Nigerianisation of the officer corps, with its consequent rapid promotion of the senior NCOs to command rank, is in contrast to the situation in the Arab countries, such as Egypt, Syria and Iraq, where the Arab officers had been a common feature of the Ottoman and monarchical armies. Military training at schools and academies had been established for years. The presence of the foreigner held the system in check, but his removal led to structural changes in which the already established army played an important part. In Nigeria the removal of the foreigner and the establishment of the army were coincidental events, and the schism between the ranks of command was as sudden as it was inevitable. It embodied the central issues of tribal advantage. In a short space of time events were to force a violent resolution of all three issues.

The schism between junior and senior ranks in the Arab

21 Miners, op. cit., Chapter 3; Luckham, op. cit., Chapter 7. G.O. Oliusanya, 'The role of ex-servicemen in Nigerian politics', *Journal of Modern African Studies*, 6, 2, August 1968.

22 Luckham, op. cit., p. 164; R. Cohen, 'The army and trade unions in Nigerian politics', *Civilisations*, 19, 2, 1969.

armies, where military tradition was established, became one of the identification of the upper ranks with the status quo and of their role as obstacles to national progress. This led to a more *ideological* development within the post-coup regimes than has so far been found in the military coups in sub-Saharan black Africa. In this region the main dividing line was the different experience and career origins of the officer ranks, expressed in disputes about how to administer the army/country, or how to ensure honesty/efficiency and how to replace the colonial systems and traditions.

The second important feature of the Nigerian army, compared to the Arab armies, was its nascent tribalistic tensions.[23] The Nigerian Federation was divided roughly into

*Table 3a Percentage regional/ethnic origins of officer/seniority cohorts in the Nigerian Army*

| Seniority cohort | Ibo | E./Mid W. | Yoruba | North | no. |
|---|---|---|---|---|---|
| pre-1952 | 14 | 14 | 57 | 14 | 7 |
| 1952-54 | 30 | 30 | 10 | 30 | 10 |
| 1955-56 | 63 | 19 | 13 | 6 | 16 |
| 1957-58 | 65 | 12 | 12 | 12 | 17 |
| 1959-60 | 34 | 15 | 27 | 24 | 41 |
| 1961-62 | 32 | 11 | 17 | 41 | 76 |
| 1963-64 | 20 | 16 | 20 | 44 | 163 |

*Table 3b Percentage regional/ethnic composition of the officer corps in 1966*

| Rank | Ibo | E./Mid W. | Yoruba | North | no. |
|---|---|---|---|---|---|
| Col. | 14 | 0 | 57 | 29 | 7 |
| Lt./Col. | 36 | 29 | 14 | 21 | 14 |
| Major | 66 | 6 | 22 | 6 | 32 |
| Capt. | 29 | 15 | 23 | 33 | 52 |
| Lieut. | 34 | 10 | 17 | 38 | 58 |
| 2/Lt. | 25 | 14 | 19 | 42 | 177 |

Source: Luckham, op. cit., Tables 36 and 37, pp. 189-90.

23 There are tribal differences among the Arabs (Sunni, Shi'i, Druzes, Alawi, and so on), but these exist within the tradition of the unifying ideology of Islam and Arabism which have no counterparts among the African tribes.

the main tribal areas, the North, the East and the West. The colonial army had been recruited tribalistically, with the Northerners providing the infantry and general soldiers, and the other regions the skilled, technical and educated specialists.[24] In the transformation of the army from pre- to post-independence the ethnic composition of the recruitment policies came to be reflected in the hierarchical composition of the different rank levels.

The entry quotas of the tribes for the seniority cohorts are reflected closely in the progress of these cohorts through the officer ranks. The most senior officers in any army generally also have seniority of service and at any time an analysis of rank would show a rough correspondence to entry into the army. Between 1955 and 1958 the Ibos predominated as a result of the recruitment policy and this shows up in their predominance in the rank of major immediately before 1966. In the January coup it was from within this rank that the murderous assault on the political and military leadership of the Federation took place. The elimination of those senior military commanders who were caught by the majors meant, after the settlement, promotion to senior rank of a cohort with heavy Ibo representation.

The January coup was interpreted by the Northern and minority tribes as an Eastern conspiracy for hegemony in the Federation. The details of the coup and how it apparently 'failed' after the liquidation of the Prime Minister, Abubaka Tafawa Balewa, and the regional premiers, and other ministers, gave credence to this view.[25] General Ironsi, an Ibo, took over command of the country by persuading the original coup leaders to surrender. Twelve of the 14 coup leaders, according to Federal evidence published later during the Biafran war, were Ibos and two Yorubas; in an additional list published by the Biafran side, a further 15 Ibo officers are named and 3 more Yorubas. There is prima facie evidence on this ground alone to justify the Northern officers in believing in an Ibo tribal attack on the North.

The Northern political (and popular) line after the July

24 Miners, op. cit., p. 24.

25 For accounts of the 1966 coups, see Luckham, op. cit., Part One; First, op. cit., pp. 278-352; Miners, op. cit., Chapter 9; Dillon, op. cit.

coup was that Ironsi was implicated in the January coup, though the evidence is circumstantial. For example, he was an Ibo like the coup leaders and was not killed, unlike similarly ranking officers of other tribes; he stepped into the leadership of the country after the Ibo majors had liquidated the political leaders and he promoted the mainly Ibo majors to the depleted senior ranks. Whatever the truth, the tribal version was believed by enough of the non-Ibo officers in the army to create unrest. The May Decrees which proposed to abolish the Federation and set up a unitary state were seen as confirmation of the Ibo plot theory, because it was believed that the Ibos had the most to gain from a unitary state under one civil service, one political system and one army command.[26] The military government faced open hostility from the North and in a series of bloody riots against Ibos in the Northern regions, in which hundreds were killed, the tribal tensions began to break through. Ironsi's solution to the regional system of government based on the tribal areas (in effect) was to try to impose a centralised state to remove the regional identities. The fact that the centralised state was being run by an Ibo-led military government, because of the over-representation in the upper ranks by Ibos, did not make this solution an attractive proposition to the other tribes. The January conspirators, who had been arrested after the Ironsi coup, were not brought to trial and this did nothing to assuage the feelings of insecurity among the other tribes.

The Northern region was not governable under the Ironsi regime without a total subjugation, requiring a massive military presence, and, of course, the existence of a firmly united military force. The tribal divisions in Nigeria in the army, stirred up by what was taken to be a tribal coup, precluded such a solution. To move troops into the Northern region would have been provocative under other conditions, and there was no hope of being able to do so with tribal tensions within the combat commands. Ibo majors with

26 Miners, op. cit., Chapter 11; Luckham, op. cit., Chapter 11; S.K. Panter-Brick (ed.), *Nigerian Politics and the Nigerian Military Rule: Prelude to Civil War*, London, 1970; a short bibliography of official Nigerian Government publications on this period is given in Miners, op. cit.

Northern captains in the same unit and a mixture of tribes in the ranks did not make for a formidable fighting force; there were therefore grave doubts as to their reliability.

On 29 July 1966, the counter-coup took place. Ironsi was executed and so were any Ibo officers that the coup makers could get their hands on, except in the Eastern region where Ojukwu managed to beat the potential rebels to the armoury and prevent them getting weapons to repeat the actions of other parts of the country. The counter-coup was entirely tribally motivated. It was a case of outright revenge for the January coup, in which Northerners had died and which the Northerners believed only the Ibos gained from. Lt. Col. Gowon, the remaining senior officer, took over the country in much the same style as Ironsi had in the midst of the January coup. There was a leadership vacuum created by the elimination of the established government and therefore the senior commander took control because there was no obvious alternative. He secured a larger measure of support among the non-Ibo tribes, first simply because he was not an Ibo (this placated the North) and secondly because he released the jailed western political Chief Awolowo, which placated the West. The massacres of Ibos on a large scale ensured that the Eastern region would be as unforgiving as they were hostile to what they regarded, with abundant justification, as an anti-Ibo pogrom.

Gowon's solution to the unsuitable tribal character of the Federation was entirely different from Ironsi's; he did not propose a unitary state but went in the other direction and put forward a new Federation based on a break-up of the three major regions into twelve smaller ones. This kept the federal structure, safeguarded some element of local interests while preventing them remaining the overwhelming problem that they were in the larger regions, and assuaged any fears that there was a tribal plan to dominate the whole of the country by one tribe. This was a brilliant constitutional scheme, at least in theory, but the Eastern leaders would not agree to it, and this disagreement and distrust was pushed by them to the point of secession.

The Biafran civil war was over irreconcilable issues: what kind of federal structure was suitable for Nigeria (the Gowon side) and the entirely separate issue of whether the Eastern region was to be a part of any form of Nigeria (the Ojukwu side).[27] Secession was not a new alternative to the Nigerian crisis, it had been mooted before — if the three regions could not stay together in peace they might as well separate, but to separate without agreement meant they could only separate by force of arms. The civil war settled this issue. There was to be a united and federal Nigeria, with a military leadership that was not dominated by any tribal group and a period of transition to civilian political rule (1976), during which time political parties on a *national* rather than a regional basis were to be created.[28]

The problems of ruling Nigeria under the old system were insurmountable, since the balance of forces made them disintegrative and in addition Nigeria had all the other problems of economic under-development. The political structure that emerged from the 1966-70 confrontations had two things in its favour: it had been created by a leadership that emerged partly by the fortune of survival and partly by rising to the events, the former creating the opportunity for the latter, and secondly, the alternatives of unitary and secessionist solutions had been violently liquidated as viable propositions, thereby removing the disturbing presence of ready-made but untried plausible Utopias.

Nigeria's post-independence constitution was unworkable and was bound to lead to a crisis. This took the form of intervention by the majors in 1966. The country was shaping up for illegal interventions from both the military and the civilian politicians in the first six years of independence.[29] There were one or two quite serious attempts at conspiracy and subversion before the majors' coup.[30] The prospects for a

27 R. Niven, *The War of Nigerian Unity*, London, 1971; M. Perham, 'Nigeria's civil war', in Legum and Drysdale, op. cit., pp. 1-12 (extracts from several important documents are included in Part 3, pp. 645-88).

28 Central Office of Information, Nigeria, op. cit., p.4.

29 B. Dudley, 'Violence in Nigerian politics', *Transition*, 5, 21, 1965; Miners, op. cit., Chapter 8.

30 J.P. Mackintosh (ed.), *Nigerian Government and Politics*, London, 1966; L.K. Jakande, *The Trial of Obafemi Awolowo*, London, 1966; see also T.N. Tamuno, 'Separatist agitation in Nigeria since 1914', *Journal of Modern African Studies*, 8, 1, December 1970.

return to civilian rule in the near future are not good (1973) and while the economic boom following the Biafran war continues, and the military leadership continues without crisis, the conditions for a change in political system are unlikely to emerge.

### 4.    Ghana

In Ghana the constitution left behind by the departing British was, in contrast, quite workable and it required the single-minded effort of Nkrumah over several years to create the conditions for military intervention.

Ghana was the constitutionalist hope in Africa.[31] It was the first British African territory to gain independence. Independence brought to power Kwame Nkrumah, a popular nationalist figure who transformed his political movement the Convention Peoples Party (CPP) from the leading political party into the only political party, with himself as absolute ruler. Nkrumah described himself as the Osagyefo (Redeemer), the Aweful, the Achiever, the Ruthless, the Valorous, the Quencher of Fires, the Fount of Honour, the Father of the Nation, the Brave Warrior, the Renewer of All Things,[32] and he was, and remains, a controversial figure in post-independence African history. He certainly regarded himself as being at the same level of importance as Nasser, Sukarno or Nehru, and if personality was the only ground for comparison there was some substance in his claim, if only in a negative way. He was also a more vulgar version of Stalin or Mao in the creation of his personality cult, and his strident, as well as naive, ideological writings bear an obvious stylistic resemblance to Marxist literature.[33]

31 E.W. Lefever, *Spear and Sceptre; Army, Police and Politics in Tropical Africa*, Washington, 1970, p. 33.

32 Quoted in Lefever, op. cit., p. 34; see also H.L. Bretton, *The Rise and Fall of Kwame Nkrumah: A Study of Personal Rule*, London, 1967, p. 101.

33 See, for example, Nkrumah's *Neo-Colonialism, The Highest Stage of Imperialism*, New York, 1966, a rather weak attempt at 'originality' suggested by Lenin's *Imperialism, The Highest Stage of Capitalism*, 1916; or his even more banal *Axioms of Kwame Nkrumah*, 'Freedom Fighters' Edition', London, 1967, blatantly modelled on Mao's 'Little Red Book'. See also K. Nkrumah, *Autobiography*, Edinburgh, 1957.

The February 1966 army and police coup ended his 'Presidency for Life' and the rule of his political machine. He had eliminated all organised opposition, all independent political life, and relied entirely on the forces of the state for survival. Once he threatened this base the outcome was inevitable.[34]

Ruth First adopts an interesting view of Nkrumah and the Ghana coup:

Nkrumah's government might have been a case of socialism badly *manqué*; but its successor regime, far from restoring the health of a dependent economy, has delivered it to the system responsible for the poverty and the exploitation of all the Third World.[35]

This type of apologetic for one-party dictatorships which are ideologically approved of is a disturbing feature of much of the writing on the Third World. Because Ghana under Nkrumah was allegedly a socialist country, her argument goes, the dictatorship and its ugly features are not of decisive importance. But to go on and judge his successors for association with something called the 'system' which is allegedly 'responsible for the poverty and exploitation of all the Third World' is absurd hyperbole. The implication that Nkrumah's *manqué* socialism was preferable to his successor's on the grounds that Nkrumah was only guilty of domestic legalistic sins while the successors were party to all the Third World's poverty and exploitation has only to be stated to be seen to be in desperate need of qualification. It would be more honest for the many scholars who think similarly simply to state their preference for certain dictators, no matter what they do, and leave it at that.

The major problem of dictatorships (right or left) is in ensuring the security of their political structure against challenges from within. This is why there is a close

34 For accounts of the coup see Lefever, op. cit., pp. 58-64; First, op. cit., pp. 363-408; A.A. Afrifa, *The Ghana Coup*, London, 1966; Bretton, op. cit.; B. Fitch and M. Oppenheimer, *Ghana: The End of an Illusion*, New York, 1966.

35 First, op. cit., p. 407; cf. I. Markovitz, 'The winter of discontent: Ghana without Nkrumah', *African Report*, 11, 4, April 1966; also in Markovitz (ed.), *African Politics and Society*, London, 1970.

association between personal paranoia and dictatorial behaviour (a condition that gets worse with time).[36] The
problem is exacerbated in a developing country by the
scarcity of a bureaucratic elite. The support apparatus of the
dictatorship in a developing country is already thin on the
ground. Through the inevitable purges of 'conspirators', real
and imaginary, the elite is replenished by inadequately
trained persons because the virtues of loyalty override their
competence. The paranoic condition also worsens through
time. The atmosphere of insecurity purveyed by the dictator
and his immediate circle permeates to the personnel whose-
function it is to provide for his safety.[37] The dictator
becomes vulnerable to the very thing he is most insecure
about.

Errors of judgment by the security forces in matters
affecting the dictator's safety are highlighted in disciplinary
measures and threats to all whom the dictator feels are guilty.
If the security services are 'terrorised' into blocking loopholes
in the security net around the dictator, and feel disgruntled
in the process, it is but a short step for them to consider the
only means of redress open to them, the coup, the mechanics

36 Stalin, Hitler and Mussolini were European dictators who
suffered from their excessive paranoia; Kassem (Iraq) was, perhaps, the
most serious case in the Arab world in recent times. The condition can
also exacerbate tendencies to personal vanity — the 'cult of the
individual' as the Russians call it — the expressions of vanity demand
reinforcement and confirmation from the followers and evidence of
'spontaneous' affection from the masses. Slights to vanity can send the
victim into uncontrollable rages particularly at those nearest to hand,
i.e. those whom the dictator depends upon most.

37 Feit, op. cit., p. 187; T.P. Omai, *Kwame Nkrumah: Anatomy of
an African Dictatorship*, London, 1970. This insecurity was not helped
by Nkrumah's creation of a special status for his Presidential Guards.
The army leadership took this as both an affront to their own abilities
and a threat to their careers. See General Afrifa's own account in *The
Ghana Coup*, London, 1966. A similar situation was provoked by Ben
Bella's attempt to create an alternative centre of official violence to the
FLN under Boumédienne. President Allende of Chile also fell victim to
the failure of a policy of arming his supporters, when the army decided
to exercise its monopoly of violence before the Allende (and other Left
party) forces were powerful enough to challenge the army in September
1973. President Cardenas of Mexico is an isolated example of the
successful pursuit of this policy.

of which they have become specialists in. The dictator is least protected if the situation in the country is insecure and hostile to the regime. The security service's function as intelligence gatherers would give them a relatively accurate picture of what was really happening in the country, and if, for many reasons, they do not pass this information on to the dictator (for fear of criticism and punishment), they increase things in their favour in planning a coup.

They are experts in the security of the regime and therefore know how to strike at its weakest points. They also know best what is the most opportune time from the point of view of the internal political situation. When the three factors of ability, conditions and motive are present, the dictatorship is vulnerable. In Ghana, Nkrumah's excesses had created the conditions of popular dissatisfaction. The chief of police and the top army leaders were in favour of action and they had also the advantage of Nkrumah's being out of the country in China. The Ghana coup of 24 February 1966 is largely explained by these circumstances.[38] It may certainly have been welcomed by Nkrumah's many international enemies, but their support was not essential to the seizure of power.

## 5.   Conclusions

The basic cause of military intervention shown up in these cases is the failure of the political structure to produce stable political parties that accept the essential rules of a parliamentary democracy. Where political parties fail, either the military must intervene or personal dictatorships must try to become established. Africa's experience to date has been in favour of the military solution. If the political leadership can be re-instated (such as in Sierra Leone's case where Dr Stevens found refuge in Guinea) the military can be replaced.[39] Where the political leadership is physically

38 For the aftermath, see R. Pinkney, *Ghana Under Military Rule, 1966-1969*, London, 1972; D. Goldsworthy, 'Ghana's Second Republic', *Australian Outlook*, 25, April 1971; E.O. Ayisi, 'Ghana and the return to parliamentary government', *Political Quarterly*, 41, December 1970.

39 Lee, op. cit., Nelkin, op. cit.; R. Murray, 'Militarism in Africa', *New Left Review*, 38, July-August 1966; D. Austin, 'The underlying

destroyed (Nigeria) there is little prospect of an early return to civilian rule. In Ghana's case the political leadership was hopelessly compromised in the defects of the Nkrumah regime or represented minority interests (such as Dr Busia) which, when given an opportunity to re-instate civilian rule, do not have wide enough support for a long enough time to establish stable civilian government. The result, in Ghana's case, was the re-intervention of the military in January 1972.[40]

---

problem of the army coup d'etat in Africa', *Optima*, June 1966; M.F. Oke, 'The army in Africa', *African Quarterly*, 9, 1, April-June 1969; R. Mathews, *African Powder-Keg: Revolt and Discontent in Six Emergent Nations*, London, 1966; J.S. Coleman and B. Price, 'The role of the military in sub-Saharan Africa', in Johnson (ed.), op. cit.; S. Andreski, *The African Predicament*, London, 1968; C.E. Welch, *Soldier and State in Africa: A Comparative Analysis of Military Intervention and Political Change*, Evanston, Ill., 1970; W. Gutteridge, 'The political role of the African armed forces', *African Affairs*, 66, April 1967.

40 See *The New Ghana*, 1, 20, 1972, Accra, Ghana.

# 6 The Military in Pakistan and Indonesia

## 1. Introduction

The military in Pakistan and Indonesia intervened as a result of the unconstitutional actions of political leaders. This chapter tries to analyse the process of political suicide that the civilian political leadership embarked upon in order to pursue its objective of absolute power. In the cases discussed here the civilian political forces attempted to ride the tiger and they became its first victims. In Pakistan the military leaders took power in a constitutional vacuum created by the civilian leadership and with the additional intention of forestalling military intervention led from the junior ranks. In Indonesia the murderous assault on the army leadership by Communist-led troops backfired, largely through incompetence, and the surviving army leaders took power and exacted a terrible revenge. In both cases the military had been built into a powerful machine by foreign assistance and were provoked into action by events rather than ambition.

## 2. Pakistan

Pakistan was from its inception a state disunited in everything except the Muslim religion. It was divided geographically by 1,000 miles of Indian territory, by ethnic and language differences, and by communal tensions (exacerbated in the East to the point of secession in 1971). One government minister, Abdul Mansur Ahmad, described Pakistan's problem as 'creating one state out of two countries and one nation out of two peoples'.[1] He could have added to the

1 Quoted in K.B. Sayeed, 'Collapse of parliamentary democracy in Pakistan', *Middle East Journal*, 13, 4, 1959.

number of peoples and countries to be united and still have been accurate. A unified Pakistan was essentially mythological and a parliamentary-governed one almost impossible. The minorities in Pakistan are quite substantial, e.g. Bengal Pakistan had over half the population within it. The activity of passionate minorities, often myopic and partisan in the perception of their own interests, will always weaken the political system and hold back nation-building (compare Nigeria). Without nation-building a divided country will be ungovernable. If the state is to continue, it must either transform the sectarian conflicts into a national interest, or reconstitute itself around an authoritarian centralist structure, such as the army.[2]

To pose the problem in this way is not to ascribe to the actual process by which it was worked out a consciousness that rose to the occasion and resolved the matter directly. Time is a ruthless eliminator of alternatives. In Pakistan it took nine years to draw up a constitution and that was operated for only two years.[3] In the period during which the constitution was being argued over, the executive of the country was moulded on the former British Viceroy system.[4] The Governor-Generals of Pakistan were: Mohammed Ali Jinnah (1947-8); Liquat Ali Khan (1948-51) (though the title belonged to Khwaja Nazimudden); Ghulan Mohammed (1951-5); and General Iskander Mirza (1955-6).

Ghulan Mohammed was the first to act unconstitutionally when he sacked Nazimudden as Prime Minister. Nazimudden had swapped the Gover鈍er-General's post for Prime Minister after the death of the powerful Liquat Ali Khan — politicians tend to gravitate towards the source of effective power. The sacking of Nazimudden by Mohammed was not challenged, and it signified the movement of the centre of power to the Governor-General. He went on to dissolve the Constituent Assembly on 24 October, 1954, with army support, and brought into the cabinet the army leader, Ayub Khan. In March 1955 he assigned to himself the right to rule by

2  K. Callard, *Political Forces in Pakistan, 1947-1959*, Vancouver, 1959.

3  G.W. Ghoudhuri, *Democracy in Pakistan*, Dacca, 1963.

4  Hurewitz, op. cit., pp. 181-2.

decree, thus consolidating executive power firmly into his hands. This was not a popular move and he was forced to resign; the country was given a last chance at parliamentary government.

The Defence Secretary, General Iskander Mirza, took over as Governor-General, and he became Pakistan's first President when the new constitution was implemented in March 1956. The new constitution did not resolve any of the difficulties in running the country, it only gave them a new form of expression. No party could get a majority and the system of blocking coalitions operated to frustrate the opportunities of party government given by the constitution.

While many of the cleavages in the country were articulated in the political system, some major ones were not, such as the problems of the landless peasant and other underprivileged groups. Personal cliques, bribery and corruption, and the ever-present system of party manoeuvring, drove Pakistan into political stagnation, the one condition that it was not suited for.

The long-awaited general election to elect a National Assembly was postponed for one reason or another under the very constitution that had been designed to ensure free elections. While there were no national elections there could be no national political parties and therefore no national cohesion or national interest. The delay in setting up a national political structure permitted local political machines to flourish and entrench themselves. Local politics in this situation tend to be negative rather than broadly representative of nationwide groupings. (They combine in a microcosm all the worst features of Third World political machines.) There can be no overlap of dissensus in such a system; it is zero-sum activity, aimed at preventing others getting anything if the locality, or sect, represented by the party is not getting what it thinks is its due. All effort is directed at stopping any change until the full (extreme) demands are met, irrespective of the overall damage to the national interest.

The national government faced external threats as well. In Kashmir it was in dispute with India, and there were tensions with Afghanistan and India over water rights. The Muslim

League and the Awami League were both in opposition to President Mirza, who was surviving in a Bismarckian style by dividing his opponents.[5] This further weakened the party system. He had formed a Republican Party to counteract the other political parties, but this identified his (small) political base more than it threatened the other parties.

Mirza wanted to be re-elected President in the forthcoming general election and he also favoured a larger role for the presidency than envisaged in most parliamentary systems. At this stage Mirza attempted the kind of activity that his predecessor, Ghulan Mohammed, had failed to carry through in 1955. Both leaders were forced to feel their way to a solution of the political crisis along the lines of a centralist Presidency. This had brought Ghulan Mohammed down. Mirza was therefore defying precedent, and he was attempting to change the constitution in a shorter time scale (two years) than the eight years it had taken to create the Governor-General system. For the plan to work, the army was required to go along with measures that dispersed the political parties and gave greatly enhanced powers to the Presidency. The army was also a much more modern army than before, having been modernised by generous American aid (negotiated by Ayub Khan). The army was stronger in 1958 and the political system weaker.

There was a virtual two-stage military coup. A brawl in the National Assembly, which fatally injured the Speaker, dragged parliamentary prestige to near zero-point and gave Mirza the opportunity to step in. On 7 October 1958, the President assumed full powers; he ended the 1956 constitution, dismissed the cabinet, dissolved the Assemblies, banned all political parties, made a few arrests and declared martial law. The army commander, Ayub Khan, was given the task of enforcing these decrees. Without a constitution it is difficult to see on what basis Mirza considered his power to rest.

The army upper-echelons were subject to the changes taking place in the country and aware of the pressures building up within their own ranks. The officer corps was a

5 C.B. Marshall, 'Reflections on the revolution in Pakistan', *Foreign Affairs*, 37, 2, 1959.

more broadly recruited class in 1958 than it had been in 1948. The European and Pacific wars had opened its ranks to lower-middle-class and land-owning families. Men of the commercial classes and academic backgrounds joined the army in the post-independence years in large numbers. In 1957 there were 3,000 applications for 80 vacancies in the officer cadets.[6] This kind of change had been taking place in other Third World armies and it had produced different solutions. In Egypt the younger officers were sufficiently different from the older officers to have completely different political and social outlooks, and after the coup in 1952 they simply retired the whole lot (a similar pattern occured in Iraq after 1958). The younger officers' solution in Egypt and Iraq did not pass unnoticed in Pakistan. The common conditions existing in each country immediately before the coups — dissatisfaction in the junior ranks with the kind of status quo that the senior officers tended to prefer — presented the senior Pakistani officers with a dilemma: either step in against the President, or have one of their junior commanders do it without them. The July 1958 Iraq coup had increased this pressure by public example.

Ayub Khan carried out President Mirza's orders of 7 October and a few weeks later he was appointed Prime Minister. On 27 October, with his position secure, the opposition dispersed and the President totally dependent upon him, he dismissed the President.[7] Mirza had created the situation with a careless abandon that defies explanation. Mirza's position as President rested on the constitution which he had overthrown, or it depended on the willingness, or otherwise, of the instruments of his power (the army and the police). He abrogated the constitution on the grounds of political chaos and technically liquidated his own legality. It was a fragile base on which to build a personal dictatorship. Only the army could enforce the fiction of his legality and this made him vulnerable to what the army, in the person of its commander, Ayub Khan, had in mind for the effective

6 M. Halpern, 'The Middle-Eastern armies and the new middle class', Johnson (ed.), op. cit., p. 298.

7 W.A. Wilcox, 'The Pakistan coup d'etat of 1958', *Pacific Affairs*, 38, 1965.

running of the state. Ayub obviously decided that the fiction was a brittle defence against potential coup-makers in the junior ranks.

If the fiction of the Presidency was left in Mirza's hands this tied the army leadership to Mirza's fortune. If Mirza was allowed to consolidate his power he might drag the army into any number of unpleasant adventures which, if they aborted, would tarnish them as targets for popular criticism (and retribution) as well. It was better by far to reorganise the political structure with the army at the head, and Ayub at the head of the army, and rely on one's own fortune.[8]

Thus the Ayub coup arose out of a defensive strategy against the unknown of personal dictatorship and the fact that the conditions for military intervention in the country were present, and which, on past and recent form, had produced actions directed, not just against the established ruler, but against the established army command. Ayub's coup prevented that scenario and for the next ten years he was to rule the country without interruption.[9]

### 3.   Indonesia

The civil-military situation in Indonesia does not lend itself to a simplistic sequence in which the military supplants the civilian power along the lines of the normal political models of the literature.[10] Indonesian politics were interwoven in such a way as to produce a defensive counter-coup against a political insurrection led by the Communist party of Indonesia, and later against the Executive (President Sukarno), in which the army as an independent social force was

8 Sayeed, op. cit., p. 404; S. Katrak, 'Coup d'etat in Pakistan', *Orient*, 4, 8, 1958.

9 For accounts of Ayub Khan's fall see: W.M. Dobell, 'Ayub Khan as president of Pakistan', *Pacific Affairs*, 42, 3, 1969; W.A. Wilcox, 'Once again at the starting point', *Asia Survey*, 10, 2, 1970; T. Maniruzzaman, 'Crisis in political development and the collapse of the Ayub Regime', *The Journal of Developing Areas*, 5, January 1971; S.J. Burki, 'Ayub's fall: A socio-economic explanation', *Asia Survey*, 12, 3, March 1972.

10 For criticism of some views on Indonesia, see U. Sundhausen, 'The military in research in Indonesian politics', *Journal of Asian Studies*, 31, 2, February 1972.

threatened with extinction. The military did not conspire to intervene and overthrow the established government. It reacted to a situation that had been developing for a long time.

It would also be simplistic to suggest that the army's intervention as the only homogeneous force was related to Indonesia's geography. The country is dispersed over a thousand miles of ocean and as many islands, and also suffers all the normal disabilities of a pre-industrial economic system. An obvious criticism of the homogeneity thesis (insofar as this homogeneity is considered to be an inherent characteristic of the military) is that the army was as bitterly divided as any other structure in Indonesia. It was a constant source of instability throughout the 1960s. The civilian political instability — a host of parties and ideological schisms — had its reflection inside the armed forces and led to internecine conflicts and clashes over issues.[11]

The factionalism in the army is, however, important to an understanding of what was happening to the military during the period and how this was preparing it for its role in 1965. The army factionalism can be compared with the equally factionalised political structure, but there were crucial differences in the effect of factionalism in both structures. Within the hierarchical army structure, factionalism purged the army of dissidents as each successive (and unsuccessful) challenge to central authority resulted in organisational retribution. When a political party splits over principle, or personality, the result is two parties in place of one. When a military structure splits, there can be only one victor and one structure remaining; the losers are paid off, killed or exiled; they are not left to set up another army and challenge the central army's monopoly of violence. Through this process the army was, by the 1960s, becoming more orderly, more professional and less ideological than it was in the early days of the republic. It was the factionalism which produced a

11 For an account of the factionalism in the Indonesian army see: R.T. McVey, 'The post-revolutionary transformation of the Indonesian army', *Indonesia*, 1, 2, April 1972; A. Gregory, 'Factionalism and the Indonesian army: the new order', *Journal of Comparative Administration*, 2, 3, November 1970.

relatively homogeneous force in the military, not its inherent nature.

The uneasy fusion of the guerrilla troops, with their ideological motivations, and the Dutch or Japanese-trained soldiers who came over to the independence struggle and out of which the Indonesian army was formed, was the single most disintegrative feature of the army in the early years. Moreover, the major issues of Communism, in all its variants, and Islam, were paralleled in the army in the confrontations and rebellions against central authority. These ideological struggles about what form of political system was to be adopted in Indonesia were compounded in many cases by outright separatist or half-way federalist tensions arising from the geographical spread of the country.

The natural selection process that was inevitable in the army, because the central authority was not successfully challenged, resulted in a decline in the number of ideo-logically committed officers, at least of the extremist variety from left and right wings, and the emergence of officers committed to centralist Indonesia. This trend coincided with, but was not necessarily in phase with, a decline in the confidence of the army officers in civilian political leaders and movements that appeared to be making a negative contribution to Indonesia and the kind of nationalism favoured by the army. The army was, then, not a ready-made unifying force, but became one through a long process of seemingly endless factionalism.[12]

At the same time the age composition of the army was changing. When General Sudirman became Army Commander in 1945 he was only 33 (about the same age as Libya's Colonel Ghaddafy when he came to power in 1971) and most of his officers were in their twenties. In 1965 a large proportion of the army officers were products of the Republic and not of the previous period of struggles against the Dutch.[13]

12 Goh Cheng Teik, 'Why Indonesia's attempt at democracy in the mid-50s failed', *Modern Asian Studies*, 6, 1972, asserts that 'personal ambition was the main impelling force behind the army unrest in 1956 and 1967'. This misses the point.

13 Sundhausen, op. cit., p. 364; Polomka, op. cit., p. 83; see also Pauker, op. cit.

For thirteen months, from March 1956 to April 1957, Indonesia had a directly elected government. It was the first and only experiment in parliamentary democracy.[14] For the rest of the time it was ruled by nominated political leaders in legislative institutions, at the head of which was President Sukarno. From 1957 to 1965, President Sukarno ruled almost entirely by executive action. However, it was not the non-elected character of Indonesia's political system that provoked military intervention. In itself the system worked, in the strict sense that it limited the damage caused by party conflicts. The problem was that the army was not represented in the political system and this exclusion was bound to cause tensions whenever the administration neglected, threatened or interfered with army interests. And these interests were increasingly articulated by an increasingly more nationalistic army.

The first major crisis occured in 1952 when military units of the Army Command took to the streets of Jakarta for a few hours on 17 October. It was meant as a display of strength for the President. The Chiefs-of-Staffs, Major-General T.B. Simatupang and Colonel A.H. Nasution, led a delegation to confer with Sukarno and requested the dismissal of the appointed parliament and the cabinet. The Defence Minister had declared his intention to cut military expenditure through a 40 per cent reduction in army strength by the end of 1953. The army leaders were not reconciled to the idea of such substantial cuts, though they did have preferences as to which kind of troops would be sacrificed if some cuts were imposed.[15]

The affair highlighted the basic weakness of the Indonesian political system: the cabinet could not claim a mandate without an election, and this made the army leaders no more and no less representative of Indonesia's interests than the

14 H. Feith, *The Decline in Constitutional Democracy in Indonesia*, New York, 1962: Feith, by using a wide definition of democracy, writes that democracy existed in Indonesia from 1949 to 1957 inclusive; Goh Cheng Teik, op. cit., p. 226, disagrees, rightly in the author's opinion.

15 The army officers were in favour of cutting out some of the troops inherited from the irregular formations, and this was used by anti-army politicians to encourage disaffection in the army.

politicians. Moreover, the army also demonstrated its ability to exert pressure on the President. This incident marks the beginning of the army's entry into politics as an institution, and it was followed up in 1955 by a declaration against civilian interference in the army's affairs.

The incident also prompted the civilian leaders in the direction of democratisation through directly elected parliaments that would answer criticism as to their being non-representative. Elections would also re-inforce the claims of the politicians to legitimacy. At the same time it placed at risk the party state, for if a democratically elected parliament failed, the political system would have to look elsewhere for stability. The Communists and the Islamic forces saw this as their opportunity to fashion Indonesia according to their images of a properly run society. The President, whose personality, ambitions and charismatic role can never be left out in understanding Indonesia at this time, may also have seen democratisation as a step towards absolute power through the party he helped found, the Indonesian Nationalist Party (PNI). While the immediate army challenge came to nothing — the President dispensed liberal dosages of sympathy towards the officers but nothing else — the turning point in the situation had been reached.

Forty parties contested the general election in 1955. The results for the major parties are shown in Table 1. The Islamic Parties, which had split out of the Masjumi in the early fifties, polled 43.5 per cent of the vote. The Communists polled 16.4 per cent, and two years later they were to continue their progress with large gains at the expense of the nationalists in local elections.[16] The position of the Communists was strengthened, as Sukarno came to rely upon them for support in the early sixties and they emerged as the major contender for power.

Given protection from army repression . . . by Sukarno, and aided by his 'revolutionary' stress, the Party grew to claim a membership of

16 D. Hindley, *The Communist Party of Indonesia, 1951-1963*, Berkeley, 1964; J.M. van der Kroef, *The Communist Party of Indonesia: Its History, Programme and Tactics*, Vancouver, 1965.

about three million by mid 1964, and another fifteen million among its affiliated mass organisations of youth, labour, women, farmers and so forth.[17]

The large number of parties that gained seats in the election made coalition government inevitable. There were three major political forces in parliament: the Nationalists, the Islamic parties and the Communists. The Islamic and Communist parties were bitter enemies and missed no opportunities for factional attacks on each other. The ensuing inter-coalition battles led to blocking coalitions such that no matter what mixture of parties was enticed into a coalition there were sufficient votes left in opposition to make such a coalition impracticable and unstable. In 1957 the attempts to form a new cabinet failed and Sukarno, wearied by the whole business of representative democracy, intervened and declared martial law.

*Table 1  Indonesia: percentage of the vote and number of seats 1955 general election*

| Party | Percentage of the vote | Number of seats |
|---|---|---|
| Indonesia National Party | 22.3 | 57 |
| Masjumi | 20.9 | 57 |
| Religious Scholars League | 18.4 | 45 |
| Communist Party (PKI) | 16.4 | 39 |
| Islamic Party Association | 2.9 | 8 |
| Christian Party | 2.6 | 8 |
| Catholic Party | 2.0 | 6 |
| Socialist Party | 2.0 | 5 |
| Ikati Pendukung Kemererdekan | 1.4 | 4 |
| Islamic Education Movement | 1.3 | 4 |
| Nationalist Rakyat Party | 0.6 | 2 |
| Others | 9.2 | 22 |
| | 100 | 257 |

Source: A. Van Merle, 'The first Indonesian parliamentary election', *Indonesia*, 9, 1956; Table adjusted.

Local rebellions and dissidence in the country combined

17 Polomka, op. cit., p. 159.

with party political in-fighting made the situation unstable.[18]
The putting down of the rebellions in Sumatra and Sulawesi
brought the army into closer affinity with the President who
at the time embodied the ethos of One Indonesia. The
President, the Communists, the Islamic Masjumi and the
army entered into a period of struggle for supremacy.

In 1958 Sukarno, with the support of the Communists,
and rival Islamic factions, banned the Masjumi, the largest of
the Islamic parties, along with the smaller Socialist Party.
This eliminated one of the contenders within the upper elite.
The Communists grew in strength and the balance of power
in the country made the President a political prisoner
alternating between appeasing the army or the Communists.
The Communists were aided in their efforts by the diplomatic assistance of the Chinese People's Republic and
Sukarno's foreign policy adventures. Sukarno's alternative to
representative democracy was 'Guided Democracy'; a thinly
disguised form of personal rule. Some of the foreign policy
adventures were a success, such as the campaign against
Dutch New Guinea (1963) but others were poor failures, the
most notable being the 'confrontation' with Malaysia which
mobilised vast resources and undermined the economy.

The defence budget increased enormously but was largely
spent on forming a modern airforce and navy. The American-
trained army became suspicious that their neglect was
deliberate and that alternative forces were being consciously
built up which could be used to neutralise the army in a
showdown. While Peking courted Indonesia as a brother
Asian power, the Russians courted Sukarno to offset the
Chinese diplomatic successes, and supplied much of the
military equipment that he wanted. A list of major weapon
exports from Russia and Eastern Europe shows the extent of
the non-army military build-up.

The army was in desperate straights even to pay its troops
and in some areas illegally 'taxed' local businesses.[19] The
'confrontation' project with Malaysia was carried out by

18 Smail, op. cit.; J.M. van der Kroef, 'The place of the army in
Indonesian politics', *Eastern World*, January 1957; also: 'Instability in
Indonesia, *Far Eastern Survey*, Army 1957.
19 Sundhausen, op. cit.

Table 2    *Russian military aid to Indonesia 1958-65*

| | |
|---|---:|
| Fighters | 108 |
| Bombers | 68 |
| Transports/helicopters | 38 |
| Missiles | 396 |
| Attack ships | 21 |
| Submarines | 4 |
| Gunboats | 73 |
| Support ships | 3 |

Source: SIPRI, *The Arms Trade with the Third World*, pp. 824-6. Thayer, *The War Business*, New York, 1969, gives slightly different figures for some of the items, e.g. 12 submarines and 8 not 6 destroyers, as well as 'helicopters, tanks, anti-aircraft guns, field artillery . . . and small arms' p.328.

them with diminishing enthusiasm. General Nasution was critical of the President's policies and was promoted 'upstairs'.[20] The drain went on and reached, according to one estimate, a military appropriation of as much as 75 per cent of the Government's budget.[21]

Nasution tried, before his 'promotion', to turn the army to a 'middle way' project of combining defence with development, and it was the effect of the President's militant foreign policy which frustrated such a role for the army that eventually turned him away from unconditional support for Sukarno.[22] The evidence suggests that the army was not directing nor gaining from the military build-up of 1963-5 and that it came in consequence to oppose the defence spending levels. This is in contrast to accepted views of the military as an unqualified force for militarism constantly seeking, irresponsibly, to increase its budget and embroil the government in foreign adventures. Governments, apparently, can drag along an unwilling military-industrial complex.

20 Polomka, op. cit., pp. 82-3.

21 B. Anderson, 'American values and research on Indonesia', paper read at the Association of Asian Studies Conference, Spring, 1971, quoted in Sundhausen, op. cit., p. 356; Stockholm International Peace Research Institute (SIPRI), *The Arms Trade with the Third World*, Stockholm, 1971, p. 460. The Institute has been used as a major source for a great deal of this book.

22 Polomka, op. cit., p. 82.

The increased military spending was accompanied by a billion dollars of Soviet equipment 'sold' to the government.[23] The Americans provided only $5 million worth up to 1952 for internal security.[24] Although the bulk of the equipment did not go to the army it was dependent after 1959 on Soviet supplies of small arms and these replaced its American and war-surplus weapons.[25] (There was also some local production under licence of the Italian Beretta 9mm sub-machine gun and the M-1 rifle.)

The Russians were no doubt wary of arming such an outspoken critic of Communism as the army.[26] The military take-over was not a consequence of the arms build-up, because this arms build-up did not place the army in a commanding position as was the case following American military exports to Turkey. Quite a different relationship exists in Indonesia between the rise of the military budgets and the army take-over. The sharp rise in defence budgets, the unpopular confrontation with Malaysia, the growth of Russian influence within the armed services (an inevitable consequence of using Russian weaponry and the associated training programme) and the alignment with Chinese foreign policy interests, contributed to a sense of paranoia in the army. They reacted ruthlessly and violently when their survival as an institution was finally made real in 1965. It was, in fact, the high defence spending and its associated policies that forced the army to fight for survival and not the growth of the parasitic army that forced the state to collapse.

The mechanics of the coups of October 1965 can only be understood in this context.[27] The first coup, of 30 September to 1 October, was directed against the army High Command in the name of the President. Six of the top

23 G. Thayer, *The War Business: The International Trade in Armaments*, London, 1969, p. 327.

24 SIPRI, op. cit., p. 462.

25 L.A. Frank, *The Arms Trade in International Relations*, New York, 1969, pp. 142-3.

26 An assessment of Russian intentions in Indonesia is given in Georgetown Research Project, *The Soviet Military Aid Programme as a Reflection of Soviet Objectives*, Washington, 1965.

27 For accounts of the 1965 coups see: Polomka, op. cit., pp. 72-8; W.F. Wertheim, 'Indonesia before and after the Untung coup', *Pacific*

ranking generals were kidnapped and executed. Generals Nasution and Suharto escaped and organised the counter-coup (which also issued orders in the name of the President). The coup was defeated and the ensuing revenge campaigns saw the physical decimation of the Indonesian Communist party[28] and the reduction of the contenders for power from these two: the President and the army. The ailing President had mass support and it was substantial enough for him to be extended the courtesies of office by the army leaders, although there was some circumstantial evidence of his complicity in the Communist coup. But within six months the decision to remove him was taken and, under army pressure, he signed away his 'powers' to General Suharto.[29] On 11 March 1966 the army took over the government of the country without opposition. They have ruled since then with undisputed title to government and are now experimenting in a new version of 'guided democracy'.[30]

*Affairs*, Spring-Summer 1966; S.W. Simon, *The Broken Triangle: Peking, Djakarta and the PKI*, Baltimore, 1969; D.S. Lev, 'Indonesia 1965: the year of the coup', *Asia Survey*, February 1966; L. Rey, 'Dossier of the Indonesian drama', *New Left Review*, March-April 1966.

28 A.C. Brackman, *The Communist Collapse in Indonesia*, New York, 1969; J.M. van der Kroef, 'Indonesian Communism since the 1965 coup', *Pacific Affairs*, Spring 1970; Polomka, op. cit., Chapter 8.

29 T. Vittachi, *The Fall of Sukarno*, London, 1967.

30 For discussion on the future of the military regime see: G. Pauker, 'Indonesia: the age of reason?', *Asian Survey*, February 1968; J.D. Legge, 'General Suharto's new order', *International Affairs*, January 1968; H. Feith, 'Suharto's search for the political format', *Australia's Neighbours*, May-June 1968; L. Palmier, 'Suharto's Indonesia', *Asian Affairs*, 57, October 1970; L. Lescaze, 'Generals are the new capitalists amid Indonesia's poverty', *Guardian*, London, 3 November 1970; H. Crouch, 'Military politics under Indonesia's new order', *Pacific Affairs*, 45, 2, 1972.

# 7 Arab Military Interventions

## 1.   Introduction

Military interventions in the Arab Middle East have been dominated in the past twenty years by the personality and leadership of Gamal Abdul Nasser. His influence extended beyond the borders of Egypt throughout his leadership up to his death in office in 1971. There were of course numerous Arab military interventions before the Free Officers seized power from King Farouk in 1952, and there have been numerous since. But Nasser's pre-eminence in the Arab world was a product of the circumstances of the transformation of the Arab countries from semi-dependent to independent states (symbolised by the great struggles against the British over the Suez Canal) and of his own concept of his special mission to be undisputed leader of the Arab nations.

This chapter discusses the rise to power of Nasser in the Egyptian coup of 1952 and his ruthless elimination of his co-conspirators in the Free Officers leadership. This period tells us a lot about Nasser's political skills. We then look at his role in the interventions and instability of two Arab countries, Syria and Iraq. The interventions in Syria and Iraq after 1958 were inter-linked at several points in the international struggles between the three main forces in the Arab nationalist movement, the Ba'athists, the Communists and the Nasserists. These internecine struggles throughout the 1960s have produced a more independent type of nationalism in Syria and Iraq than existed in the 1950s. Since the death of Nasser there have been new elements in the Arab nationalist movement — the rise of Ghaddafy of Libya, the resurgence of the Palestinian guerrilla movements, and the rivalry that is developing between Iraq and Iran.

## 2. Egypt

Nasserism is now a spent force, not just because of Nasser's death but probably in spite of it. Egypt's strategic positions and its special relationship with the Russians gave it prestige and influence up to the Six Day War. After the war Nasserism was finished as the driving force for the Arab cause; Nasser was transformed from the major leader of the cause into its 'grand old man'. The new spirit of self-reliance, and an Islamic nationalism looking in new directions (south of the Sahara and east of the Gulf), less dependent on Russian goodwill, in search of an Arab solution to the problems of the region, largely replaced the Nasserist idea as the inspiration for the young Arab officers in the armies of the region. The commercial successes of the oil producing countries in gaining larger shares of the oil revenues from the Western oil companies probably had, and will continue to have, a larger impact on the Arab cause than the Nasserist 'gains' against the British over Suez. First, the British have gone and their presence is just a memory, and secondly, the Six Day War reduced the strategic importance of Suez from international proportions to that of an anti-tank ditch across Sinai.

President Sadat is no Nasser in the Arab world. He was left with the remnants of a strategy that had reduced Egypt's ability to provide leadership against Israel to that of a purveyor of slogans and empty promises. Libya's leaders start with the singular advantage of youth. Because they have not done very much, they have not made many fundamental mistakes — their reputation is intact, and more important, it is backed by oil revenues. They do not suffer from the disadvantages of Algeria, under Boumédienne, who seized power in 1964. Algeria is distant from the confrontation with Israel, and is inevitably still influenced by its former French connections.[1] Libya can appear more Arab, more Islamic, and more often, before the Arab youth than the Algerians, and now the Egyptians, as the prototype of the Arab militant for the 1970s. But their ability to do this is a product of the

1 M.D. Pepy, 'France's relations with Africa', *African Affairs*, 69, April 1970; C. Hollingsworth, 'France still a North African power', *Daily Telegraph*, London, 12 May 1970.

previous period of Nasser's dominance in Egypt and his influence on other Arab powers.

### 3.    The rise of Nasserism

If Indonesia's army was dragged into politics by events, Egypt's stepped in with alacrity.[2] The Free Officers in 1952 were junior in rank (Lt.-Colonels and Majors) and in their early or middle thirties. Many of them had been engaged in politics since their twenties (Nasser was only 21 when he became politically active).[3] Egypt, being an occupied country, was bound to have an ideological nationalism expressed from within its officer corps in common with other elites in the country. The targets against which the army officers aimed their (largely hidden) disgust were the general enemies of Egyptian nationhood but not the monarchy as an institution. Their goal was an unspecified national resurgence and rejuvenation. The Second World War interrupted the development of the 'conspiracy', though some, such as Sadat who succeeded Nasser as President in 1971, were active throughout the war.[4]

There was plenty of fuel for nationalist dissension in Egypt after the war. The military occupation by the British, the creation of the state of Israel and the apparent inability of the monarchical regime to meet Arab and Egyptian aspirations in these matters, kindled the fires of subversion and created groups, like the group to which Nasser belonged, to move from vague idealistic notions of a Greater Egypt to determined opposition to the established regime. An attempt was made to prepare a military coup in 1948 but police surveillance was enough to confine the movement to a discussion.[5] The officers who returned from the debacle of the 1948 war against Israel were even more convinced of the necessity of action.

2 P.J. Vatikiotis, *The Egyptian Army in Politics: Pattern for New Nations*, Bloomington, Ind., 1961.

3 A. El-Sadat, *Revolt of the Nile*, London, 1957; Be'eri, op. cit.

4 Laqueur, op. cit., p. 48; Sadat was jailed for pro-German activities and later also for terrorism.

5 Be'eri, op. cit., p. 81.

In 1949 there were three military coups in Syria. The Palestinian war was the catalyst that brought the Syrian military into politics — the army was used to preserve public order against the popular need to express feelings of utter dismay at the Arab's performance against Israel.[6] Egyptian officers were conscious of the Syrian example and it is probably connected with the Syrian events that the Free Officers Movement went 'operational' from 1949.

The conspirators had potential allies with political connections to wider layers of the population than were open to the army. There was, for example, the Muslim Brotherhood who opposed the existing order (it had let down Islam). The differences between the extremist Muslim sect and the Free Officers were implicit in the Free Officers' secularism and Muslims' universalism. The officers were Egyptian nationalists first and Muslims second; the Muslims reversed that order and espoused a trans-nationalism, with the vision of Muslim nationhood rather than the narrower Egyptian nationalism. The army conspirators had to tread carefully in their dealings with the Muslim Brotherhood, organisationally separating themselves from them and, at the same time, keeping in touch with the forces that the Brotherhood had influence over, to pull them behind their own nascent revolution[7] when the time came.

Another opposition group was led by the Communists.[8] They presented a similar problem. The Communists supported the nationalist movement as a first stage in the proletarian struggle and a prelude to social change. It was a Stalinist version of the 'permanent revolution'. The Egyptian Communist party cadres were to be sacrificed by the Russians later when Soviet foreign policy interests in the Nasserite break with the West required it. The officers

6 For views on the Syrian army's role after 1948 see: Rustow, op. cit.; M. Halpern, *The Politics of Social Change in the Middle-East and North Africa*, Princeton, 1963; A. Carleton, 'The Syrian coups d'etat of 1949', *Middle East Journal*, January 1950.

7 Be'eri, op. cit., p. 87; C.P. Harris, *Nationalism and Revolution in Egypt: the Role of the Muslim Brotherhood*, The Hague, 1964; E.I.J. Rosenthal, *Islam in the Modern National State*, Cambridge, 1965.

8 Laqueur, op. cit.

maintained contact with the Communists and with other groups such as the Wafdists.[9]

The opposition groups were engaged in mass agitation, officially encouraged by the government, but the campaign got out of hand and led to serious disorders and clashes with British troops. The Farouk regime was using the disturbances to bring pressure on Britain but had no intention of allowing order to break down. The Free Officers remained aloof from these actions and watched the rapid fall of cabinets in 1952 as Farouk tried to manoeuvre out of crisis.

Farouk's administration then made a fundamental error; it added to its cabinet crisis the burden of provocative actions against those officers it suspected of plotting treason. It sentenced one of them to death for possessing incriminating pamphlets; it ordered others to be posted and appointed a Minister of Defence, related by marriage to the King but by no means of any proven capacity for the job. These measures over-stretched the regime.

The army was pushed to the point where it accepted the challenge or it permitted itself to be dispersed, with a future confined to ceremonial duties and with prospects of being called upon to back up police action against agitation campaigns with which many of the officers were basically in sympathy. Once the Free Officers refused to disperse, the monarchy was at risk, but, oblivious of the dangers, Farouk's court proceeded as if its writ ran on without question. The writ, however, stopped when the Free Officers in Cairo occupied the city and declared themselves in rebellion. Farouk was forced to give way as he did not have the forces to do anything else. Power, when it passed on, passed on without much resistance.[10]

The coup leaders were headed by Neguib, the most senior officer who supported the Free Officers. The King left Egypt and the new regime set to work to bring to fruition their plans for Egypt. The structure of government was quite simple. An all-civilian administration was set up, headed by

9 Be'eri, op. cit., p. 91, claims that Nasser managed to convince both the Communists and the Wafdists that he was in sympathy with their political positions.

10 cf. G. Nasser, *Egypt's Liberation*, Washington, 1955.

appointed ministers, but the monarchy was not abolished immediately; the Free Officers ruled as regents for the Crown Prince. All senior officers were cashiered and junior officers promoted to replace them, ensuring an infusion of new blood and, as important, gratitude and loyalty from the promoted officers to the coup leaders. A large strike was brutally suppressed in August 1952, though the strikers were acting in support of what they thought were their rights under the revolution. Several workers were killed in clashes outside the plant and subsequently others were court-martialled and sentenced either to death or imprisonment. The regime was against disorder, and strike movements were regarded as a threat that could take on a political character if not checked at the start.

Political parties were summarily stripped of their functions so that the promotors of the campaigns of unrest that helped topple the monarchy in 1952 did not remain in a position to continue their activity. By January 1953 political parties were outlawed. Popular support for the revolution was sought by the regime, but this support was to be strictly controlled by the new state and was not to be permitted any independence. Mass adulation for the revolution and its leaders was the only form of mass activity to be tolerated.[11]

The settlement of the external challenges to the regime's power left the question of who within the leadership was to prevail. The way in which this struggle unfolded is broadly as follows.[12]

The coup leaders selected Neguib as their main spokesman. He was, however, no mere figurehead and set out to ensure his primacy among the Free Officers, to whom he was senior in rank. In the June 1953 government, Neguib was President and Prime Minister and Nasser Deputy Prime Minister. A year later Nasser moved up to Prime Minister. Some of the leading figures were eliminated from office during this period by expedients ranging from arrests to appointment as ambassadors abroad.

11 Be'eri, op. cit., p. 107.
12 For an account of Nasser's role see: J. Joeston, *Nasser*, London, 1960; Nutting, op. cit.; V.B. Lutskii, 'The Revolutions of July 1952 in Egypt', in Laqueur (ed.), op. cit.

The forces in the state were the Revolutionary Council, dominated by Nasser, the Muslim Brotherhood, the broad left and Neguib, who occupied the centre balancing position. The major political force with mass support was the Muslim Brotherhood which also had allies within the army command. It was the one pre-Revolution force not banned by the regime and co-existed with the Liberation Rally, set up by the officers to channel popular support for the regime into safe activity. The implicit differences between the purist Brotherhood and the secularist officers were held in check in the aftermath of the coup as each side calculated it could use the other for its own ends. The cracks, when they came, appeared first in the Muslim Brotherhood. The Brotherhood was united only insofar as interpretation of Muslim interests was monolithic. The strains broke into open conflict in 1954 and were reflected in tensions within the army among officers, as 'represented' by Nasser (the revolution's pragmatists), and among more idealistic and (in the context of Islamic culture) more traditionalist officers 'represented' by Neguib.

Nasser became a target for the Muslim agitation, which described him as an imperialist lackey and dictator and accused him of diverting Muslim ideals into narrower egoism.[13] Nasser took action against the Brotherhood and this prompted Neguib into resignation as President. Nasser was thereby challenged from within by those officers who supported Neguib and from without by the mass political base of the Brotherhood. Nasser intensified the arrests of Brotherhood members and invoked a hard line against their activities. Neguib was placed under house arrest. The situation turned when some army units declared for Neguib and the Sudanese put diplomatic pressure on the Government. Neguib was restored to the Presidency and Nasser was forced to take a back seat for a while.

The crisis had brought to the surface the opposition to Nasser. But the tenuous nature of the forces that supported Neguib was exposed. First, there was the Muslim Brotherhood, and secondly, there was the broad Left, which was suspicious of Nasser's anti-party activities. This was not just a

13 Be'eri, op. cit., p. 114.

tenuous alliance upon which to build a political base, it was also divisive, as the Muslim and Communist movements had less in common with each other than they had with Nasser.

Nasser struck back in March with mass arrests of political figures in the Communist, Wafdist and Muslim movements. He removed in a few swoops the key cadres in the political base which rested uneasily beneath Neguib. Leaderless, these movements were much less a threat and were reduced to potential mobs rather than being disciplined political forces with distinct command structures and organisational competence. The disparate political interests of the groups would inevitably flare up without local leadership.

Nasser meanwhile turned towards a populist stance in demagogic pleas for defence of the revolution against vague threats from within. The army officers responded to Nasser's appeals and so did, significantly, the Cairo Transport Workers' Union. The official Liberation Rally was behind Nasser (it was a competitor with the opposition movement). As the pendulum swung in favour of Nasser he stepped up the arrests, forced the resignation of the remaining leftist in the Revolutionary Council, Khalid Muhialdin, and broke the back of organised opposition.[14]

He completed his coup with a well-publicised agreement over the Suez Canal reached with the British government in October 1954. This agreement was described as a betrayal by the leaderless opposition because of the clause which gave Britain re-entry powers to the canal under certain circumstances. An incompetent assassination attempt by a member of the Brotherhood gave Nasser his opportunity to settle scores with the organisation once and for all. The movement was banned, its leadership arrested (seven were hanged) and because Neguib was allegedly implicated he was placed under arrest.[15]

14 'Egypt since the coup d'etat of 1952', *World Today*, 10, 4, April 1954.
15 Be'eri, op. cit., p. 199 reports Neguib's death as August 1966; R. and W. Churchill, *The Six Day War*, London, 1967, report him as alive but under house arrest. Neguib gave interviews published in the world press in August 1973. He is very much alive and out of restriction. For Neguib's views on the revolution see M. Neguib, *Egypt's Destiny*, New York, 1955.

Nasser's victory in the factional struggle was possible because the opposition divided into sectarian factions so that, even if they did unite, they were driven inexorably into an unstable and divisive alliance. The Egyptian political movements were much less experienced than those in Indonesia. Neither of the major forces, the Muslims nor the Communists, presented the same kind of threat to Nasser as their Indonesian counterparts did to Sukarno. Nasser's base in the army was correspondingly secure. The extremism of the Muslims isolated them from becoming an effective opposition, and the Left was not a popular force (in an Indonesian sense) but was more a manipulative elite that worked within the state power structure and identified itself more with personalities than mass movements. It relied more on personal contacts than mass social pressure. For this reason alone it was vulnerable to decimation by the suppression of its leader cadres. Neguib's forces were too disparate to be concentrated, and not clear enough on what they wanted to stand up to Nasser's faction.

#### 4.    Syria and Iraq: inter-active intervention

The Nasserite victory in Egypt began a period of pre-eminence for Egypt and President Nasser in the Arab world. Nasser was to export his own version of pan-Arabism in various scenarios which had in common the premier position reserved for himself. His single-mindedness in pursuit of the goal of Egyptian (i.e. Nasserite) hegemony involved ruthless interference in the internal affairs of neighbours whenever the political position of neighbouring governments was at odds with his own.

Nasserism was more than Nasser, large as his contribution to events remained. It became symbolic of Arabism, modernity, anti-imperialism, nationalism and rejuvenation among wide layers of the Arab community in the Middle East and in particular among the army officers of Arab countries. Nasser was both myth and idol, in whose name actions were initiated, such as coups and purges, without, necessarily, a direct connection between these events and the man whose name was so liberally invoked.

Conversely, anti-Nasserists emerged from time to time, angered at Nasser's failings, jealous of his popularity, or grieved at his over-assertion of Egyptian eminence in the Arab struggle. In two countries, Iraq and Syria, the Nasserist influence in the ten years from 1958 was a source of instability:

Nasserist intervention in Syria, perhaps more than any other factor, contributed to the tensions, divisions, and hatreds that produced the coup d'états after the break-up of unity in 1961.[16]

The struggle between the nationalists, the Ba'athists and the Nasserists (sometimes self-appointed, other times not) in Syria and Iraq led to the chronic inability to maintain stable government in these countries, and due to their proximity, the interaction of the coups and attempted coups in each country only added to the problems. (These interactions can be linked with each other throughout the ten years 1958-68.) The pro-Egyptian coup of January 1958 in Syria was followed by continual pressure on Iraq, at that time ruled by a monarchy, and allied with the American Baghdad Pact. In July 1958 a military coup succeeded in Iraq and expressed a pro-Nasserist sympathy. The two movements were independent but were subject to the same kind of idealism expressed in their adulation of Nasser. Insofar as Nasser represented the Arab revolution, they were Nasserist, but this naive identity was not to last. The next few years were to produce a series of military coups for and against Nasser.

The Iraqi revolution remained 'Nasserist' for only a few weeks, but Syria went through its union with Egypt before it lost enthusiasm for Nasser.

The 1961 military coup in Syria against the Nasserists brought Syria back into agreement with the, by then, anti-Nasserist government in Iraq. A step towards rapprochement with Egypt followed the successful March 1962 Syrian coup, but a follow-through coup for reunion with Egypt a few days later was defeated.

The Syrian and Iraqi leaders were continuing their revolutions but were determined to keep the Nasserists, and Egypt,

16 Haddad, op. cit., p. 185.

at a distance. The pattern became familiar. Military coups attempted by Nasserists were resisted and the military coups that were successful moved the political systems towards more nationalist regimes.

In January 1963 another group of Nasserists tried and again failed in Syria to move the regime further towards Egypt. On 8 February 1963 Ba'athist officers in Iraq successfully seized power and made friendly overtures to Egypt and they were followed on 8 March in Syria by a successful coup identically motivated and similar in composition. Again in July 1963 pro-Nasser officers attempted to force Syria firmly into Nasser's camp and again they failed.

In November 1963, extremist Ba'athists in Iraq tried unsuccessfully to force the socialist pace of the Ba'athist party but this only provoked an anti-Ba'athist counter-coup five days later which formed a regime that survived a series of Ba'athist and Nasserist coups over the next five years. The Ba'athist regime in Syria remained the dominant political force in the country though a series of factional coups took place.

In February 1966 a successful radical Ba'athist coup in Syria was followed in March by an unsuccessful Ba'athist coup attempt in Iraq and two years later in 1968 a similar sequence of factional coups among the Ba'athists in Syria was followed this time by a successful Ba'athist coup in Iraq (see Appendix A).

We need now to look at the military interventions in Syria and Iraq in more detail. The Ba'athist experience of these countries was not repeated in other Arab countries. It both identifies their socialist nationalism and separates them from Nasserism. The perennial struggle inside the regimes between the political forces — Ba'athists, Nasserists and Communists — gave these countries an instability unequalled in the Middle East. With the anti-Nasserist monarchies, and the periodically anti-Nasserist Syrian and Iraqi governments, Nasser was restricted in the region politically and frustrated in his drive for Egyptian hegemony of the Arab Revolution. At his death Egypt was recovering from its third military defeat in twenty-four years and was in retreat in its influence among Arabs and the Russians. The frenzied interventions had been a failure.

5.   *Syria*

Syria had its borders fixed arbitrarily by the major powers in 1946 and lost about half its traditional land space. As if to compensate for this domestic contraction, it has exhibited through its leaders an obsessive interest in external affairs, particularly among its neighbours and allies. It has participated in wider union with Egypt in the ill-fated United Arab Republic, and has flirted from time to time with the idea of union with Iraq. Syrian opposition to Israel has been consistently militant and unrelenting. But external relations are a two-way process and Syria has been subjected to constant penetration by not entirely disinterested foreign powers, notably the Egyptians and the Russians.

The Syrian regime before the military coups was different from that of Egypt and Iraq, which had monarchies identified in the minds of the officers as corrupt, alien and incompetent. But Syria's independence from the French left it with a fully operational constitutional republic. The officers did not head a popular revolt against the representatives of the discredited past, they simply organised a change of government.[17] They did not announce a programme of action, only a number of slogans.

The Syrian army in the Palestine war of 1948 performed comparatively well and actually made territorial gains. These were not enough to overcome the general dismay at the debacle. Whatever the conduct of the army in specific places, overall the Arabs lost and lost badly, and defeatism was universal in all Arab countries. Defeats produce scapegoats and in most cases the ruling regime, justly and unjustly, is cast for this role. The army was as demoralised as the population, but the situation changed when the government called upon the army to restore order in a series of violent demonstrations; the army found itself in a positive role again which, with little imagination, provided them with a means for expiating their sense of guilt and at the same time gave them the opportunity for enhancing their role. The defeat of

17 This is not to say there was no discontent in the country at the time. See Be'eri, op. cit., p. 55; G.H. Torrey, *Syrian Politics and the Military, 1945-1958*, Athens, Ohio, 1964.

1948 did not *cause* the army to assert itself. It was the inability of the civilian government to cope that provided the army with its 'mission' of national salvation.[18]

The government made the incredible blunder of using the army to disperse anti-government demonstrations (November-December 1948) and followed this with an announcement of intended budgetary cuts in the military appropriations (March 1949). The necessity for the former made impractical the introduction of the latter.

The army's reaction by coup on 30 March 1949 ended the constitutional republic and began the military republic.

In two turbulent decades, the Syrian army had emerged from the role of a military force, to become the political guardian of the country. The continuous civilian interference in army politics, and the politicalisation and radicalisation of the army, increased the influence of military politicians. The army no longer acts as an arbitrator of nationalist and progressive forces. It has been persuaded of its unique and historical destiny and special political role as the 'saviour' of society from the 'corrupt' politicians. It has assumed the 'role of hero', and considers itself the key and the *only* hope for honest politics, stability, order and progress. These expectations and aspirations, now claimed exclusively by the army, have been supported in the last two decades by the civilian politicians, by the progressive forces, by the intellectuals and the academics. Because most of these groups have discredited themselves by one means or another, the Syrian army has remained the only political organisation above the battle.[19]

In 21 military coups since 1949 the Syrian army has become the political system within which the political groups in the country have fought out their differences.[20]

Syria's exposed position brought international alignments which added new conflicts to the already overburdened

18 Haddad, op. cit., p. 197, makes the valid point that the defeatist situation in the Arab world was not a direct cause of the coup; it was the government's incompetent handling of the situation that brought the army into politics. This is not to say the army's performance was any better; see Be'eri, op. cit., p. 56.

19 A. Perlmutter, 'From obscurity to rule: the Syrian army and the Ba'ath party', *Western Political Quarterly*, 22, December 1969, p. 845.

20 P. Seale, *The Struggle for Syria: a study in Post-War Arab Politics, 1945-1958*, London, 1965.

political system. Turkey and Iraq joined the Baghdad Pact; Israel was supported by America and Lebanon adopted a generally pro-Western stance. Syria's weapons supplies had come mainly from the British and the Americans before 1955 and this was a narrow and precarious base for security. The American drive to 'sign up' allies against Russia pushed Syria into a position where its moderate opinion had no resistance to demands for a closer alignment with Egypt, and through Egypt, with the Soviet Union. The political system within Syria rewarded with office those who advocated the preservation of Syrian security by friendship with the enemies of Syria's hostile neighbours.

The Table shows the extent to which the Russians responded to Syria's defence requests.

Table 1    Soviet major arms exports to Syria, 1955-58

| Item | Quantity |
| --- | --- |
| Fighters | 93 |
| Trainers | 10 |
| Transports | 8 |
| Helicopters | 7 |
| Tanks | 400 |
| Armoured cars | 100 |

Source: SIPRI, op. cit., p. 850.

Political opposition to pro-Russian 'neutrality' was eliminated between 1955 and 1957. A series of political trials were undertaken of opposition political figures, accused variously of pro-American or pro-Iraqi activities. The interests of the Syrian Ba'athist and the Communists coincided up to a point; both movements gained by the country's drift leftwards.

The union with Egypt added another political force, that of the Nasserists, who went for total integration of Syria into Egypt and the subordination of Syrian nationalism to Egyptian interests. This struck at the Ba'athist party, for Nasser did not tolerate political parties in the United Arab Republic, but it also created a nationalist trend in the country that was directed against Nasser. Poor harvests and Nasserite Egyptian socialism combined with Ba'athist socialist nationalism undermined the union. The military were humiliated by partisan retirements, transfers and postings of Syrian officers to make room for Egyptian officers; the middle class were expropriated and politicised; the masses were suffering deprivations.

The coup of 28 September 1961 ended the union and returned Syrian politics to its domestic tensions. It did not end Russian influence but gave Syria a new form of nationalism. The idealism of experimenting with pan-Arabism was replaced with a maturer determination to maintain an independent Syria.[21]

### 6.    Iraq

Hurewitz describes Iraq's and Syria's condition as 'military roulette'.[22] Before 1958, Iraq could with justice be described as 'cabinet roulette'. From 1921 to 1958 (the year of the coup) Iraq had 59 cabinets, 45 of them since 1932, and had only two chambers which completed the election term of four years.[23] There were seven military coups between 1936 and 1941, but they mainly re-shuffled the ruling coalition. No single faction had power enough to enforce itself over the others for anything but a short period. They differed on domestic policy and on foreign policy, where Iraq was embroiled in the growing tensions between Britain and Germany. The 1941 coup in fact declared for the Axis interests and provoked a British intervention, and this had the side-effect of removing the military from politics until 1958.[24]

The Iraqi military returned to political intervention in the anti-Western struggles of the 1950s. In 1948 and 1952 the military were called out to prop up the civilian Government.

21 M. Palmer, 'The United Arab Republic: An assessment of its failure', *Middle East Journal*, Winter, 1966.

22 Hurewitz, op. cit., p. 145.

23 M. Khadduri, *Independent Iraq, 1932-58: A Study in Iraqi Politics*, London, 1960; S.M. Longrigg, *Iraq, 1900-1950*, London, 1953.

24 M. Khadduri, 'General Nuri's flirtation with the Axis Powers', *Middle East Journal*, 16, 3, 1962; L. Hirscowicz, *The Third Reich and the Arab East*, London, 1966; for British military interests in the Middle East and Iraq, see Hurewitz, op. cit., p. 58.

There were serious disturbances during anti-British political campaigns arising from agitation against the British-Iraqi treaty and the encirclement policy being pursued by America against Russia. The 1948 demonstrations prompted a change in cabinet policies (as well as personnel), and the 1952 disorders required martial law to quell them. The army loyally handed over power to the newly elected Iraqi government in January 1953; it did not follow the Egyptian example and take over completely.[25]

The monarchical-civilian governments of 1952 to 1958 attempted modernisation and reforms in the context of the necessity for political balance between conflicting ideologies whose disputes were fed by the example and counter-example of the Nasserist revolution under way in Egypt.[26] Iraq was competitive with Egypt in many fields but especially in the field of leadership of the Arab world. The Egyptians regarded the Iraqi monarchy as a symbol of reaction in the Arab world, proven beyond doubt by its close Western ties which gave 'imperialism' a foothold in the Middle East for anti-Arab policies. If Iraq succeeded in economic and social reform it would become a counter-weight to Egyptian claims to Arab leadership. The courting of Syria by both Iraq and Egypt was connected with this competitive relationship between the two powers.

The relative military balance between the three countries is shown in Table 2. In population, Egypt was unchallenged even by a combination of Syria and Iraq. The military forces that were available to the countries showed that an alliance between Iraq and Syria in 1959 could have matched Egypt in military strength.

Iraq hosted the initial meeting of the Baghdad Pact in 1955 and signed alongside Turkey, Iran, Pakistan and Britain. The political alignment was complemented by a dependence upon Western suppliers for military equipment. Iraq's dependence on the West for arms supplies (see Table 3), its

25 G. Grassmuch, 'The electoral process in Iraq, 1952-1958', *Middle East Journal*, 14, 4, 1960.
26 See A.J. Meyer, *Middle-Eastern Capitalism*, Cambridge, 1959; Lord Birdwood, *Nuri as Said: A Study in Arab Leadership*, London, 1959; Haddad, op. cit., p. 82.

Table 2    Military balance, Syria, Iraq and Egypt, 1949-59

| Country | 1949 | 1954-55 | 1959 |
|---|---|---|---|
| *Military forces* (thousands) | | | |
| Syria | 25 | 25 | 60 |
| Iraq | 45 | 40 | 50 |
| Egypt | 70 | 80 | 80 |
| | | | |
| *Population* (millions) | | | |
| Syria | | 3.8 | 4.2 |
| Iraq | | 5.8 | 6.0 |
| Egypt | | 22.7 | 25.0 |
| | | | |
| *Defence* (% of GNP) | | | |
| Syria | | 4.0 | 10.8 |
| Iraq | | 6.9 | 8.8 |
| Egypt | | 4.0 | 7.0 |

Sources: M. Halpern, 'Middle-Eastern armies and the new middle class', in Johnson (ed.), op. cit., p. 292; Hurewitz, op. cit., pp. 137, 159, 160.

isolation from the Arab world (it was looking northwards rather than southwards), its monarchist government and above all its opposition to Nasser exposed it to internal and external political pressures which increased in the wave of sympathy for Egypt following the 1956 invasion of the Suez. The Iraqi government sent troops to Jordan to aid it in case of an attack by Israel, but this did not make up for the solidarity felt towards Egypt nor counter the prestige credited to Nasser after the invasion was called off. Egypt's subsequent alliance with Syria brought Nasserist pressure to the Iraqi border.

The Iraqi army was undergoing a subtle transformation in the post-war years. Men of lower-middle-class origin, and often sympathetic to Nasserism and nationalism, were gradually working their way up the promotion ladders. Their predecessors were graduating into the higher ranks and a two-tier army was forming; traditionalist, conservative and identified with the ruling oligarchy at the top and radical, young and critical below. The lower officer ranks also had the advantage of contact with the troops.

Table 3    Major weapon supplies to Iraq 1950-58

| Weapon | Quantity | Supplier |
|---|---|---|
| D.H. Vampire | 18 | UK |
| Beaufighter | 10 | UK |
| F-86 Sabre | 5 | USA |
| Hunting Provost | 6 | UK |
| Hawker Hunter | 15 | UK |
| Churchill Tank | 25 | UK |
| Centurion Tank | 90 | UK |
| M-24 Tank | 40 | USA |
| Ferret APC | 20 | UK |

Source:  SIPRI, op. cit. p. 824-43.

Nasserist propaganda was directed at the younger elements and urged them to emulate the Egyptians by overthrowing the monarchy and ending Iraq's dependence on the West and the imperialist powers that had invaded Suez. The Iraqi monarchy, allied with Israel's friends, conservative and anti-Nasserist, became identified in army circles as a major obstacle to Arab resurgence. The tradition of military intervention had been dormant for seventeen years but was therefore already established. Moreover, the army had some experience of mobilisation in the 1948 and 1956 Israeli wars and therefore was able to consider the mechanics of taking over political power.

It was the Lebanon crisis in 1958 which created the mechanical conditions for the Iraq coup. Large numbers of troops were mobilised by the government and given orders to move across Iraq. This gave a useful cover for the Free Officers' coup. Led by Brigadier-General Abdul Karim Kassem, Colonel Abdul Salaem Aref and Colonel Wasfi Taher, they executed a neat manoeuvre while passing Baghdad, entered the city and took it over.

The level of violence and the ferocity reached in the aftermath set a standard for Iraqi military coups and reprisals that was followed in later years. The entire Royal family, and their Prime Minister, General Nuri, were executed, eliminating at a stroke potential sources of loyalty for dissident forces.[27]

27 F.C.R. Bagley, 'Iraq's revolution', *International Journal*, 14, 1959; Caractacus (F.J. Snell), *Revolution in Iraq*, London, 1959.

In further moves, following the Egyptian experience, senior officers above the rank of colonel and senior civil servants of the monarchical regime were retired.

The coup leaders were mainly in their thirties (except for Kassem who was over forty) and in the main were not ideologically motivated. The forces that supported the coup were disparate and susceptible to manipulation, of which Kassem was to take advantage in his moves to supreme power.[28] The ambitious were played off against each other and the dangerous political pressures were diverted into a generality about Iraq's place in an undefined and non-existent Arab nation. In this 'new Iraq' there was also a place for the rebellious Kurds.

Opposition to Kassem was kept off balance, but enemies accumulate through time and disappointment. Kassem was pushed into action against the pro-Egyptian Ba'athist party (riding high in neighbouring Syria), the various nationalist groups, and the pro-Soviet Communist party. These groups epitomised the problem for Kassem who had ambitions of rivalling Nasser.

Traditional Iraqi-Egyptian rivalry had formally been presented as the struggle between republicanism and monarchy, or Arab nationalism and imperialist domination, but was in fact a national struggle between the two competing powers. The ascendancy of Kassem allowed for a new form of this traditional competition within a broad area of radical Arab politics. For Kassem, Nasser or his local representatives posed a threat to his build-up as an Arab leader. At the same time, Kassem's moves against Nasserism presented the sharp edge of the sword at the new regime's throat: the single most unifying feature of the anti-monarchist forces in Iraq was the pro-Nasser sympathies of the army — to offend this base was risky.

Kassem believed that the only way to compete with

28  B. Shwadran, *The Power Struggle in Iraq*, New York, 1960; A. Ray, 'Iraq after the coup', *Commentary*, September 1958; J. Troutbeck, 'The revolution in Iraq', *Current History*, February 1959; G. de Gauvy, *Three Kings in Baghdad*, London, 1961; A. Tulley, *CIA: The Inside Story*, New York, 1962; Haddad, op. cit., pp. 92-4; U. Dann, *Iraq Under Quassem: A Political History, 1958-1963*, New York, 1969.

Egyptian nationalism, and Nasser, was to indulge in an even more extreme form of Iraqi nationalism. The early honeymoon with Nasser after the coup quickly passed away to outright hostility. But Iraqi nationalism was much too narrow a power base upon which to build a revolutionary structure, especially in view of the Kurdish problem which would be reactivated by the normal expression of Iraqi nationalism,[29] and because of the likely reaction of the Egyptians, whose influence went far beyond their own borders. Just as nationalism was not strong enough to insulate Kassem from Kurdish and Nasserite hostility it was also not likely to protect him from the ideological parties, such as the Ba'athists and the Communists.

Iraqi nationalism led to a switch from Western to Soviet allies; to abandon Iraqi reliance on the friends of Israel meant reliance on Russia. This reliance is manifest in Table 4, which details the Soviet arms shipments to Iraq between 1958 and 1962. The route to the Soviet alignment came through the early declaration for Nasser; the first 19 MiG-15 fighters were flown in from Egypt in the early months of the coup.

The Russians were eager to take on the role of military supplier to Iraq. For them it was a great victory against the American encirclement. When Nasser fell out with Kassem the Russians remained aloof from the dispute, even though it was Nasser who introduced the Russians to the Iraqi leaders. At the time of the coup Nasser was in Yugoslavia, and when the news broke he flew direct to Moscow to make as much milage as he could out of the fall of the pro-Western government.[30] It raised Nasser's prestige with the Russians, and they could see that their policy of backing him was justified as, no doubt, Nasser was at great pains to tell them.

Kassem had his own ideas about breaking Nasser's monopoly of attention from the Russians and he accordingly brought Iraq out of the Baghdad Pact in March 1959. To emphasise their regard for their break with the West, the Russians made a $500 million development loan in the same

29 For accounts of the Kurdish rebellions, see: D. Adamson, *The Kurdish War*, New York, 1964; C.J. Edmunds, 'The Kurds and the revolution in Iraq', *Middle East Journal*, 13, 1959.

30 Haddad, op. cit., p. 90.

month. They appreciated Iraq's strategic importance to their strategy against American encirclement.[31]

*Table 4   Soviet major weapons exports to Iraq, 1958-62*

| Weapon | Quantity |
|---|---|
| MiG-15/17 | 71 |
| Ily-14/28 | 21 |
| Yak-11 | 15 |
| Tu-16 | 7 |
| P-6 patrol boat | 12 |
| T-54 tank | 100 |
| T-34 tank | 45 |
| JS-111 tank | 25 |
| BTR-152 APC | 200 (1960-64) |

Source: SIPRI, op. cit., pp. 842-3.

Kassem also moved against Colonel Aref, his colleague in the leadership of the coup. In a series of manoeuvres he finally got Aref on trial for treason and sentenced to death for implication in Ba'athist and Nasserist intrigues. The dispute with Aref was more than just a personality conflict, it entailed an interpretation of Iraq's relations with Egypt and Egypt's interest in Iraq. The various interpretations of Egyptian interests included the future of Iraqi oil and, however attractive Nasser's early role as a symbol of Arabic modernism and resurgence, the prospect of closer ties with Egypt looked a lot less attractive to the newly arrived officers when it implied a diminution of their newly acquired roles through submission to Nasser.

In turning against the Nasserists Kassem was forced into a reliance on the popular forces, largely under Communist influence. These forces had an armed hard-core which had acquired weapons in the confusion of the 1958 coup. However, the factional war conducted by Kassem cut his support. An attempted coup in March 1959 against Kassem was put down brutally and this drove Kassem further into the Russian camp.[32] He relied upon the Russians for weapons and upon the Iraqi communists for support.

31 SIPRI, op. cit., p. 556.
32 Haddad, op. cit., pp. 113-15.

The executions that followed the 1959 coup were supplemented by unofficial executions carried out by local Communists. These excesses drove the middle class into support of the socialist Ba'athist party. This alliance was tenuous, but the Communist excesses were extreme enough for the middle class to overcome their ideological hostility to the Ba'athist version of socialism. The Ba'athists were recognised as an indigenous force in contrast to the 'foreign' Communists. To counter this situation Kassem reduced his association with the Communists and even re-opened relations with the West (Britain supplied two vampire jets) only to have these interrupted by his military threat to Kuwait in 1961.

The economic situation deteriorated and the country was polarised. Kassem's rule was eventually toppled in a coup on 8 February 1963. His dream of emulating and surpassing Nasser collapsed. He was never able to get a dependent political force behind his rule and had to rely on others. Where Nasser smashed all political parties which he did not control, Kassem had to leave the most seditious, the Communists, operating and thereby he became associated with their actions. Where Nasser had solid support in the army, Kassem weakened his base by continuous purges, trials, and witch-hunts. Neither did Nasser have to deal with the problem of a non-Egyptian Hero in his revolution, but Kassem faced Nasser abroad and Nasserists at home. Finally his violence against his enemies drove his enemies to unite against him.

The inability of the various political factions in Iraq to gain permanent ascendency, or of the political structure to accommodate orderly transfers of power, between them meant that each change of power was accompanied by physical extermination of the losers.[33] The cost to Iraq in the destruction of the ruling elite every few years must have been enormous, especially in a country not abundant in administrative and executive talent.

33 Haddad, op. cit., p. 121, reports that in just over four years 2,000 officers and thousands of civil servants retired. A further 1,000 (some say 5,000) people were killed and another 4,000 arrested in the Ba'athist 1963 coup. See C. Hollingworth, 'The Ba'athist revolution in Iraq', *The World Today*, 19, 5, May 1963.

It was not so much a game of roulette, which is a game of chance, as an endemic conflict arising from the weaknesses of the ruling elites, worsened each time by each coup, and from the ever changing balance of forces within Iraq and within its neighbour, Syria, both subject to the pervasive influence of Nasser's Egypt.

Nasser's role in the military interventions diminished as the Arab countries developed their own political styles. With the ascendancy of Ghaddafy in Libya the same pattern of interventions in other countries as part of the bid for Arab leadership has already been established. Libyan resources and political assistance have been deployed both for allies and against enemies. The Libyan support for the anti-monarchist coups attempted in Jordan and Morocco is not unexpected from a republican regime, but its assistance to conspiracies in republican Sudan against the 'modern' Sudanese leaderships is in the classic Nasserist mould.

# 8 The Politics of Non - intervention

## 1. Introduction

We now need to take up cases where the military has been de-politicised and made either to return to the barracks (Mexico) or to stay there (Israel). Military intervention is not inevitable either in every country or in particular countries at all times.

In Israel the military has not intervened since the state was founded. In Mexico the state began in a perennial gale of interventions, but since 1940 the military have kept out of contact with the political system in other than a subordinate role. In Turkey, our third case, the military was systematically reduced in influence up to 1946, but political conditions were created by the Cold War and domestic politics which brought the tanks into the streets again. These cases will provide some pointers to the conditions that insulate a developing country from military intervention.

## 2. Mexico

The Mexican revolutionary generals were a dominant force in the country's political system after the revolutionary years (1910-20) up to 1940 and were then virtually eliminated from Mexican politics.

Mexico from 1910 to the end of the revolution in 1922 was a bloody and violent country.[1] Power rested on armed might and demonstrable cruelty. The presidents of Mexico were ex-revolutionary generals turned politicians. The last of the traditionalist revolutionary generals was Calles, whose

1 For an account of the Revolutionary years, see R. Aitken, *Revolution! Mexico, 1910-1920*, London, 1969.

term of office ended in 1936. He chose as his successor, and supported in his drive for the nomination, his protégé since the early days of the revolution, General Cardenas, who had joined the Calles army in 1913 and had risen with Calles to become his War Minister in 1933. However, he was to prove more independent than a protégé, as he broke the power, influence and proclivity for interference of the revolutionary generals and their successors.[2]

Within twelve months he had virtually eliminated Calles and his supporters from the political structure through pre-emptive purges of the state apparatus. Calles made some attempts at a come-back to reverse what Cardenas was doing, but he did not have enough support or organisation. The President had control of the patronage resources of the state, which Calles had relinquished when he ceased to be President, and potential supporters of Calles had to consider what risks they took in supporting him and thereby alienating the new President. The old revolutionary generals were comfortable with their personal positions, and the consequences of a lost rebellion set against the kind of issues that were in dispute did not make for an attractive gamble. Calles, having failed to get support, then retired from politics.

Cardenas established his ascendancy and independence and introduced a programme of reforms which reduced the potential opposition's leverage against him. These eroded the army's base of power. Promotion in the army was largely a matter of a man's record in the revolutionary wars and his loyalty to his commanding officer. This served to perpetuate the unifying mythology of the revolution to the detriment of professionalism.[3] The army officers formed a privileged political elite in the country with power bases in the local areas over which they held undisputed sway. Cardenas took

2 E. Lieuwen, *Mexican Militarism: The Political Rise and Fall of the Revolutionary Army 1910-1940*, New Mexico, 1968, and *Arms and Politics in Latin America*, New York, 1960.

3 A similar socialisation process of the new bureaucracy takes place in the Soviet Union. To advance in the Soviet State, recruits must articulate the ideology of Leninism, even though none of the leadership is actually Leninist. The mythology of the Mexican Revolution — the sacrifices of the dead, etc. — bore little resemblance to the way of life of the Generals in the 1930s.

the first step to alter this situation by introducing proficiency tests for officers below the rank of major. Most of the men in this group in 1936 were men from the junior ranks during the revolution or were post-revolution recruits. The proficiency tests were not required for senior ranks in the army (thus allaying their fears) and therefore two promotion standards were introduced which corresponded to the division in background in the officer corps that Cardenas wanted to exploit. The senior officers had little cause to oppose merit tests for their juniors, and junior officers hardly had grounds to oppose them either: it is not easy to articulate a case for a promotion system based on privileges and informal relationships.

Recruitment of suitable officers from the ranks was also introduced, to reward ability and change the class character of the junior officer corps as well, and some modest efforts were made towards providing schools for the children of enlisted men. The President was shifting the base of support for his office within the military from the priviliged clique group of the Senior leadership to the more junior, and professionally ambitious ranks, and the enlisted men.

Promotion by merit became explicit in 1936 as the sole criterion for promotion. The implications held more significance for the future than for the present. Men who rose through the ranks on one system (merit) were not likely to be happy with a change of rules to informal and unspecified criteria when they approached their senior ranks. It was unlikely that any system other than merit could be made to apply when sufficient numbers of them had reached the senior ranks. The sitting colonels and generals were secure for their service life, and time would reduce their number. To speed up the process of reducing their number, Cardenas passed laws reducing the officer career-span from 35 to 25 years. This would have retired all officers serving before 1911, and by 1940, the end of his term of office, it would retire all officers serving before 1915. In the event the law was not applied until 1945 when it had an even greater impact, retiring officers serving since before 1920. This eliminated from service the majority of the officers remaining from the revolutionary years.

Further efforts were made to align his presidency with the junior ranks by setting up military hospitals. By courting these ranks and retiring the senior ranks, Cardenas aimed to break the army as a force under the undisputed control of the local army generals, who had much in common in their relative power positions with the barons in a feudal system.

Professional armies have both active and administrative functions. Cardenas next sought to get as many of the older officers out of active command into adminstrative tasks as quickly as possible. This had two objectives. First, it would create promotion opportunities for junior ranks, firming up their association with the presidency, and secondly, it would separate local figures from their local power base and turn them into uniformed civil servants.

Active service limits were set at the age of 48 for junior officers, 58 for majors and 65 for divisional commanders. Men who had failed to reach higher rank by these ages, and under a merit system of promotion this would imply their unsuitability for active command, would be transferred to administrative functions or retired, making way for more suitable candidates from the lower rank. The most proficient professional soldiers would rise through the ranks and remain in active command (in theory).

In 1937 Cardenas made the final preparations to reduce the army's political position. He declared part-time non-military interests incompatible with army service. This made local army officers choose between their (sometimes considerable) business interests and continued active service. These officers had made good their command positions in local areas by manipulation of their position among local business interests. This new rule mainly affected the senior ranks. Cardenas in addition raised the pay of enlisted men and officers and also introduced an insurance scheme for the lower ranks. A troop ceiling of 50,000 was set.[4] Responsibility for local law and order (a potentially profitable aspect of power that some area commanders had manipulated to their advantage) was handed over to a part-time militia,

4 In 1970 the Mexican army had 54,000 troops and it had hardly changed in the post-war period.

consisting, in the main, of men from the peasant and worker classes.

The setting up of another centre of violence is a difficult and dangerous step for a government in the Third World. It has brought down a few governments in the post-war years; for example, in Algeria a similar move initiated by Ben Bella was one of the causes of the army take-over.[5] Similarly, in Ghana, Nkrumah's prestigious Presidential Guards and his Worker Brigades did a great deal to drive the army into the 1966 coup.[6]

Cardenas had already made several moves against the interests of the army commanders and this last one was a crucial test for his programme. The fact that these militants were poorly armed, badly trained, and relatively useless for a co-ordinated action, did not alter the fact that another centre of violence was being set up. In the hands of a determined political leadership, such as the Communists, who were very strongly represented in the urban centres, they posed a threat to the army should they need to intervene in the affairs of state. Carrying out a military coup against a few unguarded public buildings is an entirely different type of operation from one that risks a civil war where an armed militia exists. The army had to strike immediately if it was to strike at all. They did not and Cardenas passed on to the next stage of his confrontation with the military.

The Cardenas Presidency was radical in a number of other ways, and in broad terms Cardenas had attempted to take the revolution to the lower classes, who up to then had been neglected. The gainers from the revolution were mainly the middle classes and state bureaucrats. Land reform and higher wages through trade union militancy were directly encouraged. The land reform provoked bitter opposition and local disputes were inevitable between the vested interests and the peasants. Local law and order was now the prerogative of the part-time militia and not the army and this should have helped the peasants.

5 D. and M. Ottaway, *Algeria: The Politics of a Socialist Revolution*, California, 1970; Hurewitz, op. cit., pp. 187-99.

6 Pinkney, op. cit.; P. Hodge, 'Ghana workers brigade', *British Journal of Sociology*, 15, 2, June 1964.

The reforms were modest, but it was more significant that they took place at all, even on a small scale. The enlisted men in the army, being peasant in origin, and benefiting from the Cardenas army reforms, were an unreliable force for putting down peasant agitation. To reverse the land reform meant using unreliable troops against armed peasants. In the urban centres the same situation prevailed. The trade unions were agitating and striking for higher wages and through the militia the armed workers were responsible for order. Thus employers could not rely on terror or the use of troops to disperse their disaffected workers – they had to parley and get a compromise. The result was rising wages.

The Mexican political structure was based on the National Revolutionary Party (PNR) founded by Calles in 1928.[7] This was meant as a popular political organisation for the non-military masses to participate in, something like the Liberation Front in Nasser's Egypt. The local army commanders dominated the local machines of the PNR, and therefore Cardenas, in reducing the power of the local army command, simultaneously created the possibility of transforming the PNR into a genuine mass political force to become a counter-weight to the army. This meant re-organising the PNR.

In 1938 the PNR was re-organised into four separate sectors to represent the major interests in the country: Labour, Peasant, Popular and Army. Under this structure the army was forced to organise as a separate section in the PNR rather than dominate it entirely, or had to join one of the sections but relinquish the military base. Each sector was awarded 40 seats at the party congress, which chose the Presidential nominee for the election. The nominee was certain to become the next President given the overwhelming electoral support for the PNR. Moreover, as the incumbent President was able to choose the 40 army delegates to the conference, he was also able to ensure that they were sympathetic to his views on the role of the army in the state. This system was undoubtedly loaded against the traditional conception of what constituted army-civilian relations.

The problem for the army was that, being unable to bring

7 F. Brandenburg, *The Making of Modern Mexico*, New York, 1964.

Cardenas down on any of the single issues that had been introduced since 1934, they were now even less able to act cohesively against him, even though the sum of these issues was clearly detrimental to their established interests. There was a brief attempt at revolt by one army commander, but this was crushed.[8]

The balance of forces in the new party was against the army from the beginning. They had only 55,000 votes against 1.25 million for Labour, 2.5 million for the peasants and 55,000 for the popular sector (this section was for those not coming under any of the other categories).[9] Political power in the new party passed to the civilian groups. Moreover, whereas the peasant and labour sectors were organised on a local basis, the army was organised on a national basis, thus removing them from interference in local politics.

The *caudillo* figure in Latin America has always been based traditionally on a locality and his roots are with the local people who give him their loyalty.[10] Without this support (however it is gained — by genuine affection or terror), the *caudillo* is isolated and ineffective. The national basis for army political action undermined potential *caudillo* figures and removed local civilian political activity from overt intimidation by army commanders.

The army did not intervene as a military force but as a political force. It met Cardenas on his own ground, in a Presidential election, not so much by choice as by circumstance, and this expressed the weakness of the military more than its strength. The problem for the generals was that they could not agree on a single candidate and therefore individual generals set up their own movements, or joined established ones, to sponsor their own candidacy. This further exposed their weaknesses. A credible military intervention requires a firmly controlled and disciplined force and is not proceded

8 General Saturnino Cedillos led a rebellion in the spring of 1938 and was killed in action in early 1939; details in Lieuwen, *Mexican Militarism*.

9 ibid., p. 126.

10 W.S. Stokes, 'Violence as a power factor in Latin American Politics', *Western Political Quarterly*, September 1952, reprinted in R.D. Tomasek (ed.), *Latin American Politics*, New York, 1970.

by a sort of coup-makers' primary election. The divisive nature of the military opposition allowed the alternative civilian contestants to gain in confidence.

The army's political parties had colourful names which in a way tell their own story: The Association of Revolutionary Patriots, The Constitutional Democratic Front, The Anti-Communist Revolutionary Party, The National Union of Veterans of the Mexican Revolution, the National Vanguard and The Revolutionary Committee for National Reconstruction.

The 1940 general election ended the army's political challenge within the constitution, and it had either to submit from then on or stage a coup. Its candidate, General Juan Almazón, who had emerged in the pre-election period as the most popular of the army candidates, was the most senior army commander, and he went to the polls for the Revolutionary Party of National Unification. He had the open support of 34 senior officers who took leave to campaign for him.

The PNR was renamed the Party of the Mexican Revolution (PMR) and adopted General Camacho as its candidate. He was assured of the support of the President, the labour, peasant and popular sectors of the old PNR, as well as considerable support from within the army. Cardenas enfranchised serving soldiers in a move to split the lower ranks from the upper ranks. The choice of General Camacho was significant. He was the former Defence Minister in the Cardenas cabinet and agreed with him on the issues of civilian-army relations. He was not a revolutionary general but had served during the revolution as a junior officer and gained his promotion later. The fact that two generals were candidates in an election that was to decide whether the military were to have a role in politics is one of the ironies of the contest.

The election, which was accompanied by several murders and other bloody incidents, gave Camacho an overwhelming victory:

| | |
|---|---|
| General Camacho (pro-Cardenas) | 2.2 million |
| General Almazón (the army) | 128,000 [11] |

11 Lieuwen, *Mexican Militarism*, p. 126.

The army was now faced with a desperate decision: it was the last moment for a military coup, but it was also an unfavourable moment as the army clearly lacked a popular mandate.

Almazón and his friends accused the President of electoral fraud and claimed they had been robbed of victory. This position can only be backed by a military intervention or it simply collapses. The army waited for the signal from Almazón, but it never came. He retired quietly, and Cardenas magnanimously called upon the army officers to return to their normal duties at the end of their leave. General Camacho was inaugurated on 1 December 1940 and the country turned to other problems. The army ceased to be a sector in the ruling party (re-named again in 1945 the Institutional Revolutionary Party — PRI). The 1936 law on retirement was implemented in 1945 and 550 officers were retired in the first instance.

Table 1 brings out the extent of the decline of the army in Mexico's political system. It has been receiving a declining share of the state budget since the high point of the revolutionary wars. The levels of over 60 per cent exceed even the Arab-Israeli budgets. There was a continuing decline through the 1920s and 30s, but under Cardenas there was only a slight drop of from 24 per cent to 21 per cent, brought about by his cuts in the budget and his increases in the pay and allowances for the lower ranks and enlisted men. From 1945 the decline was dramatic, to 7 per cent by 1956. In 1970 the military budget was hovering around 10 per cent.

Mexican policy on defence has been not to try to meet the improbable: 'Military hardware is purchased neither for display nor for defence against a quite improbable external threat, but only for the purpose of preserving internal order'.[12] This view is confirmed by examining purchases of military equipment by the Mexicans since 1945. There are no advanced jet fighters and bombers and the purchases tend to be confined to transport, trainers, light patrol and helicopters. All of these types of aircraft have a counterinsurgency role.[13] Naval purchases are of light types of craft

12 ibid., p. 147.

13 SIPRI, op. cit., p. 871; International Institute of Strategic Studies (IISS), *The Military Balance, 1970-1971*, London, 1971.

Table 1 *Proportion of the state budgets allocated to military expenditure, Mexico, 1914-70*

| Year | % Total budget | Year | % Total budget |
|------|------|------|------|
| 1914 | 31 | 1944 | 14 |
| 1915 | 31 | 1945 | 15 |
| 1917 | 72 | 1946 | 15 |
| 1918 | 64 | 1947 | 13 |
| 1919 | 66 | 1948 | 10 |
| 1920 | 65 | 1949 | 10 |
| 1921 | 61 | 1950 | 10 |
| 1922 | 41 | 1951 | 10 |
| 1923 | 36 | 1952 | 8 |
| 1924 | 36 | 1953 | 9 |
| 1925 | 31 | 1954 | 8 |
| 1926 | 31 | 1955 | 8 |
| 1927 | 25 | 1956 | 7 |
| 1928 | 33 | 1957 | 7 |
| 1929 | 34 | 1958 | 7 |
| 1930 | 32 | 1959 | 7 |
| 1931 | 27 | 1960 | 7 |
| 1932 | 27 | 1961 | 7 |
| 1933 | 25 | 1962 | 7 |
| 1935 | 23 | 1963 | 7 |
| 1936 | 24 | 1964 | 7 |
| 1937 | 24 | 1965 | 7 |
| 1938 | 19 | 1966 | 7 |
| 1939 | 21 | 1967 | 10 |
| 1940 | 21 | 1968 | 9 |
| 1941 | 22 | 1969 | 10 |
| 1942 | 22 | 1970 | 10 |
| 1943 | 21 |  |  |

Sources: official sources quoted in Lieuwen, *Mexican Militarism*, p.153 (1914-40); p.142 (1940-66); and United Nations, *Statistical Yearbook 1970* (1967-70).

suitable for in-shore operations, though four frigates were purchased from the United States in 1964. Most of Mexico's armour consists of Second World War models.[14]

14 Frank, op. cit., p. 113; IISS, op. cit.

## 3.    Turkey

Turkish politics were influenced by the military establishment in the Ottoman Empire, and this tradition was followed in the early years of the Republic.[15] But for almost forty years after the foundation of the Republic the role and influence of the military were reduced, and consciously undermined, in favour of civilian-dominated political processes. As in the case of Mexico, this state of affairs was brought about by a military leader, the most illustrious of the Turkish generals, Mustafa Kemal Ataturk.[16] His views on civil-military relations were expressed many years before he was ever in a position to be tested by them. In 1909 he insisted that the relationship between the army and political activity be demarcated by a total separation of the two functions:

As long as officers remain in the Party we shall never build a strong Party nor a strong Army. In the 3rd Army most of the officers were also members of the Party and the 3rd Army cannot be called first class. Furthermore, the Party receiving its strength from the Army will never appeal to the nation. Let us resolve here and now that all officers wishing to remain in the Party must resign from the Army. We must adopt a law forbidding all future officers having political affiliations. [17]

The separation of army and political life in the midst of revolutionary changes has a long tradition going back to the seventeenth-century revolutionary general, Oliver Cromwell. In 1644, when Cromwell was wrestling with the army command and their parliamentary supporters over the conduct of the civil war, he concentrated his attack on the dual status of army commanders and Members of Parliament:

For what do the enemy say? Nay, what do many say that were friends

15  K.H. Karpat, 'The military and politics in Turkey: A socio-cultural analysis of a revolution', *American History Review*, 75, 6, October 1970.

16  For Ataturk's biography see: Lord Kinross, *Ataturk: The Rebirth of a Nation*, London, 1964; B. Lewis, *The Emergence of Modern Turkey*, London, 1961; R.D. Robinson, *The First Turkish Republic: A Case Study in National Development*, Cambridge, Mass., 1963.

17  I. Orga, *Phoenix Ascendant*, London, 1958, p. 38.

at the beginning of the Parliament? Even this, that the Members of both Houses have got great places and commands, and the sword into their hands; and, what by interests in Parliament, what by power in the Army, will perpetually continue themselves in grandeur, and not permit the War speedily to end, lest their own power should determine with it . . . I know not the worth of these commanders, members of both Houses, who are yet in power; but if I may speak my conscience without reflection upon any, I do conceive if the army be not put into another method, and the War more vigorously prosecuted, the People can bear the War no longer, and will enforce you to a dishonourable Peace.[18]

Parliament went on to pass the Self-Denying Ordnance whereby members of Parliament were precluded from being commissioned in the army. The intent was not entirely the same as Ataturk's (apart from the circumstances being different); Cromwell wanted an effective army to win a peace honourable to Parliament, Ataturk wanted both an effective army and an effective Party.

Ataturk came to power with the support of the army and the Party. Twelve of the 17 Ottoman Turkish Commanders joined the Nationalists.[19] But, once assured of power, Ataturk carried out his principles of separation of the military from civilian political life. He insisted on political leaders resigning from the armed forces, and he refrained from wearing his uniform on official occasions. His modernisation programmes did not give the army any inclination or need to intervene and his charisma ensured their loyalty. There were two plots against him, but they were isolated incidents. He alleged in 1924 that there was a number of senior officers in conspiracy against him and he secured their resignations. In 1926 a colonel went to the gallows for his part in another plot.[20]

The influence of the military in terms of numbers in the Assembly declined from one sixth in 1920 to one twenty-fifth in 1958.

18 T. Carlyle (ed.), *Oliver Cromwell's Letters and Speeches*, London, 2nd edition, pp. 128-9.

19 D. Lerner and R.D. Robinson, 'Swords and ploughshares; the Turkish army as a modernising force', *World Politics*, 13, October 1960, p.25.

20 ibid., pp. 20-2.

Table 2    *Proportion of military members in the Turkish assembly*
*1920-1958*

| Year | Proportion |
|------|-----------|
| 1920 | 1/6th |
| 1943 | 1/8th |
| 1946 | 1/9th |
| 1950 | 1/20th |
| 1958 | 1/25th |

Source:    D.A. Rustow, 'The army in the founding of the Turkish republic', *World Politics*, 11, July 1959, p. 550.

Electoral laws adopted after the Second World War disenfranchised the military and the police; they could neither vote nor stand for office nor engage in political activity.[21] This went much further than the Cardenas reforms: Cardenas shrewdly enfranchised the soldiers but depoliticised the generals. But in Turkey, by taking away the soldiers' vote, the government removed any feeling of responsibility by the military for anything that the elected civilian government did. Taking away their rights to stand for office and to engage in political activity was probably a sensible step, but to extend this to voting was a blunder of the highest magnitude. Electors are implicated in the follies of the governments they elect; those who voted for another party have a chance at another election. But if a powerful section of the community, such as the army, has neither the satisfaction of voting for a successful government nor the satisfaction of a protest vote for an alternative government, it is left only with the choice of unconstitutional action if it is politically frustrated. It is totally unrealistic to assume that because it is not permitted political rights it will automatically lose political interests. If the Turkish version of a Self-Denying Ordnance had left the army the right to vote, it might have averted the scenario of the army looking at itself as an untainted alternative to the sins of the politicians.

Turkey's political evolution up to 1946 had taken the form of a unique alliance between two opposed social forces. The ruling elite of the urban centres (leaning towards

21 Article 8, *Electoral Law*, 1946 and Article 9, *Electoral Law*, 1950; quoted in Lerner and Robinson, op. cit., p. 21.

modernisation) was allied with the ruling elite of the rural areas (leaning towards the past). The urban Kemalists were secularist, modernist and nationalist; the village Kemalists were Islamic, reactionary and universalist. Yet Kemal Ataturk held these divisive forces together, on the understanding that the modernisation proceeded without interfering with the traditional power base of the village elites. The poorer masses and the lower middle classes were more or less left out of the alliance and excluded from power.

Modernisation, economic development and structural changes operated on the Turkish social structure and undermined this alliance.[22] New social classes were appearing and growing in strength and their exclusion from the political system was less realistic as time went by. The social bonds of Islam were loosening and this also loosened the village social structure and the extended family system. The small businessman, the lowly state bureaucrat, the technician, the intellectual and the clerk were seeking political expression, but in the circumstances of the dominance of a single political party, the Republicans, they had no outlet. In 1946, President Inonu (Ataturk's successor and former colleague), in recognition of this changing situation, permitted modest reforms that included the formation of new political parties (it was these reforms that also took away the soldiers' vote).

This set off forces outside the established power system and rapidly transformed the balance of power. Political competition opened up new possibilities in the village whereby the reactionary elite could be challenged. The Republican party had been a mere symbol of modernisation around which the social remnants of the Ottoman Empire preserved their established privileges and authoritarian rule. They did not organise resistance to change, because they controlled it locally, and this made modernisation an uneven process in the country.

The 1946 constitution changed the 'understanding', and modernisation became a struggle in the country between the new forces and its previous champions whose power base

22 A.H. Ulman and F. Tachau, 'Turkish politics, the attempt to reconcile rapid modernisation with democracy', *Middle East Journal*, 19, Spring 1965.

rested in effect on the past. The old alliance made its contribution to Turkey's development, but some accommodation with the new social forces was necessary. Voters were courted and encouraged to express themselves; to campaign for votes is to mobilise groups for action, and this reached into parts of Turkey's power structure until then unaffected by the Republican revolution.

The growth of the Democratic party, led by Menderes, announced the entry of the new Turkish middle class and workers into politics. The Democrats came to power in 1952 and this rapid transformation of the political structure brought with it new tensions. The associated policies of land reform and trade unionism, and the inflation for which they were blamed and the participatory political activities of previously ignored groups, all contributed to insecurity in the established elites. This development coincided with a transformation of the recently disenfranchised armed forces.

The scenario that had extinguished the military as a political force in Mexico was repeated in Turkey, but with some significant differences that were to produce an entirely different result.

In 1948, the army was still horse-drawn, equipped with World War I weapons, ill-trained, poorly fed and inadequately clothed. It was no longer the avant-garde of modernisation it had been in Ottoman times. Nor was it now a channel of upward mobility around a frozen elite. Civilians were clearly in a position of unchallenged supremacy, politically and technologically, and it was in the civilian hierarchy that ability was most clearly recognised as a basis for promotion and power. [2 3]

The Cold War created the opportunities that changed the condition of the army.

The emergence of Russia, on Turkey's borders, as a major world power changed Turkey's peripheral pre-war position. It became what the Americans designated a 'forward area'. Turkey's ramshackle army was unsuited for the new role that was written for a country in the front line against Russian expansionism. Turkey lies across the exit for Russia's Black

᷑  23 Lerner and Robinson, op. cit., p. 28.

Sea fleet (and the entrance for America's Mediterranean fleet). It also lies across the land-strike routes from Russia to the Middle East. A weak Turkey was incompatible with any strategic defence of the area and credible policy of containment of Russia.

Table 3   Allocation of the state budget to military expenditure, Turkey, 1926-69

| Year | Percentage |
|------|------------|
| 1926 | 40 |
| 1930s | 28 |
| 1940 | 56 |
| 1946 | 33 |
| 1959 | 25 |
| 1961 | 24 |
| 1962 | 26 |
| 1963 | 22 |
| 1964 | 23 |
| 1965 | 22 |
| 1966 | 21 |
| 1967 | 21 |
| 1968 | 18 |
| 1969 | 17 |

Source:    Lerner and Robinson, op. cit., p. 27, 1926-46;
           United Nations, *Statistical Yearbook*, 1959-69.

The proportion of the state budget allocated to defence has declined (Table 3) throughout the Republic, and this is similar to Mexican experience. The massive inflow of military aid from America raised the proportion of total resources spent on defence, commensurate with its 'forward defence area' status. Table 4 brings together the state military budgets and American military aid for the years of the Cold War and the post-coup regime to put the defence spending in perspective. A NATO definition of military expenditure is used which covers defence expenditure out of the budget plus strategic investments on military highways and communications. The percentage of military aid to total military expenditure has been calculated in the final column. Using the NATO definition of military expenditure, this reduces the aid proportion a little.

Table 4   Military expenditures and military aid, Turkey 1948-62
(in millions of Turkish lira)

| Year | Military budget | Military aid | Total | Aid per cent |
|------|-----------------|--------------|-------|--------------|
| 1948 | 530 | 203 | 733 | 27 |
| 1949 | 556 | 156 | 712 | 21 |
| 1950 | 599 | 131 | 730 | 18 |
| 1951 | 652 | 165 | 817 | 20 |
| 1952 | 725 | 409 | 1134 | 36 |
| 1953 | 827 | 491 | 1318 | 37 |
| 1954 | 936 | 620 | 1556 | 40 |
| 1955 | 1077 | 465 | 1542 | 30 |
| 1956 | 1159 | 482 | 1641 | 29 |
| 1957 | 1266 | 824 | 2090 | 39 |
| 1958 | 1470 | 2264 | 3734 | 61 |
| 1959 | 2153 | 1128 | 3281 | 34 |
| 1960 | 2410 | 786 | 3196 | 25 |
| 1961 | 2718 | 750 | 3468 | 22 |
| 1962 | 2970 | 1419 | 4389 | 32 |

Source: Military budget: NATO, *Facts about Nato*, Paris, 1962, p.105; *Military Assistance Facts*, Washington, 1963, p.30; International Monetary Fund, *Balance of Payments Year Book*, 1954; United States, *Foreign Assistance 1945-62*, Washington, 1963, p.23. Quoted in F.C. Shorter, 'Military expenditure and the allocation of resources', in Shorter (ed.), *Four Studies in the Economic Development of Turkey*, London, 1967.

Military aid from the United States has been substantial; at its lowest it was 18 per cent of the total military budget in 1950, rising to 61 per cent in 1958, and normally it hovered around one fifth to one third. By 1959 $2 billion had been spent on military aid and such an injection could not help but have an important effect on the army.[24]

The army was rehabilitated from top to bottom. At first the aid was confined merely to the delivery of surplus equipment, but early American missions to Turkey, to oversee the results of the deliveries, reported that the equipment was being so abused by the ill-trained army that it

24 Lerner and Robinson, op. cit., p. 36; other sources vary this figure from $1 billion to $3 billion.

was rapidly disintegrating. Within a couple of years nearly half the trucks given to the army were non-operational through lack of proper maintenance.[25]

The American response was to put into effect an intense training programme which by 1951 had passed out 1,000 officers and NCOs. A further 300 pilots were trained on jets by 1958. All the equipment, vehicles, artillery, communications systems, machine guns and small arms for the military were provided by the United States. The airforce received Sabre jets, F-5s and F-104 supersonic aircraft, plus trainers, transport and helicopters.[26] The navy received a loan of 10 submarines and destroyers.[27] In Table 5 the share of Turkey

*Table 5    Share of American military aid to Turkey as a percentage of American military aid to 'forward areas' and to the Third World, 1949-1969*

| Years | Aid to Turkey as percentage to 'forward areas' | Aid to Turkey as percentage to Third World |
|---|---|---|
| 1949-52 | 32 | 32 |
| 1953-57 | 23 | 22 |
| 1958 | 22 | 19 |
| 1959 | 20 | 17 |
| 1960 | 12 | 11 |
| 1961 | 13 | 10 |
| 1962 | 22 | 17 |
| 1963 | 17 | 14 |
| 1964 | 13 | 11 |
| 1965 | 12 | 11 |
| 1966 | 13 | 11 |
| 1967 | 13 | 11 |
| 1968 | 10 | 9 |
| 1969 | 9 | 8 |
| 1949-59 | 23 | 21 |
| 1960-69 | 13 | 11 |

Source: Calculated from tables in SIPRI, *The Arms Trade with the Third World*, pp.146-7.

25 Lerner and Robinson, op. cit., p. 31.
26 H.A. Hovey, *United States Military Assistance: A Study of Policies and Practices*, New York, 1965, pp. 95-7.
27 Frank, op. cit., p. 113.

in American aid to 'forward areas' and to the Third World has been calculated from details in SIPRI Tables.

Before the 1960 military coup the share of Turkey in American aid to the 'forward areas' was averaging 23 per cent, and its share of Third World aid was averaging 21 per cent. After the coup the share dropped to 13 per cent (11 per cent of Third World). The major build-up of the armed forces had already taken place by 1960. The army was transformed from a stagnant force into one of Turkey's most modernised and technologically advanced elements. It regained its lost eminence of the Ottoman period.

The rapid political change expressed in the victory of the Democratic party (which was also vigorously pro-American) and the transformation of the military into a dynamic force altered the outcome of Turkey's political crisis from a civilian-political solution to Turkey's post-war problems to a military-civilian solution. The Cold War military build-up gave the Turkish army a new role in the country's defences. Its status was enhanced at the time when the factional political struggle between the Republicans and the Democrats was shaking the structural foundations of the old alliance of the elite power groups. The army, excluded from political activity, and seeing itself as the guardian of the country from Russian expansionism, to which was linked subversion and disorder inside Turkey, was able to re-enter the political arena as the country's 'saviour'.[28]

The Mexican experience diverges from the Turkish from this point. The military was removed in both cases, in Mexico after a brilliantly fought tactical struggle and in Turkey by the sheer dominance of Ataturk's charisma. Turkey's military withered away into stagnation; Mexico's was professionalised. Turkey's political system introduced the masses to political activity after the de-militarisation that had been operating for many years, while in Mexico the two events were part of the same process. By the accident of geography Turkey became eligible for massive military aid, and this revolutionised the army at a time of severe tensions in the civilian political structure. Mexico remained unthreatened and with only a

28 For an account of the 1960 coup see Hurewitz, op. cit., pp. 211-28.

nominal role for its military. In Turkey this was enough to provide the opportunity for military intervention; in Mexico, so far, there have been no new circumstances to alter its army's role. A deterioration in internal security, and the consequent security build-up, could bring Mexico's army into politics, if the civilian government cracked.

### 4.    Israel

Israel is a unique case to compare with the countries so far discussed in this book. As in Mexico, the Israeli military has been contained within the civilian political system. Unlike Turkey, a massive military build-up has not brought the military into politics. Israel has fought three wars, and myriads of smaller engagements, but these have not created tendencies towards military interference in government, nor has this military posture created authoritarian conditions within the system of government and administration.

Israel did not have a prominent revolutionary officer caste to lead it to independence. It had instead a revolutionary creed, Zionism, which united the majority of the Jewish population. The conflicting interpretations of this creed contributed to a certain amount of fragmentation in the early days, expressed to some extent in the emergence of three separate fighting forces before the formation of a single state structure in 1948.[29]

The State of Israel began as an idea and became a reality. The idea unified the historical religious tradition with the secularist political movement; there was no tortuous conflict between God and Mammon that needed to be resolved before or during the struggle for the idea.

This is in contrast to Islam, where the struggle between God and Mammon has created problems for the Islamic regimes, because the one is not a natural ally of the other. The nationalists and the Islamic sects have clashed in several countries (Egypt, Sudan, Indonesia, Algeria). Islam is at root a universalist idea that does not co-exist happily with assertative nation-states, less so in the period of their vigorous

29 For an account of early factionalism see B. Halpern, *The Idea of the Jewish State*, Cambridge, Mass., 1961.

formation. Compromise is possible between the Islamic idea and the nation-state for a short period, identified with the removal of a foreign power (imperialism), and for this purpose the nation-state can be seen by the faithful as a prelude to the wider universalistic Islamic brotherhood.

The problems emerge forcefully when the nation-state takes on essential modern forms and is forced to compromise with the idea. Both Ghaddafy (Libya) and Boumédienne (Algeria) are prisoners of this contradiction. Libyan efforts at the formation of an Islamic nation of Arab states are unlikely to develop any further than Nasser's previous efforts and no matter what temporary gains they make they will eventually have to face up to separatist nationalism from within the federations that are set up. Boumédienne came to power partly to 'purify' Algeria of atheistic Marxism but the domestic programme his government follows is little different from that of any other militant Third World power. What distinguishes the Islamic revolutionaries from other Third World countries is their hostility to Israel, whose existence is to date a more unifying force for Islam than the universalism of their religious creed.

Zionism, in contrast, brought nation and religion together; it fused rather than divided. Moreover, because of the territorial complications of Israel's foundation, the new Jewish state, in struggling to express its idea, had also to fight for its physical survival. These forces reciprocally re-enforced each other and gave the Zionist state a cohesion unmatched in the Third World. Other states have shown similar solidarity, e.g. Communist Vietnam, but these have also required authoritarian and terroristic instruments to maintain their cohesion.

Given this history of violence, why has the Israeli state not succumbed to the military?[30] Other countries with only some of the problems that Israel has faced have fallen to military intervention. One factor in the government's favour has been its consistent record of victories (this also makes it difficult to compromise in a peace settlement). Israel is also

30 A. Perlmutter, 'The praetorian state and the praetorian army: towards a taxonomy of civil-military relations in developing polities', *Comparative Politics*, 1, 3, April 1969.

governed effectively by a single party that has ruled since 1948. The opposition parties are schismatically divided and spread across the entire political spectrum. Without an effective opposition (there is no inhibition on their activity) the ruling party is secure in its coalitions. After Labour there are only two alternatives: the military or the Arabs.

The struggle for Israel was conducted on both the military and the political front. It was assisted by overseas resources and the political pressure of the Jewish communities in the rest of the world. The military struggle was divided into three major groups.[31] The largest was the Irgum Ha-Hagana (Defence) that had around 43,400 fighters (both sexes); the next largest was the Irgum Tz'vai Leumi (National Military Organisation) with about 3,000 fighters, and the smallest was the Lohomai Herut Israel (Freedom Fighters for Israel), known popularily as the Stern Gang, with about 300 fighters.[32] Another dimensional division was between the Kibbutzim-based Palmach and the official Hagana. The Palmach were ideologically leftist (Kibbutzim socialists) and preferred an Israeli army that was Kibbutzim-based, volunteer and non-professional.[33] But the provisional government set up the Israeli army on different principles. It ordered the fusion, or disbandment, of all unofficial groups and placed the army (Zahal) under a single civilian command, that of the Defence Minister, David Ben Gurion.

The issue between the unofficial fighters and the central-ised Zahal was brought to a head in 1948 (the 'Altalena' incident) when an unofficial arms delivery was intercepted and the army opened fire when attempts were made to take delivery of the weapons by one of the official groups. The army won the engagement and this settled the issue. After

31  cf. Algeria and the divisions between the FLN and the MNA, or Ulster, and the divisions between the official IRA and the provisional IRA. There are similar divisions between the anti-Portuguese forces in Angola. One of these groups is even accused of being CIA-sponsored.

32  B. Halpern, 'The role of the military in Israel', in Johnson (ed.), op. cit., p. 338; Hurewitz, op. cit., p. 365, gives the numbers as 45,000, 3,000 and 500 respectively.

33  A. Perlmutter, *Military and Politics in Israel: Nation-Building or Role Expansion*, London, 1969.

the assassination of Count Bernadotte, the United Nations representative, the other fragmentary groups were rounded up and disbanded. Civilian leadership of the armed services with the monopoly of violence being held by the government was established. Perlmutter gives the credit for this development to Ben Gurion's leadership:

The transformation of Israel's voluntary, semi-professional, and highly politicalised security organisations into a unified, compulsory, professional and de-politicalised army was accomplished by the determination and skill of David Ben Gurion.[34]

The civilian government established its legitimacy, and with the 'second chamber' represented by the Histraduit,[35] the population were able to exercise influence on, and opposition to, the political leadership. The army is centralised and monolithic; the political system stable at the centre and factional in opposition. The state is able this way to exercise a maximum of political democracy with a maximum of military response to external threats, using a skilfully combined professional and conscripted force.

The new Israeli government preferred a professional nucleus supported by a conscripted army — the professional elite would guarantee continuity and standards and the conscripts would provide the manpower. The Palmach version of an Israeli army was that of volunteer autonomous mobile fighting units localised on the Kibbutzim. This would have led to unco-ordinated responses to external threats and would have brought to the surface ideological divisions. While Zionism was a unifying idea it was also susceptible to various interpretations. The egalitarian agrarianism of the Kibbutzim, the Western elitism of the cities, or a totally religious rather than a secular state, are but a few of the possibilities. To have a military expression for each and every interpretation would have meant a factional front against the Arabs.[36] The

34 ibid., p. 54.

35 B. Halpern, 'The role of the military in Israel'. The Histraduit is the Labour and Trade Union Centre; it operates several major businesses. It is a cross between the British TUC and the nationalised/co-operative industries and the Welfare State.

36 Nevertheless there is a tendency for Kibbutzim volunteers to try

government's early test on this issue led to the disbandon-
ment of the Palmach general staff in November 1948. The
combination of professionalism and conscription did not
affect the competence of the Israeli army as a fighting force
and it has probably ensured a non-military system of
government. In Turkey this combination has not had this
effect. The conscripted army (largely rural in composition)
has been a willing tool of the professional army command in
the military interventions.

The officer corps is exclusively merit-selected and also
constantly rotated. They defend all of Israel, not just their
local version of it. It does not have long periods of separation
from the civilian way of life because it is integrated into
civilian society in many ways. Training is directed at skills
useful in both military and civilian occupations. In some
aspects of the work of the army the two are combined into
the same activity — building isolated settlements, or roads,
opens up isolated regions for settlement, and this assists the
defence of the territory.

Israel faces a 'tribal' problem in trying to fuse diverse
minorities and refugees from differential social systems into a
single nation, with a common language and common institutions. This problem is partly tackled by compulsory military
training for the youth. The army is a melting pot for the
diversity of the citizens.[37]

The professional officer corps is normally a possible source
for ambitions towards military intervention, but the Israeli
army system prevents this outcome. The demand for army
officers to take up civilian employment is sufficient to drain
off any frustrated, or politically motivated, officers. Table 6
shows the civilian occupations of retired officers of the Zahal
in 1966 by percentage distribution among categories of
employment.

Only 4.4 per cent have gone into politics and the largest

---

to get into the elite units of the forces, and whereas they constitute 4
per cent of the Israeli population, they suffered 25 per cent of the
casualties in the Six Day War.

37 The literacy rate in 1948 was 93.7 per cent, but it fell to 87.9 per
cent in 1961 due to the heavy migration; also citizens may be literate in
a foreign language and have to learn Hebrew: Hurewitz, op. cit., p. 358.

Table 6    Occupations of retired Zahal officers, 1966

| Category | Percentage |
|----------|------------|
| Private corporations | 22.4 |
| Government departments (not listed below) | 21.7 |
| Government corporations | 12.2 |
| Independent | 12.2 |
| Foreign Affairs Ministry | 6.9 |
| Defence Ministry | 5.2 |
| Higher education | 5.2 |
| Kibbutzim | 5.2 |
| Politics | 4.4 |
| Local government | 2.6 |
| Other | 2.0 |
| | 100 |

Source:   A. Perlmutter, *Military and Politics in Israel: Nation-Building or Role Expansion*, p.76; Table re-arranged.

group have become civil servants (36.4 per cent, though this rises to 53.8 per cent if those who work for government corporations and higher education are included). Non-government and private employment accounts for 39.8 per cent of the retired officers. These extensive employment opportunities in Israeli society for trained officers with educational and administrative abilities, plus the possibility of technical skills acquired from operating advanced military weapons systems, prevent the building up of fears and insecurity among the professional officers of post-service deprivation through loss of income and status. They also ensure that the Israeli state has a high proportion of ex-military personnel at all levels.

Promotion for the junior ranks is assured through rotation and retirals of senior ranks. The turnover of the officer corps also ensures a closer integration of the civilian society with the military because many of the key civilian personnel will be ex-military personnel.

There does not seem to be any grounds on which the Israeli army is likely to intervene unless it is evident that a military government would carry out a foreign, or domestic policy, that is significantly different from that being carried out by the civilian political leadership. In this context, the civilian government's eventual peace deal with the Arabs will have to take into account 'military', i.e. militant, Jewish nationalist views about possible concessions. For example, the surrender of Jerusalem to the Arabs is probably one issue that could provoke some kind of military intervention, but it is unlikely that any civilian government would be found that would contemplate such an act, unless the balance of forces in the Middle East were to alter dramatically. In 1973 the ruling Labour party government faced defections from a minority party over the prospect of the recognition of Jordanian sovereignty on the west bank of the Jordan. This defection would have reduced the government's majority to four. If the party can split over this 'concession' before direct negotiation with the Arabs the fragility of the civilian leadership is much more serious than it looks. The eventual 'peace plan' will probably need to be tested in a general election. Peace may bring more problems to Israel than the status quo.

## 5.    Conclusion

The military can be contained in a developing country. But this is already implicit in the analysis of military interventions. The military can become a political force in the state in the absence of viable alternatives. The factor that Mexico, Turkey and Israel have in common is the existence in each country of a powerful political figure at the head of an undivided party. Ataturk, Cardenas and Gurion were charismatic leaders who were able to hold together their political movements and ensure loyalty from activists in an atmosphere of revolutionary change and, in Turkey's and Mexico's cases, a class-divided nation. In Israel, society was more pluralistic, but its external security situation was severely threatened. If these leaderships had been weaker, or had diverted their ambitions to personal dictatorship of the kind attempted by Mirza in Pakistan, or Sukarno in Indonesia or Nkrumah in Ghana, then the outcome might have been different.

The three leaders were legalistic to a fault and no

substantial charges of extra-constitutional action can be brought against them. Because they were legalistic in respect of the constitution they did not threaten constitutional opposition nor invite extra-constitutional activity. It is this aspect of their political behaviour that separates them from the activities of the politicians referred to above, and also from the current behaviour of the leaders of some of Africa's one-party states, who combine their personal rule with an inability to refrain from suppressing opposition movements.[38]

When a political leadership overreaches itself, such as when it creates through time more enemies than it has friends, it is vulnerable to military intervention from a comparatively small number of armed and disciplined men. Thus the leadership may feel secure in the loyalty of its Chiefs-of-Staff (Nkrumah was even wrong in this respect) but the required force for a coup d'etat does not need the Chief-of-Staff to carry out the take-over, nor, in the initial attack, does it need the support of the rest of the armed services.

The civilian leadership can fall to intervention from another source; it can be factionalised into a stalemate (blocking coalitions). If viable government is not possible neither is viable resistance to disorder. The army is then able to intervene to 'preserve law and order'.

In Turkey, Mexico and Israel the political leadership did not fall into any of these errors. Ataturk carried out his modernising revolution in alliance with the natural enemies of change (this was a sensible policy for Ataturk but it left problems for Ionu). He stuck to the constitution and eschewed military dictatorship. Cardenas removed the military from politics and administration by asserting the supremacy of *civilian* government and not the supremacy of Cardenas. When his term of office expired he retired; he did not attempt to become 'President for life'.

Civilian government is as much a means for choosing a succession as for determining its composition. Gurion created an armed state with a single government and a population

38 In this context the Zambian leadership, for example, will not tolerate 'opposition' which compromises 'national unity'. The same can be said for Malawi. It is also increasingly evident in Sierra Leone even though there is a nominal multi-party constitution.

free to act as civilian electors (to participate in the politics of opposition) and obliged to form the bulk of the armed services. The independent armed forces were either integrated or disbanded and the closest possible relations between the professional military forces and the community were established. Practically all levels of Israeli society have personnel who have served in the armed forces or are in active reserve units. The military is constitutionally under the direct command of the civilian cabinet and, because of the composition of the armed forces, the possibility for an independent role against the civilian cabinet is extremely limited. There are conceivable circumstances in which a civilian cabinet could hand over executive powers to an army cabinet (some serious Israeli reverses in the field against the Arabs or a successful assassination action against the majority of the government), but this would not be strictly comparable to a situation in which a professional armed force took over and directed civilian activities, as in other military interventions. It would be, in fact, the civilian population of Israel in uniform.

These three cases confirm the legitimacy thesis. Where viable civilian government is present, its military form is not, and where military intervention is attempted and fails, this only serves to confirm the viability of civilian government. Where civilian governments fall and the military succeeds this expresses the crisis of civilian government and not the inherent pathology of the soldier.

# 9 Politics and Defence Budgets

## 1. Introduction

In this chapter I want to look at the allocative decisions of Third World governments. The government budget is an indicator of the allocative values of a government. We want to relate allocative decisions to the political systems in these countries and see whether any relationship exists between the type of political system and the expenditure decisions under various headings, such as defence, welfare and education. For example, do military governments spend more on defence than on welfare, or is the security situation, as perceived by the government in either political system, a more important influence on defence spending than any innate preferences for or against military spending?

Outside the textbooks, it is very doubtful if the following allocative rule laid down by Professor Pigou is of much use to any of the governments in the Third World:

Expenditure should be distributed between battleships and Poor Relief is such wise that the last shilling devoted to each of them yields the same return of satisfaction.[1]

The information necessary for such a rule to be applied is just not available in anything remotely accurate enough for a meaningful calculus of utilities to be considered. The division of resources into the budget headings is subject to the political bargaining process of each country, at each time and place. It is not reducible to a single rule or law applicable in all countries and political systems, and a great deal of time and talent is wasted in believing that it is.[2]

1 A.C. Pigou, *A Study of Public Finance*, London, 1947. p. 31.
2 See Vaizey et al., op. cit.

## 2.    Political issues

The government's budget is sensitive to the political tensions within which the government has to function. It is an expenditure that the government has direct influence over. The budget outlays also have some element of continuity in them, being affected by the decisions of previous administrations. This is of some importance to all governments. In developing countries the decisions of previous administrations, on such matters as foreign aid and loans, will continue to be budgetary burdens, long after the administration is changed, through the necessity to pay interest on the loan, and, eventually, through having to repay the principle. *Principal*

In education, decisions to introduce primary and secondary education have consequences through time due to the new age cohorts that require recurrent expenditure, and, as the population grows, due to additional expenditure to meet the demands of larger age cohorts. As the population grows so must the budgetary expenditure on education, if the original decision remains unchanged. A similar situation applies to health and social welfare expenditure.

To this type of expansion in budgetary outlays must be added the inflationary pressures, particularly those due to rising costs of capital from abroad over which the government has little control. If the physical equipment is imported from a developed country, it is subject to inflation and the developing country must increase its budgetary outlays just to maintain the quality of the educational and health provisions; and because the population pressure is also increasing the total outlays themselves, the combined effect is to raise expenditure. This reduces the areas of discretionary decision for the government.

In the case of armaments imports this problem is acutely felt by governments. Defence is undertaken by all countries. They import the great bulk of their military equipment, and the pressure of foreign prices is eventually felt, even if slowed down by subsidised political sales and by purchases of relatively obsolescent or surplus equipment. Violence has not diminished in developing countries, as has been shown, and consequently there is great pressure to maintain and expand military outlays. As security is an inter-active relationship between a country and those other countries it feels threatened by or is hostile towards, the acquisition of weapons by one country will provoke others to follow suit and invest in similar or more advanced weapons. The performance standards of weapons acquired in the Third World thereby improve through time, but so does their cost.

The elements of an arms race are not difficult to discern in several parts of the Third World (e.g. Arab states and Israel; Ethiopia and Somalia; North and South Korea; North and South Vietnam and their neighbours; Latin American Republics — and for the future, Uganda and Tanzania?).

*Table 1   Number of Third World countries with supersonic and trans-sonic military aircraft by year of acquisition*

| | Year | | | | | | | | |
|---|---|---|---|---|---|---|---|---|---|
| | *1956* | *1958* | *1962* | *1964* | *1965* | *1966* | *1967* | *1968* | *1969* |
| *No. of countries* | 1 | 4 | 5 | 8 | 14 | 21 | 25 | 29 | 30 |

Source: SIPRI., op. cit., p.8, Table 1.2.

The acquisitions of supersonic and trans-sonic military aircraft, shown by year in Table 1, illustrate the tendency for countries to increase the military sophistication of their weapon systems, as these weapons become available on the international market, or, as frequently, as their rivals acquire them. The escalation in costs matches the escalation in performance. In 1966 a sub-sonic F-86 Sabre jet fighter was priced at around $200,000 for a surplus plane but the supersonic F-4 Phantom was priced at $2.5 million.[3]

The same pressures are felt where the violence is threatened not externally but from within the country, from guerrilla and insurrectionary forces. The type of security threat ought in the long run to determine the type of response, though we can note here that governments do not always behave as if this was true. For example, Brazil and Argentina acquired aircraft carriers and air-strike capacity in the early 1960s which are only useable in conventional

3 Frank, op. cit., p. 26.

warfare. The security threat in these countries throughout the 1960s was. of an entirely different nature, and the international threat was non-existent. The value of a deep sea aircraft carrier for use against urban guerrillas is minimal. The growing interest of these countries in Counter-Insurgency (COIN) weapons suggests that this point is beginning to be understood.

The data available on the budgetary allocations in developing countries show, in effect, the vectors of a complex political process that was going on both in the years covered by the data and in previous years. Sudden shifts in allocation are rare and normally the shifts are gradual over a period of time. These shifts occur when some immediate adjustment is necessary to deal with an emergency or where the implications of previous decisions begin to take full effect. Governments in developing countries have less continuity in policies than their counterparts in the developed world and therefore the budgetary shifts in allocations usually coincide with a change in government. In Togo, for example, following the 1963 military coup the share of military expenditure out of the state budget rose from 5.4 per cent to 13.5 per cent in twelve months.

The *a priori* view that the level of insecurity felt by a government would be an important influence on that government's budgetary allocations to defence and security is one that appeals to commonsense. In Table 2 this is confirmed. The annual average defence allocation out of state budgets for periods in the 1960s shows a strong relationship between military hostilities and the size of the allocation. The effect of the Arab-Israel wars on the countries concerned has been to raise their defence allocation to extremely high levels. Syria, with 48 per cent of its budget allocated to defence, is carrying the heaviest burden, followed by Jordan (46 per cent) and Lebanon (21.2 per cent). The Nigeria-Biafra war raised the budgetary allocation from 5.2 per cent in 1961-6 to an average of 35 per cent during the war. The post-war projections for defence and security show a drop from this emergency level to 9.4 per cent.[4]

4 Nigerian High Commission, *Why Nigeria? A Businessman's Guide to Development in Nigeria between 1970 and 1974*, London, p. 8.

*Table 2    Average annual percentage allocations on defence out of*
*state budgets (41 countries)*

| Country | Date | Percentage | Remarks |
|---|---|---|---|
| Syria | 1962-69 | 48 | Arab-Israel wars |
| Jordan | 1961-70 | 46 | Arab-Israel wars |
| Nigeria | 1967-69 | 35 | Biafra war 1967-70 |
| Egypt | 1958-71 | 33 | Arab-Israel wars |
| Burma | 1963-70 | 33 | Insurgency |
| Indonesia | 1963-67 | 31.3 | Confrontation 1962-5 |
| Iraq | 1960-70 | 30 | Arab-Israel wars |
| Korea | 1960-70 | 25.7 | Korean war and high post-war tension |
| Pakistan[1] | 1960-69 | 24.9 | Indo-Pakistan wars, 1965, 1971 |
| Iran | 1961-70 | 23.1 | Persian Gulf ambitions |
| Turkey | 1961-69 | 21.8 | 'forward defence area' |
| Colombia | 1965-71 | 21.3 | Insurgency |
| Lebanon | 1961-70 | 21.2 | Arab-Israel wars |
| Ethiopia | 1964-69 | 20.9 | Ethiopia-Somalia war and separatist insurrections |
| India | 1963-71 | 20.7 | Indo-Pakistan and Sino-Indian wars |
| Brazil | 1964-70 | 17.0 | Insurgency |
| Thailand | 1961-71 | 17 | Vietnam war and insurgency |
| Peru | 1964-68 | 16.9 | Insurgency |
| Malaysia | 1966 | 16 | Confrontation and insurgency |
| Argentina | 1963-69 | 15.6 | Insurgency |
| Ecuador | 1963-69 | 15.3 | Insurgency |
| Cameroon | 1964 | 15.2 | Insurgency |
| Bolivia | 1960-68 | 14.8 | Insurgency |
| Singapore[2] | 1969 | 14 | British withdrawal |
| Tanzania | 1963-70 | 13.4 | To rise after Uganda war? |
| Sudan | 1962-69 | 13.3 | Separatist war |
| Philippines | 1961-70 | 11.5 | Insurgency |
| Togo | 1965-70 | 10.7 | |
| Guatemala | 1963-69 | 10.4 | Insurgency |
| El Salvador | 1964-67 | 10.3 | |
| Venezuela | 1965-71 | 10 | Insurgency |
| Chile | 1964-68 | 9.6 | |
| Honduras | 1964-70 | 9.1 | |
| Ghana | 1960-70 | 9 | |
| Ivory Coast | 1964 | 9 | |
| Uganda | 1965-70 | 8.8 | To rise after Tanzania war? |
| Costa Rica | 1965-68 | 7 | Army 'abolished' 1948 |
| Liberia | 1964-69 | 5.4 | |

| Country | Date | Percentage | Remarks |
|---------|------|-----------|---------|
| Kenya | 1964-70 | 5.1 | |
| Sri Lanka | 1961-70 | 3 | Uprising 1971 |
| Malawi | 1961-69 | 2.2 | |

Source: United Nations, *Statistical Yearbook 1970;* various time periods in the 1960s; some countries for one year only.

Notes: 1 Reported to be 60% in 1973.
2 Reported to be 33% in 1972.

Indonesia was allocating 31 per cent of the budget to defence during the confrontation with Dutch New Guinea and Malaysia and some reports put the proportion even higher.[5]

Korea and Turkey are major recipients of American aid and have been scheduled 'forward defence areas' in American global strategy.[6]

South Korea allocates an average of 25 per cent of the state budget to defence a decade or more after the end of hostilities with North Korea. The military posture of the Koreans has been maintained at such a high level because the governments throughout the period since the war have felt insecure with their northern neighbour. The Blitzkreig capability of the North Koreans, evidenced in their original offensive in the Korean War, where they almost pushed the Americans out of the peninsular, has been the main strategic threat to South Korea and they have kept themselves in a quasi-alert status since.[7] It also accounts for the 40,000 US

5 N.B. Indonesian statistics for the 1960s were notoriously unreliable; even the United Nations expressed caution. See United Nations, *Statistical Yearbook 1970.* The table is based on official statistics which are not always reliable. The collection and manipulation of data in many Third World countries is subject to several forms of error.

6 The American 'Forward Defence Areas' were scheduled as Greece, Turkey, Laos, Vietnam, Korea, Taiwan, Philippines, Thailand, Pakistan, India and Iran. They received, for example, 71 per cent of American military assistance in 1965, or $816 million out of $1215 millions; op. cit., pp. 12-13.

7 There were reports in 1972 that the South Koreans estimated that the North Koreans were capable of a 30-day blitzkreig on the South and that they had shortened the time needed to carry through a successful invasion from 100 days. Korea/US relations have been strained on several occasions because American estimates of North Korean intentions at particular times differed from South Korean.

soldiers permamently stationed in South Korea.

Turkey has also maintained a high proportion of the budget on defence (21.8 per cent) and in 1973 this is to be increased still further to meet the government's security preparations. These preparations are to cover eventualities with the Soviet Union, and with Syria, which is well-armed with Soviet advanced weapons, and for contingencies if there is a decline in Greek-Turkey relations over Cyprus.[8]

Pakistan is another power with a high defence allocation (24.9 per cent), and substantial American military aid. The military conflicts with India have contributed to a receptive atmosphere in the executive for military allocations. There has been an active 'defence-business' lobby close to the government.[9] There are a number of unresolved border problems with India and the effect of the successful Bangladesh separation on the communal tension within the remaining Western wing may require increased allocations to produce a well equipped and loyal force at the disposal of the central government.[10]

India has also increased its budgetary outlays on defence. It averaged 20.7 per cent of the budget in the 1960s, and this increased to 28 per cent for 1969. India has fought wars with both Pakistan and China and has also been active in a number of smaller engagements with insurgents such as the Nagas in northern India.

Malaysia and Singapore have defence allocations of 16 and 14 per cent respectively. Singapore is planning to increase its allocation to 38 per cent in the 1970s to compensate for the run-down in external military assistance from the UK, Australia and New Zealand.[11]

It is interesting to note that the Latin American republics,

8 *Financial Times*, London, 13 December 1972. The budget was to be increased 37 per cent over 1972 up to $793 millions.

9 Ahmad, op. cit., p. 67.

10 Pakistan announced on 25 December 1972 that the Government was going to make Pakistan a 'nation of arms' because the defence costs could not be met by the country. This was to take the form of a general mobilisation, including women, to supplement the 380,000 troops in the army. *The Times*, London, 26 December 1972.

11 Hon Sui Sen, Minister of Finance, *Economic Pattern in the Seventies*, Singapore, 7 March 1972, p. 27.

which have high absolute amounts to defence, are mainly located in the bottom half of the Table. They have not experienced external hostilities in the post-war years (with the exception of the so-called football 'war' between Honduras and El Salvador in 1971).[12] The main security threats have been insurgency and the present para-military role of the security forces has been sufficient to contain these types of rebellions.[13]

Of the 15 countries that have devoted to defence an average of over a fifth of their state budgets throughout the 1960s, 10 of them had military regimes for all or part of the years in question (Syria, Nigeria, Egypt, Burma, Indonesia, Iraq, Korea, Pakistan, Turkey, Colombia), and a further three, Jordan, Iran and Ethiopia, were militant monarchies. Only 3, India, Lebanon and Israel, were party states. At the other end of the scale, of the 10 countries that allocated an average of under 10 per cent of their budgets to defence, 8 were party states (Chile, Ivory Coast, Uganda, Costa Rica, Liberia, Kenya, Sri Lanka and Malawi). The two exceptions, Ghana and Honduras, were at the upper end of this bottom ranking (9 and 9.1 per cent respectively).

To see whether there is any significant relationship between the political system and the defence allocation for countries in the sample, the average annual expenditure on defence as a percentage of the state budget was calculated and listed according to whether they were military regimes (monarchical states were taken as non-military for the purposes of this exercise). The results for each regional grouping are shown in Table 3, and in the final column, the average for the whole sample in each classification is shown.

12 D. Rennie, 'The goal that started a war', *Sunday Times*, London, 3 May 1970. The 'war' was hardly a serious affair and it was quietly ended.

13 See *Journal of Inter-American Studies and World Affairs*, special issue, 14, 4, November 1972, on 'Military and guerrillas in Latin America'. There have been border incidents between some countries, Guyana-Venezuela, for example; the border claim of Venezuela was an issue in the 1973 Venezuela elections. Mexico has claims on British Honduras; so does Honduras. Guyana has claims on Surinam (Dutch Guyana); Argentina and Chile have had border disputes. Panama is pressing for the return of the Canal Zone from the United States.

In the Middle East region the military regimes have an average allocation of 27.9 per cent against the non-military regimes' 29.8 per cent. The figure for non-military governments is in excess of the military government outlay and is contrary to other regions in the Table. All other regions show a pronounced bias in favour of higher defence allocations by military regimes than by non-military regimes. The high allocations of all countries in the Middle East contributes to the higher figures in this column and there is a variety of high-allocation non-military regimes such as Jordan. If the party states alone are taken for comparison, i.e. Israel and Lebanon, the non-military average annual allocation falls to 21.9 per cent; thus monarchist Jordan is helping to raise this group's average.

*Table 3   Average annual percentage expenditure on defence out of state budgets according to political status and hostilities*

| Category | Average percentage of budget | | | | |
|---|---|---|---|---|---|
| | Middle East | Asia | Africa | Latin America | ALL |
| Military governments | 27.9 | 25.5 | 11.3 | 13.9 | 20.5 |
| Non-military governments | 29.8 | 11.4 | 6.9 | 7.5 | 14.3 |
| Belligerents (all states) | 33.1 | 23.1 | 22.9 | .. | 30.8 |
| Non-belligerents (all states) | 18.4 | 17.5 | 7.9 | .. | 13.3 |

Military governments in Asia, sub-Saharan Africa, and Latin America allocated about double the percentage allocated by non-military governments on defence out of the state budgets. The relative allocation in the Middle East group, after the adjustment of the non-military regimes (21.9 per cent), is still much closer to the military regimes than for those in other regions. This is explained by the intense pressure of Middle East insecurity, which is partly related to the Arab-Israeli war and partly also to the ever-present threats felt by the monarchical regimes who are under pressure from their republican neighbours. The former monarchical regimes of Egypt, Iraq, Yemen and Libya are an active (even evangelical) force for republicanism and consequently the monarchies invest additional resources in state security.[14] The monarchies of Iran, Morocco, Saudi Arabia and the gulf states are all heavy defence spenders.

The impact of hostilities on the defence budget can be seen in the last two rows in Table 3. The allocations in the belligerent category (taken as being a country that has been engaged in hostilities with a neighbour during the 1960s) are in every case much larger on average than those for countries that are in the non-belligerent category.

In the Asian group, neither Malaysia (including Singapore) nor Indonesia were included in the belligerent category because the 'confrontation' had an unequal effect on the countries concerned. Malaysia and Singapore received considerable logistical and material assistance from Britain, Australia and New Zealand and the effects of the war on their budgets is not entirely clear.[15]

In the Middle East and Africa the difference between the belligerents and the non-belligerents is clearly marked. War compels the government to allocate resources to ensure the survival of the territorial integrity of the country.

The impact of the political system, and the foreign relations of a country, on the proportion of the budget allocated to security has been shown to be positively related to conditions of hostility with neighbours and also related to whether a military government is in power. We now want to see if the allocations to defence expenditure are competitive

14  See J. Waterbury, 'Kingdom building and the control of opposition in Morocco: the monarchical uses of justice', *Government and Opposition*, 5, Winter 1969-1970; after the Morocco coup attempts in 1971 and 1972 Libya broadcast encouragement to the armed services to try again. Iraq has been putting propaganda pressure on both Kuwait and Iran throughout 1972/3. Iraq competes with Iran in the gulf and sees Kuwait as a rich prize for its oil revenues. See E. Downton, 'The power game in the Persian Gulf', *Daily Telegraph*, London, 5 February 1970. Border incidents occurred in 1973 between Iraq and Kuwait; see *The Times*, London, 26 March 1973.

15  See R. Strudwick (forthcoming), *Malaysia and Singapore: the Impact of Defence on Economic Development and Growth*, and R. Mills, 'Cost and determination of Malaysian defence expenditure 1963-72', mimeo, Brunel University 1973.

with some other items in the budget, i.e. whether the spending on defence reduces the amount available to be spent on education and health.

### 3.   Welfare and defence

Welfare expenditure is only one item in the state budget, but this heading is chosen because it is the heading most commonly considered by critics of defence spending as the politically sensitive sufferer from military preparations. The United States Arms Control and Disarmament Agency (ACDA) in its reports contrasts the amounts spent on military preparations with the amounts spent on education and health on a world-wide basis, on the (warranted) assumption that most readers will be applying value judgments which favour welfare expenditure in any competition between the two headings.[16]

Taking world defence expenditures as a whole, for developed and developing countries, in 1967 the education budget was only two thirds of the world military budget and public health expenditure was even lower at one third of world defence spending. This, of course, must be put in the context of the fact that the 85 per cent of all world military spending is carried out in only 7 countries, America, Russia, China, Germany, France, Canada and the United Kingdom. Half the countries in the world spend more on defence than on education and only 36 countries spend as much on public health as they do on defence.[17] Of the developing countries, 49 spend more on education than defence and 23 spend less; 22 spend more on health than defence and 47 spend less.[18]

In Table 4 percentage expenditures on defence are tested for a relationship with percentage expenditures on welfare.

16 See Arms Control and Disarmament Agency (ACDA), *Report on World Military Expenditures*, Washington (annual). This was an agency set up in the 1960s within the American administration to lobby the government on disarmament. The funds were provided by the government and high-calibre staff appointed. Ironically for the Strategic Arms Limitation Talks (SALT), its personnel were by-passed.

17 ACDA, *Report*, 1967, p. 4.

18 United Nations, *Statistical Yearbook 1970*, calculated from Country Tables on public expenditures.

The correlation coefficients for 30 countries have been calculated for the years shown in the table. The existence of a high statistical correlation does not of course necessarily prove that there is a causal relationship, nor does the reverse indicate a lack of such a relationship.

Four countries, Egypt, Honduras, Sudan and Turkey (all with military governments) have strong positive correlations between percentage defence expenditure and percentage welfare expenditure (above r = ·8). This indicates a statistical relationship between percentage movements in the defence budget and percentage movements in the welfare budget — as defence spending increases so does welfare spending. Only 4 countries, Kenya, Argentina, Korea and India, had negative coefficients, which suggests a statistical relationship such that when percentage defence spending rises percentage welfare spending falls (and vice versa). The coefficients for Korea and India were very weak correlations; the India coefficient is close enough to zero to be indicative of no correlation at all.

Twenty-six of the countries have positive correlations of which 12 are fairly strong (above r = ·5) and 14 are weak. Of the 11 non-military governments included in the Table, 4 are among the group with fairly strong correlations and 7 are weak correlations. Of the countries with the 9 lowest coefficients, 6 were non-military-governed countries. Within the limitations of the data the broad suggestion is that defence spending is not obviously competitive with welfare spending, that for military-governed countries it is less competitive than for non-military-governed countries and that for only two countries in the sample, Kenya and Argentina, is there any strong evidence of direct competition between the headings. In Kenya's case welfare spending as a proportion of the budget remained static between 1961 and 1970, while defence spending as a proportion of the budget trebled. In absolute terms the amount spent on defence quadrupled and that on welfare almost doubled. Even so, Kenya was still one of the lowest defence spenders in the sample.[19]

For all countries in the sample the state budget increased throughout the 1960s, and this enabled governments to

19 ibid. Kenya Table.

Table 4 *Correlation between percentage of the state budget allocated to defence and welfare, 30 countries*

| Country | Years | r |
|---|---|---|
| Egypt | 1963-71 | .85 |
| Honduras | 1964-70* | .89 |
| Sudan | 1962-69 | .85 |
| Turkey | 1961-69 | .81 |
| Thailand | 1961-71* | .79 |
| Kenya | 1961-70 | -.78 |
| Burma | 1963-70 | .74 |
| Nigeria | 1961-66† | .69 |
| Argentina | 1963-69 | -.62 |
| Ecuador | 1963-69* | .67 |
| Lebanon | 1961-69 | .59 |
| Philippines | 1961-70 | .55 |
| El Salvador | 1964-70 | .52 |
| Ethiopia | 1964-69 | .51 |
| Venezuela | 1965-71* | .48 |
| Pakistan | 1960-69 | .38 |
| Mexico | 1964-70* | .38 |
| Syria | 1962-69 | .35 |
| Iraq | 1960-70 | .33 |
| Guatemala | 1963-69 | .29 |
| Ghana | 1959-70 | .27 |
| Liberia | 1964-69 | .25 |
| Korea | 1966-70 | -.20 |
| Jordan | 1961-70 | .18 |
| Uganda | 1960-70 | .16 |
| Colombia | 1965-71 | .15 |
| Malawi | 1964-69 | .09 |
| Brazil | 1964-70 | .07 |
| Malaysia | 1960-69 | .06 |
| India | 1962-71 | .02 |

Source: Data calculated from United Nations, *Statistical Yearbook 1970*

* Education and defence only.

† Defence includes internal security funds.

increase expenditure on a number of headings and thereby avoid in political terms painful decisions between conflicting interests. It can still be argued (and this is implicit in much of the ACDA work) that welfare headings could be increased faster if defence spending was cut; this is true of all headings in the budget, including foreign aid repayments. The essential point to be established by its critics is that defence spending is demonstrably unnecessary and thereby wasteful. Given the pattern of violence in the Third World this hardly seems a tenable proposition[20] (see Appendix B).

Governments control their own budgets. If military governments are more prone to high proportional defence budgets and governments of all types are even more prone to high defence budgets if they face, or believe they face, external threats, the next point to examine is whether these defence allocations are competitive with education and welfare in particular cases. It is possible for a high proportional defence budget to coexist with high and low welfare proportional shares. If defence is competitive with welfare,

*Table 5    Annual average percentage expenditures on defence and welfare state budgets, 12 African countries, 1960s*

| Country | Years | Defence % | Welfare % |
|---------|-------|-----------|-----------|
| Malawi | 1964-69 | 2.2 | 20.3 |
| Zambia | 1964-67 | 5.0 | 20.5 |
| Kenya | 1964-70 | 5.1 | 15.6 |
| Nigeria | 1961-66 | 5.2 | 25.6 |
| Liberia | 1964-69 | 5.4 | 18.3 |
| Uganda | 1964-70 | 8.8 | 25.2 |
| Ghana | 1964-70 | 9.6 | 24.7 |
| Ivory Coast | 1961* | 19.0 | 26.4 |
| Tanzania | 1964-70 | 13.4 | 21.5 |
| Togo | 1964-70 | 11.1 | 24.4 |
| Cameroon | 1964-65† | 15.2 | 23.2 |
| Ethiopia | 1964-69 | 20.9 | 17.3 |
| Group average | | 8.7 | 21.0 |

Source:  Calculated from United Nations, *Statistical Yearbook 1970*.
* Data for one year only in *Bulletin Mensuel de Statistique*, June 1967.
† Data for one year only in *Cameroon Federale, Orientale Occidentale*, 1964-5.

20 There is however considerable argument about the benefits of foreign aid; see B. Ward and P. Bauer, *Two Views on Foreign Aid*, Institute of Economic Affairs, London, 1971.

then high defence allocations will be accompanied with low welfare allocations and conversely low defence allocations will be accompanied by high welfare allocations.

Table 5 shows the annual average percentages spent on defence and welfare for 10 African countries. The years for which the data apply vary due to the availability of the data. They are ranked in order of size of defence spending. The individual annual averages for each country under each heading have been averaged to give a group average. The annual average percentage expenditure of the budget spent on defence for all countries was 8.7 per cent and that for welfare was 21 per cent.

Malawi allocated the smallest amount to defence but did not allocate a proportion as great as the regional average to welfare. Indeed, of the 7 countries that allocated an above regional average for defence, 6 of them also exceeded the regional average for welfare. The below-average allocators on welfare were also below-average allocators on defence. For the 12 African countries in the sample the results do not support the *a priori* view that high defence spending is competitive with welfare spending.

The 6 countries in the Middle East group for which data was available are shown in Table 6.

*Table 6   Annual average percentage expenditure on defence and welfare state budgets, 6 Middle East countries, 1960s*

| Country | Years | Defence % | Welfare % |
|---|---|---|---|
| Lebanon | 1962-70 | 21.2 | 17.9 |
| Israel | 1964-70 | 25.8 | 15.3 |
| Iraq | 1960-70 | 30 | 18.7 |
| Egypt | 1958-70 | 33 | 20.7 |
| Syria | 1954-70 | 45 | 19.8 |
| Jordan | 1964-70 | 46 | 10.7* |
| Group average | | 33.7 | 16.8 |

Source: Calculated from United Nations, *Statistical Yearbook 1970*.
    * Estimated.

The results are conflicting. Of the three countries with below-average defence spending, Lebanon, Israel and Iraq, two had above-average welfare spending, which supports the competitive relationship. But of the three countries with average or above-average defence spending two also had above-average spending on welfare. Jordan and Israel have below-average welfare spending but have defence proportions above and below the average respectively. This ambiguity in the evidence could arise from this area's special position as an arms race region.

Israel's rate of growth in defence spending for 1949-69 was 17.7 per cent per year (in 1969 it reached an annual rate of 27.7 per cent). For the region as a whole in the same period the rate of growth in defence spending was 13.2 per cent (18.9 per cent for 1969).[21] It is not feasible for countries to sustain such a rapid growth in the defence budget without distortions appearing in the economy.

Recent suggestions from the Arab Chiefs-of-Staff that each Arab country should contribute 15 per cent of the national income to defence (i.e. for the war against Israel) indicate that the arms race could reach yet higher levels, though some element of this will actually be due to price increases. The reluctance of the Soviet Union to accede to Egyptian arms requests is forcing the Arab states to consider how to finance substitute purchases.[22]

Turning to the Latin American countries, the data are set out in Table 7.

The evidence for Latin America does show a marked leaning towards a competitive relationship between defence and welfare expenditure. Of the 6 countries with below average defence allocations, 4 have above average welfare allocations. Details for health expenditures were only available for a minority of the sample, and therefore, as the welfare figures relate to education only, this must be borne in mind when evaluating the table. Nevertheless, the 5 above-average defence spenders all have below-average expenditures on education, and this is in line with the trend among the lower defence allocators. The Latin American group is completely different in this respect from the African group.

21 SIPRI, *Yearbook 1969-1970*.
22 *Financial Times*, London, 15 December 1972.

Table 7   *Annual average percentage expenditure on defence and welfare state budgets, 11 Latin American countries, 1960s*

| Country | Years | Defence % | Welfare % |
|---|---|---|---|
| Costa Rica | 1965-69 | 7.0* | 28.6 |
| Mexico | 1964-70** | 8.4 | 21.4 |
| Honduras | 1965-70 | 9.1 | 22.4 |
| Chile | 1964-68 | 9.6 | 16.0 |
| Venezuela | 1965-71 | 10.0 | 24.0 |
| El Salvador | 1964-70† | 10.3 | 24.0 |
| Ecuador | 1963-69 | 15.3 | 18.3 |
| Argentina | 1963-69†† | 15.6 | 14 |
| Peru | 1964-69 | 16.9 | 16.4 |
| Brazil | 1964-70 | 17.0 | 7.1 |
| Colombia | 1965-71 | 21.3 | 14.8 |
| Group average | | 13.3 | 19.7 |

Source:   Calculated from United Nations, *Statistical Yearbook 1970.*
   * Includes internal security.
   ** 1967-70 estimated.
   † 1970 estimated.
   †† 1967-69 not strictly comparable.
N.B.:   Health expenditure totals were not available for all the countries and therefore only education outlays are included in welfare.

There are a number of points to make in passing about the Latin American experience. Costa Rica, for example, allocated 28 per cent of the state budget to education on average for the years 1965 to 1968 (the trend was decidedly upwards and reached a third of the budget in 1969).[23] The effect of this large proportion on the country was noted by one observer:

Nowhere in Central America or the Caribbean are there to be seen so many students wearing college badges or school uniforms, so many socks and striped shirts . . . The thirst for learning seems all consuming in Costa Rica.[24]

23 United Nations, *Statistical Yearbook 1970*, Costa Rica Tables.
24 M. Niedergang, *The Twenty Latin Americas*, London, 1971, vol. 1, p. 359.

The illiteracy rate is among the lowest in Latin America. In 1963 the illiteracy rate was 15.7 per cent compared, say, to Nicaragua's rate of 50.2 per cent.[25] One reason for the low defence allocation in Costa Rica was the unusual 'revolution' of 1948 which disbanded the armed forces, formed a national guard, and turned the main barracks into an arts museum.[26]

Mexico, like Costa Rica, makes a relatively large allocation to education (for the years 1967 to 1970 it exceeded a quarter of the state budget).[27] Defence spending has also been increasing after a long period when it was falling. The annual increase for 1949-69 was 5.4 per cent rising to 8.8 per cent in 1969.[28] Mexico has recently been purchasing large numbers of military aircraft — between 1950 and 1970 it purchased 250 military aircraft from Canada and the United States, as well as 42 small naval vessels and 55 tanks.[29]

The relatively small allotment to the military in Mexico is a consequence of a political struggle over several decades since the revolution (1912-20). The progress of that conflict is shadowed by the decline in the budgetary allocation to the military; in 1940 it received 21 per cent, in 1957, 12 per cent and in 1964 7 per cent.[30]

### 4.    Conclusion

The evidence does not suggest that high defence budgets are necessarily directly at the expense of welfare budgets. Neither does the political system appear to influence the amount spent on welfare, except in the Asian group where the average annual percentage expenditure on welfare for military regimes is 15.2 per cent compared to an annual average of 26.3 per cent for non-military regimes (see Table 8).

25 United Nations, *Demographic Yearbook 1970.*

26 SIPRI, *The Arms Trade with the Third World*, p. 691; Niedergang, op. cit., p. 364.

27 United Nations, *Statistical Yearbook 1970*, Mexico Tables.

28 SIPRI, *Yearbook 1969-1970*, Mexico Tables.

29 SIPRI, *The Arms Trade with the Third World*, pp. 871-2.

30 See E. Lieuwen, *Arms and Politics in Latin America*, New York; H. Cline, *The United States and Mexico*, Cambridge, Mass., 1953, p. 276.

Table 8   *Average annual percentage allocation on welfare for major regional groups by political system*

| | Political system | |
|---|---|---|
| Group | Non-military | Military |
| | % | % |
| Asia | 26.3 | 15.2 |
| Africa | 20.6 | 21.2 |
| Middle East | 13.2 | 18.7 |

Notes:   Asia:   Pakistan; Korea; Burma; Thailand; India; Malaysia; Sri Lanka; Philippines.

Africa:   Ghana; Togo; Uganda; Zambia; Tanzania; Malawi; Nigeria.

Middle East:   Egypt; Iraq; Syria; Turkey; Israel; Lebanon; Jordan.

In the African group military regimes have a slightly greater military allocation than welfare allocation, compared to non-military regimes. In the Middle East the military regimes have a greater average allocation on defence compared to the non-military regimes. These averages are taken from small samples for which data is available. They do not necessarily represent the whole picture and they cover countries at different stages of development.

The information regarding the relationship between defence and welfare expenditure does not produce evidence to support the normal value judgment that military spending is depriving the Third World countries of resources that could be directed to the highly valued ends of raising educational levels and improving public health. The evidence suggests that the relationships between these items of government expenditure is much more complex, not to say ambiguous.

The proposition for such a competitive relationship is, however, unexceptionable in the form that argues that whatever is allocated to welfare could be increased if there were less defence spending. But the evidence for low defence spenders does not confirm that the result is automatically to increase welfare spending. In theory, the case is sound (reduce one item and you can increase the other), but in practice something may interfere with the equation. The political bargaining system has to balance the desire for increased welfare and the necessity for security. The evidence suggests that governments have increased expenditures on all items rather than re-allocate between them.

# 10 Defence and Growth

## 1. Introduction

This chapter takes the argument about defence allocations a stage further. It concentrates attention on two indicators of economic performance, the growth rate of gross domestic product and the growth rate of per capita incomes. The proposition implicit in much of the disarmament and development literature is that the defence allocations of the Third World countries interfere with the development programmes. In the case of India, for example, the wars of 1962, 1965 and 1971 had important effects on the Five Year Plans. Resources were directed into defence activities and fiscal measures were taken to finance these expenditures. In Pakistan the wars also had effects on the development programmes. For example, in 1965 the war with India set up shocks in the economic system from which the economy never really recovered.

The analysis of the effects of wars on development is a large and neglected area of development economics. We look into this problem in later chapters. The present exercise is less ambitious. It is simply an attempt to relate the defence spending of Third World countries to their growth rates. If there is a direct relationship (implicitly a negative relationship) between defence as a burden and economic performance it might show up in the comparative growth rates of the high and low defence spenders.

Developing countries regard economic growth as a major priority. Security considerations apart, economic growth remains the one index of performance by which a developing country will measure its successes or failures and be so judged by other countries. Countries that start off from a low level of economic activity, with the associated low per capita income, unexploited resources, and desperately pressing social problems and deprivation, must find ways to expand the economy if these indices of economic backwardness are to be improved.

The Third World is also in a hurry. The material conditions of the populations of these countries would be less intolerable but for the evident affluence of the indigenous elite. Growth in the economy is necessary to spread the material advantages of a richer society to wider layers of the population; growth, at the highest feasible rate, by bringing these advantages nearer, takes pressure off the elite from the (justly) covetous.

The declaration of the Association of South-East Asian Nations (ASEAN) in 1967 is typical of the growth-directed outlook of the Third World:

> The aims and purposes of the Association shall be: *to accelerate the economic growth,* social progress and cultural development in the region through joint endeavours in the spirit of equality and partnership in order to strengthen the foundation for a prosperous and peaceful community of South-East Asian nations.[1]

It is unlikely that much progress would be made towards any of the other objectives without an acceleration of economic growth and its maintenance at a satisfactory level. Development without growth is not possible. With growth the market widens and with a widening of the market there are prospects for an ending of the dual type of enclave modern economy co-existing with a backward subsistence sector. Cultural and political variations are possible but there are broad constraints imposed by the current technology.

The gross national product is one measure of an economy. While it is a measure open to some criticism, its use is sufficiently well established for it to be helpful in this context without anybody being misled into equating economic progress, as measured by increases in the gross national

1 Association of South-East Asian Nations, *Declaration*, 8 August 1967, Bangkok; my italics. ASEAN is an alliance of Indonesia, Malaysia, Singapore, Philippines and Thailand.

product, with human happiness. The rate of growth is an arithmetical calculation found by comparing one period's product with another's. Allowing for variations in national accounting practice, the growth rate is an approximation of what has happened, taking one period with another. The trend growth rate is of some value in looking at the broader changes that are taking place, or not taking place, in an economy.

The United Nations publishes statistics each year for most countries in the world and these have been used here liberally. These figures are provided to the United Nations by government agencies and are reproduced with minimal adjustment by the UN statistical service. Thus there are two caveats for us if we use these figures. The first is that there may be errors in the collection of the data due to inefficient administrative procedures, or simply as a result of lack of coverage in a particular country. Not all countries have extensive civil administration, and consequently, whereas in some countries the data is actually collected at source (census surveys), in others it may be estimated. Access may be difficult (and dangerous) and the figures can be over- or under-estimated. The second caveat is that there may be errors in the computation of the data, largely for the same reasons as above.

If the national income accounting system is subject to criticism in countries where none of the above conditions apply, it is obvious that the criticisms are proportionately more relevant in countries where they do apply. The basic assumption made by the United Nations statisticians is that the information they receive from the national governments is fairly accurate and exception is taken to particular figures only when the discrepancies are outstanding. It would, of course, be impolitic for the UN to suggest that individual countries are unreliable collectors of information from within their own borders. Thus in using these figures caution is essential; in drawing conclusions from their manipulation it is mandatory.

## 2.   Growth and defence

If growth is important to a country it is therefore important to reduce the influence of activities that inhibit growth. Military expenditures are generally regarded as wasteful and it is worth examining the growth rates of countries to see whether there is any obvious connection between military spending and the growth rate.

Growth rates can change rather suddenly due to exceptional factors, and therefore a period growth rate is more representative than an individual year's figure alone. Military expenditures are also subject to sudden fluctuations. Where possible, then, the data have been taken for a period of years rather than for a single year.

*Table 1   Growth of GDP (%) and the percentage of GNP allocated to defence, 1960s*

| Country | Years | % growth rate | % military expenditures (GNP) |
|---------|-------|---------------|-------------------------------|
| Taiwan | 1960-69 | 10.3 | 11.5* |
| Korea | 1960-69 | 9.2 | 4.0 |
| Zambia | 1960-68 | 8.2 | 1.3* |
| Nicaragua | 1960-68 | 8.1 | 1.6* |
| Thailand | 1960-70 | 8.0 | 2.6* |
| Panama | 1960-68 | 7.9 | 0.1 |
| Israel | 1960-68 | 7.7 | 9.1 |
| Iran | 1960-67 | 7.7 | 4.8 |
| Kenya | 1964-69 | 6.8 | 0.9 |
| Ivory Coast | 1960-69 | 6.6 | 1.6* |
| Malaysia | 1960-70 | 6.0 | 2.6 |
| Honduras | 1960-68 | 5.8 | 1.3* |
| Peru | 1960-68 | 5.7 | 2.9 |
| Bolivia | 1960-68 | 5.7 | 2.3 |
| Pakistan | 1960-68 | 5.7 | 3.6 |
| Sierra Leone | 1963-68 | 5.7 | 0.8 |
| Philippines | 1960-70 | 5.8 | 1.5 |
| Guatemala | 1960-69 | 5.3 | 1.2* |
| Venezuela | 1966-68 | 5.1 | 2.2 |
| Syria | 1963-68 | 5.1 | 11.1* |
| Cameroon | 1961-68 | 4.8 | 2.4* |
| Colombia | 1960-68 | 4.8 | 1.8 |
| Chile | 1960-67 | 4.8 | 2.5 |
| Tanzania | 1964-69 | 4.7 | 0.9 |

| Country | Years | % growth rate | % military expenditures (GNP) |
|---|---|---|---|
| Sri Lanka | 1960-68 | 4.6 | 1.1 |
| Paraguay | 1960-68 | 4.5 | 2.0* |
| Ecuador | 1960-68 | 4.5 | 2.1 |
| Brazil | 1960-68 | 4.1 | 2.0 |
| Sudan | 1960-65 | 4.0 | 2.5 |
| Tunisia | 1960-68 | 3.9 | 1.8 |
| Uganda | 1966-71 | 3.5 | 1.8** |
| Zaire | 1966-68 | 3.4 | 2.7* |
| Argentina | 1960-68 | 3.2 | 2.0 |
| Indonesia | 1960-70 | 3.3 | 1.8 (est) |
| Ghana | 1960-69 | 2.2 | 1.7 |
| Egypt | 1965-63 | 1.8 | 11.7 |
| Malawi | 1960-63 | 1.0 | 0.8* |
| Uruguay | 1960-68 | 0.4 | 1.5 |

Source: Growth of GDP, United Nations, *Yearbook of National Account Statistics 1970*; Defence expenditure, United States, ACDA *Report*, 1967.
 * for 1967 only.
 ** for 1962.

Four countries, Taiwan, Israel, Syria and Egypt, have high proportions of their gross national product allocated to defence (all over 9 per cent) (see Table 1). They also have widely divergent growth rates for the period; ranging from Taiwan, at 10.3 per cent, to Egypt, at 1.8 per cent. Taiwan and Israel have received military assistance from the United States, though much of Israel's assistance' has been purchased, and Egypt and Syria have received military assistance from the Soviet Union.[2] Military expenditures are not influencing the growth rates in an identical way. Korea, for instance, receives substantial military assistance from America and has allocated substantially less than these

2 The military aid to the following countries from all sources totalled in 1967 (US dollars):
 Korean    $270 millions
 Taiwan    $92 millions
 Israel    $85 millions
 Egypt     $51 millions
 Syria     $20 millions
see ACDA, *Report*, 1969, Table 2.

countries to defence (4 per cent) and has a relatively high growth rate (9.2 per cent), Malawi allocates even less to defence (0.8 per cent of GNP) and has an even smaller growth rate than Egypt at 1 per cent.

Seventeen countries in the table cluster in a growth rate range of between 3 and 6 per cent and an allocation on defence of between 1 and 3 per cent. Of the countries in this cluster only 6 which allocated between 1 and 2 per cent on defence have growth rates between 3 and 6 per cent. This leaves 11 countries in this cluster that are allocating between 3 and 4 per cent on defence and which have the same range of growth rates. Four, Zambia, Nicaragua, Thailand and Ivory Coast, are also in the same allocative range of military expenditures and have much higher growth rates (above 6½ per cent). Panama and Kenya have had high growth rates with low military expenditures (under one per cent) but so has Iran with 4.8 per cent defence expenditure. There is no obvious relationship between growth rates and percentage allocated to defence.

### 3.    Per capita product

If growth in national product can be used as a measure of a country's economic performance, then per capita product can be used as a measure of the level of economic development (subject to the same caveats). There is no direct relationship between the amount of military expenditure and the per capita product[3] (see Table 2). Countries with high per capital incomes (over US $500) had expenditures on defence ranging from 0.1 per cent (Panama) to 2.5 per cent (Chile). Altogether there are 43 countries within this range of defence expenditure as a percentage of national product; their per capita income runs from $50 (Upper Volta) to $910 (Venezuela).

The countries in the Table have low per capita incomes because they are under-developed, not because they spend this or that amount on defence. The relationship between

3 This was also found to be true for industrialised countries; see F.L. Pryor, *Public Expenditures in Communist and Capitalist Nations*, London, 1968, p. 93; see also M. Janowitz, *The Military in the Political Development of New Nations*, p. 17.

defence spending and per capita income is much more indirect.

*Table 2   Military expenditure as a percentage of GNP and per capita GNP*

| Country | Military expenditure % GNP (1967) | GNP per capita 1967 (US $) |
|---|---|---|
| Laos | 17.8 | 70 |
| Saudi Arabia | 17.1 | 444 |
| Vietnam | 14.1 | 177 |
| Jordan | 13.4 | 286 |
| Iraq | 12.0 | 265 |
| Egypt | 11.7 | 184 |
| Israel | 10.7 | 1501 |
| Taiwan | 11.5 | 263 |
| Syria | 11.1 | 203 |
| Somalia | 6.1 | 50 |
| Cambodia | 5.9 | 150 |
| Burma | 5.7 | 70 |
| Iran | 5.6 | 285 |
| Congo | 4.8 | 145 |
| Guinea | 4.5 | 83 |
| Korea | 4.0 | 155 |
| Malaysia | 3.9 | 315 |
| Mauritius | 3.9 | 141 |
| Pakistan | 3.6 | 113 |
| India | 3.4 | 85 |
| Algeria | 3.3 | 242 |
| Brazil | 3.2 | 347 |
| Sudan | 3.2 | 108 |
| Chad | 3.0 | 79 |
| Morocco | 2.8 | 188 |
| Zaire | 2.7 | 80 |
| Thailand | 2.6 | 149 |
| Chile | 2.5 | 605 |
| Yemen | 2.5 | 104 |
| Cameroon | 2.4 | 142 |
| Venezuela | 2.4 | 910 |
| Ethiopia | 2.4 | 66 |
| Lebanon | 2.3 | 633 |
| Ghana | 2.3 | 213 |
| Bolivia | 2.3 | 164 |
| Dahomey | 2.0 | 72 |

*Table 2 (continued)*

| Country | Military expenditure % GNP (1967) | GNP per capita 1967 (US $) |
|---|---|---|
| Ecuador | 2.0 | 249 |
| Upper Volta | 2.0 | 50 |
| Uganda | 2.0 | 93 |
| Paraguay | 2.0 | 221 |
| Libya | 1.9 | 909 |
| Senegal | 1.9 | 215 |
| Zambia | 1.8 | 297 |
| Indonesia | 1.8 | 87 |
| Sri Lanka | 1.8 | 154 |
| Uruguay | 1.8 | 533 |
| Argentina | 1.8 | 649 |
| Nigeria | 1.7 | 107 |
| Malagasy ' | 1.7 | 118 |
| Philippines | 1.7 | 188 |
| Colombia | 1.7 | 288 |
| Gabon | 1.7 | 380 |
| Central African Rep. | 1.6 | 130 |
| Ivory Coast | 1.6 | 267 |
| Nicaragua | 1.6 | 360 |
| Tunisia | 1.5 | 209 |
| Tanzania | 1.4 | 73 |
| Kenya | 1.3 | 119 |
| Honduras | 1.3 | 216 |
| Togo | 1.3 | 119 |
| Liberia | 1.3 | 216 |
| El Salvador | 1.2 | 286 |
| Guatemala | 1.2 | 288 |
| Afghanistan | 1.1 | 85 |
| Niger | 1.1 | 79 |
| Guyana | 1.0 | 338 |
| Malawi | 0.8 | 52 |
| Sierra Leone | 0.8 | 156 |
| Mexico | 0.7 | 528 |
| Panama | 0.1 | 582 |

Source: ACDA *Report*, 1967, Table 11 (extracted and re-arranged).

We have already noted the relationships between low per capita income and military interventions and between military spending as a proportion of the state budget and the political system of government. The increased proneness to military coups is noticeable among low income countries, and military governments allocate more to defence out of their budgets than non-military governments. We would expect, then, some relationship between low per capita income and the proportion of the state budget spent on defence. But when this relationship is extended to the proportions of the GNP allocated to defence, it could be diluted by the influence of the overall relationship between GNP and the percentage share of the total budget.

For this exercise we are not considering the direct effect of belligerency on the defence budget. Governments, military and non-military, allocate more to defence when they are engaged in, or anticipate being engaged in, direct military confrontation, than when they are not or do not anticipate being so. Belligerency is not a function of economic development or political system.

The time period that has elapsed since most military governments came to power is quite small, and it may be that the impact of the higher defence spending associated with military governments has not had time to make an appreciable difference in a comparison with countries which have avoided military governments (and belligerency). The possible effect of the higher defence burden cannot readily be measured in terms of the per capita product until sufficient time has elapsed to allow the country's particular circumstances to be overridden by the defence factors. However, the defence burden may have a more immediate effect on the growth in per capita income.

## 4.    Growth of per capita product

Per capita product is a function of two variables: the growth in population and the growth in gross national product. If the population grows faster than the product, the per capita product will fall; if product grows faster than population, then the per capita product will increase. If defence spending is a burden on the economy and represents a diversion from productive activity — i.e. if it consumes resources rather than creates capacity — this might be reflected in a lower growth rate than would otherwise be achieved.

Population growth is subject to factors which the government does not have control of (except in the longer term and even then this is subject to government influence rather than control). Population policy is not likely to be strictly related to defence, except in the longer term through such policies as populating isolated but strategically significant areas (Russian policy towards the population of Siberia has been partly penal and partly strategic). For these reasons any conclusions from this section must be tentative; the congruence of circumstances producing higher per capita growth rates in one country compared with another country may not be measurably related to that country's defence policies.

In Tables 3, 4 and 5 the growth in per capita product and the allocation to defence have been collected for three regional groupings (the Middle East presents the problem that the belligerency status of the majority of countries for which data is available will obscure any straight relationship looked for in this section). The entries have been ranked in descending order of per capita product growth.

The African group (Table 3) all had under 3 per cent allocated to defence, yet their growth rates varied between -0.4 per cent (Ghana) and 8.1 per cent (Zambia). Of the 12 countries in the table, 6 had a per capita product growth rate in excess of 3 per cent and 6 had a growth rate of under 3 per cent. If this is taken as a crude dividing line between the relatively high and the relatively low per capita growth countries, it is interesting to note (if statistically not too meaningful) that the average of the expenditures on defence for the high per capita growth countries is 1.3 per cent and the same average for the low per capita growth countries is 1.8 per cent. The low growth countries seem to allocate on average slightly more to defence than the high per capita growth countries.

The Asian group presents some contrasts. Taiwan with 11.5 per cent allocated to defence had the highest per capita growth rate of 7.1 per cent. Vietnam, with an even higher defence allocation (and a long war), had a per capita growth of under 3 per cent. Only 4 countries in the group had defence allocations of under 3 per cent (Sri Lanka, Thailand, Philippines and Indonesia). India had a negative per capita growth rate, but this may be due to demographic factors.

*Table 3   Average annual percentage growth in GDP per capita and average annual percentage of GNP defence expenditure*

| Country | Growth GDP per capita (%) | GNP on defence (%) |
|---|---|---|
| Zambia | 8.1 | 1.3 |
| Sudan | 5.0 | 2.5 |
| Uganda | 3.8 | 1.8 |
| Kenya | 3.8 | 0.9 |
| Malawi | 3.6 | 0.8 |
| Sierra Leone | 3.6 | 0.8 |
| Ethiopia | 2.9 | 2.3 |
| Nigeria | 1.6 | 1.7 |
| Tunisia | 1.5 | 1.5 |
| Zaire | 1.0 | 2.7 |
| Tanzania | 0.7 | 0.9 |
| Ghana | -0.4 | 1.7 |

Sources: Zaire, Ghana, Kenya, Sierra Leone, Sudan: United Nations, *Yearbook of National Account Statistics 1969*, Table 4a; Malawi and Uganda, *Yearbook of National Account Statistics 1966*, Table 7a; Zambia, Nigeria, Tanzania, Ethiopia, Tunisia, *Handbook of Trade and Development Statistics 1969*. N.B.: Nigeria, Tanzania, Ethiopia, Tunisia and Uganda are given at factor cost and the rest at market prices. Defence data from ACDA *Reports* for 1966 and 1967.

The Pakistan per capita growth rate at 3.5 per cent is impressive, but a considerable amount of discrepancy existed between the two wings of the country up to their separation in 1971; there were income transfers from the Eastern wing to the Western wing throughout this period. The per capita income growth rate rose from -0.3 per cent in 1959-60 to 2.0 per cent in 1969-70 in East Pakistan, but in West Pakistan in the same period the per capita income grew from an annual average of 0.8 per cent to 4.8 per cent. The regional disparity in income which was about 20 per cent in 1949, rose to 30 per cent in 1959 and thence to 61 per cent in 1969. West Pakistan was getting richer at a faster rate than East Pakistan,

Table 4 *Average annual percentage growth in GDP per capita and average annual percentage of GNP defence expenditure*

| Country | Growth GDP per capita (%) | GNP on defence (%) |
|---|---|---|
| Taiwan | 7.1 | 11.5 |
| Korea | 5.6 | 4.0 |
| Sri Lanka | 4.6 | 1.1 |
| Thailand | 3.9 | 2.4 |
| Pakistan | 3.5 | 3.6 |
| Vietnam | 2.5 | 14.3 |
| Cambodia | 1.6 | 6.1 |
| Philippines | 1.1 | 1.5 |
| Burma | 0.6 | 6.2 |
| India | -0.1 | 3.6 |
| Indonesia | -0.2 | 1.6 |

Sources: United Nations, *Yearbook of National Account Statistics 1969,* Table 4*a*; defence data from ACDA *Reports*, 1966 and 1967.

and the consciousness of this contributed to the separatist feelings among the Bengalis.[4]

Using a 3 per cent per capita growth rate as the crude dividing line, the average defence allocation for the higher growth countries was 4.6 per cent of GNP and for the lower growth countries it was 5.5 per cent which follows the pattern for the African group.

Latin America is a group with high population growth rates, and these contributed to the lower level of growth per capita product. Three of the 4 countries with the highest per capita product growth rates had defence allocations of under 1 per cent. Costa Rica, which also had a defence allocation of under 1 per cent of GNP, is second from the bottom of the Table for per capital product growth (0.7 per cent for the years 1958-65). This is probably due to poor economic management in those years rather than to a defence burden; the army was abolished in Costa Rica in 1948 and defence is a small item in the budget. The growth rate for GDP for

4 Ahmad, op. cit., p. 34; see also H. Schuman, 'A note on the rapid rise of mass Bengali nationalism in East Pakistan', *American Journal of Sociology*, 78, 2, September 1972.

Table 5  *Average annual percentage growth in GDP per capita and average annual percentage of GNP defence expenditure*

| Country | Growth GDP per capita (%) | GNP on defence (%) |
|---|---|---|
| Mexico | 6.2 | 0.8 |
| Guyana | 4.9 | 0.5 |
| Nicaragua | 4.5 | 1.6 |
| Panama | 4.4 | 0.1 |
| Bolivia | 3.0 | 2.4 |
| Peru | 2.5 | 2.9 |
| Chile | 2.3 | 2.5 |
| Honduras | 2.4 | 1.3 |
| Guatemala | 2.2 | 1.3 |
| El Salvador | 1.9 | 1.2 |
| Argentina | 1.6 | 2.0 |
| Colombia | 1.5 | 1.9 |
| Venezuela | 1.5 | 2.2 |
| Paraguay | 1.3 | 1.8 |
| Brazil | 1.1 | 3.0 |
| Ecuador | 1.0 | 2.8 |
| Costa Rica | 0.7 | 0.5 |
| Uruguay | -0.9 | 1.5 |

Sources: United Nations, *Yearbook of National Account Statistics 1966* and *1969*, Table 4a; defence data from ACDA *Reports*, 1966 and 1967.

1968-70 was 1.2 per cent, 5.3 per cent and 6 per cent respectively, indicating a dramatic improvement.[5]

Thirteen of the 18 countries in Table 5 have per capita product growth rates of under 3 per cent, and the average of their military expenditures is 1.9 per cent of GNP. The higher growth countries have an average defence allocation of 1.1 per cent of GNP.

The three groups do produce a crude relationship between defence allocations and the growth in per capita product, but this may be due to varying rates of population growth in these countries as much as, or more than, any differences in military expenditures. If these differences are affecting the growth of per capita product, then they will eventually influence the comparative levels of per capita product. These

5 Lloyds Bank, *Economic Survey*, June, 1971.

effects of different growth rates were not appearing in the levels for the time periods in the Tables, but this may be due to the relatively small differences in growth rates, which will require longer periods of time to show significant deviations in level, and to the fact that a number of high defence spenders are also fast growers in terms of these indicators and that they are swamping the other effects of growth rate differences.

### 5.    Conclusion

Is defence a burden? The statistical evidence does not produce an unambiguous answer to that question. The growth rates for GDP of individual countries in the 1960s did not seem to have been affected by their defence allocations. There are clearly many influences working to produce the growth rate, and to seek a relationship for one of them is probably asking too much from the information available. Not all of the defence spending is likely to have the same effects on the economy. For example, the pay and subsistence provided for the armed forces (consumption) has different effects on the local economy from, say, the use of foreign exchange to purchase a tank. Unlike the use of foreign exchange to purchase a tractor (many tractors could be purchased for the price of one tank), which increases the capital capacity, the purchase of a tank does not increase productive capacity. It does not necessarily become a burden by virtue of this alone.

It may be as important to growth that the development plans can continue without interruption from lawlessness, invasion and disorder. For example, in Nigeria after the serious tensions of 1965 and before the outbreak of the Biafran war, the growth rate collapsed from 6 per cent per annum to under 3 per cent per annum. The tribal disorders disrupted output and activity; they were in fact a burden on development.[6] The import of tractors on a wide scale into Nigeria in 1965 would not have reversed this burden for the economy, but we can speculate, with some faith in our

6 M.E. Zukerman, 'Nigerian crisis: economic impact on the north', *Journal of Modern African Studies*, 8 April 1970.

conclusions, that the existence of a force under the control of the central government, inevitably·armed with weapons purchased by foreign exchange, put into action to restore law and order in the tension areas, would have been more useful than the purchase of productive capacity. It was the lack of such a force (the army was itself tribalistically divided) that allowed the disorders to develop into illegal military intervention and eventual civil war. The point being that the purchase of productive capacity cannot under all conditions be taken to be a sufficient condition for development.

The burden of defence cannot be found in its intrinsic nature alone, any more than there is the same positive return from all activities that can be described as educational: the establishment of schools to teach religious observation will have a different effect on development from the creation of colleges of technology. In what way defence spending in a particular country is contributing to, or competing with, development will depend upon circumstances and will not follow some general law applicable to all times and places.

# 11 The Economics of War: Nigeria

## 1.   Introduction

There will be little disagreement with the view that wars cost money and have economic, social and personal consequences. The dead and wounded are a more visible cost of a war than the diversion of resources. There have been a number of wars in the Third World and in this and the next two chapters we shall examine some of the economic consequences of four wars on the countries affected by them: Nigeria; Vietnam's neighbours; Israel, Egypt and Pakistan. Chapter 13 will bring together some of the conclusions from these studies by way of comparison between them.

## 2.   The Nigeria-Biafra war

The Biafran secession on 30 May 1967 was the penultimate act in the struggle between the rival factions of the Federal Republic of Nigeria over how Nigeria was to be governed. The issue was decided finally when Biafra ceased to exist on 15 January 1970. Government of Nigeria as a *nation* was decided upon by force of arms.[1]

One of the advantages to the Federalists in fighting the civil war was the successful blockade of Biafran territory. This meant that inflationary pressures, expected in the military build-up, were curbed to some extent by the diversion of goods into Federal territory, and this went some

1 W.F. Thompson, 'Nigeria's way to nationhood', *Daily Telegraph*, London, 17 July 1970.

way to reducing the inflationary gap.[2] From July 1967 the Federal side were able to enforce an effective blockade on Biafra, and a considerable amount of food imports, normally scheduled for the Eastern Region, were diverted to Federal territory. This had two side-effects, apart from the anti-inflationary one: it exerted pressure on the Biafran population (in the process it caused widespread death by starvation), and it also relieved pressure in Federal territory on food supplies. This kept food prices down in Nigeria and created a burden on the secessionists and the population they controlled.[3]

The emergency financial measures imposed by the Federal government enabled them to cut back consumer expenditure. The military spending, and the expansion of the armed forces to 250,000 at the height of the war (1969), injected a flow of demand for goods into the economy which re-appeared in the form of higher growth rates in GDP towards the end of the war.

*Table 1    Growth of real gross domestic product, Nigeria, 1958-70*

| *Year* (April-March) | *Average annual growth rate (%)* |
|---|---|
| 1958-65 | 6.1 |
| 1965-66 | 2.6 |
| 1966-67 | -4.8 |
| 1967-68 | -0.2 |
| 1968-69 | 13.0 |
| 1969-70 | 9.6 |

Source: *GDP of Nigeria, 1958/59 – 1966/67*, Lagos, 1968; *Second National Development Plan, 1970-74*, Lagos, 1970; *Economic Statistical Review*, 1970, Lagos, 1971.

The fluctuation in growth (and other indicators) is partly due to the exclusion of Biafran, or Eastern Region, figures by

2 War diverts resources into war production and normally sustains full employment. This is a problem facing any government embarking on military hostilities. It was discussed in this context by Keynes in *How to Pay for the War*, London, 1939.

3 Considerable use has been made in this chapter of Nafziger, op. cit.; all monetary details have been converted to US dollars at the rate of £N1 = $2.80. Several tables have been simplified from the original text.

the Federal authorities. The Biafran figures for 1967-9 were excluded, but thereafter they have been included, and this is bound to account for some part of the fluctuation. There is evidence, however, of a slowing down in the growth rate from 1958 to 1966, and the exclusion of Biafra in 1967 exaggerates what was an already established trend. Similarly, as we shall see, the falling growth trend was reversed during the war, and the subsequent re-inclusion of Eastern Region figures (when the Federal authorities regained control of the important areas of Biafra) merely supported an independent expansionary trend. For example, the exclusion of the Eastern Region in Nigeria's index of industrial production from the latter part of 1967 did not prevent that index from rising in the 1968-9 period. Import substitution brought about by the war, and the expansionary policies of the Federal government, contributed to this recovery and reversal of trend.[4]

The two years before the outbreak of the war were characterised by severe political and civil disturbances. The economic uncertainty (not to mention the physical liquidation of minority tribal entrepreneurs and skilled workers and the exodus of survivors to safer regions) contributed to a downward trend in indicators of economic performance. The July 1966 coup, bringing General Gowon to power, also brought to a head the tribal tensions in the country, and brought about the tribal military mobilisation to settle the issues by violence. Eventually this had the effect, in the decisive victory of the Gowon leadership, of re-creating economic confidence in the Federal territories.

The recapture of the Biafran-held oil-fields in 1968 provided the Federal authorities with the oil revenues and a fortuitous source of finance to pay for the mobilisation. This reduced the burden of the war on the population by providing a means to carry out the mobilisation without heavy sacrifices among the consumers, many of whom were

4 See a mimeographed article by A.J.M. van de Laar, 'Recent economic developments in Nigeria', Institute of Social Studies, The Hague, 1971; also S. Tornari, 'Monetary policy in a war economy: the Nigerian experience', *Social and Economic Studies*, 21, 3, September 1972.

also gaining from employment in the war-associated, and war-created, industries.

With the successes of the Federal armies in the east the problems of the war for the Federal side increased. The devastated region required food and other supplies and this reduced the counter-inflationary effect of the previous period's diversion of these commodities to the Federal area. The cost of distribution of this food to the devastated region was exorbitant; roads, rail, bridges, air strips and communications were in a state of chaos. The traditional food distribution system was disrupted and the (inevitably) bureaucratic relief organisations set-up to administer the area complicated the problem further. As a result, food prices in 1970 rose by 21 per cent.[5]

Producers' income arising from commodities that passed through the marketing boards (and thereby subject to the increased Federal taxes for the war) showed a considerable drop — about 50 per cent — in all categories, for the war years 1967-9. Part of this fall was a result of climatic factors — poor harvests — but part was due to the black market operations of speculators trying to avoid the taxes and, as important, trying to meet an expected high demand.

*Table 2   Producers' income from marketing board commodities (US $ millions) (constant prices)*

| Commodity | 1967 | 1968 | 1968 |
|---|---|---|---|
| Cocoa | 16.5 | 22.0 | 12.5 |
| Groundnuts | 87.8 | 47.8 | 24.3 |
| Seed cotton | 18.1 | 8.6 | 10.9 |
| Palm kernels and others | 15.7 | 9.4 | 10.2 |

Source: Official and Central Bank of Nigeria; Nigerian pounds converted to US dollars at rate of $2.80 = £N1; note data is for January to June for each year.

The balance of trade for the war years was positive (see Table 3), and this was almost certainly due to oil exports and rigid import controls, which did much to promote import substitution and an expanding economy. In 1968 the trade

5 Nafziger, op. cit., p. 229.

deficit on imports of non-oil goods had been reduced to a mere $3.9 million from the high $160.7 million of 1965. From December 1968 oil exports recovered rapidly and reached the production rate of 441,285 barrels a day compared to only 57,872 barrels a day in December 1967.

*Table 3    Balance of payments, Nigeria, 1965-69 (US $ millions)*

|      |       | Balance on visible trade | Surplus/ deficit |
|------|-------|------|------|
| 1965 | Oil   | 149.7  |        |
|      | Other | -160.7 | -11.0  |
| 1966 | Oil   | 202.3  |        |
|      | Other | -115.3 | +87.0  |
| 1967 | Oil   | 149.7  |        |
|      | Other | -94.9  | +54.9  |
| 1968 | Oil   | 63.5   |        |
|      | Other | -3.9   | +59.6  |
| 1969 | Oil   | 334.8  |        |
|      | Other | -99.6  | +235.2 |

Source: Central Bank, Annual Reports, 1967, 1968, 1969; Nafziger, op. cit., Table 1, p. 16 ($2.8 = £N1)

Over two millions tons of oil were exported in December 1968 and this rate was to benefit the balance of payments in 1969 by $94 million.[6]

The 1967 devaluation of sterling hit Nigeria's balance of payments at a total cost of $59.6 million. This was made up of a $36.4 million loss in revenue from primary products, priced in sterling, and a further $23.2 million in a writing down of Nigeria's sterling balance held in London.[7] Nigeria's foreign reserves reached a critically low level in 1968. They fell from $235 million in 1966 to $108.2 million in 1967[8] and were held at $136.4 million in mid-1968[9] only after the imposition of severe import restrictions and controls in January 1968.

Import licences were required for non-essential and luxury

6 Legum and Drysdale, op. cit., p. 568-9.
7 ibid. p. 568.
8 *Economic and Statistical Review*, 1970.
9 van de Laar, op. cit., Table 4.

goods and these measures replaced an earlier effort at import curbs using a surcharge system. Some commodities were banned altogether and domestic credits for import activity were also curtailed. Other measures to reduce foreign exchange costs were introduced, such as for foreign travel or for remittances abroad. Eventually the repatriation of profits and the interest on loans and capital transfers abroad were suspended.[10] Every possible measure was taken by the Federal authorities to reduce the foreign exchange costs in areas where they had discretionary powers, and the net effect of these measures was to reduce imports from $562.1 million to $484.5 million. Oil imports were also cut from $48.6 million to $37.6 million due to import substitution in the oil industry throughout 1966-9, made possible, of course, by the expanding Nigerian oil production.

The economy was, naturally, subject to distortions from these measures. Firms dependent on imports for their output — particularly those with a high import content in their products — were hit by the import restrictions policy. The licensing system and the inevitable bureaucratic tangle (plus the activity 'tax' of corruption) worked against the expansion of the economy and created some unemployment. Given that structural changes in an advanced economy are not frictionless, even in times of peace and with relatively uncorrupt administrations, the case of Nigeria is not exceptional.[11]

In Table 4 the commodity composition of Nigeria's imports for 1967 and 1968 are compared to show the effect of the import restriction policies. Key imports of crude material manufactures, machinery and transport equipment, and miscellaneous manufactures all fell substantially.

The expansion of industrial production can be seen in Table 5 (1963 = 100). By 1965, the first year of the troubles, the index reached 164.5 and had been growing by about 20 points each year. From 1965 to 1967 the index reached 172.8, an increase of about 8 points over the two years. These years covered the January and June military coups, the

10 Nafziger, op. cit., p. 233.
11 cf. attempted structural changes in the United Kingdom in coal, shipbuilding, etc.

Table 4 Nigerian imports by commodity, January-August 1967-68 (US $ in thousands)

| Import | 1967 | 1968 | % change |
|---|---|---|---|
| Food | 46138 | 23316 | -49 |
| Beverages and tobacco | 3692 | 2320 | -37 |
| Crude material | 12834 | 9313 | -27 |
| Mineral fuels | 9494 | 28608 | +201 |
| Oils and fats | 392 | 548 | +39 |
| Chemicals | 4487 | 39341 | +774 |
| Manufactures classified by materials | 145181 | 90520 | -37 |
| Machinery and transport equipment | 149971 | 98925 | -34 |
| Misc. manufactures | 33986 | 14903 | -56 |
| Misc. transactions | 5472 | 10662 | +94 |

Source: Legum and Drysdale, op. cit., p.573. Converted to US $ and final column added.

Table 5 Indices of acitivity in manufacturing, oil production and electricity consumption, Nigeria, 1963-71 (1963 = 100)

| Year | Manufacturing | Oil output | Electricity |
|---|---|---|---|
| 1963 | 100 | 100 | 100 |
| 1964 | 123.7 | 157.6 | |
| 1965 | 143.7 | 358.4 | |
| 1966 | 164.5 | 546 | |
| 1967 | 171.8 | 417.2 | 129.6 |
| 1968 | 172.8 | 185.3 | 125.8 |
| 1969 | 211.9 | 706 | 138.5 |
| 1970 | 250.2 | 1392.4 | |
| 1971 | 280.1 | 2006.6 | |

Source: Indices of manufacturing and oil production, Nafziger, op. cit., p.235; electricity consumption, van de Laar, op. cit., p.3; both sources from official statistics and Central Bank, *Annual Reports*, 1971.

Notes:    1  Production figures from 3rd quarter 1967 to last quarter 1969 exclude secessionist territory.
2  Electricity consumption figures are the arithmetical average for the quarters given in original source.
3  Indices for 1971; manufacturing is the average for the first two quarters.

massacres of Ibos in the north, and the exodus of people back to their tribal lands and the generally severe dislocation of commercial and industrial activity. By 1968 the import restrictions were in full swing (also the Eastern Region was excluded from the figures) and the import substitution programme was picking up. This is reflected in the index leaping upwards by about 40 points and following this with similar rises in the following two years.

3.   *Oil*

The crucial role of oil exports is seen in the extremely rapid expansion of crude petroleum output. From the base year in 1963 (Table 5) it increased by 57 per cent in 1964, more than doubled in the following year, and increased by 50 per cent the year after that. In 1966-7 oil output fell, and again while the oil fields were in Biafran hands in 1967-8. The Biafrans had great difficulty in selling the oil abroad due to combined pressure from Federal and British sources.[12] But in the first year of production, after the recapture of the oil-producing areas by the Federal forces, output reached record levels, seven times the 1963 figure, and went on in the following two years to even greater increases, reaching twenty times the output figure of 1963 in 1971. The role that these increases played in the balance of payments, and the earning of foreign currency, has already been mentioned; without the oil the Nigerian balance of payments, and its overseas indebtedness, would have created severe problems for the Federal government.

It may well be the case, on the other hand, that without the oil the issue would not have been pursued either by the Biafran forces in favour of secession (it is hard to see what their economy would have been based upon) or by the Federal side (oil revenues were as substantive a reason for resisting secession as the issue of principle — this made the Federal side doubly determined to resist).[13]

The indices for electricity consumption confirm the drop in activity in the first period of the Biafran war and also show

12 See Legum and Drysdale, op. cit., chapter on Nigeria.
13 See Luckham, op. cit., pp. 324-5.

the recovery that was taking place after 1968, both in domestic demand and in industrial demand.

The effects of the war on the sector origins of the GDP is shown in Table 6. A number of changes had been taking place throughout the period 1962-71, which the war interrupted (mining for instance) or gave an impetus to (manufacturing and crafts). In other cases the war appears to have had no impact at all.

Agriculture continued its decline as a source of GDP (one indicator of economic development), from 61.2 per cent in 1962 to 51.1 per cent in 1970. This sector was scheduled in the Second Development Plan to continue to decline to reach 44 per cent of GDP in 1973-4 at the end of the plan period.[14] The mining sector, which covers the oil industry, increased from 2 per cent of GDP in 1962 to 7.9 per cent in 1971. The large fall in this sector in 1967-8 is seen in the Table and its recovery in subsequent years has already been commented upon. Manufacturing and crafts almost doubled as a source of GDP in the period covered by the table.

Oil extraction need not lead to development (as the Middle East showed until recently), but it certainly can finance it. Nigeria's oil revenues financed the war by providing income to purchase essential imports (including military material) and averted a balance of payments crisis in concert with the import restriction policy. If the Biafrans had been able to hold on to the oil, and found markets, the civil war might have lasted longer and become even more bloody. Domestic manufacturing received a boost from the war but on the other hand transport was hit. Road and rail traffic were disrupted by the political instability before the war and by the pogroms against the Ibos who serviced much of the railways. During the war rail-stock, bridges, roads and vehicles were destroyed and this produced a fall in tonnages carried by the railways, as well as a fall in passenger traffic (estimated at about 20 per cent) during 1965-7. The net tonnage calling at Nigerian ports between 1966 and 1968 fell by 53.2 per cent per year.[15]

14 See Nigerian High Commission, *Why Nigeria?* p. 8; see also R.O. Ekundare, 'Nigeria's second national development plan as a weapon of social change', *African Affairs*, 70, April 1971.

15 Central Bank, *Annual Report*, 1968, p. 26.

Table 6   Sector origin of GDP by percentage (at factor cost) 1961-71, Nigeria

| Sector | 1962 | 1963 | 1964 | 1965 | 1966 | 1967 | 1968 | 1969 | 1970 | 1971* |
|---|---|---|---|---|---|---|---|---|---|---|
| Agricultural | 61.2 | 61.1 | 59.2 | 56.4 | 54.9 | 57.0 | 54.0 | 52.3 | 51.1 | 48.0 |
| Mining | 2.0 | 2.0 | 3.2 | 7.2 | 7.2 | 4.0 | 3.7 | 4.5 | 6.0 | 7.9 |
| Manufacturing | 5.8 | 5.4 | 3.3 | 5.9 | 5.9 | 7.2 | 8.5 | 9.4 | 10.2 | 10.9 |
| Transport | 4.2 | 4.3 | 4.1 | 3.4 | 3.4 | 3.3 | 3.3 | 3.3 | 3.3 | 3.1 |
| Other** | 26.9 | 26.9 | 31.2 | 28.6 | 28.6 | 28.5 | 29.5 | 29.7 | 29.1 | 28.6 |

Source: *Economic and Statistical Review*, 1970, pp.1-3, years 1962-7; *Why Nigeria?*, 1970, p.8, years 1968-71.

* The percentages for 1971 have been estimated in the source and are included as a guide to trends.

** Includes electricity and water supply, building and construction, distribution, communication, general government, education, health and other services.

### 4.    Federal and state budgets

The Federal budget was, of course, sensitive to military action and it was dislocated considerably by the war and the associated constitutional changes that broke the four-state federation into a twelve-state federation. A large transfer took place from capital expenditures by the government to current expenditures, mainly to meet the expanded defence budget. The war raised the present value of current consumption to preserve the central state, compared to the present value of uncertain future consumption.

Federal government capital expenditures for 1965-8 are shown in Table 7. Defence and law and order current expenditures increased from $40.8 million to $209.3 million, and this is probably understated.[16] The effect of this large increase in current expenditures on the capital account is shown in the 64 per cent fall in capital allocations to this heading in the table.

*Table 7    Federal capital expenditure 1965-8, Nigeria (US $ million)*

| Item | 1965 | 1966 | 1967 | 1968 | Per cent change | |
|---|---|---|---|---|---|---|
| | | | | | Capital % | Current % |
| Administration law and order | 29.8 | 26.7 | 18.0 | 10.9 | -64 | +180 |
| Social services | 12.5 | 12.5 | 4.7 | 3.1 | -76 | -34 |
| Economic services | 60.4 | 62.7 | 68.2 | 64.3 | +6 | -42 |
| Transfers | 4.7 | 42.3 | 52.5 | 18.8 | +306 | +17 |
| | 107.4 | 144.3 | 143.5 | 97.2 | -10 | -11 |

Source: 'Nigeria's post-war prospects', *West Africa*, April 1970, p.45 (Table re-arranged).

Overall    there    was    a    10    per    cent    reduction    in    capital

16 See Nafziger, op. cit., p. 230 for the suggestion that for national security reasons the true budget has not been disclosed; this position is confirmed indirectly later in this section when the wages cost of the Nigerian armed forces alone is seen to exceed the published budget in 1968.

expenditures; the two largest items cut were law and order and social services. The enormous increase in the transfer item is due to the increased public debt outlays which in 1968 led to a deficit in the Federal accounts of $185.8 million after several years in surplus.

The final column in the Table shows the percentage change in current expenditures[17] and this brings out quite clearly the transfer of expenditures in the budget caused by the emergency. Administration, law and order, etc. rose by 180 per cent, and both social services and economic services showed considerable falls in current expenditures. Transport and communication were the largest items in the economic services heading to fall and they were reduced by two thirds in 1965-8.

Table 8    *Allocation of federal budgets, Nigeria, 1967 and 1968*

| Item | 1967 (%) | 1968 (%) |
|---|---|---|
| Administration | 32 | 44 |
| (defence) | (20.8) | (35) |
| Federal contribution to states | 37.6 | 33 |
| Social and community services | 6.5 | 3.2 |
| Economic services | 6.3 | 4.6 |
| Other transfers (public debts, pensions) | 17.6 | 15.2 |
| Total | 100.0 | 100.0 |

Source:  Calculated from van de Laar, op. cit., p.4

The shift in resources in the Federal budget can be seen in Table 8. Welfare services fell from 6.5 per cent to 3.2 per cent and economic services from 6.3 per cent to 4.6 per cent. The major increase occurred in administration, mainly due to military outlays which rose from 20.8 per cent to 35 per cent, contributing to the rise from 32 per cent to 44 per cent for administration. These figures approach the normal for defence outlays in Middle Eastern countries engaged in the Arab-Israeli conflict.

17 Extracted from van de Laar, op. cit., Table 5, p 4.

Federal support for the states in the Federation is the second largest item in the budget. None of the states (with the exception of the former Eastern Region with its oil) is viable on its own, and this is the key element in the political relations between the states and the central government. In 1967 the Federal contribution to the states stood at 37.6 per cent and in 1968 at 33 per cent of the budget. Thus, whatever differences the states had with their neighbours they were united in maintaining the Federation (unless they could find a way to collect more in revenue domestically than they needed to receive from Lagos). The secessionist attempt of the Eastern Region was defeated, and therefore the central government's position as treasurer for the Federation has been strengthened since it regained access to the oil revenues.

The re-division of the states in the Federation from four to twelve also increased the power of the central government. It reduced the likelihood of new secessionist attempts because it made the individual states even less viable as small units than they were as larger units. It also added to the political problems of organising separatism because of the mechanical necessity for collusion across state boundaries if the states were to regroup before a secession was attempted.

There will inevitably be disputes between the central authorities and the local administrations in a Federation but these disputes are less likely to become critical if the sub-states are divided than if they are united into geographic regions that correspond to tribal regions. This constitutional reform came too late to avert the Biafra secession (and the war) — in one sense it precipitated both — but the defeat of the secession re-started the constitutional clock and permitted a relative peace compared to the period before the war.

## 5.    The economic cost

If the political consequences of the war were on balance positive,[18] what was the economic cost? We have seen that

18 At the time the author was sympathetic to the Biafran position. There was no evidence at the time that Nigeria as a nation was viable,

the economy and the state budgets were distorted by the war, and that the fortuitous expansion in oil extraction lessened the cost on the balance of payments. It is also clear that the special nature of the war and the way it was fought permitted the diversion of food supplies and other basic necessities into the Federal areas, holding back war inflation and damaging Biafra simultaneously, and that the stimulus to manufacturing industry started an economic boom in the country. But what was the cost in lost output? If the 1966 conflicts had been settled peacefully, or had not occurred, what would have been the peacetime growth rate in GDP?

The average annual growth rate for 1958-65 was 6.1 per cent and the 1965-6 disturbances contributed to a lower growth rate of 2.6 per cent (see Table 1). In 1966-7, the years of the coups and secession, the growth rate was negative (-4.8 per cent), and in the following year it was almost stationary (-0.2 per cent). In the midst of the war, when the military campaign was stalemated, the economy leapt forward by 13 per cent, because all the positive economic effects of the war were operating at full blast and the negative effects were postponed until the Federal forces entered Biafran territory. The first year of peace produced a growth rate of 9.6 per cent.[19]

If the 1963 GDP is taken in US dollars and the compound growth rate of 6.1 per cent calculated the expansion of GDP is as shown in Table 9. It rises from $3231.6 million to $4609.9 million in 1969 at the end of the war (there is no allowance taken of course for price inflation or the devaluation in the Nigerian pound against the dollar). The reported growth rates are applied to this same GDP for 1963 and the result is shown in column two of Table 9. (Again the actual GDP will be different due to price changes.) The third column shows the difference between the first two columns.

---

or, if it was, that it would be governable without severe repression. General Gowon's Government has, however, proved to be an enlightened and responsible administration.

19 cf. Nigerian High Commission, *Why Nigeria?*, which suggested that a much lower growth rate was attained and does not foresee a growth rate as high as 9 per cent until 1974; cf. also *West Africa*, 26 February 1973, p. 273.

Table 9   *Projected and actual performance of GDP, Nigeria 1963-69 (US $ millions)*

| Year | 6.1 per cent growth GDP | Growth GDP at recorded growth rates | Differences | % |
|------|------|------|------|------|
|      | 1    | 2    | 3 (1-2) | 4 |
| 1963 | 3231.6 | 3231.6 | 0 | 0 |
| 1964 | 3428.4 | 3428.4 | 0 | 0 |
| 1965 | 3636.7 | 3518.6 | 119.1 | 3.3 |
| 1966 | 3859.6 | 3349.2 | 510.4 | 15.2 |
| 1967 | 4092.5 | 3342.9 | 749.6 | 22.0 |
| 1968 | 4344.9 | 3797.6 | 547.3 | 14.0 |
| 1969 | 4609.9 | 4161.4 | 448.5 | 10.0 |
|      |      |      | 2374.9 | |

The original GDP figure for 1963 has been increased at a compound rate of 6.1 per cent (first column) and by the reported growth rates (second column) and the difference taken (third column). Column four is the difference in column three as a percentage of column two.

The notional costs of the war, and the political disturbances before the war, were $2374.9 million dollars. This is equivalent to 57 per cent of the 1969 hypothetical GDP or the equivalent of just over six months output. It as if the Nigerian economy stood still for seven months in economic terms. Of course, this is making the heroic assumption that the 1958-63 growth rate of 6.3 per cent would have been maintained throughout the entire period, which is by no means certain. Nevertheless it does provide a rough estimate of the possible costs.

The actual amount that can be ascribed to the war itself is a very difficult exercise and involves difficult judgments. Akene Ayida, Permanent Secretary in the Federal Ministry of Economic Development, is quoted[20] as estimating the cost of the military outlays by the Nigerian government from September 1967 to March 1969 as $840.0 million. An addition $700 million was calculated to have been lost in the destruction of physical assets, which will reduce growth in

20 A. Akene Ayida, 'Development objectives', Reconstruction and Development Conference, 1969; quoted in Nafziger, op. cit., p. 232.

the future and add further to costs and a further $211.6 million through lost exports, though some of these export losses would have been due to the adverse climatic conditions and the British devaluation.

Exports from Nigeria to Britain fell from $2293.2 million in 1966 to $1560 million in 1967 (total Nigerian exports also fell from $6212.4 million in 1966 to $5299 million in 1967).[21] The total cost of the actual fighting, according to Ayida, is $1751.6 million, or 74 per cent of the hypothetical total calculated from Table 9.

The loss to Nigeria in terms of the deaths caused by the war (mainly from starvation — though the war was relatively long contact fighting was actually a small part of it) are estimated at about two million persons, or 2 per cent of the population. The effects of this loss are near impossible to quantify; even excluding the great personal loss to their families, the cost in terms of wasted education, investment and future productive activity is incalculable. The war casualties themselves, military and civilian, represent a burden on the community for maintenance and, in many cases, hospitalisation and medical treatment. Where these casualties were formerly economically active, or likely to have been in the future in the case of children, there is also a loss of output to the community as well as a cost of sustenance. Losses among scarce, skilled and educated people will increase the economic loss to the community in the future.

### 6. The army

There are other problems arising from the period of the war which will have economic effects in the future. The most obvious is the size of Nigeria's military forces and its cost. In 1966 the army consisted of 10,500 men (511 officers),[22] and in terms of the size of Nigeria's population at 57.5

---

21 Legum and Drysdale, op. cit., p. 574.
22 IISS, *The Military Balance*, 1966-67, London, 1966; see also H. Sieve, 'Can Nigeria afford its army?', *Daily Telegraph*, London, 26 October 1971.

million this was an extremely small armed force, even by Third World standards.

The relative small sizes of the army and political elites contributed to the pre-war instability and in this respect the twelve state governments should create a more numerous political elite. In the 1966 coup, for example, the elimination of a few key personnel at the highest level of government completely broke the civilian political system. Subsequent murders within the army led to a complete change in army leadership, not without its cost in the armed forces' level of competence. The larger number of necessary targets the more secure a country's political and executive system must be.

By 1969 the army had grown to 250,000 on the Federal side alone (Biafra had an army mobilised with as many troops but they were mainly an untrained and poorly armed militia). In 1970 the Federal forces had reduced to 163,500 (army 160,000, navy 2,000 and airforce 1,500).[23] This still made it one of the largest armies in Africa. Such a rapid mobilisation in a country already divided and with a recently decimated officer corps must have diluted the leadership considerably. The lack of training facilities and the shortage of experience which characterises sub-Saharan armies must have worsened the already low efficiency levels of the military force.

To meet the heavy demands on leadership the army must have had to revert to the promotion of NCOs to provide officer material. This unavoidable aspect of Nigerianisation of the army in the late 1950s contributed to the later crisis in the army. The improvements in educational standards that had been started before the war were reversed after it. One estimate suggests that the post-commission experience in the post-war army is about 18 months on average.[24] This is hardly conducive to efficiency or to professionalism and it will take some time for the competence level to match the size of the force mobilised.

The cost to the budget of this number of men in wages

---

23 IISS, *The Military Balance, 1970-71*, London, 1971.

24 B. Dudley, 'The military and development', *Nigerian Journal of Economic and Social Studies*, 13, 2, 1971, p. 175; the implications of lack of experience before 1966 are covered in Luckham, op. cit.

alone is daunting. At $84 per man-month,[25] 250,000 men cost $252 million, 163,000 men cost $164 millions. The cost of the 1969 Nigerian army in subsistence alone exceeded the budget of $210 millions claimed by the Federal authorities to have been allocated to the military (it is also over ten times the 1965 military budget). In addition Nigeria has a 25,000-strong police force and this adds a further $25.2 millions to the wage bill.

### 7.   Conclusion

The Biafran war did not have the disastrous economic effects on the Nigerian economy that it could have had. Nigeria was assisted by the strategic circumstances of the war and the geographical factors. If Nigeria had been fighting a neighbour instead of an isolated secession these factors would not have been present and the damage to the economy might have been more severe.

Biafra was landlocked from food, materials, international aid and military resources. Nigeria was not. The oil revenues were just beginning to provide the country with the foreign exchange that it needed to finance its development programmes. A hostile neighbour at war with Nigeria would have made the oil fields a major target for bombing attacks, if not land attacks, because their strategic role in Nigeria's war effort was obvious.

The war imposed economic discipline and gave an impetus to local manufacturing and the emergency provided the kind of stimulus to economic nation-building that seven years of independence had failed to produce. The result was a cumulative force that provided the right conditions for the oil revenues to be used to push development positively. A report in 1972 considered that the transfer from the war economy generated by the secession to development activity was a major contributor to the high post-war growth rates (running at 12 per cent in 1971-2).[26]

25 Dudley, op. cit., uses a figure of £N30 per man-month.
26 'Behind the boom', *West Africa*, 26 February 1973, p. 273, quotes a Report prepared by the United Nations Economic Commission for Africa.

# 12 The Economics of War: Vietnam's Asian Neighbours

## 1. Introduction

The Vietnam war is the subject of this chapter. We are interested in the effect that this long war had on the economies of those countries that traded with it. The war is too recent to make definitive studies of the effect on Vietnam itself — there is the problem of the dearth of statistical information from a country that for long periods has had its territory in dispute. But other countries, not involved in the fighting directly, do provide statistical information on their trading links and insofar as these have been affected by the war we can examine what these effects have been. The broad conclusion that comes out of this chapter is that whatever else the war did to Vietnam, it has not inhibited the economic development of those Asian countries that supplied the imports for Vietnam's economy. We look at the Thai economy more closely to see what effects the war had due to the trading position with Vietnam and the intervention of the Americans.

## 2. Asia and the Vietnam war

The Vietnam war has had the most extensive effects on combatants and non-combatants of all wars in the Third World. The United States was riven with the political consequences of conducting the war (even more so than was the case when France was carrying the main burden of the ground fighting up to 1954), and its economic effects on the American economy were in many ways closely bound up with the political issues thrown up during the period of the war. The social and political programmes that were argued for within the American political system inevitably ended in the issue of what priorities were sacrificeable to the expense of the Vietnam war. This resulted in a diminishing credibility through time of making the war the major priority for which Americans should sacrifice the resolution of domestic problems.

The political leadership of America became increasingly divided. One side regarded the war as a moral commitment to a friendly government, in a language reminiscent of the spirit of the Korean war years, but sounding antiquated by the late 1960s. The other side raised the (other) moral issue of whether America should pour in its resources to fight a war that was an interference in another country's internal political processes; the view being that the Vietnam war was a civil war and that the choice between dictatorship from Hanoi or Saigon was one for the Vietnamese to make themselves.[1]

The vast American involvement had its effect beyond the battlefields on the economies of Asian countries, and it was on a sufficient scale to create shifts in the structure both of trade and economic activity. The economic effects of the war on the Vietnamese economy were of course substantial and will be felt for many years to come.

The demographic balance has been altered by the losses of life and other casualties occasioned by the fighting. The proportion of dependents (young, aged and disabled) has grown and the productive proportion of the population has inevitably been reduced. The nature of the fighting meant substantial losses of life among non-combatants; guerrilla war, and counter-insurgency, do not allow for non-combatants, as all are 'involved' voluntarily or involuntarily, and therefore all are open to the punitive measures of both sides. It has also led to severe dislocation of substantial numbers of the population. The presence of large numbers of foreign troops also had its social effects on the population. The

1 A.M. Schlesinger, *The Bitter Heritage: Vietnam and American Democracy, 1941-1966*, London, 1966; New York Times, *The Pentagon Papers*, New York, 1971; N. Chomsky, *American Power and the New Mandarins*, London, 1969; D. Horowitz, *From Yalta to Vietnam: American Foreign Policy in the Cold War*, London, 1965.

rebuilding of the shattered economies of North and South Vietnam will also have many problems. Very little work has so far been done on this topic, though considerable study has been carried out on the rebuilding of the European economies after the Second World War.[2]

The European economies recovered remarkably quickly given the large-scale destruction carried out during the war. The Vietnamese economy has a different set of problems because it is a different type of economy. The infra-structure created for military purposes may or may not prove to be useful in this process, as it does provide a stock of social capital. South Vietnam has had a network of major highways built, as well as harbours and airfields. The disruption of war has touched all levels of society and all corners of the country. The traditional has been confronted by the modern (sometimes in its most horrific form). The culture of Vietnam is now a hybrid of East and West. In this sense the war has disrupted the country's social, cultural and economic systems. It is not likely that aid from abroad (ironically, perhaps, from the Americans who contributed so much to the destruction) will have a similar effect on the economy as the Marshall Aid programme had in post-war Europe.

Vietnam in 1963 was a predominantly agriculture-based economy, with 70 per cent of the population engaged in agriculture. Rice was exported, and so was rubber. Exports earned $85 million in 1960 but this had fallen away to $12 million in 1970. In 1967 Vietnam imported 750,000 tons of rice, or over twice the amount of its former exports of this commodity. Agricultural output fell up to 20 per cent (either by abandoned production or insurgency 'collection'), but towards. the end of the decade output levels in secure territory had returned total output to pre-war levels by virtue

2 This topic has been of considerable interest to the disarmament lobby in the United States. The structural adjustment of the war economies after 1945 is cited as evidence that the war economies of the United States and Western Europe can adjust, without crises, to disarmament. See S. Melman (ed.), *The Defence Economy*, New York, 1963; E. Benoit and K. Boulding, *Disarmament and the Economy*, New York, 1963; United Nations, *Basic Problems of Disarmament*, New York, 1970; R.E. Bolton (ed.), *Defence and Disarmament: The Economics of Transition*, New Jersey, 1966.

of vastly improved farming methods (the Green Revolution).[3]

The import bill reached $700 million and this greatly assisted the economies of other Asian countries.[4] The military conflict also added to the expansionary force within these economies by bringing in American military spending in addition to the American military assistance provided under the aid programmes. This inflow of capital and demand into these economies ought to have had substantial economic effects and it is these that this chapter will examine.

The American military assistance delivered to Vietnam, Thailand, Philippines, Korea and Taiwan for 1960-9 was $5.8 billion or 53 per cent, out of a Third World total of $10.9 billion[5] (see Table 1).

The rank order of the recipient countries for American military assistance is Vietnam ($2509 million), Korea ($1709 million), Taiwan ($937 million), Thailand ($481 million) and Philippines ($212 million).[6] Both Taiwan and Philippines maintained a relatively steady total of annual assistance, while the other countries show marked increases over the decade. The military assistance totals for the countries have been added to the military spending by the American government for its war effort during the period and graphed in five diagrams (Figure 1).[7]

In the cases of Vietnam, Thailand, Philippines and Korea, the additional expenditure has been a substantial additional influence on total American defence-related spending. The defence-related expenditures include such headings as the purchases of local goods and services for construction of the military infra-structure (bridges, roads, airbases, harbours, camps), the payments of wages to local labour in these

3 J. Fryer, 'Home-grown food for war-torn Vietnam', *Geographical Magazine*, 42, February 1970.

4 Embassy of Vietnam, *Vietnam: Yesterday and Today*, 6, 9, October 1972, pp. 12-13.

5 SIPRI, *The Arms Trade with the Third World*, pp. 146-7.

6 ibid.

7 The details of American military assistance are from ibid. and the American military spending in the countries is from S. Naya, 'The Vietnam war and some aspects of its economic impact on Asian countries', *Developing Economies*, Tokyo, 1972.

Table 1a   US military assistance to five Asian countries, 1962-69 (US $ millions)

| Country | 1962 | 1963 | 1964 | 1965 | 1966 | 1967 | 1968 | 1969+ | 1960-69 |
|---|---|---|---|---|---|---|---|---|---|
| Thailand | 39.1 | 68.5 | 52.7 | 36.4 | 40.8 | 44.9 | 76.5 | 73. | 481.0 |
| Vietnam | 144 | 198.1 | 186.9 | 274.7 | 170 | (300) | (500) | (600) | 2509 |
| Philippines | 21.5 | 24.5 | 10.7 | 18.2 | 26.0 | 21 | 29.1 | 18.8 | 212.9 |
| Korea | 136.9 | 182.5 | 124.3 | 173.1 | 153.1 | 149.8 | 197.4 | 210 | 1709.5 |
| Taiwan | 84.4 | 85.2 | 128.1 | 84.8 | 76.5 | 71.3 | 117.2 | 55.3 | 937.2 |

Source:   Military Assistance and Foreign Military Sales Facts, May 1967 and March 1969; Military Assistance Facts, March 1968 and May 1969, in Table 3.6, SIPRI, The Arms Trade with the Third World, pp. 146-7.

Table 1b   US defence expenditures abroad for goods and services (1962-69) (US $ millions)

| Country | 1962 | 1963 | 1964 | 1965 | 1966 | 1967 | 1968 |
|---|---|---|---|---|---|---|---|
| Thailand | 28.5* | 34.0 | 70.0 | 183.0 | 286.0 | 318.0 | 278.0 |
| Vietnam | 44.5 | 64.0 | 188.0 | 408.0 | 564.0 | 558.0 | 606.0 |
| Philippines | 48.5 | 58.0 | 81.0 | 147.0 | 167.0 | 169.0 | 180.0 |
| Korea | 96.5 | 91.0 | 97.0 | 160.0 | 237.0 | 301.0 | 360.0 |
| Taiwan | 21.0 | 21.0 | 21.0 | 60.0 | 70.0 | 76.0 | 84.0 |
| Total | 239.0 | 268.0 | 457.0 | 958.0 | 1324.0 | 1422.0 | 1508.0 |

Source:   C.E. Shepler and L.G. Campbell, 'United States defence expenditure abroad', Survey of Current Business, 49,

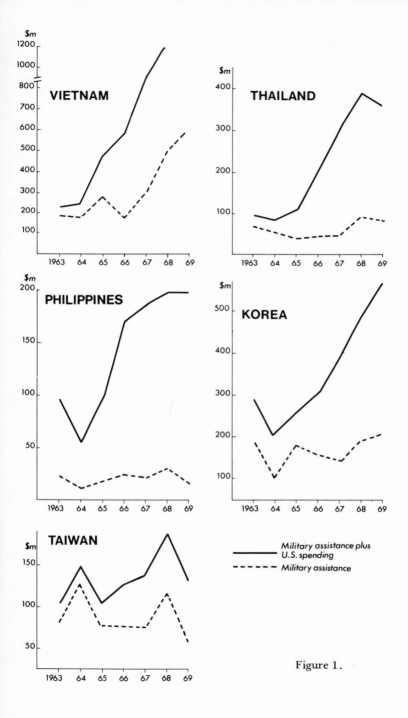

Figure 1.

installations, and the expenditures of US official personnel and their dependents in the local economies. Insofar as these figures can be accurately estimated they show an American influence several times greater than the apparent influence of the military assistance programme. The Vietnam war effort led to substantial official defence-related injections into the local economies, but the impact of the war did not end there.

The turn-around in trade balance of the Vietnamese economy, alluded to above, had the major effect of creating a massive trade deficit in Vietnam. To the extent that the Asian countries supplied the exports that Vietnam received in the period they can be said to have gained economically from Vietnam's war-induced requirements. If the former importers of Vietnam's rice exports, faced with an end to rice supplies from Vietnam, switched their imports to other Asian countries, they can also be said to have generated further economic advantages to those other countries. (Of course, this may simply have raised the price of rice for everyone and the gain may be less direct.)[8] Moreover the Americans themselves may also have increased their imports from Asia as a result of the war, and this too would have benefited the economies.

One result of the general improvement in economic performance would be an induced expansion in the economies in such indicators as per capita income or GNP, and this itself would be responsible for secondary rounds of economic activity. The defence-related expenditures additional to direct military assistance were running at over $1 billion a year from 1967, compared with under $0.2 billion in 1963 for the group of countries in Table 1b. This is a substantial intervention in their economies.

The increase in American military spending in these countries is related to their political positions over the Vietnam issue. Korea in 1965 received an American commitment to equip and train three of the ten reserve divisions of the Korean Army in exchange for the dispatch to Vietnam of 50,000 Korean troops, and in 1966 large quantities of armour and equipment began to arrive in the country,

8 There is evidence that this took place in Thailand's case. The higher price of rice (not all of it due to direct exports to Vietnam) raised producer prices and raised the incomes of Thai citizens.

pushing up the local defence expenditures due to the American military effort from $97 million in 1965 to $160 million in 1966 (Table 1*b*).

The 'Pueblo Incident' in 1968, in which a United States Navy 'spy' boat was captured by the North Koreans, raised military tensions considerably in the peninsular.[9] The Americans responded by raising their military expenditures in Korea and also by supplying new naval and airforce equipment, partly to prepare for any emergency (it was possible that the North could put pressure on the South while America was heavily engaged in Vietnam — 1968 was the year of the 'Tet' offensive by the Communists) and partly to enable the sophisticated espionage activity, using electronic devices, to continue without the risks involved in lightly armed naval craft such as the 'Pueblo'. The tension created by the incident dropped away, however; but not before the extra outlays had been made.

The Philippines were also offered special assistance in exchange for participation in Vietnam. The government accepted an American commitment to equip a Philippines engineer task-force for Vietnam (which would have uses when it rotated back to home base) and an American subsidy to cover overseas allowances in excess of Philippine regular army pay for the troops sent to Vietnam. Other offers to send extra patrol boats to the Philippines, and also to fund the equipment of three engineer construction battalions and to pay for a complete replacement unit for the troops in Vietnam, were turned down by President Marcos, even though this expense was to be met by the Americans out of its Vietnam war funds and not from the normal military assistance programme.[10]

Thailand's support for America in Vietnam, and its use of its strategic position close to the 'Ho Chi Min trail', was rewarded on an even more generous scale than either Korea or Philippines. Korea already had a substantial American ground involvement before the Vietnam war which pumped millions of dollars into the economy. Thailand's pro-American position was matched by the growth of US

9 SIPRI, op. cit., p. 417.
10 ibid., p. 459.

personnel in the country from 300 in 1960 to 45,000 in 1968. The bases from which the Americans operated were technically under the control of the Thailand government and were financed directly out of the American Department of Defence budget rather than through a Military Assistance Programme.[11] Thai forces were active in Laos and Vietnam and the Americans undertook to modernise the Thai army and train it in the use of Counter-Insurgency (COIN) techniques. In 1966 US contractors of military installations began operations on a major scale. This meant a direct grant to the Thai government of $86 million over the next five years,[12] though an even larger contribution to the Thai economy came from the personnel expenditures of the US army and officials ($800 millions).

Other countries to gain from this kind of spending were the 'Rest and Recuperation' centres for US army personnel, such as were set up in Hong Kong, Singapore, Malaysia, Japan and Australia.

The expansion of exports from Asian countries to Vietnam is shown in Table 2.

Korea increased its exports by a factor of 970 and Thailand by 635. With the exception of Taiwan and Singapore, the share of exports to Vietnam in a country's total exports is quite small (under 4 per cent).

Cambodia's trade with Vietnam fell during the period from the pre-war 1963 to the mid-war year in 1967. In every other case trade with Vietnam expanded. Japan was responsible for 40 per cent of Asian trade with Vietnam, Taiwan for 20 per cent and Singapore for 24 per cent. (Singapore's exports to Vietnam were mainly petroleum products – 70 per cent in 1968 and 88 per cent in 1969.)[13] The total of $385 million from Asia represented about half of Vietnam's imports and this is comparable with, for example, the share

11 ibid., p. 449: Foreign Assistance Act, 1969, Hearings before the Committee on Foreign Relations, U.S. Senate, 91st Congress, 1st Session, Washington, 1969, p. 290.

12 Bank of Thailand, unpublished tables, 1972 (Thai Baht converted to US dollars: US $1 = B20.80).

13 *Far Eastern Economic Review*, 'Focus: Malaysia, 1972', 26 August 1972, p. 20.

Table 2 *Exports to Vietnam by Asian countries, 1962-63 and 1966-67 ($US millions)*

| | *1962-63* 1 | *1966-67* 2 | *Increase* 2 - 1 1 | *Exports to Vietnam as % total exports* 1962-63 | 1966-67 |
|---|---|---|---|---|---|
| Total Asia | 103.8 | 385.8 | 272 | 0.9 | 2.1 |
| Taiwan | 26.4 | 79.1 | 200 | 9.7 | 13.4 |
| Singapore | 18.8 | 91.8 | 388 | 1.7 | 8.2 |
| Korea | 1.0 | 10.7 | 970 | 1.4 | 3.8 |
| Thailand | 2.0 | 14.7 | 635 | 0.4 | 2.1 |
| Japan | 46.7 | 156.5 | 235 | 0.9 | 1.6 |
| Hong Kong | 2.9 | 21.0 | 624 | 0.4 | 1.5 |
| Cambodia | 1.3 | 9.5 | -62 | 1.8 | 0.7 |
| Malaysia | 0.0 | 3.4 | — | 0.0 | 0.3 |
| India | 3.5 | 5.0 | 43 | 0.2 | 0.3 |
| Philippines | 0.6 | 2.1 | 250 | 0.1 | 0.3 |
| Pakistan | 0.6 | 1.0 | 67 | 0.1 | 0.2 |

Source: Naya, op. cit., Table 4, adjusted and re-arranged; all numbers rounded.

of Thailand's trade with Asian countries which was 54.5 per cent of its total trade in 1969.[14] The Vietnam war was not increasing Vietnam's dependence on the developed countries for imports during this period because intra-regional trade was maintained at a high level.

There were changes in the direction of intra-regional export trade. Taiwan, Korea, Thailand, Malaysia and Vietnam increased the share of their total export trade with the United States between 1962 and 1967 and, in the cases of Taiwan, Korea and Thailand, this was at the expense of Asian trade. Malaysia appears to have increased its American trade at the expense of its Japanese trade.[15]

Naya[16] examined the commodity composition of Asian trade with Vietnam to see if there were any pointers as to the economic effects of the war on their economies. His method was to take the Standard International Trade Classification and, using average export values for 1966 and 1967, to take

14 Thailand, Department of Customs, unpublished returns, 1972.
15 Naya, op. cit.
16 ibid., pp. 45-6.

each export item for Vietnam as a percentage of total exports to Vietnam and then as a percentage of total exports to all countries. By comparing these percentages it was possible to see if the item was more, or less, important in Vietnam trade than it was in total trade.

He found that for most Asian countries there was a pronounced difference in the commodity mix between their exports to Vietnam and their exports as a whole. Thai and Malaysian exports were concentrated in rice (Thailand, 74.7 per cent) and petroleum (Malaysia, 87.3 per cent). Pakistan, Philippines, Taiwan, Korea, Hong Kong, Singapore and Japan were heavily concentrated on industrial products, though both Hong Kong and Japan exported a more 'normal' mix to Vietnam in comparison with their total exports. Though Vietnam's market was limited, the concentration of its imports from Asian countries in certain lines is quite marked. For example, Taiwain directed 85 per cent of its total exports of cement, 75 per cent of its chemical fertiliser, 72 per cent of its iron and steel and nearly half of its machinery to Vietnam. Korea sent 94 per cent of its steel products, 50 per cent of its transport equipment and 50 per cent each of its chemical products and non-electrical machinery. Philippines sent 100 per cent of its iron and steel sheets (worth $33 million) and Singapore 53 per cent of its finished structural products.[17]

These commodities are of importance to the economies of the countries of origin. They are manufactured goods and as such are important to the development of a domestic manufacturing capacity. Naya attempted to analyse the linkage effects of these products on the economies of Taiwan, Korea and Japan. His conclusions are that the type of products that have been exported in high proportions to Vietnam as a result of the hostilities had, in the main, high import-inducing effects on the Asian economies. In other words, in order to produce these items for export to Vietnam these countries had to raise their imports of the inputs needed to produce them. This had the effect of introducing into these economies new imports, techniques and experiences that would otherwise not have been available.

17 ibid., p. 49.

The Vietnam conflict has provided Taiwan and Korea a greater learning effect in producing and exporting new industrial products than would have occured under normal conditions. Their production of these products is expected to be, at least in the beginning, more import-inducing than that of 'normal' exports . . . But the large import content of these products substantially reduces their net export receipts . . . more than half the value of Taiwan's exports to Vietnam is spent for induced imports in comparison with 33 per cent for its total exports. Similarly for Korea, induced imports are 40.7 per cent of its exports to Vietnam but only 11.4 per cent of its total exports. In recent years, the two largest suppliers of these countries' imports have been Japan and the US . . . Their imports from these developed countries, especially Japan, typically consist of producer and capital goods. Therefore, it is likely that a substantial share of Taiwan's and Korea's induced imports for exports to Vietnam comes from Japan and the US.[18]

### 3. Thailand

The effect of the war-related American expenditures on the Thai economy can be seen by looking at some of the important indicators of industrialisation over the period of the war. The agricultural sector of Thailand fell steadily to 29 per cent in 1970 (see Table 3). In Third World terms this is a relatively low percentage share of GDP for this sector (it approaches south European standards; compare it with Pakistan for example). Manufacturing was responsible for 14 per cent in 1966 and this rose slightly to 14.9 per cent by 1970. In absolute terms agriculture grew by about 16 per cent (1962 constant prices) and manufacturing by 50 per cent. The growth rates for the sectors are also shown in the table in brackets.

On the expenditure side public and private consumption accounted for 85 per cent of the GDP in 1960 and by 1969 this had fallen to 78 per cent. Gross investment in the same period rose from 16 per cent to 25 per cent and expenditure on the trade deficit rose from 1.4 per cent of GDP to 3.3 per cent. The rates of growth of consumption averaged 8.7 per cent for 1966-9 compared to 17 per cent for gross invest-ment. The Thailand economy was clearly on the right allocative path for sustained growth, as a result of the

18 ibid.

Table 3   Thailand: gross domestic product by sector origin percentage distribution at current market prices and growth per cent at constant 1962 prices

| Source | 1966 (%) | 1967 (%) | 1968 (%) | 1969 (%) | 1970 (%) |
|---|---|---|---|---|---|
| 1. Agriculture | 36.5 | 32.5 | 31.5 | 31.9 | 29.6 |
| Growth | (13.8) | (-5.9) | (7.3) | (10.1) | (2.9) |
| 2. Mining/quarry | 1.9 | 1.9 | 1.8 | 1.9 | 2.2 |
| Growth | (18.8) | (14.9) | (9.2) | (7.4) | (3.8) |
| 3. Manufacturing | 13.7 | 14.8 | 15.0 | 14.7 | 14.9 |
| Growth | (11.7) | (9.9) | (10.1) | (10.6) | (7.4) |
| 4. Construction | 6.1 | 6.8 | 7.0 | 6.6 | 7.0 |
| Growth | (21.5) | (19.0) | (8.9) | (4.6) | (5.5) |
| 5. Electricity/water supply | 0.9 | 1.0 | 1.1 | 1.2 | 1.4 |
| Growth | (32.9) | (21.4) | (21.0) | (20.1) | (17.7) |
| 6. Transport/communication | 6.2 | 6.3 | 6.2 | 6.1 | 6.3 |
| Growth | (7.2) | (8.5) | (5.2) | (11.3) | (6.5) |
| 7. Wholesale and retail trade | 16.8 | 17.5 | 17.3 | 17.5 | 17.2 |
| Growth | (10.2) | (12.3) | (8.6) | (9.1) | (3.7) |
| 8. Banking/insurance | 2.8 | 3.2 | 3.5 | 3.7 | 4.1 |
| Growth | (22.7) | (17.2) | (16.2) | (15.7) | (15.4) |
| 9. Ownership of dwellings | 2.2 | 2.1 | 2.1 | 2.0 | 2.0 |
| Growth | (3.9) | (4.0) | (4.1) | (4.6) | (5.4) |
| 10. Public admin./defence | 3.8 | 4.0 | 4.3 | 4.3 | 4.7 |
| Growth | (2.4) | (8.1) | (14.0) | (9.2) | (12.6) |
| 11. Other | 9.1 | 9.8 | 10.3 | 10.2) | 10.7 |
| Growth | (9.9) | (10.0) | (11.1) | (7.4) | (9.7) |
| 12. GDP Growth | (12.2) | (5.5) | (9.0) | (9.6) | (6.0) |

Source: International Bank for Reconstruction and Development (IBRD), *Current Economic Position and Prospects of Thailand*, Vol. 2, Statistical Appendix, January 11, 1972, Tables 2.1a and 2.2a.

external trading relations and the inflows into the economy, but these were threatened by the rundown in hostilities in Vietnam and the prospect of peace.

The breakdown of imports into Thailand is of interest to this aspect of the analysis. In Table 4 the increases in imports

Table 4a *Thailand: imports by end-use, 1966-70, in US $ millions*

|  | 1966 | 1967 | 1968 | 1969 | 1970 |
|---|---|---|---|---|---|
| Consumer goods | 226.7 | 256.5 | 255.9 | 284.0 | 260.1 |
| Non-durable | 155.0 | 171.1 | 165.5 | 174.0 | 167.6 |
| Durable | 71.7 | 85.4 | 90.4 | 110.0 | 92.5 |
| Capital goods | 274.1 | 362.6 | 400.9 | 441.0 | 450.5 |
| Intermediate goods | 189.5 | 227.7 | 244.5 | 282.1 | 321.8 |
| For consumer goods | 122.7 | 143.8 | 154.2 | 180.8 | 197.5 |
| For capital goods | 66.8 | 85.9 | 90.3 | 101.3 | 124.3 |
| Other | 199.4 | 219.9 | 257.5 | 241.3 | 266.1 |
| Vehicles and parts | 88.4 | 113.5 | 133.2 | 121.3 | 106.0 |
| Fuels, lubricants | 90.0 | 76.3 | 95.9 | 87.9 | 112.0 |
| Other | 21.0 | 30.1 | 28.4 | 32.1 | 48.1 |
| Total | 889.7 | 1,066.7 | 1,158.8 | 1,248.4 | 1,298.5 |

Table 4B *Thailand: imports by end-use, as percentage of total imports*

|  | 1966 | 1967 | 1968 | 1969 | 1970 |
|---|---|---|---|---|---|
| Consumer goods | 25.5 | 24.0 | 22.1 | 22.7 | 20.0 |
| Non-durable | 17.4 | 16.0 | 14.3 | 13.9 | 12.9 |
| Durable | 8.1 | 8.0 | 7.8 | 8.8 | 7.1 |
| Capital goods | 30.8 | 34.0 | 34.6 | 35.3 | 34.7 |
| Intermediate goods | 21.3 | 21.4 | 21.1 | 22.6 | 24.8 |
| For consumer goods | 13.8 | 13.4 | 13.3 | 14.5 | 15.2 |
| For capital goods | 7.5 | 8.0 | 7.8 | 8.1 | 9.6 |
| Other | 22.4 | 20.6 | 22.2 | 19.4 | 20.5 |
| Vehicles and parts | 10.0 | 10.6 | 11.5 | 9.7 | 8.2 |
| Fuels, lubricants | 10.1 | 7.2 | 8.3 | 7.1 | 8.6 |
| Other | 2.3 | 2.8 | 2.4 | 2.6 | 3.7 |
| Total | 100.0 | 100.0 | 100.0 | 100.0 | 100.0 |

Source: Bank of Thailand *Monthly Bulletin.*

according to the headings and sub-headings are shown. From this table the following points can be made. First, capital imports have doubled between 1966 and 1970, and the imports of intermediate goods and raw materials (to be processed mainly for consumer goods) have also doubled. Secondly, consumer goods have increased by less than a quarter in the same period. The picture overall is a rapid expansion of imports for capital purposes, either as finished products or as intermediate products, and a less rapid expansion in consumer imports.

The expanding economy, with its rising incomes, was working both to alter its structural composition (for the generation of the national product) and to shift its import composition towards industrialising activity: imports of capital goods prepare the base for import substitution, and imports of durable consumer goods widen the market possibilities for future manufacturing capacity.

The problem with war expenditures is that they are sensitive not to the needs of an economy but to the strategic interests of the war. The American direct involvement in the war terminated with the signing of the 'peace' agreement in January 1973. But long before then the American military presence was being run down. Those expenditures that arose directly from the combat position of the United States were greatly reduced in the two years before the 1973 cease-fire. With thousands of American troops being repatriated out of the Vietnam theatre the 'Rest and Recuperation' spending of troops in other countries declined proportionately. Thus those countries that gained from this source of income had to face corresponding adjustments over which they had no control. The problems of peace however are not likely to mean a similar economic disengagement in Vietnam itself. The Vietnam trade deficit will probably require a continuation of the import-induced activity in the Asian countries looked at so far.

The prospects for Thailand in 1969-70 did not look as encouraging as they did in 1973. The adjustment to a peace economy raised serious fears of a slide into depression.[19]

19 ibid.

Table 5    Thailand, balance of payments and international reserves

| | 1965 | 1966 | 1967 | 1968 | 1969 | 1970 | 1971 | 1972* |
|---|---|---|---|---|---|---|---|---|
| Trade deficit (million US $)** | 115 | 211 | 384 | 500 | 538 | 576 | 451 | 153 |
| Foreign exchange reserves (million US $) | 705 | 864 | 916 | 938 | 894 | 767 | 766 | 877 |
| Deficit as % of reserves | 16.3 | 24.4 | 41.9 | 53.3 | 60.1 | 75.0 | 58.8 | 17.4 |

Source: Bangkok Bank, *Monthly Review*, 13, 9, September 1972, p.410; Bank of Thailand, *Monthly Bulletin*, 12, 8, August 1972, p.72.
* Estimated.
** Converted from Thailand Bhat at $1 = 20.8 Bhat and rounded.

The trade deficit (excluding military imports) rose sharply from 1965 to 1970, but this was covered by the foreign exchange reserves, though the deficit ratio rose alarmingly in 1970. The pressure on Thailand to expand its exports in the face of possible reductions in US military spending was urgent because reserves were vulnerable if the capital grants from America were withdrawn. The foreign exchange reserves provided a possible cushion for the transformation period, but this was dependent upon the managerial competence of the government.

There was a change in government in 1971, with the object of getting these economic problems under control. A National Executive Council emerged with strong powers to conduct the economic transformation. This in itself set off some new problems with particular reference to the massive Japanese intervention into the Thai economy.[20] Thai nationalism in economic affairs is not an entirely abstract concept; it is felt acutely among business and middle-class circles and is a source of criticism if the government is not seen to be handling Thai interests with partisan diligence. As it was, several external events took place that gave the Thai

20 B. Roberts, 'Thailand's economy: in need of a positive lead', *Financial Times*, London, January 1972.

economy some smaller boosts which, along with the not entirely unexpected decision of the Americans to continue their presence in Thailand beyond the termination of the Vietnam war, set the economy on an optimistic line of development.

The Philippines experienced severe flooding in 1971 necessitating rice imports of 300,000 metric tons and this had a major impact on Thai exports of rice in the region. Thailand's rice exports rose 56.2 per cent in volume in 1971.[21] The Indo-Pakistan war in 1971 and food shortages in Cambodia had similar beneficial effects on Thai rice exports. Other benefits to Thailand's commodity trade were the jute scarcities from the Bangladesh war, a shortage of American maize (Thailand's exports in 1971 rose 33.4 per cent in volume and 21.2 per cent in value) and a shortfall in the Cuban sugar harvest. The 1971 increases in Thai exports over 1970 are shown in Table 6.

*Table 6    Thailand, percentage increases in volume and value of major exports 1971 over 1970*

|            | Volume | Value |
|------------|--------|-------|
| Rice       | 56.2   | 15.3  |
| Rubber     | 11.7   | -14.8 |
| Maize      | 33.4   | 21.2  |
| Tin        | -2.4   | -3.5  |
| Jute       | 5.2    | 29.8  |
| Teak woods | 38.2   | 30.6  |
| Tapioca    | -16.2  | 0.5   |

Source:   Bangkok Bank, *Monthly Review*, op. cit., pp. 411-13.

The windfall gains of rising commodity export prices helped reduce the trade deficit in 1971 and this process continued in 1972. The other helpful push to the economy was the American decision to retain its airforce and army personnel in the country. This meant that the American economic input into Thailand in 1973 would be worth US $201 million[22] which is comparable with the peak year of

21 Bangkok Bank, *Monthly Review*, pp. 394-5.
22 ibid., p. 383.

1968 of US $206 million and nearly double the 1971 total of US $115 million.

Thailand's new strategic significance in south-east Asia for American foreign policy, following the withdrawal from Vietnam, and the increased pressure on the Thai government from the Communist insurgents in the north-east of the country, means that the Thailand economy is set to continue its insurgency-generated economic inflow for the next few years.

### 4. Conclusion

Vietnam faces the enormous problem of redressing the deficit on the balance of payments and adjusting from a war-distorted economy to a peaceful line of development. In 1968 the deficit on the balance of payments came to something like 20 per cent of the GNP,[23] and it was even larger in 1971. About a sixth of this deficit was made up of non-essential imports such as motorbikes, clothing, radios and television sets, which accounted for nearly US $100 million in 1968.[24] The government also announced a policy of utilising the social overhead capital provided as a by-product of the war (airfields, port facilities, warehouses, hospitals, barracks, communications equipment etc.) by combining it with the pool of trained and skilled men in the armed services to commence a programme of reconstruction. This programme should feature an austerity drive against consumer luxuries by heavy taxation of imports of these items along with determined efforts to modernise agriculture, particularly in rice production.

The plans are one thing and their implementation another. Vietnam's notorious corruption may make the import tax

23 Pham Kim Ngoc, *Economic Independence for Vietnam*, Saigon, 1970, p. 2.

24 The mass import of consumer durables was a deliberate war policy of the Saigon government. If the population accepted Western goods they might reject those who would take them away, i.e. the Viet Cong. The scheme was probably too subtle and it also added to consumption and war weariness — none of these alternative consumer goods were available 'up country' where the fighting was concentrated, which increased the attractions of avoiding war service.

policy ineffective. Increased rice production presupposes that the countryside is secure. The heavy capital investment required to meet the needs of development is bound to be a difficult problem for a country in which the political issues are not yet settled and where the destruction of human and capital resources by the war has created a major development gap between potential and actual possibilities. This must make questionable the immediate future of economic development in Vietnam.

This war certainly benefited economically Vietnam's Asian trading partners (Korea, Japan, Malaysia, Singapore, Thailand, Philippines), and from the experience of Thailand the war's end does not necessarily signify an economic crisis. It will be some time however, before it is clear whether Vietnam itself will be able to turn the positive benefits of the war into development against the overwhelming negative costs of the destruction wrought in the fighting.

# 13 The Economics of War: Israel, Egypt and Pakistan

## 1. Introduction

The two wars discussed in this chapter are both marked by their shortness: the 1967 six-day Israeli-Arab war and the 1965 seventeen-day Indo-Pakistan war. But the effects of these wars on the countries concerned were much more long-term. The Israeli war had an immediate and beneficial effect on the economy, but the aftermath of occupation and continuous alert status for the armed forces has had less beneficial effects. The Egyptian economy neither gained nor lost economically from the war — it simply continued to lag in every field. For Pakistan the 1965 war was a costly mistake — the military imperatives overrode the economic necessities. A downturn in the economic indicators is marked by this war. In this sense the 'Six Day' and 'Seventeen Day' wars were misnamed.

## 2. Israel

Military preparations and the nation-building process are inseparable in the Middle East. The existence of Israel as a non-Arab state is a reference point for the nationalist and pan-Arab forces. In Israel the fragmented political groups are at least united on the issue of the survival of Israel. The record of achievement of the two opposing forces in the region is to some extent a measure of the relative successes of each side in the task of nation-building. The Israelis have shown a consistent capability in defending their state's right to exist (contrast this with the performance of the South Vietnamese), while the Arab states have shown a poorer record and were probably further away from success than they were in 1948. This does not mean that the current balance of capability will continue indefinitely.

The older generation in Israel have been totally committed to the survival of the state; they have been divided, and sometimes violently divided, but their overriding concern was how to ensure the existence of Israel. With the younger generation the picture is less clear. A minority of them are not immune to world trends among politically motivated left-wing youth and they are less committed to the survival of Israel by the old methods of victory in battle. They tend to support policies of reconciliation and, equally significant, they may indulge in activities aimed at extending what they understand as social justice, secularism and social change, which in the context of beleaguered Israel undermines the monolithic unity against the Arabs. It is by no means surprising that the Israeli public's reaction to the discovery of Jewish nationals involved with a Syrian spy ring in 1973 should have been one of disbelief followed by dismay.[1]

In the Arab states a reverse process is at work. The older generation are identified with defeatism and the younger generation with militant opposition to Israel. The political leadership, facing the impasse of the poverty of their policies, are confronted by a rebellious youth demanding a policy of no concessions to Israel. The guerrilla groups are staffed and inspired by young and educated Arabs:[2] the governments are composed of the previous generation. While the Israeli generation gap pushes against the monolithic determination to survive at all costs, the Arab generation gap pushes the Arabs into greater intensities of hostility to Israel and more determined activity. The youthful Colonel Ghaddafy of Libya

1 The discovery of the complicity of some young Jews in a Syrian spy ring in December 1972 is reported to have shocked Israeli public opinion. It is interesting to note that the Jewish members of the spy ring were in their twenties, that one of them was the son of a well-known Communist and that upon conviction in the Court to terms of imprisonment they sang the 'Internationale'. The disaffection of a minority of young Israelis from the official policy of the survival of the State of Israel, as conceived by its founders, has become a matter of serious concern to the Israeli population as a whole.

2 Y. Kuroda, 'Young Palestinian commandoes in political socialisation perspective', *Middle East Journal*, 26, 3, 1972.

has attempted to get to the head of this generation and in so doing must fight for Arab leadership against the veteran Sadat of Egypt. The next years in the Middle East will to a large extent be a contest between the new generations on either side of the divide, and both will be working under different pressures from those faced by their forebears.

In this section we will look at the economic effect of the 1967 war on the economies of Egypt and Israel. This war was in many ways the crowning success of the first generation of Israelis — everything they represented in tenacity, valour, skill and superiority over the Arabs, was epitomised in the military successes of the Six Day War. In the same way the inability of the government to get a political settlement after their military victory, and the 'neither-war-nor-peace' status of the belligerents that has continued to 1973, are also an expression of the weakness of the Israeli state as conceived in its current form. Israel has survived up to now against overt Arab hostility because its nationalism has proven superior in organisation and determination to Arabic nationalism. As long as this is true the Arabs cannot defeat the Israelis in battle.[3] But Israel cannot get a peace, or security, without the co-operation of the Arabs.

3 See R. Verna, 'Z'va Haganah be Israel', 1 and 2, *Armies and Weapons*, London, 1 and 2, 1972-1973. The Israeli armed forces are geared to blitzkreig strategy — i.e. lightening thrusts at an opponent to gain a quick decision. The Israelis might not be able to sustain a front war, especially if the Arabs could keep them fighting for over a month. The Germans faced the same military problem in 1941; see A. Millward, *The German War Economy*, London, 1968. There is no sign that the Arab armies could hold the Israelis for a long enough time to alter the military balance. Israel's troops are psychologically and militarily geared for assault deep into enemy territory and the seizure of defensive positions (Suez, Golan, West Bank) which become major obstacles for Arab counter-attack. But if an Arab army could hold and engage the Israelis in a static way for some weeks, or if the Israelis advanced beyond where they could be serviced, the military decision could go to the Arabs. Israel, for example, may have reached the territorial limits that it can hold for the time being — to try to capture North Africa, for example, would turn the war into a prolonged affair. See also C. Douglas-Home, 'Long-term pressures on a nation in arms', *The Times*, London, 18 November 1970.

The 1973 War has borne out this analysis: the capability gap between Israel and Egypt is closing.

The Israeli economy was in recession for the two years before the 1967 war.[4] The growth rate of GNP had fallen from 10.8 per cent (1961-4) to 8.4 per cent (1965), and it fell again to 1.5 per cent in 1966. In Table 1 the percentage change in some of the economic indicators is shown. 1967 is the dividing line in performance. The per capita GNP, gross and net investment, and employment either had negative growth rates compared with 1961-6 or worsened already negative growth rates. Other indicators, such as growth of output, growth of output per worker, and growth of public consumption compare unfavourably in 1966 with 1965 and the evidence for 1967 supports the view that the economy was slowing down. After the war the 1968 growth rates of the indicators show strong recovery. GNP leapt from a 1.4 per cent growth rate to 14.2 per cent and in 1969 this was followed by a 12 per cent growth. GNP per capita, which stagnated into a negative growth in 1967, jumped to 11 per cent growth rate in 1968. Gross investment reached the staggering growth rate of 45.2 per cent in 1968 while net investment hit 87.6 per cent. Output was up 28.6 per cent and output per worker up 11.9 per cent. Diamond exports, which are important to Israel's trade balance, raised their growth rate from -4.4 per cent to 22.9 per cent and other industrial exports trebled their growth rates.

Public consumption rose dramatically in 1967 from 8.3 per cent to 26.8 per cent which is to be expected following the war mobilisation. High growth rates were also sustained for public consumption in the succeeding two years, and this is also to be expected in the circumstances of the occupation of vast territory and the stand-by status of the military before and after the cease-fire. The expansion in the money supply may be partly due to this situation.

The 'Resources' heading is composed of the GNP and the import surplus, and this confirms the general picture of a

4 Kanovsky, op. cit. Much use has been made in this chapter of Kanovsky's thesis, though my conclusions are not necessarily the same as Kanovsky's. See also: M. Allen, 'Israel gears her economy to siege conditions', *The Times*, London, 22 September 1970; D. Spanier, 'Budgeting for guns and butter', *The Times*, London, 18 November 1970.

slow-down to 1967 and a rapid expansion of available economic resources following the war. All in all, the picture of the Israeli economy in the post-war period is one of economic boom.

Table 1 *Israel: average annual percentage change in selected economic indicators 1961-1969*

|  | Pre-war | | | Post-war | | |
|---|---|---|---|---|---|---|
| *Indicator* | *1961-64* | *1965* | *1966* | *1967* | *1968* | *1969* |
| GNP | 10.8 | 8.4 | 1.5 | 1.4 | 14.2 | 12.0 |
| GNP per capita | 6.5 | 4.8 | -1.1 | -1.8 | 11.0 | 8.0 |
| Private consumption per capita | 6.5 | 4.6 | 0.5 | -1.7 | 7.4 | 8.5 |
| Public consumption | 10.6 | 10.5 | 8.3 | 26.8 | 13.4 | 10.0 |
| Output | 15.2 | 9.9 | 1.4 | -3.1 | 28.6 | 18.0 |
| Output per worker | 6.3 | 8.3 | 3.4 | 2.4 | 11.9 | 6.0 |
| Gross investment | 14.5 | -1.3 | -14.8 | -28.1 | 45.2 | 25.0 |
| Net investment | 12.9 | -8.2 | -25.3 | -22.4 | 87.6 | 35.0 |
| Employment | 5.2 | 3.0 | -0.6 | -4.2 | 9.0 | 11.0 |
| Diamond exports | 20.5 | 11.6 | 25.1 | -4.4 | 22.9 | 13.0 |
| Other industrial exports | 15.9 | 12.7 | 14.3 | 9.1 | 26.1 | 17.0 |
| Wages | 12.0 | 18.4 | 19.8 | 3.3 | -0.3 | |
| Cost of living index | 7.3 | 7.7 | 8.0 | 1.6 | 2.1 | |
| Money supply | 19.8 | 9.0 | 7.3 | 20.3 | 19.0 | |
| Resources | 11.6 | 6.0 | -0.4 | 1.3 | 16.3 | |

Sources: Bank of Israel, *Annual Reports*, Israel; *Israel's Economic Development − Past Progress and Plan for the Future*, Jerusalem, 1968; Central Bureau of Statistics, *Monthly Bulletin of Statistics*, September 1969; quoted in Kanovsky, op. cit., Tables 1, 3 and 4, pp.87, 103 and 108 (data re-arranged).

Notes: Average annual changes 1961-64 refer to annual averages for these years; employment refers to changes in annual average number employed, including employers and self-employed, but not to hours worked; the cost of living index refers to changes in annual average.

The government attempted to reflate the economy in the latter part of 1966 and authorised public works programmes to take up the slack in the employment sector. Without the war the time period from recession to boom might have been stretched into 1968, or longer;[5] the war speeded the process up considerably.

While the war may have had fortuitous consequences for the economy in moving the country from recession to an earlier boom, it was not of course without costs. Table 2 shows the costs of the Six Day War in non-recoverable losses. These totalled $91.6 million and can be compared with the nominal value of captured munitions and military hardware, estimated at $167 million.[6] These costs do not include the defence costs themselves for the war, nor the costs of the subsequent occupation or the costs of continuing confrontation with the defeated Arab states. The magnitudes of these costs are uncertain, but there is no doubt as to their upwards direction.

The Finance Minister made various estimates of the total cost of the war during 1967: his July figure was $567 million, his November figure $750 million and his December figure $950 million, all of them influenced by the occupation and associated costs after the six days of actual fighting.[7] In this sense the 'cost' of the Six Day War is an inadequate calculation because the war created additional and burdensome costs to the economy which cannot really be separated.

In 1968 the Israeli defence budget reached $657 million or 18 per cent of GNP, and this rose to $833 million for 1970. The arms purchase abroad accounted for half of the balance of payments deficit in 1968 (standing at $696 million).[8] The post-war arms race in the region ensured that defence spending remained at a high level; the deficit rose to $880 million in 1969, of which $450 million was due to arms

5 Minister of Commerce and Industry, *Jerusalem Post Weekly*, 2 January 1967, p. 3, quoted in Kanovsky, op. cit., p. 38.

6 The cost of the casualties of the war, compensation, pensions, hospitalisation and so on are not included in this table. They are paid out of defence funds and are not separately identifiable. Kanovsky, op. cit., p. 49.

7 See *Israeli Economist*, June-July 1967, p. 137; *New York Times*, 16 November 1967; *Maariv*, 18 December 1967, quoted in Kanovsky, op. cit., p. 42; A. Szeskin, 'The areas administered by Israel: their economy and foreign trade', *Journal of World Trade Law*, 3, September-October 1970.

8 Kanovsky, op. cit., Table 2, p. 94.

Table 2    *Israel: non-recoverable losses of the Six Day War*

| Item | US $ million |
| --- | --- |
| Compensation for war damage | 5.7 |
| Damage to churches in Jerusalem | 2.9 |
| To US families for attack on US Liberty | 6.9 |
| Loss of production in the economy | 60.0 |
| Loss of tourist traffic by El Al | 3.0 |
| Loss of exports (adjusted) | 14.0 |
| Total | 92.5 |

Source: Kanovsky, op. cit., pp. 42, 43, 44, 45; tourism is estimated to have fallen during 1967 but this was already falling in 1966 and the tourist earnings of $5 million have not been included in the above.

purchases.[9] With about a fifth of the GNP allocated to defence to meet the occupation costs, terrorist activity and the general alert for future hostilities, the economy while bouyant was, and still is, under strain.

The Arabs are inflicting severer economic difficulties on the Israelis by maintaining the posture of 'neither war nor peace' than they have been able to inflict with outright hostilities or any of the sensational terroristic actions. A reduction in the tension in the region would be as helpful to the Israeli economy as was the emergency provoked by the 1967 war.

The growth rate in GNP has been higher post-war than pre-war but this has brought with it problems of a different kind. Rising per capita incomes have maintained the share of private consumption in GNP at the same time as the share of public consumption, mainly on defence, has risen. The adjustment has had to be made in the form of a deficit on the balance of trade and through foreign indebtedness and aid from abroad. An Israeli economist wrote in 1970, after studying the economic boom of the post-war period:

The data demonstrate clearly that the 'economic miracle' of a peace economy in times of war, with a rising standard of living, was no

9 ibid., Table 7, p. 121.

miracle at all: it was paid for by an ever-increasing import surplus, which resulted in a rapid increase of the foreign debt.[10]

This is the problem of the Israeli government today: it must maintain a credible defensive posture, sufficient to defeat determined armed attacks from all the Arab armies combined, even though the actual threat may only be located on any one border at a time, and it must also direct the economy into a growth path, which means restraining the growth in consumption and directing resources into investment. The longer the full alert defence allocation is not tested – i.e. the longer there is no actual outbreak of fighting – the more resistance there is to restraining consumption.[11] At some point in time, in the absence of peace, the external debt will reach a natural ceiling and the economy will have to choose, in effect, between guns and butter. For the Israelis this is a pressing reason for peace.

### 3.    Egypt

Egypt's economy in 1967 was performing below capacity and was also suffering from mismanagement. The war did not produce a reversal of economic fortune as it did with the Israelis. In fact the war, and the defeat, only served to exacerbate the negative features of the bureaucratically managed economy. The Egyptian economy has known few periods of successful operation and the post-war situation did not change anything. The end of the Korean war hit the 1952 cotton boom and from then on depressed per capita income (which returned to the 1913-28 levels) in the wake of a collapse in cotton prices to half their 1950 level.[12] The new military government after the 1952 coup was able to stave off part of the effects of this crisis at the expense of Egypt's Sterling balances. But reserves once committed and not replaced

10 E. Berglas, 'Defence, the standard of living and the external debt', *Israeli Quarterly Journal of Economics*, Spring 1972, p. 38.

11 For a more optimistic view see A. Vice, 'Massive outlays on defence do not hinder expansion', and M. Brilliant, 'Industry develops under stress of war', *The Times*, London, 28 Setpember 1971.

12 C. Issawi, *Egypt in Revolution*, London, 1963.

allow only a short-term strategy of economic management.

In 1956 the Suez invasion was partly a cause of the policy of 'Egyptianisation' of assets. It also coincided with a swing towards to Soviet Union and away from the West. In other developing countries the nationalisation of assets has not always been followed by a pro-Soviet foreign policy and the two events are not inevitably related — e.g. Uganda, 1972-3 or Thailand, 1971. In 1960-1 Egyptianisation was taken a stage further by widespread nationalisation measures in line with Nasser's 'Arab Socialism'. The application of these measures to the Syrian part of the United Arab Republic provoked Syrian secession from the union. The living standards of the Egyptians had regained their 1952 levels just before the wave of 'socialism' and this recovery is all the more remarkable when it is noted that these standards had dropped below their 1950 levels by up to about 18 per cent.[13]

The nationalisation policy meant that 'in effect the industrial, commercial, financial and landowner classes were dispossessed of most of their property'.[14] The problem for a developing country which embarks upon this type of social programme is that it does not have a surfeit of administrative and managerial talent which it can call upon to take over and run the enterprises. This means either importing foreign managers (in Egypt's case from the Soviet bloc) or accepting a lower level of managerial competence than was previously practised. As the socialisation measures are political rather than economic in motivation, they create an even more restricted layer of managerial talent than in an open society; managers are chosen for their political loyalty rather than for their competence. Viewed from the top, this is necessary and inescapable; from below, it is alienating — the brunt of scarcities and low quality is borne by the poorer sections of the community; and viewed from the outside, it appears wasteful and inefficient.

The government had ambitious plans for the future which became even more ambitious as the leadership tried fren-

13 D.C. Mead, *Growth and Structural Change in the Egyptian Economy*, I.U. Homewood, 1967, p. 224.

14 Kanovsky, op. cit., p. 210.

ziedly to make up for the gap between plan and reality. The first Five Year Plan aimed to double national income in 20 years; this was revised on political grounds to a demand for doubling of income in only ten years, followed, in 1965, with Nasser's demand to do the job in only seven years.[15] In the context of the managerial performances of the Egyptian bureaucracy these 'aims' were totally unrealistic.

Productivity in industry and agriculture was well below any level that would make even the modest aims of the Plan realistic. One report put labour productivity increases in the first year of the plan at 7.3 per cent, and at only 0.9 per cent in the second year and nil in the third year.[16] That this was representative of the trend is confirmed by semi-official indices of productivity.

*Table 3    Egypt: productivity indices 1959-65 (1959-60 = 100)*

| Year | Index |
|------|-------|
| 1959-60 | 100 |
| 1960-61 | 101.7 |
| 1961-62 | 97.6 |
| 1962-63 | 100.6 |
| 1963-64 | 98.5 |
| 1964-65 | 98.5 |

Source:  *L'Egypte contemporaine*, July 1967; quoted in Kanovsky, op. cit., p. 231.

Agricultural productivity fell below the first year's perform-ance in subsequent years, except for 1964-5 when product-ivity reached 1.2 per cent above the first year.[17]

The government, with worthy intentions but disastrous consequences, adopted labour policies which were at variance with the economic realities. It cut the working week from 48 to 42 hours and raised money wages by 31 per cent during

15 ibid., pp. 215, 250.
16 B. Hansen and G. Marzourk, *Development and Economic Policy in the UAR*, Amsterdam, 1965, pp. 133-5.
17 A.S. Gerakis, *United Arab Republic: A Survey of Developments During the First Five Year Plan, 1960/61 – 1964/65*, International Monetary Fund Staff Papers, November 1967.

the Plan.[18] It also adopted employment targets for each sector in a bid to reduce unemployment. This only served to extend the labour surplus in the country — calculated to be as high as 40 per cent in agriculture and services[19] — into industry. Industrial employment expanded during 1959-65 at an annual average rate of 8.1%. Employment targets are easier to meet than output targets — industrial output was 25 per cent below target in the same period.

The policy of industrial absorption of surplus labour contributed to rising costs in addition to the costs of a shorter working week and a money wage increase. This added to the burden of costs on the input side without creating additional output. It made domestic production even less competitive than it already was and did this in the context of expectations of doubling income in twenty or ten or seven years. Something, of course, had to give, and the result was another round of inflation.

The Egyptian bureaucracy represents the major obstacle to achievement of the Plan targets. A bureaucracy is a complex organisation which creates and nurtures a system of delineation of tasks and decisions on principles that minimise initiative and maximise caution in decision-taking.[20] Economic management is already subject to lags in the decision process — a problem has to be noticed, evaluated and deliberated upon; corrective policies have to be searched for, agreed upon and implemented. These policies take time to have their effects. If delays and buck-passing are introduced — a bureaucracy perfects this type of behaviour — the lags are extended. Another unwelcome feature of bureaucratic administration is that some problems are 'ignored' by the decision makers because of the implications for the lower levels of drawing the attention of decision makers higher up in the hierarchy to the failures lower down, or, what is as negative, the problem is covered up through corruption. This situation adds to the managerial costs of programmes apart

18 Kanovsky, op. cit., p. 230; see also; M.H. Nagi, *Labour Force and Employment in Egypt: A Demographic and Socio-Economic Analysis*, New York, 1972.

19 Mead, op. cit., pp. 80-98.

20 See T. Burns, *Industrial Man*, London, 1969.

from the costs of wrong decisions. Moreover, wrong decisions are not necessarily corrected in this system by the right decisions. It is also extremely difficult for lower ranks openly to criticise the errors of upper ranks. The atmosphere of mutal deception prevails amidst mutual cynicism.

In Egypt the nationalisations and the presence of the military in a function for which they were not trained, the conflict between political reliability and competence, the insecurity from the political purges of the apparatus, together with all the normal problems of a developing country, increased the burdens on the system. The result contributed to the pre-war deterioration in the economy. The foreign debt, for example, grew to $4.3 billion, which according to one report exceeded the estimated GNP for 1966 of $3.8 billion.[21] The debt payments on this to foreign creditors (allowing for Soviet military grants and Kuwait 'loans') were $200 million a year, or 22 per cent of foreign currency earnings. The trade deficits were $414 million in 1964, $328 million in 1965 and $465 million in 1966. This forced Egypt to default on its loan repayments to the International Monetary Fund and to other foreign creditors.

The only successful feature of Egyptian performance was in the Suez Canal. The net trade deficit was reduced considerably in each year up to the closure of the canal (see Table 4). The war resulted in the closure of the canal and this part of Egyptian enterprise ceased to make any contribution to the economy. While the future of the canal was under discussion at the time because the new super-tankers were expected to lead to a drop to some extent in canal revenue, the contribution of the canal in terms of foreign currency was likely to have been a major feature of the Egyptian economy for many years after 1967.

The Israeli occupation of Sinai cut off another source of revenue for the Egyptians. Oil production was worth $56 million a year to Egypt from Sinai. Fortunately this was made up by the opening up of new fields and the increased output of current fields in the non-occupied part of the country, and these restored income from oil by 1969. Egypt

21 Kanovsky, op. cit., p. 253, quoting *The Economist*, London, 10 June 1967.

Table 4    *Egypt: trade deficit and the Suez canal operation earnings 1960-68 (US $ millions)*

| Year | Deficit | Receipts Suez canal | Net deficit |
|------|---------|---------------------|-------------|
| 1960 | 99 | 144 | +45 |
| 1961 | 215 | 147 | -68 |
| 1962 | 342 | 154 | -188 |
| 1963 | 396 | 163 | -227 |
| 1964 | 416 | 180 | -236 |
| 1965 | 329 | 198 | -131 |
| 1966 | 466 | 219 | -247 |
| 1967 | 226 | 66* | -160 |
| 1968 | 70 | 0 | -70 |

Source: United Nations, *Monthly Bulletin of Statistics*; National Bank of Egypt, *Economic Bulletin*, 22, 2, 1969; recalculated from data quoted in Kanovsky, op. cit., p. 344.
* Three months only. April, May not available.

came off worse in the post-war exchange of shell fire when the Suez oil refineries were hit by the Israelis in October 1967. This cost a reported $230 million worth of damage. In 1969 the refineries were put out of action altogether. Israel attacks on Egypt up to the cease-fire were aimed at economic targets and included bridges and a power station.

The estimated cost of the war to Egypt was about $500 to $600 million up to 1969, much of this in the form of hard currency earnings.[22] To make up the loss, Egypt was forced to lean heavily on Arab neighbours for subsidies (Kuwait and Libya, for example, have supplied help).

Egypt's arms procurement was assisted by the Soviet Union with an estimated $2-3 billion worth of armaments. Nevertheless domestic defence expenditures have risen to match the Israeli arms programme. Defence budgets in the early 1960s were 7 to 8 per cent of GDP, and these rose to 13 per cent of GDP in 1966 and 18 per cent in 1969.[23]

In 1972 the Egyptian Chief-of-Staff, Lt. General Saad-Eddin Shazli, claimed that Egypt was spending 23 per cent of her national income on defence and called upon the other

22 Kanovsky, op. cit., pp. 256-60, 283-5.
23 ibid., p. 288.

Arab states to spend at least 15 per cent each or contribute the equivalent amount to those that were.[24] To describe these amounts as extremely high is no exaggeration. In the context of indifferent economic performance they are a heavy burden. Whereas Israel has been able to shoulder the burden with difficulty, it is clearly beyond the Egyptians to shoulder it at all without severe political stress and low efficiency.

### 4.  Pakistan

The economic performance of Pakistan before and after the 1965 hostilities with India will now be examined.[25] The hostilities were of a short duration, 17 days (and only 21 days in the Bangladesh war), but the economic impact of the military posture was considerable. The economic distortions set off by the war in 1965, plus the West wing's dominance of economic affairs in Pakistan, contributed in no small measure to the disintegrative tendencies between West and East Pakistan that finally led to the separatist war for Bangladesh.[26]

From 1954 to 1960 the annual average growth rate of GNP was 2.4 per cent, and from 1960 to 1969 it was 5.4 per cent. The annual average growth of GNP per capita in the same periods rose from nil growth to 2.7 per cent respectively.[27] The growth rate of GNP in the two wings of Pakistan showed a disparity in the West wing's favour. The East wing's growth rate in the first decade 1949-50 to 1959-60 was 0.2

24 *Financial Times*, London, 15 December 1972.

25 The following section is confined to the impact of the war on Pakistan. India is not included, not because it is uninteresting, far from it, but because Veena Agarwal (Delhi and Brunel), in a forthcoming study on the impact of the defence budgets on Indian development planning, has covered the subject in detail.

26 For an account of the break-up of Pakistan see: Ahmad, op. cit.; F.M. Innes, 'The political outlook in Pakistan', *Pacific Affairs*, 26, 4, December 1953; M.S. Rajon, 'Bangladesh and after', *Pacific Affairs*, 45, 2, 1972.

27 J.J. Stern and W.P. Falcon, *Growth and Development in Pakistan, 1955-1969*, Harvard, 1970, p.9, calculated from *Statistical Bulletin*, Karachi.

per cent, and in the second decade it was 5.4 per cent, compared with the West wing's performance in the same periods of 3.6 and 7.2 per cent respectively. In per capita terms the 1959-60 compound growth rate in the East wing was negative (-0.3 per cent) rising to 2 per cent in 1969-70 (before the war), compared with the West wing's 0.8 per cent and 4.8 per cent respectively for the same years.[28]

The sectoral growth rates show the changes that are essential for an understanding of the Pakistan economy. Agriculture grew at 1.4 per cent during 1954-60 and 3.4 per cent during 1960-9; in this latter period the agricultural growth rate exceeds the population growth rate of 2.8 per cent. Large scale manufacturing (firms employing 20 or more persons and using power) contributed an 8.4 per cent growth rate in the first period and a 10.9 per cent in the second.[29] The sectoral contributions to GNP are shown in the Table for both wings separately for the three periods: 1949-50, 1959-60 and 1964-5.

*Table 5  Percentage contribution by sectors to GNP, Pakistan (1959-60 factor cost)*

|  | 1949-50 | | 1959-60 | | 1964-65 | |
|---|---|---|---|---|---|---|
|  | *West* | *East* | *West* | *East* | *West* | *East* |
| Agriculture | 54.0 | 65.0 | 47.0 | 58.0 | 43.0 | 56.0 |
| Mining | 0.2 |  | 0.4 |  | 0.5 |  |
| Manufacturing | 7.9 | 3.8 | 12.8 | 6.1 | 13.7 | 7.9 |
| Construction | 1.4 | 0.4 | 2.5 | 1.4 | 4.5 | 4.1 |
| Electricity etc. | 0.2 | 0.05 | 0.5 | 0.1 | 0.7 | 0.5 |
| Transport and communications | 5.0 | 5.1 | 5.6 | 6.0 | 5.8 | 6.1 |
| Trade, finance, etc. | 30.5 | 25.3 | 31.8 | 25.8 | 31.8 | 25.8 |

Source: Percentage calculated from T.M. Khan and W.A. Bergon, 'Measurement of structural change in the Pakistan economy,' *Pakistan Development Review*, Summer, 1966, in Ahmad, op. cit., p.32.

The East wing is clearly more dependent on agriculture

28 Ahmad, op. cit., pp. 29-30.
29 Stern and Falcon, op. cit., p. 9.

than the West wing. It is less industrialised and has both a smaller trade and a smaller financial contribution to GNP. It has near-parity in electricity production and a slight advantage in transport and communications as contributors to GNP. Agriculture is a declining sector in Pakistan and has contributed less than 50 per cent to GNP in the whole country since 1962; this fell to 45.4 per cent in 1968. Manufacturing, particularly through expansion in the West wing, grew from 8 per cent of GNP to 11.8 per cent in 1969. The proportion of large scale manufacturing in the manufacturing sector grew in the same period from 45.1 per cent to 71.4 per cent.[30]

The pre-war (1965) period from independence produced a rate of increase in investment in Pakistan sufficient to double every five years the amount of investment available to the economy.[31] By 1965 the proportion of gross investment to GNP stood at 18.8 per cent, having doubled twice from 9.2 per cent in 1954 and 4.4 per cent in 1949.[32]

The 1965 war broke the growth trends in the Pakistan economy. The rate of growth in investment for the years 1964/5 to 1968/9 was only 4 per cent, or under $30 million. The investment/GNP ratio and the savings/GNP ratio also fell in the same years (see Table 6).

Table 6   *Performance indicators, Pakistan 1954-69*

| Indicator | 1954-55 | 1964-65 | 1968-69 |
|---|---|---|---|
| % GNP in agriculture | 56.1 | 48.1 | 45.4 |
| % GNP in manufacturing | 8.0 | 11.5 | 11.8 |
| Investment/GNP (%) | 9.2 | 18.8 | 13.3 |
| Savings/GNP (%) | 6.7 | 12.2 | 9.7 |
| Imports/GNP (%) | 7.1 | 11.1 | 6.2 |
| Exports/GNP (%) | 8.0 | 4.9 | 4.1 |
| Average increase industrial production | 31.1 | 11.3 | 7.4 |

Source:   Stern and Falcon, op. cit., Tables II-1; II-2; II-3; II-4; II-6; II-7; II-8; and III-3, adjusted and combined.

30 ibid., pp. 9-10.
31 G.F. Paanek, *Pakistan's Development*, London, 1966, p. 8.
32 Ahmad, op. cit., p. 26.

The marginal savings rate, which had been at a low 6.4 per cent between 1954 and 1960, increased to 24 per cent in the period of the Second Development Plan, 1960-5, and this helped to double the contribution of savings to GNP from 6.5 per cent to 12.2 per cent. One effect of the war was to reduce the proportion of savings in GNP to 9.7 per cent and to reduce even further the marginal savings rate from 24 per cent to 5.7 per cent.

Tax revenues were raised as a percentage of GNP between 1960 and the war. In money terms they went up from 1.6 million rupees to 5.4 million rupees. This was achieved by raising the rates for all categories of imported goods.[33] The increase in the tax revenues did not compensate for the fall in savings because expenditures on defence increased enormously in the period: in 1965-6 defence expenditures doubled. In fact, in 1965-6 the surplus for development expenditures in the government accounts fell 45 per cent. Foreign aid funds fell and debt financing by the government almost trebled.

The war, and its attendant consequences, set up inflationary strains in the economy, and these dominated the Third Plan period. Taking the fiscal year of 1959-60 as a base price, changes up to 1968-9 were as shown in Table 7. The pre-war position was relatively stable, but after 1965 the rate of increase became substantially higher, with jumps in the GNP price deflator, food prices, and raw materials prices. Fuel and manufacturing prices remained relatively steady. By 1969 the increase was substantially higher than for the Second Development Plan period. The general five point increase for the years 1960-4 was replaced by increases of 22, 29, 19, 20 and -5 points respectively.

The 1965 war was followed by two very bad harvests, in 1966 and 1967, to which was added the burden of a reduction in food imports. Export performance in the Third Plan period did not meet expectations and the rise of the price index was partly a cause of the blunting of Pakistan's competitive edge in world markets. The reduction in foreign

33 See G.M. Rahdu, 'The rate structure of indirect taxes in Pakistan', *Pakistan Development Review*, 4, 1964; Stern and Falcon, op. cit., pp. 12-19.

Table 7    Prices indexes, Pakistan 1960-69

| FY | GNP | Food | Fuel | Manufactures | Raw materials |
|----|-----|------|------|--------------|---------------|
| 1960 | 100 | 100 | 100 | 100 | 100 |
| 1961 | 105.1 | 100.5 | 99.2 | 101.2 | 119.2 |
| 1962 | 104.1 | 106.6 | 98.7 | 102.1 | 107.3 |
| 1963 | 106.5 | 104.9 | 99.0 | 104.9 | 105.1 |
| 1964 | 105.1 | 104.9 | 104.8 | 105.8 | 105.3 |
| 1965 | 110.9 | 112.1 | 104.8 | 107.1 | 121.4 |
| 1966 | 115.6 | 117.3 | 108.5 | 113.4 | 125.2 |
| 1967 | 129.0 | 139.6 | 118.0 | 116.7 | 124.8 |
| 1968 | 126.9 | 134.7 | 120.0 | 120.2 | 106.4 |
| 1969 | 132.5 | 141.8 | 123.2 | 127.8 | 116.7 |

Source:    Stern and Falcon, op. cit., Table II-7, p. 17. The table has been re-arranged and abridged. Dotted line indicates 1965 war.

aid and the decline in the increase in exports contributed to a shortage of raw materials, which pushed up prices and reinforced the negative effects on the economy.

The cumulative trade deficit for the two Plan periods created a difficult situation for the economic managers. The deficit in 1960-5 was 9.4 billion rupees and for 1965-9 it was 6.8 billion rupees. The balance of payments was continually worsened by the burden of foreign loan repayments, equivalent to 20 per cent of Pakistan's export earnings in 1968-9. The loan element in foreign assistance, with future repayment burdens, rose from 86 per cent in the Second Plan period to 94 per cent in the Third Plan period.[34] It is little wonder that the new Bangladesh government was advised not to include heavy foreign loans in its development plans.[35]

Pakistan made some attempts to redistribute the foreign aid burden. The aid consortium countries (United States, Germany, Japan, United Kingdom, Canada, Italy, France, Netherlands, Belgium and Sweden) were responsible for 95.1 per cent of aid during the Second Plan and 87.7 per cent in the Third Plan. There are two groups of 'non-consortia'

34 Stern and Falcon, op. cit., p. 29.
35 K.U. Ahmad, 'New priorities and old biases: the first budget of Bangladesh', South Asian Review, 6, 1, October 1972; also Break-Up of Pakistan, Chapter 6.

countries: Denmark, Australia, New Zealand, Switzerland and Turkey in one group, responsible for 1.3 per cent and 1.9 per cent in each period; and the Communist bloc, which raised its aid contribution from 3.6 per cent to 13.4 per cent. The rise in total aid from non-consortia countries of from 4.9 per cent to 15.3 per cent reflects Pakistan's policy of trying to spread the aid sources as widely as possible.

The economic difficulties set off by the 1965 war have not been controlled in the Third Plan period. If anything they got worse. The decline in investment, and in growth rates, with, at the same time, an increase in inflationary pressure, brought strains inside the economy that were felt disproportionally in the country, the poorest sections and the poorest (East) wing being most adversely affected. The large scale disturbances and industrial strikes in late 1968 eventually brought a change in the military leadership. Ayub Khan, who had ruled since 1958, gave way to General Yahya Khan in March 1969. The new regime cracked down hard on the disorders but did not resolve the economic crisis – in fact the evidence shows that the burden was pushed on to the Eastern wing of the country, eventually driving it into secession, when the impact of a series of natural disasters on top of the government's policies finally broke the religious ties that had held Pakistan together.

Pakistan's Kashmir gambit in 1965 had proved a serious error of judgment, for not only did it fail in its immediate obectives but it was the single most important event in creating a situation whereby the inherent weaknesses of the 1947 state of Pakistan were brought to the surface.

## 5. Conclusions

The economic impact of war is not uniform. In Israel, Nigeria and the countries that traded with Vietnam, the economies were not disrupted by the hostilities in any way that could be described as detrimental to development. Egypt and Pakistan, however, can be seen to have come out of their wars with their economic programmes severely damaged. It may be coincidental that they were both the losing side militarily.

The connection between war and development may not be

simply a matter of whether the country wins or loses. A country can win a war but at immense cost, such as, for example, the economic cost of the Second World War to the United Kingdom. The First World War weakened all the European combatants but strengthened the position of the United States. In the Second World War the British economy was severely damaged, and a large part of British overseas investments had to be liquidated. The political strain of the war on the Empire was enough to make inevitable its separation into independent countries.

The wars discussed in these three chapters were in no way of comparable dimensions to the First or Second World Wars. The largest, and longest, the Vietnam war, has been confined to a relatively small area and a relatively small population. The war was costly, from the American point of view, mainly because of the expensive technology assembled by the Americans to fight the war, but it was not a war fought on a European or Pacific scale. Engagements in the field were confined mainly to small numbers of men on either side and were not battles between 20 or 30 divisions. The South Vietnamese thrust into Cambodia in 1970, probably the largest mobilisation of troops into one campaign, was a short campaign over in a few weeks. There were few sustained ground-combat battles, such as in the 1971 and 1972 Communist offensives, which were stand-up battles of a conventional kind but of limited duration.

Counter-insurgency warfare is expensive, but it is not as expensive as a logistically sustained front-to-front war. The Third World countries are, in the main, unsuited to conventional front-to-front campaigns.[36] There are a number of reasons for this. Few of the combatants are willing to fight in this way. It takes considerable organisation, discipline and training to mobilise tens of thousands of troops to fight this kind of war. The logistical problems of placing these large forces into a particular geographical place, and sustaining them, are enormous. These problems increase if the troops

36 In many cases the armies are not technically proficient. They have been modelled on conventional armies but are not in fact suited to this role both because of their inadequacies and because their opponents are not of the conventional kind.

move even limited distances, let alone if they move under combat conditions. The organisational skills required to sustain an army in a temporary place — the front and rear areas will cover tens, if not hundreds, of square miles — are a formidable drain on managerial resources. It is no accident that a number of wars in developing countries have been reduced to armoured thrusts a few miles in one direction and then have stalemated or have seen the use of aircraft to drop 'terror' bombs on undefended civilian targets.

Guerrilla warfare is partly a response to this problem.[37] The guerrilla bases are not just fighting units but administrative training areas. The central army has all the trappings of a modern conventional army and it is a formidable instrument against urban or isolated rural disorder. In engagements against armed attacks from small groups, it has the advantage in fire power. But it is not as formidable a fighting force as it appears on paper for sustained engagements of a conventional type. The insurgents do not have the resources to fight these kinds of wars — the Vietcong for example had to be supported by the bulk of the North Vietnamese regular army after 1967 — and the central authority does not have a fighting force with the experience for that kind of warfare either.

Guerrilla warfare is, in effect, a product of the organisational inadequacies of the Third World in general rather than some special characteristic of revolutionary strategy. Guerrilla warfare is not a panacea for revolutionaries: it is a necessity. A mobile response to guerrilla warfare, which strikes at the administrative functions of the guerrilla bases, is more likely to be successful than the search for military

37 See P. Sanger, *Insurgent Era*, Washington, 1967; L.E. Campbell, 'The historiography of the Peruvian guerrilla movement, 1960-1965', *Latin American Research Review*, 3, 1, 1973; Vegas, op. cit.; B. Davidson, 'Advance in Angola: guerrillas head for the Atlantic', *Sunday Times*, London, 16 August 1970, and 'Angola in the tenth year: a report and analysis', *African Affairs*, May-June 1970; *The Economist*, 'The guerrillas for whom the tide is ebbing', 6 February 1971; T.E. Skidmore, 'Failure in Brazil: from popular front to armed revolt', *Journal of Contemporary History*, 5, July 1970; R. Debray, *Revolution in the Revolution? Armed Struggle and Conflict in Latin America*, London, 1967.

'victims'. It is not dead guerrillas that decimate an insurgency movement but administrative deprivations. Guerrilla warfare is an opportunity for insurgents and central authorities to develop administrative capacity. In a quiescent political situation the central authority can relax and rely on its para-military forces to maintain order. The outbreak of guerrilla operations will force it to change. Either the central state sets up its administration (complete with the welfare services, justice, law and order), or the guerrillas will do it instead. Populations give loyalty to such 'states'. If the guerrilla movement succeeds in this work, the actual fighting between it and the central authority is a detail. The converse is equally true.

For these reasons the wars discussed above have had differential effects on the countries concerned. The countries with the least ability to produce an effective conventional army, and to create the administrative apparatus to sustain it in conventional battle, have not only lost in a military sense, but this organisational inability has been part of the economic mismanagement of the country.

Egypt and Pakistan did not abort their development programmes because of war alone. The seeds of disaster were already well-established in each country. In Egypt the economy was distinctly unhealthy before the war. In Pakistan the economic crisis was hidden by the exploitative relationship between the West and East wings of the country. Egypt had no means of financing its economic incompetence — the Suez Canal provided too small a revenue due to the limitations of traffic — and consequently the situation was clearly unsatisfactory before the war. Of course, if both countries had kept out of their respective wars they would have been better off financially, but low-grade managerial ability is often accompanied by fanatical problem-shifting cadres at the centre. The wars were diversionary adventures of failed political leaders.

The Vietnamese case is different. The war itself was (and is) a civil war between competing elites. Which elite will prove superior will eventually be settled. It does not follow that either side will win due to 'history' or suchlike — basically it is a question of which side deploys its violence most effectively. In civil wars there can be no calculus of economic gains or losses for the contestants. For the trading partners who have gained from the war and its economic consequences (the large trade deficit in Vietnam and the American involvement) the calculus of advantage was positive.

Nigeria's civil war is a different case from Vietnam's. The opposing elites in Nigeria fought along tribal lines in a frontal confrontation. We have already noted the unsuitability of Third World military forces for such a role. But it must also be noted that in such a conventional role the balance of advantage must be with the central authorities, especially in conditions where the insurgents are landlocked and blockaded. Bringing the Federal army to a single place to fight created enough technical problems for the Federal authorities: for the Biafrans it was a near impossibility. The fact that the war dragged on so long was in many ways due to the organisational and logistical incompetence of both sides, but particularly the Federal side. As the advantages were with the Federal side, delays in getting a decision in battle must be taken as a criticism of them rather than their opponents. The economic consequences of the war were in every sense beneficial. It provided the shock needed to the system to set Nigeria on a growth path. In this the oil played a large part. Above all the war Nigerianised Nigeria's political structure. Without this element an exploitative relationship of the Eastern Region similar to that of Pakistan might have been created and certainly the political instabilities of the past would have continued.

# 14 Local Arms Races

## 1. Introduction

This chapter looks at the arms trade with the Third World. The industrialised countries are the main suppliers of armaments and there is a thriving trade between these countries and the developing world. Armaments spending is a relatively small part of its defence budgets of Third World countries – in the main the major item of expenditure is manpower. There is a large element of politics in the arms trade as suppliers have tended to use their weapon exports as part of their foreign policy.

## 2. General situation

Seven countries (Russia, China, America, Canada, Britain, France and Germany) account for 85 per cent of the world's defence spending.[1] The military procurement decisions made in these seven countries determine, directly and indirectly, the trends in military spending in the bulk of the remaining countries in the world. These countries are also inter-related and interdependent in their military decisions, and each country's actions have to take account of possible reactions by the others – this is the classic oligopoly relationship.

The oligopolistic nature of international arms supplies arises because armaments policies are extensions in effect of the policies of governments. The governments in the arms business are in an oligopolistic relationship of a special kind (not often duplicated in private oligopolistic industries). The oligopolistic participants in the international arms business are divided into broad coalitions. The Russian and Warsaw

1 United Nations, *Basic Problems of Disarmament*.

Pact countries form one coalition and the American and NATO countries another. (China is at present a 'coalition' of itself.) The major competitive tensions are between the three powers Russia, China and America.

Triadic competition played an important role in the post-war arms trade. For example, American military support for the (South) Vietnamese was balanced by Chinese and Russian support for the (North) Vietnamese and Vietcong, but Russian and Chinese support was subject to their mutual hostility. During the war it reached the stage of the Chinese refusing overland facilities for Russian war material across Chinese territory, forcing the Russians to extremely inconvenient detours to supply a friendly government. Chinese support for Pakistan against India, endorsed by Chinese opposition to Bangladesh separatism, was matched by Russian support for India and Bangladesh. The Americans regarded Pakistan, in spite of its Chinese affinities, as a major ally and supplied it with large amounts of military material. Pakistan was also a member of American-dominated military alliances (the Baghdad Pact and CENTO) and at the same time a friendly power to China. Russian and Chinese arms supplies to Indonesia were motivated by their competition in the Pacific rather than their estimations of the political progress of Communism in Indonesia.

Within the American coalition there is supplier competition between the members. British and French competition in arms supplies took place in Biafra, Nigeria and South Africa, where France has sought to replace Britain as an arms supplier. Britain competes with America in the Middle East (Saudi Arabia) and Latin America. The arms supply policies of the two blocs take into account the activity of the members of the other bloc, and increasingly the possible moves of China. Arms policies are therefore bloc-oriented. In addition, the members of the coalition decide their individual arms policies, taking into account the policies and potential gains of other members of the coalition. This may lead to members of the same bloc coalition being on opposite sides in a Third World conflict. Arms policies are therefore partly nationally oriented. In the American coalition there is more room for competing national arms policies than in the

Russian coalition. France in this context is the most tenuous of members of the American coalition. As war is a continuation of politics by other means, an arms supply capability is one of the main instruments of political intervention.

In 1966 world military expenditures were $159 billion compared to $111 billion spent on education, $52 billion spent on public health and $8 billion spent on foreign aid.[2] The Third World with 72 per cent of the world's population spent only 11 per cent of the world's education budget and 10 per cent of the world's health budget. The military spending of the two major military alliances, NATO and the Warsaw Pact, is shown in Table 1, for 1964 to 1969. The percentage share of the two blocs has remained steady at around 87 per cent. The 'Other' category includes the Third World and the developed part of the world not in either of the two Pacts, such as Australia, New Zealand, China, the Asian Communist countries, Japan, South Africa, and the neutral European countries. The share of the Third World in this category is approximately 53 per cent, or 7 per cent of the world's defence expenditures ($13 billion).[3]

Table 1    World military expenditures, 1964-69 ($ billions)

|  | 1964 | 1965 | 1966 | 1967 | 1968 | 1969 |
|---|---|---|---|---|---|---|
| NATO | 73 | 74 | 86 | 100 | 105 | 108 |
| (%) | (52.5) | (52) | (53.5) | (55.2) | (55) | (54) |
| Warsaw Pact | 49 | 51 | 54 | 57 | 60 | 63 |
| (%) | (35.2) | (35.6) | (33.7) | (31.5) | (31.4) | (31.5) |
| Other | 17 | 18 | 20 | 24 | 26 | 229 |
| (%) | (12.2) | (12.5) | (12.7) | (13.3) | (13.6) | (14.5) |
| TOTAL | 139 | 143 | 160 | 181 | 191 | 200 |

Source: ACDA, Report, 1969, p.1 (N.B.: since 1967 most of the increases are due to inflation).

2 ACDA, Report, 1967, p. 5; the 1971 Report estimated world defence spending as $216 billion, of which $31 billion was spent in the developing world (up from $23 billion in 1968. Military aid in addition was $4 billion). N.B. The ACDA definition of 'developing world' is more extensive than that used here.

3 Calculated from ACDA Reports using the definition of developing countries used in this study.

Disarmament is fundamentally a problem of the relations between the major blocs, and not a problem that can be solved in the Third World. The NATO and Warsaw Pact countries take up the bulk of the world's defence expenditures; they account for the largest share of the world's supplies of armaments; and they dominate the political institutions that could sponsor disarmament.

The security problems of Third World governments are relatively more serious than those of the major supplier countries.[4] Many of the governments of the developing world are under constant pressure from insurgency or the territorial claims of neighbours. Some of the conflicts are part of the Cold War and others have a localised origin (the Israeli-Arab conflicts). These security problems are reason enough for expenditures on defence. Without security no nation will disarm.

It cannot be assumed that a bilateral arrangement between the Russians and the Americans to de-escalate their commitments to preserve their spheres of influence in the Third World would reduce tension in these countries to the point that they could curtail their defence expenditures significantly. The withdrawal of the Americans from Vietnam will not prevent the civil war from continuing. Until the issue separating the Communists from the non-Communists is resolved, there is a basis for war and insurgency. The same applies to Thailand and South Korea. The withdrawal of the British from India did not lead to a peaceful independence, and the withdrawal of the bloc powers from their foreign bases and client relationships is not likely to be a prelude to lower defence expenditures.

The presence of the bloc powers is bound up with the way in which the conflicts in these territories unfolds at any particular period of time, but the conflicts are not dependent on the role assigned to these countries in the larger conflicts

4 By 'more serious' is meant that they are under more constant challenge internally and externally. The power blocs may be in implicit conflict with each other, but this is a cold war rather than a simmering one that threatens to become 'hot'. After all, the NATO and Warsaw pact countries do have a final deterrent, which is something a government in Asia, Africa or Latin America, not to mention the Middle East, does not have.

between the major powers. The vulgar myths of 'American imperialism' and 'Russian (or Chinese or Cuban) Communist conspiracy' as explanations of the violence in the Third World survive all the counter-evidence that is there for all to see. For this reason it is unlikely that an arrangement could be devised in which the blocs themselves guaranteed the integrity of the developing countries and thereby, as the argument goes, enable them to reduce their defence expenditures.[5]

The developing countries as independent political units have to survive against internal and external threats, and they require an effective security force against potential and actual challenges to their right to rule. This monopoly of violence is an inescapable part of the burden of government. To this end they devote a portion of their available resources, or sacrifice some of their political independence, or both, to acquire military hardware and know-how from the world's suppliers. It is the purpose of this chapter to examine this trade in arms with the Third World.

### 3.    *The major suppliers*

In Table 2 the percentages of total Third World supplies of major weapon exports from Russia and America have been calculated. There are some interesting points. The Far East (including Vietnam) has received over a third of the Russian supplies and 54 per cent of American supplies during 1950-69. This region has been a high tension region throughout this period. The Korean war, the Vietnam war, the Indo-Pakistan and Sino-Indian wars, Laos, Thailand and Cambodia, the Formosa 'war' with mainland China, and the military build-up through the CENTO, SEATO Pacts and the armament of Indonesia by Russia and America, all contributed to this concentration of war supplies from the two major powers on this region.

The Middle East was the second largest customer for Russia and America. Russian supplies were exclusively delivered to the Arab countries, while American supplies

5 For one such proposal, see A. Rivkin, *Africa and the West: Elements of a Free-World Policy*, London, 1962, pp. 105-6.

*Table 2 Major weapons supplies by region from USSR and USA (1950-69) as percentages of their total Third World supplies*

|  | USSR (%) | USA (%) |
|---|---|---|
| Far East (including Vietnam) | 37.3 | 54.4 |
| Indian sub-continent | 16.0 | 7.2 |
| Middle East | 37.5 | 19.9 |
| North Africa | 3.0 | 1.0 |
| Sub-Saharan Africa | 1.2 | 1.4 |
| Cuba | 5.4 | — |
| Latin America | 0.0 | 14.7 |
|  | 100.0 | 100.0 |

Source: SIPRI, op. cit., pp. 190-1 and 144-5 (American percentages have been adjusted to exclude American aid to Greece and Turkey). Numbers rounded.

were divided between a major portion to Israel and smaller supplies to Jordan, Saudi Arabia and Iran.

The relative importance of the Indian sub-continent to Russia is shown by the share of 16 per cent delivered to this region, compared with only 7.2 per cent from America. Britain was the traditional Western supplier to India and Pakistan. In contrast, whereas America sent 14 per cent of her arms supplies to Latin America (including pre-Castro Cuba), the Russians sent 5 per cent of theirs (almost totally to Cuba). Russia has a 'special relationship' with Cuba and its weapon exports to this small island exceeded by a considerable margin all its weapon exports to Africa (4 per cent). A similar balance between American weapon exports to Latin America and its exports to Greece and Turkey can be drawn: America sent almost twice as many arms to these two countries as to the whole of Latin America. As Greece and Turkey are on Russia's doorstep, and Cuba is on America's, it is not difficult to draw the inference that the strategic interests of the major powers play the crucial role in the determination of export policy. Both these powers must have regarded these particular customers as 'forward strategic areas' to justify the size of the arms deliveries.

Africa, north and south (excluding Egypt and south of the Zambesi) is a relatively neglected area for arms exports from the major powers. There are two main reasons for this 'neglect'. First, the African continent is not regarded as a strategic zone in the Cold War. The case of South Africa and the shipping routes round the Cape introduced a strategic element into the area but this is a 'frozen' factor. The Russians have no interest in arming South Africa and the Americans, for all kinds of delicate political reasons, cannot. Therefore, while the strategic importance of the Cape routes has increased because of the closure of the Suez Canal and the growing popularity of giant oil tankers, the Americans cannot respond to Soviet naval patrolling of the Cape routes by aiding South Africa without creating political problems domestically and with other African countries. The north African coastline is also closed to the Americans and therefore their naval response to the Russians has to be handled by the NATO Mediterranean fleet. Secondly, the newly dependent African powers already have traditional links with the European suppliers and this relationship has been of sufficient (if waning) strength to reduce the Russian and American opportunities to establish footholds. Nigeria, during the Biafran emergency, was an exceptional opportunity for the Russians in this respect.

The five major arms suppliers are America, Russia, Britain, France and China, and in the period 1950-69 they delivered to the Third World regions $14.8 billion (1968 prices) worth of major weapons.[6] This was distributed between the regions in the following way:

| Far East | Middle East | Indian sub-continent | Latin America | Africa |
|----------|-------------|----------------------|---------------|--------|
| 5.6 | 4.3 | 2.6 | 1.9 | 0.4 |
| | | | | (US $ billions) |

The arms have flowed to the regions most affected by hostilities.

Africa's weapons deliveries have only been counted from when the countries became independent and thus the total is probably understated for this region. Most of the independence changes did not take place until after 1960, and this region will take some time to reach weapon delivery levels

6 SIPRI, op. cit. p. 11.

comparable with other regions that have not been affected by outright hostilities, such as Latin America.

For the years 1950-69 the annual average major weapon deliveries of the major suppliers to the Third World have been distributed as follows:[7]

| USA | USSR | UK | France | Other (including China) | Total (US$) |
|------|------|------|--------|-------------------------|-------------|
| 322 | 264 | 124 | 56 | 111 | 877m. |

The United States led the field over the period, but to some extent this position was due to the later arrival of the Russians as major weapon exporters. Their real impact as a major supplier did not take place until after the mid-1950s (post-Suez). Soviet weapons were exported to Korea during the Korean War and there were substantial deliveries to the new Chinese People's Republic. But supplies to non-Communist developing countries did not get under way as early as American supplies. Recent (post-1965) Russian delivery trends suggest that Russia will be the premier arms supplier overtaking America in the 1970s.

*Table 3 Major weapons supplies by region and supplier, 1950-69 (%)*

| Region | USSR | USA | UK | France | China | Other | |
|--------|------|------|------|--------|-------|-------|------|
| Far East | 34.9 | 49 | 2.8 | 0.8 | 6.2 | 6.3 | 100 |
| Indian sub-continent | 31.4 | 13.8 | 36.9 | 9.9 | 1.1 | 6.9 | 100 |
| Middle East | 45.8 | 23.5 | 12.4 | 11.6 | | 6.7 | 100 |
| Africa | 15.1 | 16.7 | 30.2 | 11.1 | | 26.9 | 100 |
| Latin America | 15.0 | 39.2 | 21.1 | 3.2 | | 21.5 | 100 |

Source: SIPRI, op. cit., pp. 405, 469, 508, 582, 608, 689; the figures have been rounded; Africa excludes Rhodesia, South Africa, Portuguese Africa, and North Africa; Latin America includes Cuba.

The distribution of the major arms deliveries in each region among suppliers is shown in Table 3. The former British

7 ibid.

imperial connection with the Indian sub-continent and sub-Saharan Africa is shown by Britain's major share in arms exports to these regions. The importance of India to Russian interests after the 1962 war with China is seen in Russia's 31 per cent share in arms deliveries to this region. Bearing in mind the extremely short time which Russia had to develop its arms exports to India (five years) compared with Britain's (since independence), the Russian performance is both significant and remarkable. India's alignment with Russia for arms supplies in such a short period of time must be regarded as a success for the Russians. In Africa the British domination was complete. The north African situation (not covered in the Table) was one of competition between France, America and Russia. Latin America was dominated by American exports (39 per cent), followed by Britain. The Russian interest was mainly confined to the Cubans, but the Allende government in Chile presented them with a new potential customer. In the Middle East the Russian domination of arms supplies was complete.

### 4.    *The regional balance*

The change in the importance of particular regions as recipients of arms supplies followed the changes in the hostilities, and threats of hostilities, throughout the post-war years. This can be seen by examining Table 4. The largest shift in importance was from Latin America and Greece and Turkey to the Middle East and Vietnam. The Latin American countries have been a war-free region throughout the post-war years and the 'forward area' status of Greece and Turkey in the early 1950s assured them of priority in the restructuring of their armed forces with modern American arms.

The Far East, excluding Vietnam, received 34 per cent of world arms exports at the height of the Korean war (1950-4), dropping to 25 per cent in 1955-64 and to 12 per cent in 1965-9. This region would have been a relatively 'normal' region for arms supplies if it had not been for the Vietnam war. The first two rows in Table 4 show conclusively the role that the Vietnam war played in keeping this region a major weapon importer. As the percentage share of the Far East, excluding Vietnam, fell, the percentage share of Vietnam rose and the total share of the Far East, including Vietnam, as a result remained at about 32 per cent for1950-69. World arms imports in the Third World rose from an annual average of $349 million to $1421 millions.

*Table 4   Regional imports of major weapons by Third World countries as a percentage of the total arms imports (five year moving average)*

|  | 1950-54 | 1955-59 | 1960-64 | 1965-69 | 1950-69 |
|---|---|---|---|---|---|
|  | % | % | % | % | % |
| Far East | 34.1 | 25.8 | 25.6 | 12.1 | 20.9 |
| Vietnam | 0.6 | 1.5 | 6.7 | 22.4 | 11.1 |
|  | (34.7) | (27.3) | (32.3) | (34.5) | (32.0) |
| South Asia | 12.0 | 18.5 | 15.5 | 13.4 | 14.9 |
| Middle East | 10.6 | 23.3 | 20.7 | 31.3 | 24.5 |
| North Africa | — | 0.6 | 1.4 | 3.0 | 2.4 |
| Africa | 2.0 | 1.2 | 3.6 | 2.6 | 2.4 |
| South Africa | 2.3 | 2.0 | 2.7 | 3.8 | 2.9 |
| Latin America | 18.3 | 12.1 | 16.0 | 6.3 | 10.8 |
| Greece/Turkey | 20.1 | 15.0 | 7.9 | 6.1 | 10.0 |
|  | 100 | 100 | 100 | 100 | 100 |
| Total US $ m. annual average | 349 | 855 | 864 | 1421 | 877 |

Source:   SIPRI, op. cit., p. 16 (extracted from Table 4); North African average in final column is for 1956-69; 'Africa' is sub-Saharan Africa. Numbers rounded.

The growth of the Vietnam arms imports was not at the expense of imports into the rest of the Far East region but in addition to them. The region without Vietnam imported an average of $119 millions per year in the first five years, 1950-5, and at the end of the period, 1965-9, the annual average import of arms was $172 million. Vietnam raised its imports of arms from $2 millions per year in the first five years to $318 millions in the last five years. In other words its annual average imports in 1969 were not far short of the total imports into the Far East in 1950.[8]

South Africa imported the same amount of arms as black Africa in 1950 ($7 million), but, by 1960-4, the five years during which many black African states became independent, its annual average imports were about $10 million less than black Africa's. However, in the years 1965-9, South Africa overtook black Africa and was importing nearly $20 million more arms per year. On a population basis this discrepancy is quite remarkable.

There is an obvious relationship between the importance of a region as a major arms importer and the incidence of hostilities. Both the Middle East and Vietnam have increased their shares of the imports of arms throughout 1950-69 and both have been areas of high military tension. All regions have been increasing their military imports by value but these regions have also increased their shares. The expansion of military sales from the industrialised suppliers has been due to a large extent to the demands of these regions and their military needs (as perceived by them).

### 5.    The Middle East

The arms trade with the Middle East has both increased in volume and changed in source of supply. The British dominated this region's arms supplies up to the mid-1950s, providing 54 per cent of its requirements. After Suez (1956) and the formation of the Iraqi Republic (1958), Britain was replaced by Russia, which exported almost $2 billions worth of arms from 1955-69, compared with Britain's $535 millions between 1950-69 (almost the same figure as France's at $498 millions). America's exports of arms have totalled $1 billion in the period.

The Russian arms exports to this region have been stimulated by the military failures of its clients. The Egyptians, Russia's main customers, have lost two wars since they switched suppliers. The losses of equipment have been on a scale not matched in any other Third World country,

---

8 ibid. The value of arms imports to the various regions and from the various suppliers is taken from several parts of the SIPRI study. All references unless otherwise specified are from this work.

not even Vietnam, and this contrast is very much to the point given that the Egyptian armed forces count their fighting literally in hours while the Vietnamese can count in years.

Replacements for military equipment used up in general service are an accepted part of military costs. Equipment deteriorates through use, misuse, accidents and low maintenance standards. In one report, the estimates of replacement equipment to meet attrition due to all reasons placed the rate as high as 60 per cent for combat aircraft and 33 per cent for armoured fighting vehicles in the developing world between 1965 and 1969. This period spans the Six Day War and takes into account the substantial Arab losses incurred in 1967. The more normal rate of attrition is calculated to be 10 per cent for combat and trainer aircraft, 7½ per cent for transport and utility aircraft and 5 per cent for armoured fighting vehicles and naval vessels.[9]

Arms imports are therefore not cumulative — there is always some element of replacement for attrition and also for obsolescence. Israel, which has developed an efficient maintenance, repair and recovery capability (necessary for a domestic capability in aircraft production), has not had enormous losses in combat, and has therefore less need to import merely to replace and replenish equipment. Moreover, the Israeli domestic arms capability, which provides it with $30 million per year in export earnings for small arms, ammunition, spare parts and explosives — exceeding the annual French exports to the region for 1965-9 — has meant that her dependence on outside supplies is confined to the sophisticated weapons, such as sonic combat aircraft and missiles.[10]

The reported combat aircraft losses of Egypt and Syria are shown in the above Table. Egypt lost 274 aircraft and Syria 57, and most of them were destroyed while on the ground in the early minutes of the war. A further 36 aircraft were lost by Jordan, Lebanon and Iraq. Soviet deliveries after the war had to make good these losses. Israel lost 50 aircraft and

9 A.C. Leis, 'The transfer of conventional arms to less developed countries', *Arms Control and National Security*, 1, 1969.

10 Frank, op. cit., p. 126-7. See also S. Peres, *David's Sling: The Arming of Israel*, London, 1970.

Table 5    Egyptian and Syrian combat aircraft losses, June 1967

| | Pre-war number | Egypt Losses | Replace-ments | Pre-war number | Syria Losses | Repl ment |
|---|---|---|---|---|---|---|
| MiG-21 fighter/ interceptor | 110 | 95 | 175[1] | 36 | 32[2] | 11 |
| MiG-19 fighter/ interceptor | 120 | 40[3] | 50 | — | — | — |
| MiG-15/17 fighter | 168 | 82 | — | 101 | 23 | 5 |
| Su-7 ground attack fighter | 14 | 10 | 64[4] | — | — | — |
| Tu-16 bomber | 25[6] | 30 | —[7] | — | — | — |
| IL-28 bomber | 89 | 27 | 20 | 7 | 2 | — |
| Totals | 526 | 284 | 309 | 144 | 57 | 16 |

Sources: SIPRI, op. cit., pp. 838-9, 850-1 for pre-war deliveries and replacements: Interavia, *International Defence Review*, Geneva, November 1967, p. 1638, for losses in the June war.

Notes:    1    A further 150 MiG-21s (J) were delivered in June 1970.

2    SIPRI, op. cit., quotes 33 for losses, but Interavia figure is used.

3    Interavia gives only 20 lost, but SIPRI gives 40. SIPRI's later figure taken. R. and W. Churchill, op. cit., quote 20 lost.

4    A further 20 Su-7s were delivered in 1969-70.

5    20 Su-7s were delivered in 1969.

6    The SIPRI delivery total is 5 less than the Interavia losses total.

7    10 Tu-16s may have been delivered in 1970.

these included French Mirage IIIs, Sud-Vautour fighter/ bombers and Magister Strike Trainers (being used in a combat role).[11] The French imposed an arms embargo on Israel, which was particularly difficult for Israel, as almost all its aircraft were of French origin. Fifty Mirage fighters ordered and largely paid for were cancelled unilaterally by the French, which obligingly lifted its other arms embargo on the Arab states, and this forced the Israelis to purchase combat aircraft from the United States at a much higher cost.[12]

11 Frank op. cit., p. 38.

12 Kanovsky, op. cit., p. 127; the cost of the French Mirages was $70 million and the cost of the 50 Phantoms from America was $260-300 million.

General De Gaulle was able by this switch in policy to divert potential Arab hostility towards France as the major supplier of the aircraft that did so much decisive damage to the Arabs' military position in the fighting. The result of the French shift in arms policy towards the region is shown in Table 6.

*Table 6    French arms supplies to Middle East to 1969*

|  | Combat aircraft | Utility aircraft | Heli-copters | Armour | Missiles | Naval craft |
|---|---|---|---|---|---|---|
| Pre-war: |  |  |  |  |  |  |
| Arab countries | 18 | 14 | 15 | 82 | 15 | 4 |
| Israel | 247 | 65 | 66 | 330 | 902 | 6 |
| Post-war: |  |  |  |  |  |  |
| Arab countries | 167 | 8 | 36 | 360 | 48 | 0 |
| Israel | 25 | 0 | 7 | 0 | 0 | 12 |

Source:   Compiled from SIPRI, op. cit., country registers for Syria, Iran, Iraq, Lebanon, Saudi Arabia, Algeria, Libya, Egypt and Israel, pp. 838-52.

Israel was clearly France's major customer in the region before the 1967 war. In all weapons except naval craft it received substantially more from France than all the Arab countries combined together. It was particularly dependent on France for combat aircraft, armoured fighting vehicles and missiles. After the embargo the position was reversed. The Arab countries became France's major customers for combat aircraft, armoured fighting vehicles, missiles and helicopters. These French deliveries also had the advantage of being the most up-to-date versions in the French range.

The helicopters included the Sud Super Frelon and the Alouette III; the combat aircraft the Dassault Mirage and the Fouga Magister; and the armour the world rated AMX-30 main battle tank and the Panhard AML-90. These are the kind of weapons that the Arabs needed most — the AML-90, for example, is suitable for anti-aircraft activity, which in the past has been a notorious weakness in the Arab armies. The combat aircraft figure for the Arab states included the programmed deliveries to Libya scheduled for 1970-4. France was also reported to be negotiating the sale of 50 Dassault Mirage F1 fighters to Iraq for 1974-5 deliveries.[13]

Israel switched from French to American and British supplies after the war and the French embargo. The 25 combat aircraft delivered from France in 1968 were actually ex-German Bundeswehr Fouga Magisters, which had been refurbished under a contract in France. Israel also produced a local version of the Magister under licence — the Potez/Badek CM-170 Magister. Twelve gunboats (*saar* type) were 'smuggled' out of France by Israeli agents, as their delivery was contrary to French declared policy at the time. These were effectively the terminal deliveries in the French arms relationship with Israel.

There have been large-scale Russian arms exports to the Arab states and this does not leave a great deal of room for the French suppliers to grow in. The Russian interest in the region has always been political. Table 7 shows the numbers of major weapons delivered from the Soviet Union to the Arab states pre- and post-war. Deliveries of combat aircraft and armour after the debacle of 1967 were at a higher rate of delivery than pre-war. Half as many aircraft were delivered to the Arab countries listed in the three years 1967-70 as were delivered in the previous ten years, and for armour the comparable proportion is 60 per cent in three years of the amount delivered in ten.

Egypt, Syria and Iraq are of political importance to Russia because of their geographical positions in the region. They flank Turkey, America's regional 'forward defence' area, and lie in a belt across the region between the pro-Western powers of Turkey, Iran, Jordan and Saudi Arabia. The eastern Mediterranean is important to Russian policy because it is a gateway to the southern flank of NATO. Friendly governments on the north African coast suit Russian interests if only to keep out America, but they have the additional attraction of providing naval base facilities. To this end Russian arms exports have been generous to those governments that wanted them. The fact that this was a high-

13 *Flying Review International*, March 1970, p. 9.

*Table 7 Russian major weapon exports to Arab countries 1949-70, before and after 1967*

|  | Before 1967 | | | After 1967 | | |
|  | Aircraft | Armour | Naval craft | Aircraft | Armour | Naval craft |
|---|---|---|---|---|---|---|
| Egypt | 750 | 1160 | 85 | 497 | 900 | 10[1] |
| Syria | 110 | 565 | 30 | 130 | 450 | 0[2] |
| Algeria | 122 | 310 | 10 | 17 | 0 | 2 |
| Iraq | 201 | 370 | 21 | 55 | 50 | 0 |
| Yemen | 30 | 0 | 0 | 27 | 30 | 0 |
| Morocco | 19 | 45 | 0 | 0 | 80 | 0 |

Source: SIPRI, op. cit., Country Registers; Frank, op. cit., pp. 86, 87, 92.

Notes: 1 Frank lists an additional 3 submarines on order in 1969.

2 Frank lists an additional 2 submarines on order in 1969.

tension area due to the local dispute between Arab and Jew made this aspect of Soviet policy dangerous.

The regional division created the possibility for a Russian interest — the super-powers had either to remain neutral or take sides, and taking one side left the other side free to align with the other power. The conflict in the Middle East is by no means big-power initiated, and it would continue if the powers withdrew. But the intervention of the big powers for their own ends, or through force of circumstance, does add another dimension to this potentially explosive situation. The post-Gaullist regime of President Pompidou continued the policy of not sending arms to belligerent countries; but the French readiness to meet arms requests from the Arabs, the difficulties that the Russians have recently had with the Arabs, and the emergence of the Libyan leadership as a counter to post-Nasser Egypt, do create the possibility of major French inroads into the big powers' current positions in the region.

## 6. *The Indian sub-continent*

The hostilities that have taken place on the Indian sub-continent have played a role in the demand for weapons in both India and Pakistan and now, of course, Bangladesh. The

Soviet Union has been able to use its armaments industries to make its presence felt across the Himalayas. The picture is the same to some extent as in the Middle East. Britain, the major imperial power in the region, dominated politically and militarily in the early post-independence years. Until 1959 British arms sales accounted for 65 per cent of the total imported into the region (worth $102 millions a year in arms exports), but by 1969 this share had dropped to a mere 13 per cent (or $24 million in value). That this was a real transfer of interest is indicated by the fact that the total arms imports into the region rose in the same period from $158 million per year for 1955-9 to $191 millions per year for 1965-9. Arms imports went up by $33 million per year, but Britain's share dropped by $78 million. American exports fell even more dramatically from $24 million per year to $1 million in the same period, or from 15 per cent to a derisory 0.5 per cent. France also dropped its share of the arms market from $22 million to $14 million, though the percentage fall was not as high as for Britain and America.

It was the Soviet Union that made the big gains in the period. It raised its share from a low 3 per cent to 68 per cent in the ten years, or from an annual average of $5 million to $129 million in value terms.[14] Russian arms diplomacy made these gains by skilfully playing its cards in support of India, the major power in the region. For the Indians the relationship was just as fruitful. It assured them of needed arms and technical know-how which they were able to turn to domestic advantage in their national arms industry.

The basic tension in the region is between India and Pakistan. The states formed at the end of the British rule in 1947 did not create the differences between the Muslim and Hindu peoples — they only provided a modern vehicle for centuries-old antipathies. The Pakistan state, geographically divided, was a religious state that attempted to override communal differences with a common religion. The secession of Bangladesh was the product of the failure of the religious state permanently to bind together peoples with fundamentally opposed interests.[15] There have been other sources of

14 SIPRI, op. cit., p. 469.

15 For an account of the history of Hindu-Muslim hostilities, the

tension in the years since independence. India has had considerable border difficulties with China and with some of its northern neighbours. Afghanistan has also had differences with the Pakistan government over the rights of Pathans resident in its territory.

India's military strategy was based on the assumption that it would not be attacked by its neighbours with a force of sufficient strength to create problems for the armed forces. India also regarded itself as being 'above' the use of force in the settlement of differences between nations. Somehow India's prestige as a neutralist country dedicated to world peace was supposed to ensure its invulnerability to aggressive designs on its integrity. The Sino-Indian war of 1962 rudely put paid to these illusions.

Pakistan was not regarded as a major threat militarily. India had acquired the bulk of the armed forces and their equipment upon partition through the segregation of army units into Hindu and Moslem components. Pakistan acquired the major British military installations in the north-west frontier region and in West Pakistan, but these were immobile defence installations and presented no threat to India, especially when manned by depleted army units. From this disparity major differences in arms procurement policies emerged between the new states. Pakistan regarded India as a major threat. The geographical separation of Pakistan presented defensive and logistical problems. The population balance was also in India's favour.

Pakistan sought and found a friendly power (America) to provide it with the arms it felt it needed and in return accepted the need to be bound into alliances, which had the political aims of mutual security. The American interest in these alliances was that they formed a barrier to Russian expansion; the Pakistani interest was that they helped guarantee its integrity against India. Whether in fact the

transfer of power, and post-independence developments see: L. Mosley, *The Last Days of the British Raj*, London, 1961; C.H. Philips and M.D. Wainwright (eds), *The Partition of India: Policies and Perspectives*, London, 1970; Government of Pakistan, *Chronology of Pakistan, 1947-1957*, Karachi, 1958; V.P. Menon, *The Transfer of Power in India*, London, 1957.

alliances could have achieved either, or both, the objectives of America and Pakistan is not as important as the fact that they were thought to be able to achieve them. That Pakistan was not pursuing a consistent ideological foreign policy is evidenced by its close relations with China. The Chinese had their difficulties with India over the border issues and were competitive with India over broader issues of influence among the developing world. Russia's aid to India after the 1962 war, and the fact that the Chinese were hostile to India, pushed Pakistan into alliance with both America (against the Russians) and China (against both the Russians and the Indians).

The Indians dropped their neutralist strategy after the 1962 war. Until then India had relied on its international prestige, its weight of numbers and its feelings of moral superiority to prevent major incursions into its territory. Moreover, it responded to threats to its territory and challenges in disputed areas (Kashmir, Nagaland, northern borders) with a passionate zeal that belied its actual military position. The governing elite was civilian/intellectual biased (it was also backed by the Indian civil service) and had a corresponding conviction in its superiority over other elites in India. The position of the army reflected this attitude. It was treated as a second-class necessary evil, with low status, low pay and low budgets. Nothing that the army could achieve by violence could not be achieved by the politicians by speeches and good intentions.

India began independence with the lion's share of the old British army of India. Through neglect in the intervening years this became a shadow of its former self. The humiliation of 1962, when the Indian army broke before the Chinese, forced upon the political elite a less naive attitude towards infallibility.

In Pakistan the leading elite was less experienced than the Indian in the crucial middle ranks. The Indian political tradition had produced a more successful political force and the administrative competence of the Indian civil service, which India held on to after independence, provided it with a first class state apparatus (probably unmatched in the Third World). Pakistan got the smaller part of the army, the remnants of a civil service and political force based more on separatist xenophobia than on an all round political position.

The army in Pakistan was to play a greater role because of this situation. While India's army languished through neglect, Pakistan's moved into central government. The Indian army was defeated outright in 1962, but the government learned the lessons of the defeat quickly. Pakistan's army was built up by generous American aid, and after the 1962 defeat of India it considered itself superior. If it had struck in 1962 it might have been able to take advantage of its superiority (on paper). But it attacked in 1965 when the Indian army had been receiving assistance from abroad for three years.

With the Chinese attack in 1962 a number of things altered in this region. In the first place the defeat of the Indian army (which in many places did not put up a creditable perform- ance but, given the circumstances, it is surprising that any units managed to make a fight of it) brought a reversal of priorities. The army was re-equipped on a large scale. This brought to a head the Pakistani issue. The arms build-up against the Chinese was interpreted as a threat to Pakistan. The resulting interaction was an arms race by both countries.

The Indian defeat in 1962 exposed the lamentable deficiencies of the Indian army.

The army was short of 60,000 rifles, 700 anti-tank guns, 200 two-inch mortars. Supply of artillery ammunition was critically low; 5,000 field radio sets were needed, thousands of miles of field cable, 36,000 wireless batteries. If vehicles of pre-1948 vintage were considered obsolete (and most were below operational requirements) the army was short of 10,000 one-ton trucks and 15,000 three-ton trucks. Two regiments of tanks were unoperational because they lacked spare parts.[16]

The SIPRI estimation of the Indian army's fitness for combat echoes this view:

The army still possessed Second World War mortars, artillery and howitzers and its standard rifle was the .303 Enfield, a weapon which entered service during the First World War . . . India possessed no radar, except the systems at Delhi and Calcutta airports. Harvard trainers and

16 Maxwell, op. cit., pp. 245-6.

Vampire fighters were grounded through lack of spares. The aircraft base repair depot at Kampur did not have sufficient foreign exchange for spares and was unable to perform its primary function of repair . . . The navy was in an even worse state. The government did not provide funds for spares and repairs. The only adequate repair and docking facilities were at Bombay and Cochin on the west coast.[17]

The re-equipment of the armed services was undertaken with the assistance of the USA, the British, other Commonwealth countries, France and the Soviet Union. It was a rapid delivery schedule in the early days. Eight flights a day of twenty-two tons of equipment were flown in by the Americans alone.[18] The switch from a neo-pacifist non-aligned posture was not direct and, in deference to the previous image, the appeals for help went out to all friendly nations, including Russia and Israel.

The major emphasis of the arms build-up was in the field of transport. Short take-off aircraft and helicopters were in great demand for they were most suited to the rugged terrain of the Sino-Indian border. A determined effort was made to set up a domestic arms industry. The multi-national sources of supply — balanced between East and West — and a domestic capability were to be the bridge between naive non-alignment (re-affirmed by Nehru a few weeks before the policy was reversed) and sophisticated non-alignment.[19]

The Pakistan government, sensitive to Indian military capability, was not willing to regard Indian re-armament as a purely isolated action to contain the Chinese. The view was that what India could deploy against China she could also deploy against Pakistan. The Americans who were helping India under the programme of containing world Communism matched their aid to India with the delivery to Pakistan of 12

17 SIPRI, op. cit., p. 476; see also Kavic, op. cit., and S.S. Khera, *India's Defence Problems*, Bombay, 1968.

18 Maxwell, op. cit., p. 419.

19 Nehru rejected military aid and declared it unacceptable 'even if disaster comes to us at the frontier'. When the 'disaster' arrived the policy was changed. See Government of India, *Prime Minister on Sino-India Relations*, 1, ii, pp. 118-19, New Delhi, 1961-3; quoted in Maxwell, op. cit., p. 411.

supersonic fighters (the F-104) in 1962. The Russians delivered 6 supersonic MiG-21s to India.

The Indians set up six new infantry divisions, specially trained and equipped for fighting in mountainous border country. This did not pass unnoticed by Pakistan, whose army faced the Indians across this type of terrain in Kashmir. The Indian capability to fight the Chinese in that type of country was transferable to Kashmir. The Indians also took measures to integrate Kashmir into the Indian state, and in the circumstances this was regarded as provocative by Pakistan. In 1965 war broke out on this front between the two sides.

In the 1965 war Pakistan lost 250 tanks (including advanced Paton tanks) and 20 combat aircraft (including some F-104 Starfighters) in the 17 days of fighting.[20] The peace forced some serious rethinking in both countries. The Pakistanis had attempted a pre-emptive strike against India, which was growing visibly stronger militarily. It was only a matter of time before India would have the balance of advantage. The incompetence of the Pakistani army in the use of their sophisticated American equipment was exposed by their performance. This lack of relative competence counterbalanced the Indian tactical disadvantages. India was vulnerable to attack on two fronts (three if China joined in) and had to deploy considerable troops to block an armoured thrust across the plains to the capital, as well as to engage a possible Chinese attack on the northern borders.

American aid to Pakistan between 1954 and 1965 amounted to over $1 billion, largely in the form of combat aircraft (120 F-86 Sabres, 26 Canberra Bombers and 12 F-104 Starfighters), armoured fighting vehicles (460 Patton tanks, 200 Shermans, 50 Bulldogs and 50 M-113 personnel carriers) and financial assistance to pay for the defence forces.[21] The Americans imposed an arms embargo on both

20 Frank, op. cit., p. 38.
21 SIPRI, op. cit., Country Register; see also Thayer, op. cit., p. 226; the figure quoted by Thayer is $730 million which agrees with a figure quoted in SIPRI, op. cit., but the SIPRI authors have added on $565 million for defence assistance received between 1959 and 1963; see Committee on Foreign Relations, *Hearings Before the Sub-*

sides during the 1965 war, but they both turned to other suppliers to replace the lost equipment. This suggests that unilateral arms embargoes are not necessarily useful instruments of foreign policy. The Chinese sent into Pakistan 80 T-59 main battle tanks (a Chinese version of the Russian T-54), 40 MiG-19s, 6 IL-28 bomber/transports, 4 MiG-15s and 5 Mi-6 helicopters. Even Russia sent Pakistan 100 T-54 main battle tanks. The result of the American embargo policy was that the Pakistan and Indian armies were supplied with Soviet-designed armour. Behind the arms follows influence, and, of course, its converse. In 1970, Indian sources were claiming that Pakistan was trying to acquire 50 MiG-21s from Russia, which suggests that the felt need for arms will drive countries into unpredictable alliances.[22]

The Russian policy on arms exports proceeds entirely from its foreign policy objectives. Its relationship with India was the most fruitful and it gave them a greater opportunity to extend their influences than a similar relationship with Pakistan would. It had no need to rush arms to Pakistan. China's interest in Pakistan was clearly aimed at keeping India off balance — every division tied down along a hostile border with Pakistan was one less on China's border.   The Russian 'exchange' in tanks with Pakistan coincided with the deterioration in Pakistan's relations with America. Pakistan became a less secure member of the American alliances against Russia. It moved, in effect, from alignment towards non-alignment.[23] Meanwhile, Russia's exploitation of the Chinese attack on India helped to move India from non-alignment towards alignment with the Soviet Union. On both counts the Russians made progress in their diplomatic activity. They weakened the American ring around their country and drew a friendly power into closer ties through the shipment of weapons and expressions of sympathy.

*Committee on Near Eastern and South Asian Affairs*, US Senate, March-June 1967, p. 50; also IISS, *The Military Balance 1964-1965*, London, 1966, p. 26.

22 *Flying Review International*, March 1970, p. 10.

23 A.M. Rajasekhariah and V.T. Patil, 'Soviet arms supply to Pakistan: motives and implications', *Modern Review*, 123, October 1968.

Set alongside the arms diplomacy of the programme towards the Arabs and the Indonesians, both of whom were to prove poor clients (the Arabs lost twice and the Indonesian Communists fluffed their chances), the Indian record from 1965 to 1972 must surely make India the post popular friendly power to Russia outside the Communist bloc itself. It is as if the 'jewel' of the British Empire has become the 'jewel' of the Russian foreign ministry.

### 7.    Africa

The situation regarding arms supplies to black Africa has already been noted. The countries that make up this group became independent relatively later than other Third World countries. That this has affected the rate at which arms have been supplied to these countries can be seen in Table 8.

*Table 8    Black Africa: share of increase (%) in major arms imports by groups of countries achieving independence in 1955-64*

| Countries achieving independence in: | Percentage share of increase in arms imports | | |
|---|---|---|---|
| | *1955-59* | *1960-64* | *1965-69* |
| 1955-59 | 47 | 52 | -138 |
| 1960-64 | — | 63 | 217 |

Source:  SIPRI, op. cit., adapted from Table 19.3, p. 602.

A newly independent country faces the task of running its armed forces, which have recurrent costs (pay, allowances, etc.) and equipment costs. It can choose to run the army on a low priority budget (India) and to equip it with limited means of violence. But even the most restricted view of an army's role, such as an accessory to the civil authorities for civil order, would mean that some equipment would need to be purchased. This would inevitably mean purchasing from without the country, either directly from a manufacturer or indirectly on the used arms market. The group of countries that achieved their independence during 1955-9 accounted for 47 per cent of the increase in arms imports during that period. In the following period, 1960-4, they accounted for

52 per cent. The next group of countries, independent during 1960-4, accounted for 63 per cent of the increase in arms imports and 217 per cent of it in 1965-9. (The countries that were already independent before 1955 had a falling share of the arms import increase in the 1960-4 period.) The arrival of new states led to more arms imports, but to regard this with dismay is, in effect, to regret the fact that these countries became independent.

The major influence on arms procurement in Africa (and elsewhere) is the possibility, and actuality, of military conflict. Africa has had its share of military conflicts; Sudan (1960-71), Ethiopia (1960-9), Somalia (1960-9), Zaire (1960-4), Nigeria (1967-9) and Uganda (1972). There has also been localised activity in some of the former French colonies and, of course, there is the sustained guerrilla warfare going on in Guinea, Angola and Mozambique and the occasional outbreaks of fighting in Rhodesia and South Africa. Conflicts affect arms procurement, as can be seen in Table 9.

Table 9  Black  Africa:  arms  imports  (in  US$m.)  related  to conflict

| Recipient | Prior to conflict | | During conflict | |
|---|---|---|---|---|
| | Annual average | % of total arms imports | Annual average | % of total arms imports |
| | $m | | $m | |
| Ethiopia | 2 | 1.8 | 4 | 11.2 |
| Somalia | — | — | 2 | 6.0 |
| Zaire | — | — | 5 | 16.4 |
| Nigeria/ | | | | |
| Biafra | 2 | 6.9 | 10 | 36.6 |

Source: SIPRI, op. cit., Table 19.5, p. 604.

Black Africa's conflicts are mainly *internal* conflicts between the central government and secessionist or insurgency challenges. This has not been the case in the Middle East and the Indian sub-continent. Vietnam and Latin America are closer to African experience in this respect.

The arms 'races' have been one-sided affairs because of the

nature of the conflicts. The central government increased their official arms imports from whoever would sell to them whenever they had to deal with emergencies. The 'rebels', on the other hand, had to make do with what they could get from friendly sources or with what they could steal from the central government. The expansion in arms imports was therefore kept below comparable arms races in other parts of the world. The suppliers were not competitively bidding for customers — either they had a relationship with the recipient government or could develop one, while supplying the irregular forces is generally such a difficult logistical problem that the natural barriers to supply act as a brake on the race becoming two-sided. There is, however, considerable evidence of Russian and Chinese weapon supplies to insurgency movements in Africa. Libya also became a source for supplies on a considerable scale.

Ethiopia has received substantial military aid from the United States. Between 1953 and 1969 this aid totalled $147 million. Before 1962 this was almost the entire American aid programme to Africa and even after 1962 it was running at 70 per cent of this programme.[24] Total US military aid from 1953 to 1963 to 13 other tropical African countries was only $34.8 million.[25] This preference for Ethiopia is difficult to explain in military terms. It is true that the Americans operate a high frequency radio communications station at Kagnew in Ethiopia (leased until 1978). The base cost $60 — $70 million to set up and is sited in a former Italian radio station. It costs $13 million a year to operate and employs 1800 US military personnel.[26] The base plays a role in the American world-wide communications system, but it is not regarded as a major priority in American defence. American military assistance may be concentrated on Ethiopia for the simple reason that European suppliers are still the major source for military hardware for most of the

24 SIPRI, op. cit., p. 651.

25 Lefever, op. cit., p. 157; Ethiopian military aid was supplemented by a further $19.6 million in excess stocks and $5.9 million in other general aid. Lefever gives Ethiopian aid for 1954-68 as $118 million.

26 Lefever, op. cit., p. 158 and SIPRI, op. cit., p. 651. The total number of US citizens at the base in 1969 was 3,000.

other independent countries. American interest in Ethiopia may be promoted simply by the Ethiopian need for arms.

Ethiopia has faced secessionist activity on two fronts since the 1960s. Eritrean and Somali separatists have caused a heavy drain on Ethiopia's military budgets. The Eritrean problem reflects religious differences — the separatists are Muslim and the central authorities Christian. The Arab nationalists have aided the Eritrean separatists through religious identification. Sudan gave the rebels the right of sanctuary up to the late 1960s and arms were passed through Arab sources to keep the rebellion going. Ethiopian/Sudan relations improved sufficiently to make the border more secure and the rebels had to re-direct their arms to seaward rather than landward routes.[27]

The irredentist claims of the Somalis on the south-eastern border to wide areas of Ethiopia (and also to parts of northern Kenya) led to a two-day war between Ethiopia and Somalia in February 1964. The result from a military point of view was inconclusive and a cease-fire was arranged by the Organisation of African Unity. US military aid had given a paper superiority to the Ethiopians. The Imperial Ethiopian Air Force (IEAF) had 14 F-86 Sabres and some squadrons of SAAB bombers. Against them the Somalis had some ex-Second World War Mustangs (ex-Italian) and 6 MiG-15 trainers. The armoured fighting vehicle disparity was also in Ethiopia's favour. They had over 100 tanks and armoured personnel carriers, and Somalia had only 35 personnel carriers and 5 obsolescent tanks. Neither side was prepared for a campaign, and neither had the logistical ability to sustain fighting on any scale for any length of time.

To make a serious attack requires considerable planning and organisation. In the absence of such an objective, or more correctly, in the absence of an ability to back up such an objective, the 'fighting' must degenerate into spoiling engagements rather than determined pursuance of a military

27 During the border dispute between Yemen and South Yemen in 1972 the Yemen authorities took over a Red Sea island in October and reported their discovery of £1 million ($2.4 million) worth of small arms and other supplies allegedly en route for the Eritrean rebels from Libya. *Financial Times*, London, 18 October 1972.

strategy. It is reported that both sides ran out of fuel for their aircraft and armour and that the fighting came to an end on a face-saving formula.[28] But before it is concluded that this performance was actually a success in that the futility of war would become obvious to all concerned, it would be well to see what the consequences of this situation were for both sides.

After the two-day war the Somalis increased their arms imports rapidly. Presumably they were determined not to be let down by the lack of material in the future. They planned to increase the army from 4,000 to 20,000 with Russian assistance. (Its strength in 1972 was 13,000.)[29] Its airforce was to be modernised by Mig-15/17s. The progress of the Sovietisation of the Somali armed forces can be seen below:

| a) *Aircraft* | *1960-63* | |
|---|---|---|
| Fighters | 8 | WWII Mustangs, ex-Italy |
| Transports | 7 | ex-Italy |
| Trainers | 10 | ex-Italy and ex-Egypt |
| Helicopters | 2 | ex-Italy |
| | *1963-71* | |
| Fighters MiG-15/17 | 20 | ex-Soviet |
| Trainers MiG-15 | 22 | ex-Soviet |
| Transports | 8 | 4 ex-Italy, 4 ex-Soviet |
| b) *Naval* | *1963-71* | |
| Patrol boats | 14 | ex-Soviet |
| c) *Armour* | *1960-63* | |
| Tanks | 5 | ex-UK |
| APCs | 35 | ex-Egypt and ex-UK |
| | *1963-71* | |
| Tanks | 82 | ex-Soviet |
| APCs | 65 | ex-Soviet |

Source: SIPRI, op. cit., Country Registers, p. 859; IISS, *The Military Balance*, 1971-72, p. 37.

28 Lefever, op. cit., pp. 155-6.
29 IISS, *The Military Balance, 1971-72*, London, 1972, p. 37.

The Somalis ended up with the fourth largest combat air force in black Africa, and the highest proportion of military expenditure to GNP; they also had one of the lowest per capita incomes of the group of countries with substantial combat airforces (see Table 10).

Table 10    Black Africa: combat aircraft and economic indicators for 1971

| Country | Number of combat aircraft | US$ per capita income | Military expenditure as a percentage of GNP |
|---------|---------------------------|------------------------|---------------------------------------------|
| Ethiopia | 48 | 66 | 2.4 |
| Nigeria | 32 | 107 | 1.7 |
| Zaire | 32 | 80 | 2.7 |
| Somalia | 20 | 50 | 6.1 |
| Uganda | 19 | 93 | 2.0 |
| Zambia | 12 | 247 | 1.8 |
| Guinea | 5 | 83 | 4.5 |

Source: IISS, *The Military Balance*, 1971-72, Country Tables; per capita incomes and military expenditure percentages from ACDA, *Report*, 1967.

The Ethiopians also increased their arms imports, but not on such a large scale, as they already started off from quite an advantage. They imported about 30 helicopters after 1965 which are the mainstay of the counter-insurgency type of warfare. The Americans provided the IEAF with a squadron of F-5 'freedom fighters' and Britain sent a squadron of Canberra bombers (surplus RAF). The imports were in direct response to the separatist pressure and its relations with Somalia. The Somali imports were directly related to its irredentist claims and the failure in 1964. That the Russians supplied Somalia was probably inevitable, given the Americans' supplies to Ethiopia. Both sides now have disporportionate military capabilities compared with other African countries.

Following the 1972 Uganda-Tanzania 'war', where the vulnerability of Tanzania to Ugandan air attacks and the difficulties of making decisive land attacks against each other were clearly exposed, it is to be expected that both sides will build up their armed forces in the next five years. A government must defend its people from attacks, and Tanzania's open skies situation (it had no combat aircraft to protect its skies in 1972) put the government under pressure from its own people. From the Ugandan point of view the bombing and strafing at will of undefended Tanzanian villages exerted enormous leverage on the Tanzanian government. The 'invasion' by Obote[30] supporters was contained by the Ugandan army, but this highlights the weakness of the kind of wars that Africa is capable of fighting. To put together a fighting force, to directs its efforts at a point, to supply it with ammunition, fuel and leadership over distances even as small as five miles, is often beyond the logistical organising ability of most African military machines (regular and irregular). War exposes inefficiency in professional instruments of violence. Just as the 1962 war taught a lesson to India, and the 1964 war a lesson to Somalia, so it is to be expected that the 1972 war has taught a lesson to Tanzania. In this situation the arms salesmen are bound to be called upon.

The military experience of Nigeria in the Biafran war brought Russian arms imports into the country in a big way. The hostilities mobilised tens of thousands of men on both sides, caused high civilian casualties (by bombing, strafing, ground fighting and starvation) and led to a heavy demand for weapons. The British government responded to the Nigerian request for arms on a large scale, but the Nigerian needs (as seen in Lagos) exceeded even what the British government willingly sent. To some extent the British were forced to match whatever the Russians were willing to deliver in order that the Russian influence might not entirely replace that of the British.[31]

30 President Obote was overthrown by military coup in January 1971 and attempted to return to power by military action in 1972.

31 The Official British reasons were given by the Foreign Secretary, Michael Stewart, in the House of Commons on 18 December 1968 (see *Hansard*, column 846). These included the fact that Nigeria was a member of the Commonwealth, that the Federal government was

Whatever the reasons for the British arms policy, the Nigerians responded to the emergency with massive demands. Major weapons imports were running at an annual average of $2.4 million before 1967, and this rose to $8.8 million during the war. If all arms imports are included (small arms and ammunition, etc.) the arms import for the years 1968-9 rose to $164 million a year. The British share of this was reported to be $6.8 million in 1968 and $25 million in 1969.[32] The bulk of the balance was provided by Russia, Czechoslovakia and Egypt. There was some specialisation between the British and the Russian suppliers to Nigeria. The Soviet bloc tended to supply the combat aircraft and the British and French the small arms and armour. (France played a dual role in the war — for a large part of it the French were unofficially supplying Biafra.) The Russian group sent 63 aircraft to the Federal government between 1967 and 1970. These were composed of 42 MiG-15/17s, 12 L-29s, 5 IL-28s and 4 Su-7s.[33] These were collected from Russia, Czechoslovakia, Egypt and Algeria, with the latter providing pilots and ground crews.

Biafran arms imports were comparatively modest. Many arms suppliers placed an embargo on arms to both sides, but the open-door policy of the British and the Russians made this a onesided form of 'neutralism'. In this context an arms embargo can be seen to be indirectly aiding the side that can get some arms. The Federal authorities got all the arms they could handle, but the Biafrans had to make do with what they could get by quasi-legal means.

---

recognised as the sole government and was facing a secessionist rebellion, that the Soviet Union would merely step in to meet any arms supply demands that the British did not respond to and that the British government supported the Federal point of view. This is presumably a consistent policy, as no doubt any British government would take a dim view of any Commonwealth government that supplied arms to the IRA in Northern Ireland or equivocated on the British government's legitimacy.

32 SIPRI, op. cit., p. 630; *The Economist*, London, 31 January 1970.

33 SIPRI, op. cit., Country Register; two MiG-19s may also have arrived in 1969; IISS, *The Military Balance, 1971-1972*, p. 37, lists the current strength of the Federal airforce as 8 MiG-17s, 6 IL-28s, 8 L-29s and 10 P-149 trainers.

The Russians complimented their arms drive with economic aid to the Federal authorities. Soviet exports to Nigeria increased from $20 million to $28 million, a rise of 40 per cent.[34] The Biafrans were left to their own devices. One report claims that the French supplied up to 10 per cent of the Biafran arms in 1968 and up to 50 per cent in 1969.[35] Once they lost the oil fields and were blocked from using the revenues, the Biafran cause was doomed.

The campaign highlighted the potential of counter-insurgency aircraft as effective weapons against ground and air attacks. Led by Count Gustav von Rosen, a Swedish pilot, Biafra put into the air 5 Swedish Malma light planes in May 1969. The highest number of these aircraft operational was 16 to 18 and they were adapted to their new role by field engineering with modest little six-round rocket launchers on each wing. These little planes were up against what ought to have been a totally Federal-dominated sky. The morale-boosting psychological shock to the Federal side was only matched by the apparent incompetence of the Federal airforce. Lagos lost 20 planes in flying accidents alone to one plane in hostilities between 1967-9.[36] The multi-national personnel flying for Nigeria (Egyptians, Russians, English, Nigerians and South Africans), the hurried training, the poor liaison (they shot at their own aircraft regularly), low maintenance standards and the general terrain, contributed to the ineffectiveness of the Federal airforce. But in spite of this the sheer weight of the Federal side and the isolation of the Biafrans led inevitably to a victory for Lagos. Without the arms imports, the war might have dragged on even longer. In this sense the arms imports shortened the war.


## 8.   Conclusion

Arms imports are available from the major supplier countries

34 J. Stanley and M. Pearton, *The International Trade in Arms*, London, 1970, p. 184.

35 S. Diamond, *New York Review of Books*, 26 February 1970, in SIPRI, op. cit., p. 263.

36 K. Sissons, 'MiGs versus Minicons', *Flying Review International*, February 1970.

for a number of reasons. They can be commercially advantageous to the supplier either because they dispose of surplus requirements, thus reducing the cost of replacement, or because they permit economies of scale in production. Arms sales are also politically advantageous and can be used as part of a foreign policy. Major weapons sales to a Third World country create openings for influence. The training programmes, at home or in the supplier country, to enable a Third World army to operate the equipment, are bound to have influence, even if unintentional, on the service personnel. The provision of spares and replacements enhances the relationship. The selection of weapons itself can assist a foreign policy objective, in that some weapon systems fit into certain strategic concepts but not into others. For example, the provision of COIN equipment rather than supersonic fighters is probably more relevant in some countries (e.g. Latin America, Africa) than others (Middle East, India), but this may conflict with commercial interests.

Increased imports are likely following independence and also following a war emergency, especially if the inefficiency of the armed services is exposed in the engagements. There is little evidence that arms imports promote military situations: the relationship appears to be the other way round.

# 15 Arms Production: The Issues

## 1. Introduction

The domestic production of military hardware in the Third World can be looked at from two angles. From one view the use of resources of capital, management, technical skills, labour and raw materials, the foreign exchange costs of imports and licenses to manufacture certain items, and the high risk of investments necessary to develop sophisticated weapons, can be regarded as a diversion of critically scarce inputs available to the economy. From this point of view the whole exercise is wasteful, and, given the urgent human problems of the developing world, probably *criminally* wasteful as well. Even if it is conceded that defence itself is necessary to some extent, the establishment of a domestic defence industry is seen as a broadening out of wasteful expenditure beyond the already committed resources of manpower and foreign exchange which are the two major items in Third World defence budgets.[1]

The other viewpoint would regard the establishment of a domestic industry as part of the programme of industrialisation. Without the industrialisation programme, the country cannot become independent politically. A defence industry helps achieve the former — it develops administrative skills in modern management — and guarantees the latter. The greater costs in terms of resources used up in a domestic defence programme, compared with the costs of purchasing the weapons from abroad, is no different from the problem faced in developing any other manufacturing capacity. If the least-cost approach is sacrosanct, i.e. that one should only

1 United Nations, *On the Economic and Social Consequences of Disarmament*, p. 12.

produce domestically if the import cost is greater than the domestic production cost, there can be no arguments about the inevitable status of a peripheral region as an importer of manufactured goods.

The major arms suppliers, as we have seen, use their arms sales for political ends. The fact that overseas arms sales have a sound economic justification is often of secondary import-ance to the political weight that those sales give the producer in foreign policy. Arms sales can be wrapped around a political purpose, either to bind a country to a particular line of policy or to counter-balance the influence of a rival major power. The United States, Britain, France and Russia have a long record of tempering commercial interests with their political objectives. After twenty or more years of this policy operating in the Third World, it is not surprising that some countries regard the power which the arms sellers have unashamedly exercised with something less than equanimity.

The newly independent countries are sensitive to what they regard as continuing dependence on the metropolitan powers. The arms trade is an acutely sensitive area in this respect. The counter-policy of an arms industry under their own control is extremely attractive. Of course, the wish is not sufficient to create a domestic arms capability, any more than mere wishing will create any other kind of domestic manufacturing capability. But once the political will is present, especially if it is brought to life by some local tension or an inconvenient embargo, the country may attempt to bring together the necessary resources. The (few) successes (and many failures) of the experiments in this type of policy are not being considered here; we are concerned only with the long-term potential consequences.

The original objective for domestic arms production may have been political independence from foreign suppliers; it may have been to save foreign exchange costs, or simply to increase the war potential of the country. But it is not *necessary* for the economic managers to be aiming at industrialisation; nor for them to have any recognisable objectives.

A domestic arms capability requires pre-requisite con-ditions and implies probable consequences. Movement from one form of dependence to another may result instead; from dependence upon foreign suppliers of weapon systems to dependence upon foreign suppliers for parts. This may also be accompanied by increased foreign exchange costs rather than lower ones — parts may cost more than systems. The war potential and efficiency of the armed forces may be reduced through lower quality or through insufficient quantity. But in this chapter and the next we are not looking at the efficiency by which a country achieves the objectives of the ruling elite. Instead, we will look at the consequences of a policy of import substitution (for whatever objective), in the specific case of the defence industry, on the potential development of the countries concerned. But first we must look at some general matters.

## 2.   Some problems of development

Let us look at some of the more obvious problems facing a Third World country which is anxious to import substitute in manufactured goods. The industrialised economies are complex and sophisticated structures which have been built up over many decades. The markets for their products are extensive within these countries, and they are produced by work forces that are literate, skilled, trained and socialised within that type of production system. Few of these circumstances exist in the Third World (which is why it is *developing*). The industrial structure that exists is a minority activity which is often isolated from the rest of the economy. It is often dependent on the peripheral needs of an extractive type of activity, which exists in enclaves (not always foreign owned) within the subsistence (majority) economy.

The market for manufactured articles is limited by the low per capita income (and the even lower actual incomes of the bulk of the population), and in the case of capital goods the market is even more limited. Much of the economic activity of the country is in subsistence agriculture, with low yields and backward technology. The land system varies from landlordism, with its debtor blight on peasant initiative, to small-holding farming and its reactionary attachment to traditional methods. Over-population (and its accompanying under-employment) on the land is a burden which the agricultural surplus, such as it is, has to carry before any remainder is passed to the city or overseas as a cash crop. Rising agricultural yields are essential if living standards are also to rise, and without an increase in dietary intake there can be no increase in physical effort to conduct a modern agricultural work programme.[2] Abject poverty produces physical incapacity for work and this incapacity is a barrier to change. The manufacturing base is extremely narrow and often tends to be dominated by a few monopolistic families who naturally eschew the development of the broad entrepreneural base which is necessary to administer a development programme. Political solutions to this problem may do little to help and much to hinder.[3]

Contrary to a popular impression, the Third World is not universally overcrowded. Most of the black African countries have populations of under 10 million. The GNP that these countries have at their disposal is far below that which is necessary to finance industrialisation. This reduces the potential market even further.

The population of black African states is shown in Table 1. While population statistics should be used cautiously, they nevertheless show that the population base of many of these countries is extremely narrow. There are 16 countries with under 3 million in the population and, even allowing for inaccuracy in the data, given the low per capita income this does not leave much scope for developing a market. Thirty-four of the countries have populations under 10 million and only Nigeria stands out with nearly 54 million.[4]

The available labour force is pitifully small. This must not be confused with the numbers living in the urban centres. Men must be both available and able to work, even supposing jobs were open to them. The urban masses of the Third World are often illiterate and untrained and would require

2 See Myrdal, op. cit; for criticism see P.T. Bauer, *Dissent on Development: Studies and Debates in Development Economics*, London, 1971.

3 See Seers, op. cit.

4 There is much controversy about Nigeria's population and for some years it has been a political issue.

Table 1 Black Africa: population of the independent states (1969)

| Country | Population (millions) | Country | Population (millions) |
|---|---|---|---|
| Angola | 5.36* | Malawi | 4.4 |
| Burundi | 3.48 | Mali | 4.8 |
| Botswana | 0.6 | Mauritania | 1.14 |
| Cameroon | 5.74 | Mauritius | 0.8 |
| CAR | 1.52 | Mozambique | 7.27* |
| Chad | 3.62 | Niger | 3.9 |
| Zaire | 17.03 | Nigeria | 53.7 |
| Congo (B) | 0.92 | Guinea (P) | 0.55 |
| Dahomey | 2.62 | Reunion | 0.44 |
| Ethiopia | 24.77 | Rwanda | 3.48 |
| Gabon | 0.48* | Senegal | 3.78 |
| Gambia | 8.74 | Sierra Leone | 2.51 |
| Ghana | 8.74 | Somalia | 2.73 |
| Guinea | 3.83 | Sudan | 15.31 |
| Eq. Guinea | 0.29 | Swaziland | 0.4 |
| Ivory Coast | 4.21 | Togo | 1.82 |
| Kenya | 10.51 | Uganda | 8.36 |
| Lesotho | 0.89 | Tanzania | 12.93 |
| Liberia | 1.15 | Upper Volta | 5.28 |
| Malagasey | 6.6 | Zambia | 4.3 |

Source: United Nations, *Demographic Yearbook 1970*, Table 4.
    * Figures for 1968.

substantial investment to prepare them for adaptation from peasant working relationships, or prolonged urban idleness, to modern factory and manufacturing relationships.

Illiteracy rates in some Third World countries are shown in Table 2. These rates of illiteracy per hundred persons are often crude estimates (the decimal points ought not to be taken too seriously) but, like population statistics, they show the general pattern. At illiteracy rates over 50 per cent the decimal point is not important anyway — the situation is desperate enough. A poor illiterate population is a crushing burden for a developing country.

The result of poverty and illiteracy is paucity in the market and a miniscule administrative elite. It produces external dependence, and, in some cases, a violent political

Table 2    Illiteracy rates per 100 persons, over 15 years old: estimates and census data, various years 1965-70

| Country | Percentage | Country | Percentage |
|---------|-----------|---------|-----------|
| Mali | 97.8 | Cambodia | 59.0 |
| CAR | 97.9 | Honduras | 55.0 |
| Sudan | 95.6 | Turkey | 54.0 |
| Dahomey | 95.4 | Zambia | 53.5 |
| Chad | 94.4 | El Salvador | 51.0 |
| Cameroon | 94.0 | Nicaragua | 50.2 |
| Morocco | 88.8 | Singapore | 50.2 |
| Nigeria | 88.5 | Burma | 42.3 |
| Iraq | 85.6 | Brazil | 38.9 |
| Zaire | 84.6 | Mauritius | 38.4 |
| Congo | 83.6 | Peru | 38.9 |
| Algeria | 81.2 | Reunion | 37.4 |
| Pakistan | 81.2 | Venezuela | 36.7 |
| Libya | 78.3 | Vietnam | 35.5 |
| Iran | 77.2 | Ecuador | 32.7 |
| Malawi | 77.9 | Thailand | 32.3 |
| Malaysia | 76.5 | Korea | 29.8 |
| Uganda | 74.9 | Philippines | 28.1 |
| Egypt | 73.7 | Taiwan | 27.6 |
| India | 72.2 | Colombia | 27.1 |
| Guatemala | 70.6 | Paraguay | 25.5 |
| Syria | 69.2 | Sri Lanka | 24.7 |
| Tunisia | 67.8 | Mexico | 23.8 |
| Jordan | 67.6 | Chile | 16.4 |
| Malagasy | 66.5 | Uruguay | 9.4 |
| Indonesia | 61.0 | Argentina | 8.6 |
| Bolivia | 60.0 | | |

Source:   United Nations, Demographic Yearbook 1970.

structure with a savagery of its own — for example, Papa Doc's Haiti, or the tribal bestiality of Rwanda and Burundi, and, latterly, Amin's Uganda.[5] But a large population and

5 This relationship between violent extremes and poverty has not been tested here but it is an observable characteristic. The Sicilian Mafia is one well-known example. 'Papa Doc' Duvalier ruled Haiti with a brutal dictatorship for years up to his death in 1971. In Rwanda and Burundi the tribal cleavage, roughly following the previous dominance pattern, has resulted in mass killings on both sides — on one occasion the entire parliament was wiped out (see Legum and Drysdale, op. cit.).

high illiteracy can be accompanied by problems no less serious. The food crisis diverts scarce administrative talent to face the constant pressures of ignorance and hunger: a situation summed up as 'running fast to slow down the slide backwards'.

The magnitude of the difficulties involved in industrialising a country are a measure of its backwardness. No social and economic system so far devised has been able to overcome these problems by reliance on a purely primary economy, whether agriculturally based or confined to the extraction of raw materials. These types of economies must, sooner or later, face up to the need for a domestic manufacturing capacity. The ideal of the world economically segmented according to the principle of comparative advantage — in which each country specialises in those products for which it has a relative advantage over other possible suppliers, exchanging its surplus for the specialised outputs of other countries — is not suitable, nor probably even attainable. The theory of comparative advantage ignores the *costs* of specialisation. R. Prebisch has shown how the specialist strictures are a cruel deception to a developing country and how attempts to organise world production in the basis of comparative advantage enhances the peripheral dependence of the Third World on the industrialised economies.[6]

One of the obstacles to industrialisation is the relatively inelastic supply of manufacturing capacity to meet demand. To overcome this the economic managers must induce (or introduce) domestic manufacturing capacity. This sector will have to increase in size, proportionately and absolutely,

General Amin's regime in Uganda received considerable publicity for several incidents, including the blowing up by the army of a house occupied by prisoners and the 'disappearance' of several dozen prominent people who were thought to be less than ethusiastic about the military coup of 1971. All these countries have low per capita incomes. See R. Tanter, 'Dimensions of conflict behaviour within and between nations, 1958-60', *Journal of Conflict Resolution*, 10, 1, March 1966.

6 R. Prebisch, 'Commercial policy in the underdeveloped countries', *American Economic Review*, May 1959; United Nations, *The Economic Development of Latin America and its Principal Problems*, New York, 1950.

throughout the development period. (This is recognised implicitly in the arguments for 'infant industry' protection.)

Even the most vigorous land reform programmes will disperse insufficient numbers of urban unemployed back to the land to make much difference to the cities. Modernisation of agriculture, through the use of fertilisers, new strains of seed, mechanisation and irrigation technology, not only raises yields but also reduces manpower. The net effect may be a continuation of urbanisation. In these conditions to raise income per head it is necessary to broaden the base of the modern manufacturing sector. Both the output per head of food production and the income per head from activity have to grow faster than the natural rate of population growth if the economic market is to expand to justify domestic manufacturing capacity. It is not so much a necessary circle as an imperative spiral.[7]

Developing countries are constrained by these problems. There are other problems. Import substitution reaches natural limits for every stage of technical ability. The simpler and more basic products can be substituted relatively quickly. For example, in Thailand, domestic manufacturing of cement represents a major proportion of the manufacturing capacity of the country. But the barriers of technological complexity are reached rapidly. One way round this problem is to use tariff protection on a cascade basis, as in Mexico. A programme of tariff levels for different stages of manufacture is introduced, and the level is raised through time to induce domestic manufacturing processes to take over the process of assembly until the whole product is produced locally. The local price of the product will be higher in the initial stages than the import price to consumers but the employment results may be considered to counter-balance this effect.[8]

7 See Bauer, op. cit., for criticism of the 'vicious circle' theories.

8 Mexico, Chile, Australia are examples of countries that have pursued a 'cascade' policy successfully. The employment generating effects of the policy, and the training aspects of the policy in new techniques, are the obvious objectives. A later stage of this type of policy is to go over from foreign ownership of the domestic capacity to national ownership, again by stages of acquisition of the equity until it has majority domestic ownership. For some countries 'partnership' control is another objective. Thailand, for example, had some local problems in joint Thai-Japanese enterprises.

Regional common markets have also been tried — East Africa, South-East Asia, Central and South America — but these have often been plagued with political problems, largely over the issue of the imbalance between the gains and losses anticipated by members. The ideal solution is for a group of developing countries to form a common market to combine their markets for manufactured goods and to assign production roles to each other for specific products. The division of the production rights has to be decided by political bargaining and this is where some of the agreements have foundered.

The proposition is quite simple, though: where a single country does not have a viable market potential to justify import substitution, several countries together may reach the critical level. Tariff-free entry to each other's markets may make competition with non-member imports a possibility. Each member should gain something from the employment creating aspects of the agreement. The reality, however, is that the industrialisation process has uneven effects — different industries do not have the same input mix, technological level, investment requirement and so on. The strains of the transition period during the re-direction of trade flows invite conflict. These problems are not unknown to the industrialised powers in the EEC.


## 3. Features of military development

Military production introduces new dimensions to the solution of the industrialisation problem, at least for those countries that have reached some level of domestic manufacturing capacity and have had some experience of import substitution. First, in the nature of the product. The government exercises a monopoly of violence, and therefore the instruments of violence have a ready and assured monopsonistic market. The low per capita product is no longer a constraint because the market for arms is dependent on the budget not the individual. That governments have large markets for weapons can be seen in the size of some of the military establishments of the Third World (see Table 3).

The military procurement sector of the governments of these countries must have a substantial domestic impact.

Table 3    Size of the armed forces in some developing countries, 1970 (numbers in thousands)

| Country | Army | Navy | Airforce | Para-military |
|---|---|---|---|---|
| India | 860 | 40 | 80 | 100 |
| Korea | 593 | 16 | 24 | 1 million |
| Vietnam | 429 | 31 | 40 | 555 |
| Taiwan | 425 | 35 | 80 | |
| Turkey | 420 | 38 | 50 | 75 |
| Pakistan | 365 | 10 | 17 | 280 |
| Egypt | 275 | 14 | 25 | 120 |
| Israel* | 275 | 8 | 17 | 10 |
| Indonesia | 250 | 34 | 35 | 100 |
| Nigeria | 240 | 5 | 7 | |
| Iran | 150 | 9 | 22 | 40 |
| Thailand | 130 | 21 | 23 | 18 |
| Burma | 130 | 7 | 6 | 25 |

Source:  IISS, *The Military Balance 1971-72*, London, 1971, Part One.
        * When fully mobilised.

Large numbers of men have to be fed, clothed, sheltered, trained and supervised. The administrative systems required just to control their location and their movement will require all kinds of inputs from the economy. The arming and supplying of these troops with even simple weapons, and maintaining and repairing them, should provide a substantial market for a domestic industry, even if confined to small arms and ammunition.

Secondly, because military security is a prime objective of a government, the production of weapons for the national forces is automatically protected from competition. The new industry does not face competition of the kind which a local durable consumer goods factory would have to face. The armed services, for all kinds of obvious reasons, are limited in the range of weapon systems that they can absorb and remain effective with. Thus long production runs are assured once the government decides to purchase locally. If the weapons are produced under licence the country can also combine the benefits of modern design and performance standards and the advantages of establishing domestic manufacturing activities.

Thirdly, because the decision to set up, or support, a

domestic defence industry is partly a political one, it is not subject to normal competitive commercial criteria. The object is some kind of self-sufficiency, and therefore mistakes and failures are likely to be set against the hoped for future political benefits of independence. Where a commercial project in difficulties would be terminated, it may be that the arms project will be continued by the political leadership when it runs into trouble. This is also where the main weakness of political control can do the most damage. The politicians may be chasing something unattainable in the time-scale, and on the budgets, available. Instead of concentrating on technologically feasible projects the government may insist on prestigious projects which succeed only in diverting resources into wasteful projects. The contrast between Israel and Egypt in this respect highlights the two extremes of capability.

Fourthly, the arms industry both diverts labour, especially skilled and technically competent labour, and also produces a demand for this type of labour which makes large-scale training programmes feasible. Labour diversion has to be set against labour creation.[9] This is probably the most important dimension in domestic arms production: it is not present with a policy of arms imports or a policy of reliance on commercially induced domestic manufacturing — the former uses the labour of foreign countries and the latter is subject to all the difficulties already mentioned. Because the government gives priority to arms production it also has to face up to the shortages in human resources. To meet its military ambitions it has to tackle some of the social barriers to development.

## 4. The arms producers

Twenty-two countries in the Third World are known to be

---

9 The analogy is with customs unions and the diversion and creation of trade. See R.G. Lipsey, 'The theory of customs unions: A general survey', *Economic Journal*, 60, 1960, pp. 496-513. In many cases the diversion of labour sources tends to be the only factor considered, but this must also be netted against the creation of labour caused directly and indirectly by the armaments programme.

Table 4    Domestic arms production in the Third World, 1969

| country | arms | naval craft | aircraft |
|---|---|---|---|
| Argentina | * | * | * |
| Brazil | * | * | * |
| Chile[1] | * | * | * |
| India | * | * | * |
| Indonesia | * | * | * |
| Israel | * | * | * |
| Turkey | * | * | * |
| Egypt[4] | * | * | |
| Burma | * | * | |
| Cuba[2] | * | * | |
| Dominican Republic | * | * | |
| Korea (North)[3] | * | * | |
| Korea (South) | * | * | |
| Mexico | * | * | |
| Peru | * | * | |
| Thailand | * | * | |
| Sri Lanka[5] | * | * | |
| Pakistan | * | | * |
| Taiwan | * | | * |
| Colombia | | * | |
| El Salvador | * | | |
| Iran | * | | |
| Nigeria | * | | |

Sources: SIPRI, op. cit., p.725; Frank, op. cit.
Notes:    1    Frank, op. cit., p.138: 'Chile has no indigenous arms production' but SIPRI, op. cit., lists it for all three categories.
2    Frank, op. cit., lists Cuba as shown but not confirmed by SIPRI.
3    Frank, op. cit., p.143; Korea (North) 'may have constructed some submarine chasers recently'.
4    Frank, op. cit., p.136: 'There is one major shipyard at Port Said (Castro) which reputedly built a Soviet-type "Komar" patrol boat in 1963'. SIPRI does not list Egypt for naval construction.
5    Not listed in SIPRI; see Frank, op. cit., p.138.

producing small arms, i.e. hand-guns, rifles, automatics, mortars and light artillery. This is about a third of the countries that import these weapons. Eighteen countries have produced naval craft of one sort or another and ten countries have produced aircraft either under licence or from their own designs. (Five of these countries have worked on missile projects.) Four countries have also produced armoured vehicles or have substantially modified vehicles that have been imported or captured.

In Table 4, the known domestic arms producers in the Third World are listed and the discrepancies between the sources are noted.

The levels of skills required for the production of small arms, naval vessels and aircraft will vary considerably. Small arms production requires machine-shop skills such as are found in tool-makers, machinists, fitters, drillers, borers, lathe-operators, forgers, reamers, press-workers, heat-treatment specialists and so on. The workers would need to work to fine tolerances and, for operational effectiveness, the parts would need to be interchangeable. Naval hull production is a relatively simple type of work using the metal fabrication trades. The power sources, however, unless imported, will require highly skilled workers of an even more technically advanced type than those necessary for producing small arms. In the case of aircraft production the requirements are much higher than for both the other sectors. The metal fabrication is more critical and the instrumentation and power source much more advanced.

It is also a fact that those products (such as light naval craft) which are within the competence of many Third World countries to produce are also products which the industrialised economies can offer at very competitive prices.[10]

## 5. The manufacturing base

As manufacturing capacity in Third World countries is a small proportion of their total economic activity, it is impossible, on the information available, to make judgments on the size and growth of the arms sector. For example, 10 African countries had under 5 per cent of their Gross Domestic Product produced in the manufacturing sector and only 4 could show a share of above 14 per cent.[11] The share of

10 SIPRI, op. cit., p. 724.
11 United Nations, *Economic Bulletin* 10, 1, June 1970. (Economic Commission for Africa, New York).

manufacturing in the formation of GDP ranged from 1 per cent (Mali, Togo and Upper Volta) to 17 per cent (Egypt). The range for Asian countries was from 6 per cent to 28 per cent and for Latin America it went from 12 per cent to 34 per cent.[12] The manufacturing base in Africa was smaller than either Asia's or Latin America's. A relatively large manufacturing base was approximated by only two countries (Nigeria and Egypt) in Africa, and both had a domestic defence industry, but by nine countries in Latin America and twelve countries in Asia.[13] Does this suggest some relationship between arms production and manufacturing share of GDP? Intuitively this would seem to be the case. To produce weapons requires manufacturing skills and this presupposes some experience, or minimum threshold of capacity, even for the most simple weapons.

The United Nation's classification of manufacturing industry in 1969 covered thirty-three sub-categories. The great bulk of them have no obvious connection with the production of small arms, naval craft or aircraft. The sub-categories do not list armaments in an identifiable way and therefore, to get some idea of the relationship between arms production and manufacturing, an indirect, and necessarily approximate, method had to be used.

Armaments, naval craft and aircraft are all heavily dependent on the metal trades. They have a high dependence on metal processing, metal fabrication and metal machining. Therefore we can assume that where armaments production is undertaken there will be some call upon the metal manufacturing and engineering sectors of the manufacturing sector. There are seven sub-categories of the United Nations manufacturing classification which are possible contributions to the defence programme. These are:

1. iron and steel
2. non-ferrous metals
3. metal products, not machinery
4. machinery, not electrical

12 United Nations, ibid., footnote.
13 The United Nations place all North African countries into Africa; Israel, Turkey and so on into Asia.

5. electrical machinery
6. shipbuilding and repairing
7. motor vehicles[14]

If we call this metal and engineering group the *potential defence capacity* (PDC) of the country, we can take it as a percentage of the country's total manufacturing capacity and see if it is relatively important in that country's output. Then the countries that are known to have a domestic defence industry can be compared with those that do not. As we are assuming that defence production is heavily biased towards this group of metal and engineering trades, we can see whether the defence production is associated with any obvious differences between the defence producers and the defence importers. The method is crude and therefore insensitive, but it is a guide, and, while not conclusive, may point to the general trends in each group.

The share of the PDC in the total manufacturing capacity of a country can be measured in several ways. The United Nations data for 1969 gives several sets of figures such as the wage bill for each sub-category, the contribution to fixed capital formation, the proportion of the value added, the numbers employed and the value of the output produced. The last two were chosen for this exercise because they indicate two important aspects of economic activity which are likely to be more meaningful than the others, given the general poor quality of the data available from the Third World. Summing the numbers employed is a reasonably unambiguous task. Estimating the wage bill for different grades of labour, or the fixed capital formation and value added for different definition of capital, would present statistical and conceptual problems even for an industrialised economy. In conditions where the data are unreliable, it makes the already crude procedure of this exercise even less meaningful. As employment and output are the least difficult figures to estimate, they are used here.

Information was available for 30 developing countries and 17 of them are known to be arms producers. The data were

14 United Nations, *The Growth of World Industry*, New York, 1969, vol. 2.

Table 5  Percentage relationship between potential defence capacity (PDC) and total manufacturing capacity, 30 countries, annual averages 1965-68

| | Arms producers | | | Arms importers | |
|---|---|---|---|---|---|
| Country | PDC % of total manufacturing employment | PDC % of total manufacturing output | Country | PDC % of total manufacturing employment | PDC % of total manufacturing output |
| Chile | 24.1 | 28 | Jordan | 15.5 | 8.2 |
| India | 23.9 | – | Philippines | 14.6 | – |
| Israel | 23.7 | 22.1 | Algeria | 14.5 | – |
| Brazil | 23.3 | 28 | Malaysia | 13.9 | – |
| Taiwan | 23 | 18.4 | Tunisia | 7.3 | – |
| Turkey | 20 | 22 | Libya | 7.3 | – |
| Korea | 16 | 14.9 | Iraq | 6.6 | 9.4 |
| Colombia | 15.9 | 12.1 | Honduras | 4.2 | 4.2 |
| Egypt | 13.7 | 11.7 | Malawi | 2.9 | 2.2 |
| Pakistan | 13.4 | 11.4 | Ethiopia | 1.8 | 4.4 |
| Iran | 12.7 | 10.6 | | | |
| Nigeria | 11.7 | 24.4 | | | |
| Sri Lanka | 9 | 9.6 | | | |
| El Salvador | 4.4 | 6.2 | | | |
| Dominican Republic | 2.2 | 2.2 | | | |
| Peru | 1.7 | 18.6 | | | |

Source: Calculated from United Nations, *Growth of World Industry*, 1969, vol.2.
– indicates no data available.

taken for the years 1965 and 1968 inclusive for each category in the metal and machinery trades. The totals for each year were then taken as a percentage of the total manufacturing capacity and the arithmetic mean calculated. This shows the percentage of total manufacturing capacity that is credited to the PDC for each country. Table 5 shows the results for the known defence producers and the arms importers.

The lack of data for arms importers limits the value of the striking visual difference between the two columns, for there is a clear tendency for arms producers to have a larger proportion of their manufacturing capacity in the metal and machinery, or PDC, group than for the arms importers, expressed in terms of percentage employment and percentage output. Metal working activity is an essential part of the industrialisation process, and countries with a small share of their manufacturing sector in the metal trades are not likely to be able to diversify into general arms production. But exceptionally, there are small countries, like Dominican Republic, Cuba, El Salvador, who have had a specialist interest in small arms and have been able to pursue these interests for some years without significant metal manufacturing activity.

The next thing to look at is whether the arms producers have tended to hold back their metal manufacturing capacity by the diversion into arms production, and what effect, if any, the PDC may have had on the growth of the metal and machinery sectors.

In Table 6 the growth performance of the manufacturing and PDC sectors for 15 countries is shown for countries where information was available. Thirteen of these countries had defence industries and only two were from the group of arms importers. It is clearly insufficient information to make even a crude comparison. Of the arms producers 9 of them have a PDC sector growing faster than their manufacturing sector. Arms production is not apparently inhibiting the expansion of the metal and machinery categories. Israel, El Salvador, Colombia, and Peru show the reverse relationship. Taking Israel on its own — as it can be argued that the other three countries are special cases of minor arms producers —

the relationship is interesting because Israel has been the most successful of all countries in the Third World in arms production. This creates some ambiguity in the picture; defence industries do not seem to slow down growth by diverting resources, but Israel's case weakens the implications of this conclusion; though it will be noted that the differences in Israel's case are marginal — 11.3 per cent for manufacturing and 10.6 per cent for the PDC sector.

*Table 6    Annual average rates of growth of manufacturing output and PDC, 15 countries, 1960-68*

| Country | Total manufacturing sector (%) | Potential defence capacity sector (%) |
|---|---|---|
| Sri Lanka | 5.2 | 21.9[1] |
| Taiwan | 16.6 | 21.7 |
| Turkey* | 13.6 | 21.2[2] |
| Korea | 18.2 | 19.4[3] |
| Egypt | 11.7 | 18.1 |
| Iran | 11.7 | 12.2[4] |
| India | 5.8 | 11.5[3] |
| Israel | 11.3 | 10.6[3] |
| Dominican Rep. | 1.5 | 9.4[5] |
| El Salvador | 11.5 | 8.2[1] |
| Peru | 8.2 | 8.1 |
| Chile | 4.9 | 6.9[3] |
| Colombia | 6.0 | 5.2 |
| Ecuador** | 11.4 | 20.5[6] |
| Honduras* | 11.9 | 17.9[7] |

Source:  United Nations, *Growth of World Industry*.
          * 1960-66.
          ** For ship building and repair 1964-68.
Notes:    1 Iron and steel, non-ferrous metals and metal products only.
          2 Iron and steel and non-ferrous metals.
          3 Excludes shipbuilding and motor vehicles.
          4 Excludes iron and steel and non-ferrous metals.
          5 Excludes metal products and machinery groups.
          6 Excludes iron and steel, non-ferrous metals and machinery.
          7 Excludes machinery.

## 6.    Conclusion

Domestic military production is not necessarily a diversion from the industrialisation programme of a Third World country. There is no evidence that it wastes resources or holds back growth of the manufacturing sector. From an economic point of view it has a number of attractive features because it tackles some of the structural obstacles to development. The market is monopsonistic and the technology transferable. The potential defence sector is associated with and integrated into the metal and engineering sector, and there appears to be some positive association between the expansion of both sectors.

# 16 Arms Production : The Products

### 1.  Introduction

In this chapter the products of the arms producers in the developing world will be looked at more closely. In examining some of the products we will be able to bring out some of the policy issues involved and some of the consequences for the industrial structure of taking on aircraft, armour and naval construction.

By using an estimate of the normal maintenance requirements for the weapons that are used in the Third World we can estimate the labour inputs needed to keep these weapon systems operational. As these modern military products require considerable maintenance and repair facilities it seems intuitively sensible to look for a connection between the estimated size of the maintenance and repair workforce that a country might need and its ambitions as a defence producer.

The skills and technical know-how that a country accumulates from the maintenance of supersonic aircraft, modern fast surface boats and destroyers, and from large formations of heavy armour, are a necessary first stage in creating the minimum ability to produce some of the weapons domestically. The evidence seems to confirm this commonsense view of the connection between current military maintenance capability and the establishment of domestic arms production.

### 2.  Small arms

About a third of the Third World countries produce some of their own small arms and ordnance. Of these India, Israel,

Egypt, Pakistan and North Korea claim to be self-sufficient. From the technical point of view small arms and their ammunition are the simplest weapons to produce. The basic work involves light machining (lathe, drill, bore, ream, grind and press machines) and metal forming. A country that has a metal manufacturing sector has the basic resources to go into small arms production. Countries such as Dominican Republic, Argentina, Turkey, India and El Salvador have considerable experience in the production of small arms; in Turkey's case since 1890.

The large armies and para-military forces of the Third World constitute a large and constant demand for small arms and ordnance, and each country has to meet this demand out of the budget and has to import them unless they are produced locally. The full-time work of gunsmiths in keeping these stocks operational is a first step towards the setting up of workshops to manufacture parts and assemble them. For some countries this may not be an attractive alternative wherever they have open access to supplies from the major manufacturing nations and relatively peaceful situations. But countries such as India, Pakistan, Israel and Egypt, which have considerable access to the major arms suppliers and have also been engaged in military action, have taken the political decision to achieve self-sufficiency in small arms production.

Some of the weapons are produced under licence from foreign manufacturers, but some are indigenously designed, such as the Israeli Uzi sub-machine gun and the Argentinian sub-machine gun series.[1] The Egyptians produced a modified Swedish-designed rifle (renamed the Hakim 7.92mm.), and after this experience they went on to produce their own rifle, the 'Rashid', and a sub-machine gun, the 'Port Said'. Dominican Republic produces the Cristobal .30 carbine in a plant established by the Italian Beretta company. India's small arms experience was gained under the British and the Ishapore factory produces a local rifle as well as the Belgian FN Nato 'assault' rifle. During the Second World War over 690,000 Enfields and thousands of Vickers machine guns were manufactured in India. In Indonesia the work of re-boring thousands of captured weapons started the national

1 SIPRI, op. cit., p. 725.

small arms industry, and in Iran the experience gained from manufacturing Czechoslovakian small arms in the 1930s and the licensed manufacture of Russian sub-machine guns during the Second World War (similar arrangements still continue) established the small arms industry which continues its activities today. Mexico's arms industry produces the Obregon .45 hand gun and the Mendoza 7mm. machine gun. Turkey produces a German designed hand gun (the 'Walther PP').[2]

It is likely that this trend will continue. A country that uses its monopsonistic buying status to develop a local arms capability can realise wider ambitions by exports to other Third World countries. The Egyptian leaders in 1972, for example, were strongly in favour of all the Arab countries pooling their resources to establish an Arab defence industry capable of producing enough arms to outpace Israel's arms output by 1977. The motivation was clearly political rather than economic, as the Egyptians were in favour of arms production 'even if the cost of production is double the price of imported arms'.[3] Israel, however, is considerably further advanced in domestic arms production and already exports some of its models, earning the ultimate accolade for design and performance in that some of its weapons are manufactured under licence in Europe.[4]

### 3.    Armour

The conventional armies of the Third World have strong armoured elements. Many of the para-military formations are heavily armed with tanks, armoured personnel carriers, helicopters and even ground-attack aircraft. In many cases the kind of weapons that the army of the para-military forces have at their disposal depends upon the roles that the government assigns to them. Internal security is a more

2 Frank, op. cit., chapter 4.

3 Lt.-General Saad Eddin Shazli, Egypt's Chief of Staff, quoted in *Financial Times*, London, 21 December 1972.

4 Frank, op. cit., p. 126; Israel offered domestically produced missiles for export in March 1973, which represents a fairly advanced stage in domestic arms production.

pressing problem in most countries than external threats, and armour is a key element in controlling cities. It tends to make or break an attempted military coup.

Some of the countries with large armoured forces have been engaged in conventional tank battles. Egypt, Israel, Jordan, Syria, India and Pakistan have made substantial use of armour in their wars, especially India and Israel who have done this to devastating effect. Somalia is extremely well endowed with armour compared to its neighbours. Its 13,000 strong army has four tank battalions and nine mechanised infantry battalions, which have 250 medium tanks and over 200 armoured personnel carriers between them.[5] Most of this armour is of Russian origin and arrived after the border war with Ethiopia in 1964.

Heavy armour deteriorates quickly. Operating the vehicles has a punishing effect on the mechanical efficiency of the moving parts. If they are also being shot at or mined, this makes the problem much worse. Even under the ideal conditions of peace-time training, using skilled operators, the costs of maintenance are extremely high. The ideal conditions seldom exist in the Third World. The terrain is difficult, the climate unsuitable, the operators inexperienced and the maintenance function almost non-existent, at least at near-adequate standards of efficiency. This situation gives the country with well-trained and disciplined troops, using properly maintained armour, striking advantages over potential opponents. To a large measure this explains the failures of the Arabs and the Pakistanis in their military confrontations — it is not a question of valour but of preparation; the Israelis and the Indians simply worked harder at being operationally efficient.

SIPRI has compiled estimates of the maintenance costs and manpower requirements for armour, aircraft and naval craft to keep them operational to Swedish standards. Now there are few countries in the Third World that are able to match Swedish standards, but we can nevertheless use these figures to estimate what these countries would require if they were to maintain and operate their military equipment at these standards. By using these model standards we can set

5 IISS, *The Military Balance, 1971-72*, London, 1972, p. 37.

them against the registered military hardware that the country has credited to it in the various international publications and see what this would mean in terms of man-hours of skilled work to keep these pieces operational. We can convert the estimated maintenance hours into man-year equivalents for ease of manipulation. Man-year equivalents are not a real world requirement — this would assume that every hour in a working year was used on maintenance by an extremely dedicated workforce — but it makes rank order comparisons between countries easier.

The Third World puts its vehicles through quasi-combat conditions. In combat the maintenance function is disrupted by organisational breakdowns, enemy actions and fatigue. The climatic conditions of the Third World — heat, humidity and dust — intensify the wear and tear on the vehicles. The absence of proper roads means that the vehicles are being driven over rough country for most of their working life and the lack of systematic maintenance, inevitable in warfare conditions, is a permanent condition of peace.

An efficient armoured unit requires 150 trained mechanics for every 100 tanks, another 50 mechanics for every 100 APCs and 5 mechanics for every 100 trucks.[6] The cost in spare parts alone for tanks is estimated to be $10 for every kilometre that they are driven.

Few Third World armies will reach these manpower standards. Some armies are nowhere near these standards. The Indonesian army for example had a large part of its equipment non-operational in 1969. Only a third of the navy was seaworthy, 42 of the 122 aircraft were grounded and about a third of the army was engaged in non-military duties.[7] This kind of situation will lead to steady deterioration of performance. The burden of service will fall on a smaller number of vehicles which will raise the rate of wear and tear and put yet more out of action. The result is to reduce the military effectiveness of the forces.

The difference in the number of mechanics needed to maintain a hundred tanks and those needed to maintain a hundred trucks is a measure of the tanks' greater mechanical

6 SIPRI, op. cit., p. 806.
7 IISS, *The Military Balance, 1971-72*, p. 47.

complexity. Tanks will use up the services of skilled mechanics even after they go for a drive along a city road. The training costs of maintenance mechanics are very high — excluding upkeep it cost $6,000 in Sweden to put a man through a six-month training programme.[8] There might be some additional return to the economy if the skills are ultimately transferable to the civilian sector. Vehicle maintenance has an important role in the development of mechanised agriculture and transport.

Training in repair of tank transmissions may be valuable to a man who will repair Mack trucks when he returns to civilian life, but the training will not have been nearly as valuable as it would have been had it been training in repairing Mack trucks.[9]

The question is not as simple as that.

Countries have and, for the foreseeable future, intend to keep armed forces. They are going to continue to equip their forces with mechanised vehicles which will require maintenance. The real issue is not whether the civilian spill-over effects could be achieved by different methods — that they clearly could — but whether, in spite of the existence of a theoretical alternative, the necessity to allocate resources to internal and external security leads to spill-over effects and, if it does, whether these spill-over effects are qualitatively greater in countries that have the largest investment in military security. In this case we are measuring the potential contribution to the civilian goals of society of the military capability that a country purchases or acquires, though the amount of military investment does not directly relate to the amount of security that a country achieves from such acquisitions.

A large armoured force requires mechanics. It must also have available the means to train considerable numbers of mechanics and, of course, the facilities for them to carry out their functions. The issue, therefore, is whether this process will have any spill-over effects, intended or otherwise, on the civilian sectors, either from the trained men leaving the army

8 SIPRI, op. cit., p. 807.
9 Hovey, op. cit., p. 125.

at the end of their service, or from the work opportunities it creates for private and public firms. If there is a spill-over from military activity and military activity is irreplaceable in the world as we know it, then the spill-over is a positive contribution in itself and ought not to be set against alternatives that are not available.

Is there a relationship between military strength and the potential defence capacity of a country (i.e. the engineering manufacturing sectors)? Five countries in the Third World are known to have some domestic manufacturing experience of armoured fighting vehicles. These are: Argentina, Brazil, Israel, India and Egypt. Turkey is also reported to be planning to produce tanks and other armoured vehicles. Argentina has assembled 30 French-designed AMX-13 tanks; Brazil has designed its own armoured reconnaissance vehicle (for counter-insurgency operations); India produces a version of the Vickers tank, the 'Vijayanta'; Israel had produced a hybrid tank – a Sherman (US) chassis with a AMX-13 (French) 75 mm. gun; and Egypt has also modified Sherman tanks.[10]

Where information is available on the armoured fighting vehicle strengths of countries, it is possible to calculate the manpower equivalents to maintain the vehicles to Swedish standards, using the SIPRI figures. (With the exception of truck production, because the figures are not available.) A country with domestic truck production or assembly facilities can easily switch to military production with a few modifications. These trucks tend to be designed for 'up country' use, and they are adaptable for military purposes with little effort. As trucks require the least manpower to maintain, the absence of the truck maintenance figures will not effect the figures a great deal.

Using the Swedish figures – 150 mechanics for 100 tanks and 50 mechanics for 100 APCs – Table 1 has been constructed. The countries are ranked by the estimated number of man-years equivalent to maintenance required for their known rank strengths in 1970. The administrative personnel and managerial staffs that are necessary to establish and operate maintenance functions have not been included in

10 SIPRI, op. cit., p. 726.

the figure. The figures show what is required to repair, service and maintain the tanks as a purely technical function.

The first three countries in the Table, Egypt, India and Israel, which have the largest maintenance requirements in manpower, happen to be countries which also have some domestic armour production or substantial modification capabilities. India has carried out domestic production on the largest scale. The 'Vijayanta' tank, a modified version of the Vickers Armstrong Chieftain, is scheduled to be produced at a rate of 200 tanks per year from the Madras works in the early 1970s. Between 1967 and 1970 India produced 200 tanks of this type, which makes India the Third World's foremost producer of armoured fighting vehicles. Approximately 43 per cent of this tank has been made domestically and the rest is imported.

*Table 1   Maintenance man-year equivalents required for declared armoured strength at Swedish standards in the developing world, 1970*

| Country | Maintenance man-years required | Country | Maintenance man-years required |
|---------|-------------------------------|---------|-------------------------------|
| Egypt | 3075 | Somalia | 401 |
| India | 2175[+] | Saudi Arabia | 390[+] |
| Israel | 2120 | Cuba | 340 |
| Iran | 1995 | Sudan | 257 |
| Korea (N) | 1600[+] | Peru | 240 |
| Pakistan | 1455[+] | Libya | 181[+] |
| Iraq | 1445 | Brazil | 150 |
| Syria | 1225 | Lebanon | 150[+] |
| Algeria | 850 | Vietnam (S) | 125 |
| Vietnam (N) | 600[+] | Thailand | 100[+] |
| Jordan | 547 | Argentina | 90 |
| Morocco | 490 | | |

Sources: SIPRI, op. cit., p. 806 for the maintenance standards per 100 vehicles: IISS, *The Military Balance 1970-71* and *The Military Balance 1971-72*, London, 1971 and 1972, for the armoured strengths of the countries.

[+]From incomplete details.

Israeli armoured production was exclusively from the cannibalisation of ex-American Shermans. The technical aspect of this effort is ingenious (a combination of welding and fitting skills), but the domestic production side has not been developed. The useable debris of the 1967 war gave Israel considerable numbers of tanks, including the capture without a fight of a whole brigade of Russian T-54s in Sinai.[11] Such windfall gains do not encourage the use of Israeli resources to produce tanks, though there is little doubt that they could do so if they felt it necessary. The Egyptians have relied on imported Soviet armour rather than develop their own tank production, and this decision not to produce domestically is a consequence of easily acquired material. The modification of heavy and medium tank bodies, their tracks, engines and firing systems is probably within the capability of most of the countries in the Table.

The interesting positions in the Table are occupied by Brazil and Argentina. Brazil's tank force is relatively large by Latin American standards — about 100 tanks — but given the size of the country it is relatively modest in comparison with other large developing countries, e.g. India. Yet Brazil is the only developing country to attempt to design and build an armoured personnel vehicle, the Cutia 'Vete' T 1A1. APCs are much lighter than tanks, more manoeuvreable and much faster — the Vete T 1A1 can reach 80 mph on paved roads.[12] The design and construction of APCs is quite different from that of tanks and it is not so anomalous that the Brazilians have made these efforts in view of their place in the armour maintenance Table.

Brazil's transport sector produces about 6 per cent of the manufacturing output. These APCs would be compatible with that kind of commercial and light-vehicle experience. The political estimates of the Brazilian government as to where the major threat to their security is coming from have led to the development of the APC rather than the heavy battle tanks. Imported tanks probably meet the needs of the government for heavy armour to back up the civil authorities against disorders in the cities. APCs have specifications, such as high speeds and long range, which are ideal for urban troop deployments in counter-insurgency operations. The experi-

11 R.S. and W.S. Churchill, op. cit., p. 167.
12 SIPRI, op. cit. p. 726.

ence gained in producing a reconnaissance vehicle is a first step to developing a vehicle for counter-insurgency. This aspect of domestic arms production in the Third World is likely to grow in importance.

Third World governments face internal security problems on a growing scale. The arms they need are not necessarily the type so far sold to them by the industrialised countries, where different strategic considerations determine the feasibility of weapon systems. Arms imports of obsolete weapon systems from areas with different requirements are less likely in future to look attractive to security conscious Third World governments. Argentina's work on the IA 58 counter-insurgency aircraft is part of this trend of switching to weapons more suitable to local needs.

Heavy tanks, supersonic aircraft and aircraft carriers have been imported on a grand scale into the Third World and probably provide less security per dollar than more expensive domestically produced security equipment that at least has the design advantages of being made to order. Those countries that have been engaged in conventional warfare no doubt need the traditional type of weapons, but other countries, such as are found in Latin America and Africa, would have much to gain from a change in emphasis; they might also discover that there is a lucrative export potential in this type of equipment.

Argentina's armoured vehicle programme developed from its domestic commercial automobile industry. There has also been a close linkage in Argentina between the aircraft industry and the motor vehicle industry. The state-owned Fabrica Militar Aviones, which sponsored some of the post-war aircraft projects, went over almost entirely to motor vehicle production in its plants in 1954. This shift in output was significant enough to show up in a spurt in Argentinian manufacturing industry in the early 1950s. Until 1954 employment in the vehicle sector was almost entirely confined to garage and maintenance work, but after 1954 it grew dramatically as a result of the expansion of vehicle manufacturing.[13] This was due to the shift from aircraft to

13 J.M. Katz, *Production Functions, Foreign Investment and Growth: A Study Based on the Argentine Manufacturing Sector, 1946-1961*, New York, 1969, p. 130.

motor vehicles production decided upon by the FMA. The skills, techniques, plant and experience of the one field are useable in the other — and presumably in reverse too. This process is underlined by the experience of Industries Kaiser Argentina which also switched from aircraft to motor vehicle production. Through a French acquisition of this company (by Renault) an arrangement was made for it to diversify into production, under licence, of the French AMX-13 tank.

The situation appears to be one where the major armour users in the Third World are well placed, by virtue of the large scale technical maintenance requirements of heavy tanks, to go over to the production of armoured vehicles, if they decide politically to do so. In India's case this has been undertaken successfully. India has large territories to defend and has used tanks in the three conventional wars she has fought in the past ten years. Israel and Egypt have the capacity, but so far they have used it only to modify vehicles because the alternative supplies are fairly open — Israel from war booty and Egypt from Russian generosity. Countries with substantial mechanical experience from motor vehicle production such as Brazil and Argentina have been able to develop a domestic light armour industry, suited to their security needs.

### 4. *Naval construction*

Argentina and India have produced some sophisticated naval vessels, such as destroyers and frigates, but the normal type of craft produced in the Third World is patrol boats and light craft. Sri Lanka, India, Indonesia, Mexico, Thailand and Turkey produce patrol type craft ranging in size from the 37 ton 'Polimar' in Mexico to the Turkish 412 ton 'Kochisar'. But the major portion of the naval supplies come from abroad in every case. Sri Lanka imported 19 small patrol boats between 1955 and 1967 (and two frigates and a minesweeper) but assembled 12 motor launches in 1968. It has the ability therefore to replace some of its imports of naval craft but has not chosen to become self-sufficient. India's imports between 1950 and 1970 included an aircraft carrier, a cruiser, 6 destroyers, 9 frigates, 7 submarines, 18 patrol boats and some smaller craft, but its own yards built 3 frigates and some light boats between 1960 and 1968. This pattern was followed by Indonesia which imported 23 heavy ships, 14 submarines and 185 light patrol boats between 1950 and 1965 and build 28 patrol boats domestically. Thailand and Turkey similarly imported the heavier craft and built some local patrol boats.[14]

The small proportion of local shipbuilding that is undertaken in the Third World is partly explained by the smallness of their shipbuilding facilities. In Table 2 the size of the shipbuilding facilities as a proportion of total manufacturing capacity for 14 countries is shown. Those countries that do build some of their naval requirements domestically tend to have a larger share of their manufacturing capacity in ship-building than those that do not. The naval construction countries have a marginal lead of an average of 1.04 per cent of manufacturing employment and 0.82 per cent of output in shipbuilding, against 0.93 per cent for employment and 0.23 per cent for output for the non-naval constructing powers.

Countries like Ghana (1.1 per cent), Iraq (1.2 per cent), Pakistan (1.4 per cent) and Tunisia (1.2 per cent) with comparable employment levels to the constructors probably had the potential to become viable domestic producers of military vessels. But for most countries the

Table 2   Shipbuilding facilities as a percentage of manufacturing capacity, 14 countries, 1965-68

| Naval constructors | | | Non-constructors | | |
|---|---|---|---|---|---|
| Country | Employment % | Output % | Country | Employment % | Output % |
| Chile | 2.1 | 0.7 | Algeria | 0.4 | 0.2 |
| Colombia | 0.3 | 0.1 | Ecuador | 0.6 | — |
| India | 0.7 | — | Ghana | 1.1 | 0.01 |
| Korea | 1.4 | 2.5 | Iraq | 1.2 | 0.3 |
| Peru· | 0.6 | — | Nigeria | 0.6 | 0.03 |
| Turkey | 1.3 | 0.4 | Pakistan | 1.4 | 0.6 |
| Egypt | 0.9 | 0.4 | | | |

Source:   United Nations, *Growth of World Industry*.

14 SIPRI, op. cit., p. 734 and Appendix 6.

proportion of GDP arising from shipbuilding is quite small, and it is not apparently an activity that the Third World has undertaken in a substantial way.

The techniques and skills required for shipbuilding and repairs are relatively simple (compared to much of the metal manufacturing sectors, such as vehicles and aircraft). They are also skills that must be present if the industrialisation process is to be undertaken. The metal trades of fabrication, welding and metal forming are needed primarily, as well as draughting and design. The need for a power source is the major problem and this is probably the major obstacle to Third World naval construction. The engines and their parts can be imported and assembled but the benefits from domestic manufacture of the hulls and superstructure, when the high-valued components still have to be imported, are marginal.

Countries with some naval capacity have a base upon which to build. Naval vessels require considerable maintenance to keep them seaworthy. The standards of maintenance in the Third World vary from abysmal to tolerable.[15] We can carry out the same exercise on shipping as we have on armour. In the case of naval vessels the maintenance in man hours varies considerably for each type of vessel. The Swedish standards have been set out below:

Table 3    *Maintenance man-hours for naval vessels*

| Type | Man-hours per year |
|---|---|
| Destroyers | 45,000 |
| Submarines | 19,000 |
| Minecraft | 56,000 |
| Motor torpedo boats (small) | 11,250 |
| Motor torpedo boats (large) | 10,000 |
| Gunboats | 12,250 |

Source: SIPRI, op. cit., p.807.

The details of the naval strengths of the Third World given in the source publications create a special problem for this type of exercise. The vessel types do not always fit clearly

15 See R. Dumont, *Fresh Start in Africa*, London, 1966.

into the maintenance categories in the Table. For example, corvettes, cruisers and frigates have to be treated as if they were destroyers, and patrol boats which come in a whole range of sizes have had to be lumped together. Many other ships such as tankers, oilers, supply ships, landing craft and training ships are not listed in the Swedish data. In the case of aircraft carriers, also not listed, this has a significant effect on the totals for they require large-scale maintenance programmes. Only a handful of countries have aircraft carriers (India, Brazil, Argentina) and they have large navies as well. The non-inclusion of aircraft carriers reduces their maintenance totals, though they are still near the top of the table.

The annual maintenance hours for each country's naval force have to be converted into man-year equivalents required. This was arbitrarily chosen to be a working year of 50 weeks at 45 hours per week (2250 hours) which was divided into the annual total man-hour maintenance requirement for the fleets that each country had. This calculation is subject to all the qualifications already mentioned: maintenance standards are not the same in every country; the fleets have a different composition and some of their craft have been assigned arbitrarily; the ships are of varying age and design, and therefore the hours of work even for similar jobs will be different; and the annual hours of work figure assumes a constant work pace at a fixed working week for 50 weeks. It is nowhere suggested here that the figures in Table 4 are the actual or even realistic maintenance hours for any of the countries. The calculation is aimed at a rough index to order the different countries; the order is more important than the figures.

The maintenance work force figures produced in the Table will vary considerably with the composition of the fleets. Naval firepower is not directly related to maintenance. Submarines require 19,000 hours a year to remain operational which is about one third that required by minesweepers (56,000 hours). Gunboats have more maintenance hours than heavy torpedo boats. Thus a country with minesweepers and gunboats may have a larger maintenance input requirement than another country armed with destroyers and submarines, though the firepower difference would reverse the relationship.

Table 4   Workforce requirements in man-year equivalents to maintain declared naval strengths of 48 developing countries, 1970

| Country | Man-year equivalents required | Country | Man-year equivalents required |
|---|---|---|---|
| Indonesia* | 1503 | Syria | 143 |
| Taiwan* | 1176 | Uruguay | 143 |
| Brazil* | 849 | Tunisia | 142 |
| India* | 717 | Iraq | 122 |
| Argentina* | 705 | Nigeria | 120 |
| Korea (S)* | 666 | Ecuador | 109 |
| Korea (N)* | 658 | Cambodia | 88 |
| Egypt* | 634 | Morocco | 75 |
| Pakistan | 423 | Tanzania | 65 |
| Burma* | 380 | Saudi Arabia | 58 |
| Philippines | 378 | Paraguay | 43 |
| Cuba* | 360 | Zaire | 43 |
| Malaysia | 341 | Somalia | 32 |
| Colombia* | 339 | Sudan | 32 |
| Peru* | 338 | Guinea | 32 |
| Thailand* | 335 | Guatemala | 27 |
| Iran | 319 | Lebanon | 27 |
| Algeria | 304 | Nicaragua | 26 |
| Venezuela | 281 | Kenya | 21 |
| Chile* | 254 | El Salvador | 20 |
| Mexico* | 240 | Honduras | 16 |
| Dominican Republic* | 217 | Ivory Coast | 10 |
| Libya | 196 | Malagasy | 10 |
| Israel* | 187 | Senegal | 9 |

Source:   IISS, *Military Balance*, *1969-70* and *1970-71*, London.
     * Known naval craft producer.

Indonesia tops the Table for maintenance requirements. It was also reported to be a country with only a 33 per cent seaworthiness in its fleet.[16] The 17 naval producers in the Table (marked by an asterisk) are all in the top 24 countries.

16 IISS, *The Military Balance, 1971-72*, p. 47.

The average man-year equivalent workforce requirement of the naval producers is 562 men and the average for the non-producers (i.e. the importers) is 118. The average is reduced considerably by the range of the importers, from 9 men in Senegal to 423 in Pakistan. If we exclude all the smaller navies in countries below Libya in the Table and take the average for the remaining countries (i.e. those above Israel) the average for the importers rises to 320. The conclusion is therefore the same: naval producers have on average naval forces which require higher maintenance inputs than naval importers, and thereby, at least on paper, more extensive maintenance and repairs experience. Seven countries, Pakistan, Philippines, Malaysia, Iran, Algeria, Venezuela and Libya, have maintenance requirements on one measure comparable to the naval producers and are probably potentially capable of moving into naval construction. The strategic placement of some of these countries (Malaysia, Algeria, Iran) suggests that the trend for them towards the year 2000 will be to develop some experience in this field.[17]

A criticism of Third World countries in the past is that they have based their naval development on an immitative model of the conventional navies of the industrialised powers. Brazil and Argentina are two cases in point. In 1956 Brazil paid $35 million for a second-hand British aircraft carrier. The delivery of the ship provoked a civil war between the navy and the airforce as to which service was to control the carrier. The crisis caused trouble for four Presidents and led to the resignations of ten admirals and ministers. On several occasions pitched battles actually broke out between

17 Malaysia and Indonesia are separated by 24 miles of sea at the closest point and in 1972 both countries were making suggestions that the Straits might cease to be international waters and presumably become subject to a charge for useage. This particularly affects Japan whose oil passes through these waters from the Middle East; Algeria is placed at an important end of the Mediterranean which is at present patrolled by NATO and Warsaw Pact fleets; Iran is emerging as a new power in the Middle East and naval dominance of the Gulf will be necessary if it is to be made secure, especially in its conflict with Iraq. See E. Downton, 'The power game in the Persian Gulf', *Daily Telegraph*, London, 5 February 1970; P. Martin, 'Iraq: eyes on the gulf', *The Times*, London, 3 April 1970.

the two services. The eventual compromise was arrived at in 1965: the navy ran the carrier and the airforce the aircraft. But this was not the only repercussion. Within weeks of the original sale Argentina followed suit and bought another re-conditioned ex-British carrier. Its only problem was 'that the ship was so obsolete that it could not accommodate modern jet aircraft'.[18] Apart from these aspects of the fiasco the purchases themselves were open to grave criticism as being of little use to either country in dealing with its security problems. Carriers have limited use in dealing with insurgency in urban centres.

Developing countries can build up their naval interests on a more modest scale by gaining experience on small craft. As their maintenance function increases, carefully prepared orders for smaller craft from the government can set up a shipbuilding facility that can turn to larger craft, and eventually commercial craft, in due course. If the government works for industrialisation on a sound basis, rather than becoming diverted into prestigious exercises, it can assist the programme along in this way. The fact remains, however, that even the acquisition of prestige vessels and the need to keep them operational will also provide a pool of experience for the industrialisation programme. It is not entirely negative, but acquiring naval vessels that have a useful security role as well as a training role clearly is more advantageous than the acquisition of 'useless' vessels.

## 5.    Aircraft production

Aircraft production is the highest stage of the military industrialisation process; the technology represented by the aircraft is for a Third World country the Matterhorn of sophistication. The airframe construction is similar in concept to that of a boat, but the tolerances are much finer and the fabrication process much more complex, and it has to meet rigid design standards. The airborne failure of aero-engines has fatal consequences and therefore the main-tenance standards are critical. Aircraft maintenance is

18 See Thayer, op. cit., p. 268.

measured in hours of flying time rather than on an annual service basis. Because air traffic is international, the ground systems and the maintenance facilities tend to approach a common standard throughout the world.

Almost all developing countries have airforces. These can vary from the huge combat forces of India (625 planes) and Egypt (523 planes) to the tiny forces of Tanzania (12 non-combat planes) or Senegal (10 non-combat planes).[19] As with the navy, the composition of the airforce will determine the maintenance requirements. The larger the combat element in an airforce the larger the airforce itself tends to be, but large numbers of utility planes can alter the ranking for maintenance. Maintenance hours are assigned according to flying time, but as flying times for a country's airforce are not available we have to use a circuitous route to carry out the calculations.

The SIPRI estimates show a ratio of 30 hours maintenance for every hour of flying time for interceptors, ground-attack and reconnaissance aircraft. For trainers and transports the ratio is 20 hours per hour of flying time. Helicopters also have 20 hours.[20] On this basis two mechanics would have to work for a year just to allow Algeria's 142 combat aircraft to fly for one hour.

SIPRI makes the further point that it takes four mechanics to maintain one aircraft and six completely to overhaul it.[21] We can use this rough measure to rank the maintenance requirements of the airforces in the Third World. Allowing for the fact that different types of aircraft have different requirements, we can nevertheless arrive at some indication of the maintenance inputs of these airforces. Again these figures do not include the back-up organisation to run a maintenance function. This is estimated to be about 50 men per aircraft. Airforces are clearly consumers of manpower.

These figures were applied to the declared air strengths of 60 developing countries, taking into account combat and non-combat aircraft and helicopters. The results are set out in Table 5. The known aircraft producers are indicated by an

19 See IISS, *The Military Balance, 1971-72*, pp. 33-46.
20 SIPRI, op. cit., p. 808.
21 ibid.

asterisk. From the Table the aircraft producers tend to have the largest airforces, and therefore the largest maintenance forces as measured by the SIPRI figure. Eleven of the highest work force requirements belong to countries with some

Table 5   Aircraft maintenance requirements for declared air strengths of 60 developing countries, 1970

| Country | Required work force | Country | Required work force |
|---|---|---|---|
| Egypt* | 5466 | Philippines | 612 |
| Brazil* | 5142 | Malaysia | 600 |
| India* | 4632 | Libya | 588 |
| Korea (N) | 4110 | Uruguay | 576 |
| Argentina* | 3672 | Bolivia | 486 |
| Vietnam (S) | 3450 | Burma | 468 |
| Israel* | 2976 | Zaire | 402 |
| Taiwan* | 2772 | Nigeria | 396 |
| Pakistan* | 2400 | Sudan | 354 |
| Turkey* | 2160 | Tunisia | 342 |
| Venezuela | 1920 | Ecuador | 324 |
| Iraq | 1800 | Uganda | 324 |
| Iran | 1782 | Ghana | 312 |
| Chile* | 1746 | Zambia | 300 |
| Cuba | 1740 | Singapore | 300 |
| Peru | 1740 | Nicaragua | 294 |
| Korea (S) | 1620 | Honduras | 282 |
| Thailand | 1452 | El Salvador | 276 |
| Syria | 1416 | Cambodia | 258 |
| Vietnam (N) | 1368 | Paraguay | 246 |
| Indonesia* | 1272 | Jordan | 240 |
| Algeria | 1230 | Lebanon | 216 |
| Mexico* | 1140 | Kenya | 210 |
| Morocco | 1098 | Somalia | 198 |
| Colombia | 984 | Guatemala | 192 |
| Afghanistan | 888 | Ivory Coast | 126 |
| Saudi Arabia | 732 | Tanzania | 108 |
| Ethiopia | 684 | Guinea | 66 |
| Dominican Republic | 636 | Malagasy / | 60 |
| Laos | 618 | Senegal | 60 |

Sources: Air Strengths from IISS, Military Balance, 1970 and ibid., 1971; maintenance conversion figures from SIPRI, op. cit., p. 808.

domestic aircraft industry. The average required work force of these countries is 3034, compared with an average for the aircraft importers (in the top twenty-three countries) of 1969 men. Taking all the airforces into account, the importing countries average falls to 811 men. Aircraft production capability is clearly related to aircraft industry activity. The larger the aircraft maintenance requirements, the more likely the country will be developing some local capacity to assemble or even design its own aircraft.

Some countries have a maintenance requirement for their airpower commensurate with that of countries that have domestic air production in some form or another, yet choose to import aircraft rather than attempt ·their own output. Eight of these countries Korea (North and South), Vietnam (North and South), Iraq, Thailand, Syria and Cuba are in relative tension areas — they perceive some threat externally. Venezuela, Peru and Algeria are not in any obvious way threatened externally and their large airforces defy justification on those grounds. Iran is coming under increasing pressure from its neighbour Iraq as each challenges for the leadership of the Gulf.[22]

At the end of the European ·war in 1945 a number of German designers became refugees and this gave an opportunity to some of the Third World countries to acquire highly qualified design teams with proven records of ability. Argentina, Brazil, India and Egypt made use of these services. Indonesia appears to have been an exception and to have developed its aircraft production from its own resources. However, the success rate for indigenous-designed aircraft has not been very good. The developmental costs for new aircraft are very high and their lead-times were often beyond that which some of these governments had the patience for. The government needs a strong political will to carry through a development programme in such high risk ventures. These difficulties were made worse by the habit of concentration on prestige projects — jet aircraft before they had experience of non-jet technology — which were not within the available technology nor the available capacity. The planes were within the design capabilities of the designers — after all they were

22 The points made in note 17 apply.

previously part of the world's foremost aircraft producing teams — but were outside the local capacities of the plants set aside to manufacture them. Egypt, Argentina and Brazil fell victim to this problem for many years. Israel and India tried a different route. They went for planes within their capabilities and gradually extended themselves into higher technology.

The political difficulties of the aircraft ventures are no less serious for the sponsors. Attracted by the prospect of a modern jet industry, they are vulnerable to the set-backs and failures which are an inescapable part of a development programme. The pressure is put on to produce quick results, but the reality is for results to be delayed. This provides political ammunition for opposition; in democracies this is a gift to the opposition parties and in dictatorships it is a gift to conspiring rivals within the bureaucracy.

India set itself the target of self-sufficiency in aircraft production for both military and civilian use within a period of 20 years (by 1967). Argentina, under Perón, went through a similar nationalistic fervour until it was re-directed into more modest, and eventually more successful, projects after 1954. The result by 1972 was not self-sufficiency, or anywhere near it, but both countries had built a substantial capability in aircraft production which is beginning to bear fruit in the 1970s.

The Hindustan Aeronautics Company (HAL) grew out of the maintenance work and repairs to British aircraft during the Second World War. It assembled its first aircraft in 1948 and subsequently produced Vampire fighters and Folland Gnat trainers for the Indian airforce. In 1969, HAL is reported to have been making a profit of $5 million on a gross turnover of $87.4 million.[23] But the early attempts at producing fighters were total failures. The ill-fated HAL HF-24 started off as a 'low cost' fighter at $1.5 million in 1956. By 1969 only 16 had been produced and the individual cost had risen to $7.4 million, with three major changes in engine. HAL achieved much more success with its licensed production of Russian MiG-21s, and delivery began to the

23 SIPRI, op. cit., p. 745.

Indian airforce in 1970. Local inputs into the MiG is about 60 per cent.

The most successful Indian-built aircraft is the Folland Gnat, powered by imported Bristol Orpheus turbo-jets. Over 85 per cent of the components are manufactured in India, including 60 per cent of the engine. This must have had a beneficial effect by spreading technology and guaranteeing risk projects in India's manufacturing sector.[24]

The Argentinian case history is like India's, but with less successful results. It started during the Second World War, but went straight into local design and prototype production. The power of airpower was demonstrated by the combatants in the war, and the acquisition of this power was an attractive proposition to Argentina. But 8 of the 13 aircraft built in Argentina were cancelled before the production stage.[25] Two of the planes that were successful were the IA-35 multi-purpose aircraft, of which 100 were built, and the IA-46 light agricultural monoplane, of which 114 had been built up to 1970.

Other activities of the Argentinians included the licensed production of foreign-designed aircraft, mainly trainers. The counter-insurgency aircraft, the IA-47 and the IA-55, were field-tested in 1970, and it was upon these that the aircraft industry was pinning its hopes for large export sales to other Latin American countries in order to break into major production.

Argentina uses its military aviation to extend and maintain communication links with outlying areas of the country which are not easily accessible by, or commercially profitable for, civil air companies. A similar task is given to the Colombia airforce by the government. Once airstrips are constructed and the country opened to air-traffic, the routes can be handed over to commercial operators.[26]

The major lesson from these cases is that licensed assembling is the best first-stage activity for a developing country wishing to set up on aircraft capability. The arrival of emigré designers from Europe was not the fortuitous gift

24 ibid., p. 752.
25 ibid., p. 763.
26 *Flying Review International*, February 1970, p. 52.

that it appeared to be. Ambitious projects beyond the capability of the country's technology are likely to be wasteful of resources. The Brazilian government appeared to have taken this point when they set up a joint state-private company to assemble the Aeromacchi MB-326G light strike/ trainer in 1969.

Israel's state-owned aircraft industry (IAI), like India's, grew out of maintenance capability and is an organisation employing over 10,000 people in 1972.[27] Israel has had the advantage of a large pool of expatriate labour to draw upon plus the pressure of external threats to security. It took the route from repair work to production and used glider work to learn the basic aerodynamics. This type of thoroughness has paid off in exports of the IAI Avra light transport and its executive jet. It is suggested that the next project will be a small interceptor.[28] Although the light transport has commercial selling points, it should be noted that its short take-off — 590 feet — in temporary land strips and its adaptable pay load — including a jeep and occupants — has military applications which have not been missed by the Israelis nor for that matter by the Arabs.

Egyptian aircraft production seems to be still in the early Argentinian stage. It used German designers (including Willy Messerschmidt), but their projects have been cancelled for cost reasons. Its successes have been in modest light monoplanes, but its greatest disasters have been in attempts at missiles and rockets. (These were also subject to Israeli sabotage.) By 1969 the Egyptians had advanced no further than where they were in the 1950s with light aircraft, and their ambitions in jet planes and missiles had been frustrated. Egypt has all the advantages of the aircraft producers in the other countries of the Third World — a large airforce and resident skills — but it has not managed to overcome the

27 SIPRI, op. cit., reports that some of its employees came from Israel's motor car industry, which is interesting in view of the experience of Argentina where the reverse process took place. Metal manufacturing skills are transferable between these types of industry.

28 *Air Force Space Digest*, Washington, November 1968, quoted in SIPRI, op. cit., p. 776. For an account of Israel's military production see Peres, op. cit.

political direction from the government that provides the will, but not the means, for setting up consistent domestic production of aircraft.

## 6.   Conclusion

Third World countries have accumulated experience in military technology through the use of imported weapons in a relatively short space of time. The largest users of military equipment have been the first, in the main, to go in for domestic production. There seems to be some associative, if not causal, link between the maintenance function and the attempt at domestic production. This is probably because maintenance, by its very nature, is residential, even if the weapon system is sophisticated and imported. The use of expatriate engineers in the early stages does not present a permament solution to the maintenance problem. Sooner or later local maintenance terms must be trained. The combination of experience and ambition will suggest to the governments that they seriously consider proposals to develop their own weapon systems.

# 17 Disarmament

## 1. Introduction

In this final chapter we will consider the question of disarmament as it relates to Third World countries. This is an obvious question to consider in a book on the military. It is not, however, as obvious a solution to the problems of the Third World as it appears to be. World disarmament is an indivisible problem, affecting all countries and not just some of them. It also presupposes the solution of conflicts of right and interest by some hitherto untried method that breaks completely with the recorded history of human society. If this millennarian peace is to be established within the time-scale that the Third World will benefit from it in a developmental sense, i.e. within the next twenty or thirty years, the first stages of the peace will have to start appearing within the next decade. It is not being too cynical to describe the prospects of such a development in societal relations as being founded more on hope than experience.

It does not follow, of course, that the world community ought to abandon efforts to find new ways of resolving conflicts. It is certainly not the task of this chapter to argue that proposition. But, what must be faced up to is the question of whether these efforts confined to Third World countries would be meaningful in the short term and, given the likely time-scale of the change over from violence to non-violence, whether the Third World need wait so long before the natural development process will raise their economies to comparable levels with the industrialised countries.

## 2. The world armaments situation

Total world expenditures for military purposes rose from $120 billion in 1960 to $216 billion in 1971. This was equal to about 9 per cent of the world's annual output of goods and services. The bulk of this spending (over 90 per cent) was in the world's industrialised countries (including China). It represented the equivalent of two-thirds of the entire national income of all underdeveloped countries.[1] The burden of this defence spending was carried in the industrialised countries. This must be borne in mind when considering the case for disarmament on the grounds of the economic plight of the Third World.

U Thant, then Secretary General of the United Nations, discussing the costs of world defence expenditures, wrote in 1970:

> This unproductive and wasteful diversion of the world's resources and energy has exacted a heavy toll on the living conditions of the peoples of the world both in the developing and developed countries.[2]

But the underdeveloped world has spent only one tenth of the amount on defence of the non-Communist world, and it cannot follow from this that the defence burden is equally shared between the countries that make up the Third World and the industrialised world (including the European Communist countries). It is only an assumption that defence spending in the developed world has an opportunity cost outside these countries. If the resources allocated to defence are, in the main, non-transferable (due to political realities) outside the countries that make these expenditures, then it is not relevant to ascribe to these expenditures opportunity costs for other parts of the world.

General disarmament between the major powers would certainly release resources within these countries, but

1 ACDA *Report*, 1969. See also: 'Statement on the economic and social consequences of the arms race and military expenditure', *Pugwash Newsletter*, 9, 1, July 1971, pp. 4-6; E. Benoit and H. Lobell, 'World defence expenditures', *Journal of Peace Research*, 2, 1966.

2 United Nations, *Economic and Social Consequences of Disarmament*.

whether their political systems would tolerate massive shifts of resources to other countries is a matter upon which doubt must exist.

The studies that have been conducted of the economic and social effects of disarmament show considerable strains upon the economies concerned in the transition period (even assuming that all the political issues are resolved between the super-powers). Any large-scale unemployment arising from disarmament will have repercussions — it is naive to assume that a spirit of goodwill will flow so freely that the political oppositions in these countries (however formed) will refrain from making political capital out of the transitional difficulties. The life-span of governments in the party democracies is shorter than the feasible transition period that disarmament would require. It is not just a technical question of how to dismantle the weapon systems, but also a political question of how to lower tension and ensure security for all concerned.[3] Even in the dictatorships the differences between the life-span of the bureaucracies and the length of the transition period is a problem for the personnel concerned. Thus the process will create periods of vulnerability for the governments and they are likely to try to offset these with domestic programmes that will take up most of the resources as they are released.

The studies by Seymour Melman on the defence conversion tasks suggest that the problem is somewhat different from that faced by the economies involved in the European and Pacific war in 1945. These countries had war economies converted from civilian economies at the outbreak of hostilities. Today's problem is altogether different:

At the present time, the bulk of military production is concentrated in industries, firms or plants that have specialised for this work, and frequently have no prior history of civilian work.[4]

3 See D. Belouski, 'Security through disarmament', *Review of International Affairs*, 19 October 1968.

4 S. Melman, op. cit., and *The Peace Race*, New York, 1962; *The War Economy of the United States*, New York, 1971; G. Piel, 'Can our economy stand disarmament?' *Atlantic Monthly*, 210, 35, September 1962; R.G. Kokat, 'Some implications of the economic impact of disarmament on the structure of American industry', *Kyklos*, 19, 1966; A.C. Enthoven, 'Defence and disarmament: economic analysis in the department of defence', *American Economic Review*, 53, May 1963.

There is no reason to believe that the situation is any different in the Soviet defence plants.

Melman calculated the cost of the kind of alternative spending programmes that were desperately urgent within the United States. These came to $76 billion alone, or *twice* what the United States was spending on defence at the time (1960); it is also the equivalent of the entire 1970 Federal budget. Moreover, as the $76 billion was an annual cost and as the disarmament programme would be phased over several years, it would mean a considerable movement of resources from other budget headings if the programme was to be met.

Experience of public discussions on alternatives to current spending shows that the list of alternatives rapidly outpaces the funds that would be released. In the context of a world disarmament programme, which could hardly be carried out in secret, the domestic pressure from the pressure groups in the political lobbies to allocate the released resources could create severe social tension through the inevitable disappointments. Now the issue for us is this: would there be much left over, if anything, for the Third World?

This is not an argument against the major powers trying to get agreement on weapon and force levels, though such an argument could be made.[5] The Strategic Arms Limitation Talks (SALT) have been aimed at something along these lines; that 'something', however, needs close scrutiny, for the evidence so far from the talks is that the Soviet Union and America are in reality only drawing up a set of rules to conduct their own arms race at a lower cost to themselves. Nor is it an argument against attempting nuclear disarmament or curtailment of future production of nuclear and chemical weapons. The issue that we are attempting to look at is whether there is anything in such activity that will manifestly benefit the Third World, or whether, in fact, the whole issue is of marginal relevance to these countries and the problems they face.

5 See Chamberlain, op. cit.; 'If what everyone says he wants (peace and disarmament) is eventually achieved, the consequences are almost certain to be the end of 500 years of Western world supremacy.'

### 3.    Disarmament and development

The great bulk of the saving from disarmament and defence expenditures as a result of general disarmament would be concentrated in a few, already rich, countries. The major military expenditure in developing countries tends to be on manpower rather than equipment. Savings in foreign exchange for the purchase of military equipment could also be made, but the main effect would be to discharge into the labour market skilled and unskilled men, which, as the United Nation's report notes, may 'aggravate the already difficult problem of unemployment and under-employment'.[6] The irony is that the resulting social tensions arising from general disarmament may require additional para-military forces to maintain order.

The report links the solution to these problems to the goodwill of the industrialised economies:

The realisation of the great potential gains from disarmament in the underdeveloped countries would depend on a major intensification of efforts to promote economic development. Such efforts would be facilitated insofar as military spending were channelled to development expenditure and as scarce foreign exchange reserves were freed for development purposes; *and still more to the extent that aid were forthcoming from the industrially advanced countries in the form of both capital equipment and technical assistance.*[7]

For some countries with high defence budgets (the Middle East for example) there would be an undoubted impact from the re-allocation of their defence funds to development projects. For many other countries the benefit would be marginal. If the real gain would come from an increased assistance from the industrialised countries (and the gains from this assistance are by no means so obvious as to be unchallengeable),[8] then this could theoretically be achieved without disarmament. If general disarmament is not likely to provide funds in itself for the Third World the likely gains for the Third World are less impressive.

6 United Nations, *Basic Problems of Disarmament*, p. 14.
7 ibid., author's emphasis.
8 See Bauer, op. cit.

Why a policy of 'goodwill' should achieve what manifest self-interest (i.e. the gains from tying Third World countries by aid to the political blocs of the competing industrialised countries) has failed to do is not explained. The assumptions behind the United Nations Report are themselves suspect. The authors assume that the shortages of capital and foreign exchange are the major barriers to development and that the industrialised countries only have to pour in resources (released by disarmament) and the Third World countries would develop. These are assumptions clearly accepted by vast numbers of people, but they are none the less questionable for that. No amount of capital will make less necessary the change in the social structure, and it is in this process that the political and social tensions manifest themselves.

Cross-national studies have shown that the rate of socio-economic change is an important contributory factor to political instability. In one study 70 per cent of the countries that were experiencing high rates of socio-economic change were politically unstable and 63 per cent of the countries with low rates of change were politically stable.[9]

To disarm *and* step up the pace of change is a contra-dictory policy. It might call for intervention on a large scale by the armed forces of other countries (imperialism?). To disarm and stop the process of change — assuming that a policy of stagnation can be brought about deliberately or even that it could be imposed — is also eventually likely to lead to violence due to disparities in aspirations and reality. Disarmament is not feasible in conditions of violent challenge to the existing, or the incoming, order. Because the armies of the Third World play a much more central role in maintaining internal order than they do in the advanced countries, their absence following disarmament will have more serious effects on political life than their absence in the industrialised countries. But even this difference is changing fairly rapidly in the industrialised countries.

Urban violence and confrontation in the industrialised countries can reach levels of intensity where only the

9 Kirkham, Levy and Crotty, op. cit.; N. Brown, 'Underdevelopment a threat to world peace', *International Affairs*, 47, 1971.

intervention of troops in a para-police role has any chance of containing the conflicting forces. In Northern Ireland this situation has existed for several years; France in 1968 was poised for the intervention of the French army if the para-military riot police showed signs of wavering. The threshold of intervention by heavily armed and organised troops in Third World countries is much lower than in the developed countries in general, and there is no reason to assume that disarmament arranged through the United Nations is likely to raise that threshold in current circumstances.[10]

If the gains from disarmament depend on the aid programmes of the industrialised countries then the implications of this have to be made clear. Disarmament, it may be argued, releases resources in the developed economies, some of which can be diverted to the Third World. There is no evidence to suggest that this would in fact be the case. On the contrary there is much to suggest that the political case for disarmament in the developed countries will prove acceptable only on the basis that the diverted resources can be seen to be of direct benefit to the domestic economies and the social lives of the people within them (this is after all what Melman and his colleagues have been concentrating their attentions upon and showing to informed American opinion). If the urban crisis is making disarmament more palatable, and this is what is achieved when the trade-offs are written about, then the amelioration of the problems of the urban crisis must inevitably be shown to be the major result of a disarmament programme, and not the amelioration of the problems of the Third World.[11]

10 See Appendix B.

11 See J. McDonagh and S. Zimmerman, *A Programme for Civilian Diversification of the Air Space Industry*, US Senate, 1964; ACDA, *Survey of Economic Models for Analysis of Disarmament Impacts*, Washington, 1965; *Defence Industry Diversification: An Analysis with 12 Case Studies*, Washington, 1966; *The Implications of Reduced Defence Demand for the Electronics Industry*, Washington, 1965; *Convertibility of Space and Defence Resources to Civilian Needs*, US Senate, 1964; E.J. Mosbaek, 'Information on the impact of reduction in defence expenditures on the economy', *Quarterly Review of Economics and Business*, 5, Fall 1965; J. J. Hughes, 'Disarmament and regional unemployment', *Journal of Regional Science*, 2, 1964.

Disarmament is often written about as if it is a state of nature that modern man has been diverted from by fallacious politics. It is nothing like this at all. It would be an entirely new arrangement in human society, never tried before in recorded history. It is not likely to come about within the next few years, or even decades. In the Third World it is not even an option. There can of course be a lowering of tension between countries and this alone would make significant contributions to the lowering of the proportions allocated to defence in the budgets of many countries. But the lowering of tension, say, in the Middle East, is not a problem that will find an easy solution. The end of the Korean war did not lead to a drop in the military budgets; fear does not wither away while its cause remains. Nor does the 'umbrella' strategy offer an alternative.

The argument for the umbrella strategy is as plausible as it is false. The idea is that the developing countries need only so much defence as is necessary for them to handle internal security problems. Their external problems, which contribute the larger part of the heavy defence budgets of the high military spenders and promotes the arms races, can be defused, it is believed, if the major powers were to make it clear that they would 'guarantee' each and every country against external aggression. The full might of the big powers would be brought to play against any power which used military force to intervene in another country. With this umbrella guarantee, the argument goes, the developing countries could withhold from massive military budgets, put the resources to work for development and live in peace. It may be that some people believe it would work, but a listing of the difficulties that the strategy ignores surely exposes its hopeless naivety.

In the first place the borderline between external aggression and insurgency is extremely blurred, and the examples of Vietnam and Palestine only have to be mentioned to illustrate the point. How the major powers could 'guarantee' anything in such situations is open to question.

The second obstacle to the umbrella plan is that agreement is unlikely by the big powers on which countries and whose integrity they were jointly guaranteeing. In the Middle East,

Asia and Latin America they have conflicting loyalties to most of the contenders. Even if America and Russia miraculously found agreement, the presence of China (and the emerging European alliance) would stretch the incidence of miracles to a degree where the whole idea is hypothetical and utopian.

The third obstacle is that the plan required the recognition of the status quo — all countries and all boundaries are recognised as permanent. It is precisely the inability for a status quo to emerge, except by force of arms, that will prevent the umbrella plan from implementation.[12]

The fourth obstacle, is that countries that are independent are loath to hand over their protection to others. Where this happened, Korea, Taiwan, and Vietnam for example, the protection of the military power was accompanied by the supply of the means for self-protection. It is a debatable proposition whether the taxpayers of the developed countries are likely to be persuaded to support the military protection of other countries where a self-help contribution is negligible or non-existent. It must always be borne in mind when devising schemes to solve the world's problems that solutions which expose those in power to challenge from oppositions, or rivals, are not really viable.[13]

If some degree of self-help is necessary, and partisanship in allocating protection inevitable, it follows that the power providing the umbrella of protection is more than likely to provide the means for self-help. This situation is the one that obtains at the present, i.e. the partial umbrella system is the

12 There are border disputes between the following countries, just to mention a few examples: Morocco, Algeria, Mauritania and Mali; Mexico and Honduras; Honduras and British Honduras; Guyana and Venezuela; Guyana and (Dutch) Surinam; Argentina and Chile; India and Pakistan; India and China; Pakistan and Afghanistan; Iran and Iraq; Iran and Gulf States; Yemen and South Yemen; Israel and Jordan; Israel and Syria; Israel and Egypt, Sudan and Ethiopia; Ethiopia and Somalia; Somalia and Kenya; Malaysia and Philippines; Indonesia and Australia, Japan and Russia and so on. In these circumstances who can guarantee what?

13 See Rivkin, op. cit., for an example of an 'umbrella' plan for Africa. See also Chamberlain, op. cit.; B. Singh, 'Some problems and prospects of international peace forces', *Australian Journal of Politics and History*, 17, 2, August 1971.

one that the big powers already operate. The generalised umbrella plan is, however, unrealisable for the reasons we have suggested. The partial umbrella system has nowhere reduced the arms race (in fact it is part of it). This route to a quasi-disarmament is clearly not open as it flies in the face of reality.

The final argument against the umbrella strategy is that it presupposes that the major powers remain armed and everybody else disarms. This is not a very feasible proposition. Many Third World countries feel threatened as it is by one, or both, of the major powers and they are unlikely to accept that their enemies, or potential enemies, should have the means to violence and they should not. Racial, and political, differences are not so easily disposed of.

### 4. Conclusion

Violence is endemic and takes a variety of forms in different parts of the world. Human conflict is pervasive; governments and insurgents alike resort to violence because it is the normal means of settling human conflict. To ascribe to violence, and to the means by which violence is institutionalised, the status of a major barrier to development is to re-write the political realities of human experience. This is the final dilemma of mankind: war and violence have been man's way of resolving conflicts and the search for alternatives is rational man at his finest but also at his most impotent. The conquest of hunger, disease and want, the conquest of space and environment, the solution to every technical problem that intelligence can dream up, are minute problems compared with the solution to the problem of war and violence.[14]

A world disarmed, whatever else it might achieve, might become the most dangerous place for life that man could create. It might also become something more pleasant, but the pessimists have over 25,000 years of experience on their

14 There is a considerable literature on war and peace. See M. Penrose (ed.) *Pathogenesis of War*, London 1963, esp. the article by G. Sharp, 'The need for a substitute for war'; also Chamberlain, op. cit.

side. Robert Ardrey summed up the dilemma most pointedly in his book *African Genesis*:

Deprived of the contest of weapons that was the only bough he knew, man must descend to the canebreaks of a new mode of existence. There he must find new dreams, new dynamics, new experiences to absorb him, new means of resolving his issues and of protecting whatever he regards as good. And he will find them; or he will find himself lost. Slowly his governments will lose their force and his societies their integration. Moral order, sheltered throughout all history by the judgment of arms, will fall away in rot and erosion. Insoluble quarrels will rend people once united by territorial purpose. Insoluble conflicts will split nations once allied by a common dream. Anarchy, ultimate enemy of social man, will spread its grey, cancerous tissues through the social corpus of our kind. Bandit nations will hold the human will a hostage, in perfect confidence that no superior force can protect the victim. Bandit gangs will have their way along the social throughfare, in perfect confidence that the declining order will find no means to protect itself. Every night we shall build our nostalgic family nest in tribute to ancestral memories. Every day we shall pursue through the fearful canebreaks our unequal struggle with extinction. It is the hard way, ending with a whimper.[15]

There is no sign anywhere on the planet that any country is prepared to risk extinction with a whimper to avoid extinction with a bang. And this is probably the best place to let the argument rest in the meantime.

15 Robert Ardrey, *African Genesis*, London, 1969.

# Appendix A
# Military Interventions in the Third World 1945-72

The lists for the four regions, Middle East, Latin America, sub-Saharan African and Asia, have been compiled from various sources (books, articles, newspapers, and notes). They are not exhaustive; some of the alleged coup attempts are doubtful and owe more to the propaganda needs of the governments against whom the alleged coups were directed than to any basis of fact. Also, some other incidents which are listed as coups or attempted coups are loose interpretations of what a coup d'etat consists of and therefore require subjective agreement on when a sudden change in leadership or a local insurrection can be characterised as a coup.

The army mutinies in Kenya, Uganda and Tanzania are listed as attempted coups, though the evidence suggests that they were not motivated by a desire to change the government. The removal of Nasser from the leadership of the Free Officers in 1954, and then his counter-stroke against Neguib a few months later, are counted as coups. But the guerrilla actions against King Hussein in Jordan in 1971 are not listed as attempted coups. All these reflect the subjective judgment of the author. Differing views of readers will be welcomed, though whether a definitive list could be agreed which would secure universal endorsement is open to doubt.

1. *Latin America 1954-72 (*S = *success,* F = *failure*)

| Date | Country | Remarks | Outcome |
|------|---------|---------|---------|
| October 1945 | Venezuela | | S |
| October 1945 | Brazil | | S |
| October 1946 | Argentina | | S |
| May 1947 | Nicaragua | | S |
| May 1948 | Costa Rica | Anti-army | S |

| Date | Country | Remarks | Outcome |
|------|---------|---------|---------|
| June 1948 | Paraguay | | S |
| October 1948 | Peru | | S |
| November 1948 | Venezuela | | S |
| December 1948 | Paraguay | | S |
| December 1948 | El Salvador | | S |
| 1949 | Paraguay | | S |
| November 1949 | Panama | Police-led | S |
| 1950 | Paraguay | | S |
| May 1951 | Panama | | S |
| March 1952 | Cuba | | S |
| 1952 | Bolivia | | S |
| May 1954 | Paraguay | | S |
| June 1954 | Guatemala | US aid | S |
| November 1955 | Brazil | | S |
| 1955 | Argentina | | S |
| May 1957 | Colombia | | S |
| January 1958 | Venezuela | | S |
| May 1958 | Bolivia | | F |
| October 1958 | Bolivia | Socialist | F |
| April 1959 | Panama | Cuban aid | F |
| April 1959 | Bolivia | | F |
| 1959 | Cuba | Castro | S |
| December 1959 | Paraguay | Cuban aid | F |
| May 1960 | Paraguay | Invasion | F |
| January 1960 | El Salvador | | S |
| January 1960 | Dominican Republic | | F |
| October 1960 | El Salvador | | S |
| November 1960 | Guatemala | | F |
| November 1960 | Nicaragua | | F |
| January 1961 | El Salvador | | S |
| February 1961 | Venezuela | | F |
| November 1961 | Ecuador | | S |
| November 1961 | Dominican Republic | | S |
| January 1962 | Dominican Republic | | F |
| May 1962 | Argentina | Anti-Frondizi | S |
| May 1962 | Venezuela | Naval mutinies | F |
| June 1962 | Venezuela | Marines | F |
| August 1962 | Argentina | Right-wing | S |
| September 1962 | Argentina | Factional | F |
| March 1963 | Argentina | Right-wing | F |
| April 1963 | Argentina | Anti-Perón | F |
| March 1963 | Peru | | S |

| Date | Country | Remarks | Outcome |
|------|---------|---------|---------|
| March 1963 | Guatemala | | S |
| October 1963 | Honduras | | S |
| July 1963 | Ecuador | | S |
| September 1963 | Dominican Rep. | | S |
| November 1964 | Bolivia | | S |
| April 1964 | Brazil | | S |
| May 1965 | Bolivia | Factional | S |
| May 1965 | Colombia | | S |
| January 1966 | Bolivia | Factional | S |
| March 1966 | Ecuador | | S |
| June 1966 | Argentina | | S |
| October 1966 | Venezuela | | F |
| January 1967 | Nicaragua | | F |
| July 1968 | Bolivia | Military cabinet | S |
| August 1968 | Bolivia | | F |
| October 1968 | Panama | | S |
| October 1968 | Peru | | S |
| 1968 | Bolivia | | S |
| December 1969 | Panama | | F |
| June 1970 | Ecuador | | S |
| June 1970 | Argentina | Military junta | S |
| August 1970 | Bolivia | | F |
| October 1970 | Bolivia | | F |
| October 1971 | Bolivia | | S |
| January 1971 | Bolivia | Right-wing | F |
| March 1971 | Ecuador | Foiled | F |
| March 1971 | Argentina | | S |
| April 1971 | Bolivia | | F |
| May 1971 | Argentina | | F |
| August 1971 | Bolivia | | S |
| October 1971 | Argentina | | F |
| February 1972 | Ecuador | | S |
| March 1972 | El Salvador | | F |
| December 1972 | Honduras | | S |

## 2.    *Asia 1945-72*

| Date | Country | Remarks | Outcome |
|------|---------|---------|---------|
| 1947 | Thailand | Army counter-coup | S |
| January 1949 | Cambodia | | F |
| February 1949 | Thailand | Naval | F |

| Date | Country | Remarks | Outcome |
|------|---------|---------|---------|
| February 1949 | Cambodia | | F |
| 1949 | Pakistan | 'Pindi' plot | F |
| June 1951 | Thailand | Marines | F |
| November 1951 | Thailand | Army | S |
| October 1952 | Indonesia | | F |
| 1955 | Indonesia | Anti-cabinet | S |
| 1956 | Indonesia | | F |
| 1957 | Indonesia | Sukarno | F |
| Sept./Nov. 1957 | Thailand | | S |
| September 1958 | Burma | | S |
| October 1958 | Pakistan | | S |
| October 1958 | Thailand | Factional | S |
| August 1959 | Laos | | S |
| March 1960 | Indonesia | Anti-Sukarno | F |
| April 1960 | Korea | Anti-Rhee | S |
| May 1961 | Korea | | S |
| January 1962 | Ceylon | Police/army | F |
| March 1962 | Burma | Anti-U Nu | S |
| June 1962 | Korea | Foiled | F |
| December 1962 | Brunei | UK aid | F |
| March 1963 | Korea | Factional | F |
| November 1963 | Vietnam | Anti-Diem | S |
| January 1964 | Vietnam | | S |
| February 1964 | Burma | Socialist | S |
| April 1964 | Laos | Right-wing | F |
| January 1965 | Vietnam | | S |
| January 1965 | Laos | Right-wing | F |
| March 1965 | Laos | | F |
| April 1965 | Laos | | F |
| October 1965 | Indonesia | Communist | F |
| October 1965 | Indonesia | Army | S |
| March 1966 | Indonesia | Fall of Sukarno | S |
| February 1969 | Pakistan | Anti-Aya | S |
| March 1969 | Thailand | | S |
| March 1970 | Cambodia | | S |
| December 1970 | Laos | Right-wing | F |
| March 1971 | Thailand | | S |
| April 1971 | Laos | | F |
| December 1971 | Pakistan | Army quit | S |

3.    *Middle East  1945-72*

| Date | Country | Remarks | Outcome |
|------|---------|---------|---------|
| March 1949 | Syria | | S |
| July 1949 | Lebanon | Syria aid | F |
| August 1949 | Syria | Pro-UK | S |
| December 1949 | Syria | | S |
| November 1949 | Syria | | S |
| July 1952 | Egypt | | S |
| September 1952 | Lebanon | | S |
| August 1953 | Iran | Anti-cabinet | S |
| February 1954 | Syria | | S |
| February 1954 | Egypt | Pro-Neguib | S |
| March 1954 | Egypt | Pro-Nasser | S |
| April 1954 | Jordan | | F |
| January 1958 | Syria | Pro-Egypt | S |
| July 1958 | Jordan | Foiled | F |
| July 1958 | Iraq | | S |
| October 1958 | Lebanon | Civil war | S |
| November 1958 | Sudan | | S |
| March 1959 | Iraq | Anti-Communist | F |
| March 1959 | Jordan | Foiled | F |
| May 1959 | Sudan | | F |
| November 1959 | Sudan | | F |
| May 1960 | Turkey | Anti-Menderes | S |
| November 1960 | Turkey | Anti-Socialist | S |
| September 1961 | Syria | Anti-Nasser | S |
| December 1961 | Lebanon | Syrian aid | F |
| February 1962 | Turkey | | F |
| March 1962 | Syria | Pro-Nasser | S |
| March 1962 | Syria | Nasserist | F |
| June 1962 | Algeria | Anti-Boumédienne | S |
| July 1962 | Algeria | Pro-Bella | S |
| September 1962 | Syria | | S |
| September 1962 | Yemen | Republican | S |
| December 1962 | Tunisia | Foiled | F |
| January 1963 | Syria | Nasserist | F |
| February 1963 | Iraq | Nasserist | S |
| March 1963 | Syria | Ba'ath/Nasser | S |
| May 1963 | Turkey | | F |
| July 1963 | Iraq | Communist | F |
| July 1963 | Syria | Ba'athist | S |
| July 1963 | Syria | Nasserist | F |
| July 1963 | Morocco | Foiled | F |

| *Date* | *Country* | *Remarks* | *Outcome* |
|---|---|---|---|
| September 1963 | Algeria | | F |
| November 1963 | Iraq | Ba'athist | F |
| November 1963 | Iraq | Anti-Ba'athist | S |
| 1964 | Egypt | Muslim | F |
| June 1964 | Algeria | Islamic | F |
| September 1964 | Iraq | Ba'athist | F |
| October 1964 | Sudan | Anti-army | S |
| June 1965 | Algeria | Anti-Bella | S |
| September 1965 | Iraq | Nasserist | F |
| October 1965 | Iraq | Nasserist | F |
| December 1965 | Syria | Ba'athist | S |
| February 1966 | Syria | Factional | S |
| March 1966 | Iraq | Ba'athist | F |
| June 1966 | Iraq | Nasserist | F |
| September 1966 | Syria | Anti-Ba'ath | F |
| December 1966 | Sudan | Communist | F |
| August 1967 | Egypt | Amer | F |
| November 1967 | Yemen | | S |
| December 1967 | Algeria | Colonel Zbiri | F |
| February 1968 | Syria | Ba'athist | S |
| March 1968 | Syria | Factional | S |
| March 1968 | Yemen | Leftist | F |
| July 1968 | Iraq | Ba'athist | S |
| July 1968 | Iraq | Factional | S |
| August 1968 | Syria | Factional | F |
| August 1968 | Yemen | Leftist | F |
| January 1969 | Yemen | Leftist | F |
| March 1969 | Iraq | Anti-Ba'ath | F |
| May 1969 | Sudan | | S |
| September 1969 | Libya | Republican | S |
| June 1970 | S. Yemen | | S |
| July 1970 | Sudan | Communist | F |
| November 1970 | Syria | Nationalist | S |
| March 1971 | Turkey | Anti-cabinet | S |
| April 1971 | Egypt | Anti-Sadat | F |
| June 1971 | Syria | | F |
| June 1971 | Morocco | Republican | F |
| July 1971 | Sudan | | F |
| September 1971 | Iraq | Leftist | S |
| August 1972 | Morocco | Republican | F |
| November 1972 | Egypt | | F |
| November 1972 | Jordan | Republican | F |

4.   *Sub-Saharan Africa  1960-72*

| Date | Country | Remarks | Outcome |
|---|---|---|---|
| April 1960 | Guinea | Foiled | F |
| December 1960 | Ethiopia | Republican | F |
| 1961 | Liberia | Communist | F |
| September 1961 | Zaire (K) | Mobutu | S |
| November 1961 | Guinea | Foiled | F |
| September 1962 | Nigeria | Awolowo plot | F |
| December 1962 | Senegal | | F |
| January 1963 | Togo | | S |
| January 1963 | Ivory Coast | Foiled | F |
| February 1963 | Liberia | Foiled | F |
| August 1963 | Congo (B) | | S |
| 1963 | Chad | Foiled | F |
| September 1963 | Ivory Coast | Foiled | F |
| October 1963 | Dahomey | | S |
| 1963 | Zaire (K) | | S |
| December 1963 | Dahomey | French aid | F |
| January 1964 | Kenya | Mutiny | F |
| January 1964 | Tanzania | | F |
| January 1964 | Uganda | | F |
| February 1964 | Gabon | French aid | F |
| January 1965 | Burundi | | F |
| October 1965 | Burundi | Republican | S |
| November 1965 | Zaire | | S |
| November 1965 | Dahomey | | S |
| December 1965 | Dahomey | | S |
| January 1966 | CAR | | S |
| January 1966 | Upper Volta | | S |
| January 1966 | Upper Volta | | S |
| January 1966 | Nigeria | | S |
| February 1966 | Ghana | Anti-Nkrumah | S |
| February 1966 | Uganda | | F |
| June 1966 | Zaire | | F |
| July 1966 | Nigeria | Counter-coup | S |
| July 1966 | Burundi | | S |
| July 1966 | Zaire | Gendarmerie | F |
| Setpember 1966 | Liberia | Foiled | F |
| November 1966 | Chad | Foiled | F |
| November 1966 | Burundi | | S |
| November 1966 | Ethiopia | Foiled | F |
| January 1967 | Togo | | S |
| March 1967 | Sierra Leone | | S |

| Date | Country | Remarks | Outcome |
|------|---------|---------|---------|
| March 1967 | Sierra Leone | Counter-coup | S |
| April 1967 | Ghana | | F |
| October 1967 | Malawi | 'Invasion' | F |
| December 1967 | Dahomey | | S |
| March 1968 | Guinea | Military-led | F |
| April 1968 | Sierra Leone | NCO-led | S |
| September 1968 | Congo (B) | | S |
| November 1968 | Mali | | S |
| March 1969 | Eq. Guinea | | F |
| April 1969 | CAR | | F |
| August 1969 | Mali | | F |
| September 1969 | Burundi | | F |
| October 1969 | Somalia | Army/police | S |
| November 1969 | Ethiopia | Foiled | F |
| December 1969 | Dahomey | | S |
| January 1970 | Lesotho | | S |
| April 1970 | Somalia | Factional | F |
| August 1970 | Togo | Foiled | F |
| September 1970 | Kenya | Foiled | F |
| October 1970 | Sierra Leone | Foiled | F |
| November 1970 | Guinea | 'Invasion' | F |
| January 1971 | Ghana | Anti-Busia | S |
| January 1971 | Uganda | Anti-Obote | S |
| March 1971 | Sierra Leone | | F |
| March 1971 | Malagasy | | F |
| April 1971 | Mali | | F |
| May 1971 | Somalia | | F |
| July 1971 | Guinea | Foiled | F |
| July 1971 | Uganda | | F |
| July 1971 | Burundi | Foiled | F |
| August 1971 | Chad | Foiled | F |
| February 1972 | Ghana | Anti-Busia | S |
| February 1972 | Congo (B) | Leftist | F |
| February 1972 | Dahomey | | F |
| May 1972 | Malagasy | | S |
| 1972 | Burundi | Monarchist | F |
| November 1972 | Dahomey | | S |

# Appendix B

The following Table has been constructed from details in *The Times* (London) Index for the years 1968-71. Under the headings a list was made of the reported incidence that could be broadly described as political: Riots and Demonstrations; Guerrilla Activity; Judicial Executions; and Estimated Numbers Killed. A strike in itself was not included as a political act unless it led to a riot or violent demonstration in which police or troops were involved. Guerrilla activity covered incidents such as kidnapping, arson, jail break or law defiance. Judicial executions covered mainly those executions by due legal process but in some cases also those where state authorities killed guerrillas in unspecified incidents. The estimated numbers killed were those numbers reported killed, and the plus sign (+) indicates that an unspecified number were killed, sometimes in addition to the numbers known.

Two points must be made about the Table. First, it is not a scientifically accurate Table in the sense that it does not represent the whole picture. The published news reports in an (albeit) eminent British newspaper are subject to the Editor's bias as to what to report on and what not to report on. Thus, because British readers of *The Times* appear to be interested in Indian events, judging by the news space accorded to India, greater detail on Indian political violence is available. India may therefore appear to be an exceptionally violent country in contrast to other countries which receive less attention in *The Times*.

Secondly, because of the inevitable bias and the selection of news for publication the Table shows only a sample of the facts, and it is therefore an underestimate of political violence rather than an overestimate.

The Table is only a guide to the trend of political violence in these Third World countries. It shows that deaths from political conflict are quite substantial, that guerrilla action is fairly widespread and that judicial executions are also a common feature of public life.

The number of deaths does not include those killed in wars or civil wars. Thus the deaths caused by the Vietnam war, Indo-Pakistan wars, the Arab-Israel wars and the Nigeria-Biafra war have been excluded.

*Political Violence in the Third World, 43 Countries, as Reported in* The Times (*London*) 1968-71

| Country | Incidents | | | |
|---|---|---|---|---|
| | Riots/ demonstrations | Guerrilla/ terrorism | Judicial executions | Estimated numbers killed |
| Algeria | 2 | 3 | 7 | 9+ |
| Afghanistan | 1 | 1 | - | 2 |
| Argentina | 14 | 20 | - | 18 |
| Brazil | 11 | 21 | 7 | 184 |
| Bolivia | 3 | 13 | + | 13 |
| Burma | 1 | 10 | - | 101 |
| Chad | 2 | 10 | - | 16+ |
| Chile | 9 | 12 | - | 5 |
| Cameroon | - | - | 1 | 4 |
| Congo (B) | 1 | 1 | 1 | 3 |
| Dahomey | - | - | 1 | 4 |
| Ecuador | 3 | 3 | - | 7 |
| Ethiopia | 4 | 8 | - | 12 |
| Ghana | 5 | 1 | - | - |
| Guinea | - | 4 | 2 | 59+ |
| Guatemala | 1 | 20 | - | 16+ |
| Honduras | - | 2 | - | 1+ |
| India | 55 | 22 | + | 923+ |
| Indonesia | 8 | 8 | - | 33+ |
| Iran | 4 | 6 | 3 | 11 |
| Iraq | - | 4 | 1 | 122 |
| Jordan | 1 | 21 | 1 | 54+ |
| Kenya | 7 | 2 | - | 86+ |
| Korea | 8 | 8 | 1 | 30 |
| Lebanon | 7 | 9 | 1 | 16 |
| Malaysia | 7 | 16 | - | 8+ |

| Country | Incidents | | | Estimated numbers killed |
|---|---|---|---|---|
| | *Riots/ demonstrations* | *Guerrilla/ terrorism* | *Judicial executions* | |
| Mexico | 7 | 9 | - | 43 |
| Nigeria | 3 | 4 | - | 13 |
| Pakistan | 13 | 3 | 7 | 27+ |
| Panama | 1 | 2 | - | 2 |
| Philippines | 12 | 27 | 1 | 206+ |
| Sierra Leone | - | 2 | 1 | 4 |
| Somalia | - | 2 | - | 1 |
| Sudan | 1 | 6 | 2 | 125+ |
| Sri Lanka | 8 | 4 | 2 | 16+ |
| Thailand | - | 17 | 1 | 4+ |
| Turkey | 11 | 11 | 2 | 20+ |
| Tanzania | - | 1 | 1 | 24 |
| Uganda | 2 | 5 | - | 600+ |
| Uruguay | 1 | 17 | - | 3 |
| Venezuela | 9 | 9 | - | 2 |
| Zambia | 8 | 5 | - | 7 |
| Zaire | 4 | - | 1 | 6 |
| TOTALS | 234 | 349 | 44 | 2840 |

# Bibliography

Arms Control and Disarmament Agency, *Report on World Military Expenditure*, annual, Washington.

Adamson, D., *The Kurdish War*, New York, 1964.

Afrifa, A.A., *The Ghana Coup*, London, 1966.

Agarwal, V., *The Indian Development Plans and Defence Spending*, forthcoming.

Ahmad, K.U., *Break-Up of Pakistan: Background and Prospects of Bangladesh*, London, 1972.

Ahmad, K.U., 'New priorities and old biases: the first budget of Bangladesh', *South Asian Review*, 6, 1, October 1972.

Aitken, R., *Revolution! Mexico, 1910-1920*, London, 1969.

Albino, O., *The Sudan: A Southern Viewpoint*, London, 1970.

Ali, T., *Pakistan: Military Rule or Peoples Power*, London, 1970.

Allen, M., 'Israel gears her economy to siege conditions', *The Times*, London, 22 September 1970.

Andreski, S., *The African Predicament*, London, 1968.

Andrzejewski, S., *Military Organisation and Society*, London 1954.

Apple, R.W., 'A third front in Indo-China', *New Statesman*, London, 24 April 1970.

Arasartman, S., 'The Ceylonese insurrection of April 1971: Some causes and consequences', *Pacific Affairs*, 45, 3, 1972.

Ardrey, R., *African Genesis*, London 1969.

Association of South-East Asian Nations, *Declaration*, 8 August 1971, Bangkok.

Austin, D., 'The underlying problem of the army coup d'etat in Africa', *Optima*, June 1966.

Ayisi, E.O., 'Ghana and the return to parliamentary government', *Political Quarterly*, 41, December 1970.

Badgley, J.H., 'Two styles of military rule: Thailand and Burma', *Government and Opposition*, 4, 1, 1969.

Baer, G.W., *The Coming of the Italian-Ethiopian War*, Cambridge, Mass, 1967.

Bagley, F.C.R., 'Iraq's revolution', *International Journal*, 14, 1959.

Bauer, P.T., *Dissent on Development: Studies and Debates in Development Economics*, London, 1971.

Be'eri, E., *Army Officers in Arab Politics and Society*, London, 1970.

Belouski, D., 'Security through disarmament', *Review of International Affairs*, 19 October 1968.

Benoit, E. and K. Boulding, *Disarmament and. the Economy*, New York, 1963.

Birdwood, Lord, *Nuri as Said: A Study in Arab Leadership*, London, 1959.

Berglas, E., 'Defence, the standard of living and the external debt', *Israeli Quarterly Journal of Economics*, Spring 1972.

Berindranath, D., *War and Peace in West Asia*, New Delhi, 1969.

Beshir, M.O., *The Southern Sudan: Background to Conflict*, London, 1968.

Boca, A.D., *The Ethiopian War, 1935-1941*, Chicago, 1935.

Bolton, R.E. (ed.), *Defence and Disarmament: The Economics of Tradition*, 1966.

Brackman, A.C., *The Communist Collapse in Indonesia*, New York, 1969.

Brandenburg, F., *The Making of Modern Mexico*, New York, 1964.

Bretton, H.L., *The Rise and Fall of Kwame Nkrumah: A Study of Personal Rule*, London, 1967.

Brilliant, M., 'Industry develops under the stress of war', *The Times*, London, 28 September 1971.

Brown, N., 'Underdevelopment a threat to world peace', *International Affairs*, 47, 1971.

Bulloch, J., 'Taming Jordan's guerrillas', *Daily Telegraph*, London, 5 March 1970.

Burki, S.J., Ayub's fall; a socio-economic explanation', *Asia Survey*, 12, 3, March 1972.

Burns, T., *Industrial Man*, London, 1969.


Callard, K., *Political Forces in Pakistan, 1947-1959*, Vancouver, 1959.

Campbell, L.E., 'The historiography of the Peruvian guerrilla movement, 1960-1965', *Latin American Research Review*, 3, 1, 1973.

Caractacus (F.J. Snell), *Revolution in Iraq*, London 1959.

Carleton, A., 'The Syrian coups d'etat of 1949', *Middle East Journal*, January 1950.

Carlyle, T. (ed.), *Oliver Cromwell's Letters and Speeches*, London, 2nd edition.

Cartwright, J.R., 'Party competition', *Journal of Contemporary Political Science*, 1972.

Cartwright, J.R., *Politics in Sierra Leone 1947-67*, Toronto, 1973.

Cheng, J.C., *The Politics of the Red Army: A Translation of the. Bulletins of Activities of the People's Liberation Army*, California, 1966.

Chiang, D.W., 'The military and nation-building in Korea, Burma and Pakistan', *Asia Survey*, 15, 11, 1969.

Chomsky, N., *American Power and the New Mandarins*, London, 1969.

Churchill, R. and W., *The Six Day War*, London 1967.

Clive, H., *The United States and Mexico*, Cambridge, Mass., 1953.

Cohen, R., 'The army and tradè unions in Nigerian politics', *Civilizations*, 19, 2, 1969.

Coleman, J.S. and B. Brice, 'The role of the military in sub-Saharan Africa', J. J. Johnson (ed.), *The Role of the Military in Underdeveloped Countries*, Princeton, 1962.

Crawley, A., *De Gaulle*, London, 1969.

Cross, C., *The Fall of the British Empire, 1918-1968*, London, 1968.

Crouch, H., 'Military politics under Indonesia's New Order', *Pacific Affairs*, 45, 2, 1972.


Daalder, H., *The Role of the Military in the Emerging Countries*, The Hague, 1962.

Dalby, D., 'The military takeover in Sierra Leone', *The World Today*, August 1967.

Dann, U., *Iraq Under Quassem: A Political History, 1958-1963*, New York, 1969.

Davidson, B., *The Liberation of Guiné: Aspects of an African Revolution*, London, 1969.

Davidson, B., 'Angola in the tenth year: a report and analysis', *African Affairs*, May-June 1970.

Davidson, B., 'Advance in Angola: guerrillas head for the Atlantic', *Sunday Times*, London, 16 August 1970.

Davidson, B., 'The guerrillas for whom the tide is ebbing'. *The Economist*, 6 February 1971.

De Gauvy, G., *Three Kings in Baghdad*, London, 1961.

Debray, R., *Revolution in the Revolution? Armed Struggle and Conflict in Latin America*, London, 1967.

Deutscher, I., *The Prophet Armed*, London, 1954.

Deutscher, I., *The Prophet Unarmed*, London, 1959.

Deutscher, I., *The Prophet Outcast*, London, 1963.

Dillon, W., 'Nigeria's two revolutions', *African Report*, 11, March 1966.

Dobell, W.M., 'Ayub Khan as president of Pakistan', *Pacific Affairs*, 42, 3, 1969.

Douglas-Home, C., 'Long-term pressures on a nation in arms', *The Times*, London, 18 November 1970.

Downton, E., 'The power game in the Persian Gulf', *Daily Telegraph*, London, 5 February 1970.

Drysdale, J., *The Somali Dispute*, London, 1964.

Dubois, V.C., 'The role of the army in Guinea', *African Report*, 8, 1, January 1963.

Dudley, B.J., 'Violence in Nigerian Politics', *Transition*, 5, 21, 1965.

Dudley, B.J., 'The military and development', *Nigerian Journal of Economic and Social Studies*, 13, 2, 1971.

Dumont, R., *Fresh Start in Africa*, London, 1966.


Edmunds, C.J., 'The Kurds and the revolution in Iraq', *Middle East Journal*, 13, 1959.

El-Sadat, A., *Revolt on the Nile*, London, 1957.

Enthoven, A.C., 'Defence and disarmament: economic analysis in the department of defence', *American Economic Review*, 53, May, 1963.

Feit, E., 'Military coups and political development: some lessons of Ghana and Nigeria', *World Politics*, January 1968.

Feith, H., *The Decline in Constitutional Democracy in Indonesia*, New York, 1962.

Feith, H., 'Suharto's search for the political format', *Australia's Neighbours*, May-June 1968.

Fife, C., *Sierra Leone Inheritance*, London, 1964.

Finer, S.E., *The Man on Horseback: The Role of the Military in Politics*, London, 1962.

Finer, S.E., 'The one-party regimes in Africa: a reconsideration', *Government and Opposition*, 2, July-October 1967.

First, R., *The Barrel of a Gun: Political Power in Africa and the Coup d'Etat*, London, 1972.

Fisher, H., 'Elections and coups in Sierra Leone', *Journal of Modern African Studies*, 7, December 1969.

Fisher, S.N., *The Middle East: A History*, London, 1960.

Fisher, S.N. (ed.), *The Military in the Middle East: Problems in Society and Government*, Ohio, 1963.

Fitch, B. and M. Oppenheimer, *Ghana: The End of an Illusion*, New York, 1966.

Frank, L.A., *The Arms Trade in International Relations*, New York, 1969.

Fryer, D.N., *Emerging South-East Asia: A Study in Growth and Stagnation*, New York, 1970.

Fryer, J., 'Home-grown food for war-torn Vietnam', *Geographical Magazine*, 42, February 1970.

Gailey, H.A., *A History of Gambia*, London, 1964.

Georgetown Research Project, *The Soviet Military Aid Programme as a Reflection of Soviet Objectives*, Washington, 1965.

Gerakis, A., *United Arab Republic: A Survey of Developments During the First Five Year Plan, 1960/1-1964/5*, International Monetary Fund Staff Papers, November 1967.

Ghonduri, G.W., *Democracy in Pakistan*, Dacca, 1963.

Gittings, J., *The Role of the Chinese Army*, London, 1967.

Goh Cheng Teik, 'Why Indonesia's attempt at democracy in the mid-50s failed', *Modern Asian Studies*, 6, 1972.

Goldsworthy, D., 'Ghana's second republic', *Australian Outlook*, 25, April 1971.

Gott, R., *Guerrilla Movements in Latin America*, London, 1971.

Graham, R., 'Yemen unity; the raising of the veil', *Financial Times*, London, 15 December 1972.

Grassmuch, G., 'The electoral process in Iraq, 1952-1958', *Middle East Journal*, 14, 4, 1960.

Gregory, A., 'Factionalism and the Indonesian army: the new order', *Journal of Comparative Administration*, 2, 3, November 1970.

Gutteridge, W.F., 'The political role of the African armed forces', *African Affairs*, 66, April 1967.

Gutteridge, W.F., *The Military in African Politics*, London, 1969.

Hadaun, S., *Bitter Harvest: Palestine between 1914 and 1967*, New York, 1967.

Haddad, G.M., *Revolutions and Military Rule in the Middle East*, vol. 2: *The Arab States*, New York, 1971.

Hain, S.G., 'Islam and the theory of Arab nationalism', in W.Z. Laqueur (ed.), *The Middle East in Transition: Studies in Contemporary History*, London, 1958.

Halliday, F., 'The fighting in Eritrea', *New Left Review*, 67, May-June 1971.

Halliday, F., 'The Ceylonese insurrection', *New Left Review*, 69, September-October 1971.

Halpern, B., *The Idea of the Jewish State*, Cambridge, Mass., 1961.

Halpern, B., 'The role of the military in Israel', in J.J. Johnson (ed.), *The Role of the Military in Underdeveloped Countries*, Princeton, 1962.

Halpern, M., 'The Middle-Eastern armies and the new middle class', in J. J. Johnson (ed.), *The Role of the Military in Underdeveloped Countries*, Princeton, 1962.

Halpern, M., *The Politics of Social Change in the Middle East and North Africa*, Princeton, 1963.

Hammer, E.J., *The Struggle for Indo-China*, Stanford, 1954.

Hansen, B. and G. Marzouk, *Development and Economic Policy in the United Arab Republic*, Amsterdam, 1965.

Harris, C.P., *Nationalism and Revolution in Egypt: The Role of the Muslim Brotherhood*, The Hague 1964.

Hatch, J., 'Kaunda's one-party state', *New Statesman*, London, 29 December 1972.

Hazelhurst, P., 'Obsession with war on the sub-continent', *The Times*, London, 25 October 1971.

Hicks, J., *A Theory of Economic History*, London, 1968.

Hindley, D., *The Communist Party of Indonesia, 1951-1963*, Berkeley, 1964.

Hirskowitz, L., *The Third Reich and the Arab East*, London, 1966.

Hodge, P., 'Ghana workers' brigade', *British Journal of Sociology*, 15, 2, June 1964.

Hodgkin, T., *African Political Parties*, London, 1961.

Hollingworth, C., 'The Ba'athist revolution in Iraq', *The World Today*, 19, 5, May 1963.

Hollingworth, C., 'France still a North African power', *Daily Telegraph*, London, 12 May 1970.

Hon Hui Sen, *Economic Pattern in the Seventies*, Singapore, 1972.

Horowitz, D., *From Yalta to Vietnam: American Foreign Policy in the Cold War*, London, 1965.

Horowitz, I.L., 'Political legitimacy and the institutional crisis in Latin America', *Comparative Political Studies*, 1, 1, 1968.

Horowitz, I.L., 'The norm of legitimacy: the political sociology of Latin America', in I.L. Horowitz, J. de Castro and J. Gerassi (eds), *Latin-American Radicalism: A Documentary Report on Left and Nationalist Movements*, New York, 1969.

Hopkins, K., 'Civil-military relations in developing countries', *British Journal of Sociology*, 17, 2, June 1966.

Hovey, H.A., *United States Military Assistance: A Study of Politics and Practices*, New York, 1965.

Howe, R.W., 'Togo: four years of military rule', *African Report*, May 1967.

Hughes, J. J., 'Disarmament and regional unemployment', *Journal of Regional Science*, 2, 1964.

Huntingdon, S.P., *The Soldier and the State*, Cambridge, Mass., 1957.

Hurewitz, J.C., *Middle-Eastern Politics: The Military Dimensions*, New York, 1970.


Innes, F.M., 'The political outlook in Pakistan', *Pacific Affairs*, 26, 4, December 1953.

Issawi, C., *Egypt in Revolution*, London, 1963.


Jakande, L.K., *The Trial of Obafemi Awólowo*, London, 1966.

Janowitz, M., *The Military in the Political Development of New Nations: An Essay in Comparative Analysis*, Chicago, 1964.

Janowitz, M., *Sociology and the Military Establishment*, New York, 1965.

Joeston, J., *Nasser*, London, 1960.

John, R. and S. Hadaun, *The Palestinian Diary*, Beirut, 1970.

Johnson, J. J. (ed.), *The Role of the Military in Underdeveloped Countries*, Princeton, 1962.

Johnson, J. J., *The Military and Society in Latin America*, Stanford, 1964.


Kanovsky, E., *The Economic Impact of the Six Day War: Israel, the Occupied Territories, Egypt, Jordan*, New York, 1970.

Karpat, K.H., 'The military and politics in Turkey: a socio-cultural analysis of a revolution', *American Historical Review*, 75, October 1970.

Katrak, S., 'Coup d'etat in Pakistan', *Orient*, 4, 8, 1958.

Kavic, L.J., *India's Quest for Security: Defence Policies 1947-1965*, Berkeley and Los Angeles, 1967.

Kennedy, P., *The Economic Impact of Portugal's Colonial Wars*, forthcoming.

Khadduri, M., *Independent Iraq, 1932-1958: A Study in Iraqi Politics*, London, 1960.

Khadduri, M., 'General Nuri's flirtation with the Axis powers', *Middle East Journal*, 16, 3, 1962.

Khan, T.M. and W.A. Bergon, 'Measurement of structural change in the Pakistan economy', *Pakistan Development Review*, Summer, 1966.

Kilner, P., 'Sudan: a year of revolution', *African Affairs*, 69, October, 1970.

Kim, C.I.E., 'The military and political change in Asia', *Pacific Affairs*, 15, 1 and 2, 1967.

Kinross, Lord, *Ataturk: The Rebirth of a Nation*, London, 1964.

Kirkham, J. F., S. G. Levy and W. J. Crotty, *Assassination and Political Violence: A Report to the National Commission on the Causes and Prevention of Violence*, New York, 1970.

Kokat, R.G., 'Some implications of the economic impact of disarmament on the structure of American industry', *Kyklos*, 19, 1966.

Kuroda, Y., 'Young Palestinian commanders in political socialisation perspective', *Middle East Journal*, 26, 3, 1972.


Lachicen, E., *The Huks: Philippine Agrarian Society in Revolt*, New York, 1971.

Lamb, A., *The McMahon Line*, London, 1966.

Laqueur, W.Z., *Communism and Nationalism in the Middle East*, New York, 1956.

Laqueur, W.Z. (ed.), *The Middle East in Transition: Studies in Contemporary History*, London, 1958.

Lasswell, H., 'The garrison state', *American Journal of Sociology*, 46, January 1941.

Lee, J.M., *African Armies and Civil Order*, London, 1969.

Lefever, E.W., *Spear and Sceptre: Army, Policy and Politics in Tropical Africa*, Washington, 1970.

Legge, J.P., 'General Suharto's new order', *International Affairs*, January 1968.

Legum, C. and J. Drysdale, *African Contemporary Record: Annual Survey and Documents 1968-9*, London 1969.

Leis, A.C., 'The transfer of conventional arms to less developed countries', *Arms Control and National Security*, 1, 1969.

Lescaze, L., 'Generals and the new capitalists amid Indonesia's poverty', *Guardian*, London, 3 November 1970.

Lev, D.S., 'Indonesia 1965: the year of the coup', *Asia Survey*, February 1966.

Lewis, B., *The Emergence of Modern Turkey*, London, 1961.

Lieuwen, E., *Arms and Politics in Latin America*, New York, 1960.

Lieuwen, E., *Mexican Militarism: The Political Rise and Fall of the Revolutionary Army, 1910-1940*, New Mexico, 1968.

Lipset, S.M., 'Political sociology', in R.K. Merton, L. Broom and L.S. Cottrell, *Sociology Today: Problems and Prospects*, New York, 1959.

Lipset, S.M., 'Some social requisites for democracy: economic development and political legitimacy', *American Political Science Review*, 53, 1, March 1959.

Lipset, S.M., *Political Man*, New York, 1960.

Lissak, M., 'The military in Burma: innovations and frustrations', *Journal of African and Asian Studies*, 5, 1969.

Little, T., 'The nature of the Palestinian resistance movement', *Asian Affairs*, 57, June 1970.

Lomax, D., 'A diary of the Jordan civil war', *Listener*, London, 10 October 1970.

Longrigg, S.M., *Iraq, 1900-1950*, London, 1953.

Luckham, R., *The Nigerian Military: A Sociological Analysis of Authority and Revolt, 1960-1967*, London, 1971.

Lutskii, V.B., 'The revolutions of July 1952 in Egypt', in W.Z. Laqueur (ed.), *The Middle East in Transition: Studies in Contemporary History*, London, 1958.

Luttwak, E., *Coup d'Etat*, London, 1968.


Mabrui, A.A. and D. Rothchild, 'The soldier and state in East Africa: some theoretical conclusions on the army mutinies in 1964', *Western Police Quarterly*, 20 March 1967.

Mackintosh, J.P. (ed.), *Nigerian Government and Politics*, London, 1966.

Maniruzzaman, T., 'Crisis in political development and the collapse of the Ayub regime', *Journal of Developing Areas*, 5, January 1971.

Mao Tse Tung, *Selected Works*, London, 1954.

Markovitz, I., 'The winter of discontent: Ghana without Nkrumah', *African Report*, 11, 4, April 1966; also in I. Markovitz (ed.), *African Politics and Society*, London, 1970.

Marshall, C.B., 'Reflections on the revolution in Pakistan', *Foreign Affairs*, 37, 2, 1959.

Mathews, R., *African Powder-Keg: Revolt and Discontent in Six Emergent Nations*, London, 1966.

Maxwell, N., *India's China War*, London, 1970.

McDonagh, J. and S.Z. Zimmerman, *A Programme for Civilian Diversification of the Airframe Industry*, US Senate, 1964.

McVey, R.T., 'The post-revolutionary transformation of the Indonesian army', *Indonesia*, 1, 2, April 1972.

Mead, D.C., *Growth and Structural Change in the Egyptian Economy*, Homewood, Ill., 1967.

Melman, S., *The Peace Race*, New York, 1962.

Melman, S., *The Defence Economy*, New York 1963.

Melman, S., *The War Economy of the United States*, New York, 1971.

Menon, V.P., *The Transfer of Power in India*, London, 1957.

Merrican, A.P., *Congo: Background to Conflict*, Evanston, Ill., 1961.

Meyer, A.J., *Middle-Eastern Capitalism*, Cambridge, 1959.

Miller, H., *Jungle War in Malaya: The Campaign against Communism 1948-60*, London, 1972.

Millward, A., *The German War Economy*, London, 1968.

Miners, N.J., *The Nigerian Army, 1956-1966*, London, 1971.

Mondlane, E., *The Struggle for Mozambique*, London, 1969.

Morrison, G., *The Southern Sudan and Eritrea: Aspects of Wider African Problems*, London, 1971.

Mosbaek, E.J., 'Information on the impact of reduction in defence expenditures on the economy', *Quarterly Review of Economics and Business*, 5, Fall 1965.

Mosley, L., *The Last Days of the British Raj*, London, 1961.

Murray, R., 'Militarism in Africa', *New Left Review*, 38, July-August 1966.

Myrdal, G., *Asian Drama: An Inquiry into the Poverty of Nations*, London, 1969.


Nafziger, E., 'The economic impact of the Nigerian civil war', *Journal of Modern African Studies*, 10, 2, 1972.

Nagi, M.H., *Labour Force and Development in Egypt: A Demographic and Socio-Economic Analysis*, New York, 1972.

Nasser, G., *Egypt's Liberation*, Washington, 1955.

Naya, S., 'The Vietnam war and some aspects of its economic impact on Asian countries', *Developing Economies*, Tokyo, 1972.

Neguib, M., *Egypt's Destiny*, New York, 1955.

Nelkin, D., 'The economic and social setting of military takeovers in Africa', *Journal of African and Asian Studies*, 2, 3-4, June 1967.

Newman, K.J., 'The new monarchies of the Middle East', *Journal of International Affairs*, 13, 2, 1959.

Niedergang, M., *The Twenty Latin Americas*, London, 1971.

Nigerian High Commission, *Why Nigeria? A Businessman's Guide to Development in Nigeria between 1970 and 1974*, London.

Niven, R., *The War of Nigerian Unity*, London, 1971.

Nkrumah, K., *Autobiography*, Edinburgh, 1957.

Nkrumah, K., *Neo-Colonialism, the Highest State of Imperialism*, New York, 1966.

Nkrumah, K., *Axioms of Kwame Nkrumah*, London, 1967.

Nutting, A., 'A new Biafra looms behind Sudan's grass curtain', *Sunday Times*, London, 29 November 1970.

Nutting, A., *Nasser*, London, 1972.


O'Brien, C.C., *To Katanga and Back*, London, 1964.

Oke, M.F., 'The army in Africa', *African Quarterly*, 9, 1, April-June, 1969.

Oliusanya, G.O., 'The role of ex-servicemen in Nigerian politics', *Journal of Modern African Studies*, 6, 2, August 1968.

Omai, T.P., *Kwame Nkrumah: Anatomy of an African Dictatorship*, London, 1970.

Orga, I., *Phoenix Ascendant*, London, 1958.

Ottaway, D. and M., *Algeria: The Politics of a Socialist Revolution*, California, 1970.


Paanek, G.F., *Pakistan's Development*, London, 1966.

Palmer, L., 'Suharto's Indonesia', *Asian Affairs*, 57, October 1970.

Palmer, M., 'The United Arab Republic: an assessment of its failure', *Middle East Journal*, Winter, 1966.

Panikkar, K.M., *The Founding of the Kashmir State*, London, 1953.

Pankhurst, E.S., *Ethiopia and Eritrea: The Last Phase of the Reunion Struggle, 1941-1952*, London, 1953.

Panter-Brick, S.K. (ed.), *Nigerian Politics and the Nigerian Military Rule: Prelude to Civil War*, London, 1970.

Pareto, V., *The Mind and Society: A Treatise on General Sociology*, New York, 1963.

Pareto, V., *The Rise and Fall of Elites: An Application of Theoretical Sociology*, Totowa, N.J., 1968.

Park Chung Hee, *The Country, The Revolution and I*; *Our Nation's Path*; *Major Speeches*, all Seoul, 1962.

Pauker, G.J., 'The role of the military in Indonesia', in J. J. Johnson (ed.), *The Role of the Military in Underdeveloped Countries*, Princeton, 1962.

Pauker, G.J., 'Indonesia: the age of reason?' *Asia Survey*, February 1968.

Peres, S., *David's Sling: The Arming of Israel*, London, 1970.

Perham, M., 'Reflections on the Nigerian civil war', *Journal of International Affairs*, 46, April 1970.

Perham, M., 'Nigeria's civil war', in C. Legum and J. Drysdale, *African Contemporary Record*, London, 1969.

Perlmutter, A., *Military and Politics in Israel: Nation-Building or Role Expansion*, London, 1969.

Perlmutter, A., 'The praetorian state and the praetorian army: toward a taxonomy of civil-military relations in developing polities', *Comparative Politics*, 1, 3, April 1969.

Perlmutter, A., 'From obscurity to rule: the Syrian army and the Ba'ath party', *Western Political Quarterly*, 22, December 1969.

Pepy, M.D. 'France's relations with Africa', *African Affairs*, 69, April, 1970.

Pham Kim Ngoc, *Economic Independence for Vietnam*, Saigon, 1970.

Philips, C.H. and M.D. Wainwright (eds), *The Partition of India: Policies and Perspectives*, London, 1970.

Piel, G., 'Can our economy stand disarmament?' *Atlantic Monthly*, 210, 35, September 1962.

Pigou, A.C., *A Study of Public Finance*, London, 1947.

Pinkney, R., *Ghana Under Military Rule, 1966-1969*, London, 1972.

Polomka, P., *Indonesia Since Sukarno*, London, 1971.

Prepisch, R., 'Commercial policy in the underdeveloped countries', *American Economic Review*, May 1959.

Pryor, F.L., *Public Expenditures in Communist and Capitalist Nations*, London, 1968.

Pye, L.W., *Guerrilla Communism in Malaya: Its Social and Political Meaning*, Princeton, 1956.

Pye, L.W., 'Armies in the process of political modernisation', in J. J. Johnson (ed.), *The Role of the Military in Underdeveloped Countries*, Princeton, 1962.

Rahdu, G.M., 'The rate structure of indirect taxes in Pakistan', *Pakistan Development Review*, 4, 1964.

Rajasekhariah, A.M. and T.V. Patil, 'Soviet arms supply to Pakistan: motives and implications', *Modern Review*, 123, October 1968.

Rajon, M.S., 'Bangladesh and after', *Pacific Affairs*, 45, 2, 1972.

Ray, A., 'Iran after the coup', *Commentary*, September 1958.

Rennie, D., 'The goal that started a war', *Sunday Times*, London, 3 May 1970.

Rey, L., 'Dossier of the Indonesian drama', *New Left Review*, March-April, 1966.

Rivkin, A., *Africa and the West: Elements of a Free-World Policy*, London, 1962.

Roberts, B., 'Thailand's economy: in need of a positive lead', *Financial Times*, London, January 1972.

Robinson, R.D., *The First Turkish Republic: A Case Study in National Development*, Cambridge, Mass., 1963.

Rosenthal, E.I.J., *Islam in the Modern National State*, Cambridge, 1965.

Rustow, D.A., 'The army in the founding of the Turkish republic', *World Politics*, 9, July 1959.

Rustow, D.A., 'The military in Middle-Eastern society and politics', in S.N. Fisher (ed.), *The Military in the Middle East*, Ohio, 1961.

Sanger, P., *Insurgent Era*, Washington, 1967.

Sayeed, K.B., 'Collapse of parliamentary democracy in Pakistan', *Middle East Journal*, 13, 4, 1959.

Sayle, M., 'Cambodia: why Nixon went in', *Sunday Times*, London, 3 May 1970.

Schlesinger, A.M., *The Bitter Heritage: Vietnam and American Democracy, 1941-1966*, London, 1966.

Schuman, H., 'A note on the rapid rise of mass Bengali nationalism in East Pakistan', *American Journal of Sociology*, 78, 2, September 1972.

Seale, P., *The Struggle for Syria: A Study in Post-War Arab Politics, 1945-1958*, London, 1965.

Seers, D., *A Theory of Inflation and Growth in Underdeveloped Countries Based on the Experience of Latin America*, Oxford Economic Papers, 14, 2, 1962.

Se-Jin Kim, *The Politics of Military Revolutions in Korea*, Chapel Hill, N.C., 1971.

Sharif, M.B., *Strangers in Paradise*, London, 1970.

Shepler, and L.G. Campbell, 'United States defence expenditure abroad', *Survey of Current Business*, 49, December 1969.

Shorter, F.C., 'Military expenditure and the allocation of resources', in F.C. Shorter (ed.), *Four Studies in the Economic Development of Turkey*, London, 1967.

Shwadran, B., *The Power Struggle in Iraq*, New York, 1960.

Sieve, H., 'Can Nigeria afford its army?' *Daily Telegraph*, London, 26 October 1971.

Simon, S.W., *The Broken Triangle: Peking, Djakarta and the PKI*, Baltimore, 1969.

Singh, B., 'Some problems and prospects of international peace forces', *Australian Journal of Politics and History*, 17, 2, August 1971.

Sissons, K., 'MiGs versus Minicons', *Flying Review International*, February 1970.

Sklar, R.L., 'Political science and national integration: a radical approach', *Journal of Modern African Studies*, 5, 1, May 1967.

Sklar, R.L., 'Nigeria's politics in perspective', *Government and Opposition*, 2, 4, July-October 1967.

Skidmore, T.E., 'Failure in Brazil: from popular front to armed revolt', *Journal of Contemporary History*, 5, July 1970.

Smail, J.R., 'The military politics of North Sumatra, December 1956-October 1957', *Indonesia*, October 1968.

Smith, W.C., *Islam in Modern History*, Princeton, 1957.

Spanier, D., 'Budgeting for guns and butter', *The Times*, London, 18 November 1970.

Stanley, J. and M. Pearton, *The International Trade in Arms*, London, 1970.

Stern, J. J. and Falcon, W.P., *Growth and Development in Pakistan, 1955-1969*, Cambridge, Mass., 1970.

Stevens, S., *Broadcast No. 3: The Honourable Prime Minister*, no date, Sierra Leone High Commission, London, 1971.

Stockholm International Peace Research Institute, *The Arms Trade with the Third World*, Stockholm, 1971.

Strudwick, R., *Malaysia and Singapore: The Impact of Defence on Economic Development and Growth*, forthcoming.

Sundhausen, U., 'The military in research in Indonesian politics', *Journal of Asian Studies*, 31, 2, February 1972.

Szeskin, A., 'The areas administered by Israel: their economy and foreign trade', *Journal of World Trade Law*, 3, September-October 1970.


Tanter, R., 'Dimensions of conflict behaviour within and between nations, 1958-1960', *Journal of Conflict Resolution*, 10, 1, March 1966.

Thayer, G., *The War Business: The International Trade in Arms*, London, 1969.

Thirlwall, A.P., *Growth and Development*, London, 1972.

Thompson, W.F., 'Nigeria's way to nationhood', *Daily Telegraph*, London, 17 July 1970.

Tordoff, W., 'Tanzania: democracy and the one-party state', *Government and Opposition*, 2, 4, July-October 1967.

Torrey, G.H., *Syrian Politics and the Military, 1945-1958*, Ohio, 1964.

Totten, G.O., 'Models and the problems of internal legitimacy', in W.A. Beling and G.O. Totten (eds), *Developing Nations: Quest for a Model*, New York, 1970.

Trotsky, L., *Permanent Revolution*, London 1963.

Trotsky, L., *Problems of the Chinese Revolution*, London 1963.

Troutbeck, J., 'The revolution in Iraq', *Current History*, February 1959.

Tully, A., *CIA: The Inside Story*, New York, 1962.

Turley, W.S., 'Civil-military relations in North Vietnam', *Asia Survey*, 9, 12, December 1969.


Ulman, A.H. and F. Tachan, 'Turkish politics: the attempt to reconcile rapid modernisation with democracy', *Middle East Journal*, 19, Spring 1965.

United Nations, *The Economic Development of Latin America and its Principal Problems*, New York, 1950.

United Nations, *Basic Problems of Disarmament*, New York, 1970.

US Army, *Area Handbook for Angola*, Washington, 1967.


Vaizey, J. et al. *The Political Economy of Education*, London, 1972.

Van de Laar, A.J.M., 'Recent economic developments in Nigeria', Institute of Social Studies, The Hague, 1971.

Van der Kroef, J.M., 'The place of the army in Indonesian politics', *Eastern World*, January 1957.

Van der Kroef, J.M., 'Instability in Indonesia', *Far Eastern Survey*, April 1957.

Van der Kroef, J.M., *The Communist Party of Indonesia: Its History, Programme and Tactics*, Vancouver, 1965.

Van der Kroef, J.M. 'Indonesian Communism since the 1965 coup', *Pacific Affairs*, Spring 1970.

Van der Mehden, F., *Politics of Developing Nations*, Englewood Cliffs, N.J., 1964.

Van der Mehden, F. and C.W. Anderson, 'Political action by the military in developing areas', *Sociological Research*, 28, Winter 1961.

Van Merle, A., 'The first Indonesian parliamentary election', *Indonesia*, 9, 1956.

Vatikiotis, P.J., *The Egyptian Army in Politics: Pattern for New Nations*, Bloomington, Indiana, 1961.

Vegas, L.M., *Guerrillas in Latin America: The Techniques of the Counter-State*, New York, 1970.

Verna, R., 'Z'va Haganah Le Israel', *Armies and Weapons*, London, 1972-1973.

Vice, A., 'Massive outlays on defence do not hinder expansion', *The Times*, London, 28 September 1971.

Vietnamese Embassy, *Vietnam: Yesterday and today*, 6, 9, October 1972.

Vittachi, T., *The Fall of Sukarno*, London, 1967.


Ward, B. and P. Bauer, *Two Views on Foreign Aid*, Institute of Economic Affairs, London, 1971.

Warner, D., 'Cambodia's Achilles' Heel', *Daily Telegraph*, London, 21

June 1971.

Waterbury, J., 'Kingdom building and the control of opposition in Morocco: the monarchical uses of justice', *Government and Opposition*, 5, Winter, 1969-1970.

Welch, C.E., 'Political modernisation and the African military', in C.E. Welch, *Political Modernisation: A Reader in Comparative Political Change*, London, 1967.

Wertheim, W.F., 'Indonesia before and after the Untung coup', *Pacific Affairs*, Spring-September 1966.

Wheeler, D.L., 'The Portuguese army in Angola', *Journal of Modern African Studies*, 7, 3, October 1969.

Whitaker, P.M., 'The revolution of Portuguese Africa', *Journal of Modern African Studies*, April 1970.

Whitsan, W.W. (ed.), *The Military and Political Power in China in the 1970s*, New York, 1972.

Wilcox, W.A., 'Once again at the starting point', *Asia Survey*, 10, 2, 1970.

Wilcox, W.A., 'The Pakistan coup d'etat of 1958', *Pacific Affairs*, 38, 1965.

Young, E., *The End to Arms Control?* London, 1972.

Zolberg, A., *Creating Political Order: The Party States in West Africa*, Chicago, 1966.

Zukerman, M.E., 'Nigerian crisis: economic impact on the North', *Journal of Modern African Studies*, April 1970.

# Index

Aden, 13, 43

Afghanistan, 40, 91, 183, 320

Africa, 11, 14, 25, 32, 46, 57, 59, 62, 64, 87, 153, 163, 164, 170, 173, 184, 206, 255, 258-9, 264, 273-81, 291, 296, 311

Afrifa, General, 86

Agriculture, 198, 210, 219, 236, 241-2, 285, 286-90

aid, 9, 142-5, 210, 213-17, 233, 238-9, 244-5, 270-2, 275, 330-1

Algeria, 13, 32, 33, 41-3, 45, 46, 105, 131, 147, 181, 265, 288, 298, 309, 313, 316-17, 319, 320-1

Allende, President, x, 39, 86, 258

Almazón, General, 134-5

America, 2, 11, 18, 42, 51-2, 100, 102, 113, 117, 118, 123, 124, 136, 141-2, 160-1, 165, 172, 178, 208-9, 210-11, 214, 222, 224, 244, 246, 250-4, 258, 260, 262, 264, 268-70, 275, 284, 308-9, 329, 332

Amin, General, 62, 74, 288

Angola, 10, 274

Arab, 7, 11, 34, 40-3, 47, 78, 104-26, 154, 157, 158, 163, 170, 201, 227-40, 263, 273, 304, 305

Arakanese, 46

Aref, Abdul Saleem, Colonel, 121, 124

Argentina, 45, 48, 157, 166-7, 171, 180, 182, 288, 294, 303, 308, 309, 310-11, 312, 315, 316, 318, 320, 322-4

armed forces, 1, 7, 17, 19, 23, 31-54, 56-68, 73, 76-84, 92-3, 95, 100-3, 105, 108-9, 115, 120-1, 128-30, 135, 141-2, 143-4, 148-51, 193, 205-7, 224, 234, 268-70, 279, 285, 292, 305

arms trade, 8-9, 100-3, 117, 119, 123-4, 156-7, 170, 172, 178, 212-14, 239, 250-82, 284

Asia, 11, 14, 25, 32, 37, 47, 163-4, 173, 184, 211, 214, 217-18, 259, 296, 334

Ataturk, Kemal, President, 7, 32, 44, 137-40, 145, 152, 153

Australia, 47, 161, 164, 216, 245

Awolowo, Chief, 82

Ayida, Akene, Minister, 204

Ba'athist party, 104, 113-14, 117, 122-25

Baghdad pact, 25, 119, 123, 125

balance of payments, 194-7, 214, 222-3, 225, 238, 244, 249

Balewa, Abubaka Tafawa, Prime Minister, 80

Baluchistan, 41, 45

Banda, Hastings, President, 63

Bangladesh, 8, 37, 40, 44, 50-1, 61, 161, 185, 224, 240, 244, 249, 251, 265-6

Belgium, 244

belligerence, 163-4, 183, 184, 265

Ben Bella, 86

Bernadotte, Count, 149

Bhutto, President, 40, 44

Biafra (Nigeria), 49-51, 76-84, 158-9, 188, 190-207, 249, 251, 274, 279, 280-1
blitzkreig, ix, 160, 229
Bolivia, 29, 45, 159, 182, 187, 288, 320
Boston, Sir Henry Lightfoot, 72
Boumédienne, President, 86, 105, 147
Brazil, 45, 157-9, 171, 180, 182, 187, 288, 294, 298, 308, 310, 312, 315, 316-17, 320-2, 324
Britain, 3, 37, 62-3, 65, 74, 77-8, 90, 105, 106, 117, 118-19, 125, 149, 164, 165, 197, 205, 244, 246, 250-1, 255, 260, 264, 266, 268-70, 273, 278, 280, 281, 284, 303, 317-18
budget, 73, 101, 135-6, 142-3, 162-3, 164-73, 186, 200-2, 206-7, 291, 333
bureaucracy, 23, 65, 78, 86, 131, 236-7
Burma, 45-6, 51, 159, 162, 173, 181, 186, 288, 292, 294, 316, 320
Burundi, 45-6, 288
Busia, Dr, 88

Calles, General, 126-7, 132
Camacho, General, 134-5
Cambodia, 35, 36-7, 45, 47-9, 181, 186, 216-17, 224, 246, 254, 288, 316, 320
Cameroon, 33, 35, 39, 65, 159, 168, 179, 182, 288
Canada, 165, 172, 244
Cardenas, President, 7, 44, 86, 128-36, 139, 152-3
CENTO, 251, 254
Central African Republic, 45, 58, 182, 288
Ceylon, see Sri Lanka
Chad, 36, 39, 45, 74, 182, 288
Chile, x, 39, 159, 162, 171, 179, 180, 182, 187, 258, 288, 294, 298, 313, 316, 320
China, 17, 19, 32, 35, 46, 87, 100-2, 161, 165, 250-1, 254, 258, 267, 268-73, 275, 327, 334
Colombia, 36, 159, 162, 170, 179, 182, 187, 288, 294, 298, 299, 313, 316, 320, 323
Communism, 10, 16-17, 18-20, 35-6, 37, 43, 45-9, 52, 84, 95, 96, 97-8, 99-100, 100-3, 107, 111, 112, 114, 117, 122, 124, 147, 215, 251, 253-4, 257
Congo, Brazzaville, 45, 181, 288
consumption, 4, 8, 31, 57, 60, 191, 200, 219, 230-1, 233, 285
corruption, 31, 56-8, 91, 115, 116, 130, 195, 225
Cortadellas, General, 74
Costa Rica, 1, 39, 159, 162, 171, 186, 187
counter-insurgency, 38-9, 45-7, 158, 216, 246-9, 282
coup, military, 7, 8, 14, 22, 23-4, 25-30, 33, 38, 59, 62, 69, 72-4, 79, 84-8, 89, 92-3, 94, 102-3, 106, 107, 108-9, 113-26, 128, 134, 135, 145, 181, 188-9, 192, 195, 206, 223, 234, 245, 305
Cromwell, Oliver, 137-8
Cuba, 10, 18, 224, 255, 258, 294, 299, 309, 316, 320, 321
Cyprus, 161
Czechoslovakia, 19, 280

Dahomey, 45, 182, 288
defence expenditure, 5, 8, 9, 21, 30, 37, 47, 57-8, 73, 97, 100-2, 116, 135-6, 142-3, 155-74, 175-89, 200-1, 211, 214-15, 222, 223, 232-4, 252, 283, 293, 333
De Gaulle, 13, 263-5, 333
Denmark, 245
development, 3, 4-5, 9, 20, 27, 31, 123, 140, 143, 175, 180-1, 183, 188-9, 207, 235, 245, 248, 285-95, 321, 330-6
diamonds, 230-1

disarmament, 9, 165, 253, 326-36
Dominican Republic, 10, 294, 298-9, 300, 303, 316, 320

Ecuador, 29, 45, 159, 167, 171, 180, 182, 288, 300, 313, 316, 320
education, 5, 24, 80, 99, 151, 156, 165-74, 189, 205
Egypt, 7, 8, 2, 32, 40, 42, 44-5, 61, 77, 93-126, 132, 146, 158, 162, 163, 166-7, 169-70, 173, 178, 180, 181, 190, 234-40, 245, 248, 255, 260-5, 280-1, 288, 292, 293, 294, 296, 298, 300, 302, 304-5, 308-9, 310, 312, 313, 316, 319, 320-2, 324
El Salvador, 45, 159, 162, 167, 171, 182, 288, 294, 298-9, 300, 302, 316, 320
elections, 62-5, 71, 75, 91-3, 98, 118, 133-5, 139
elites, 3, 6, 8, 13, 23-4, 31, 44, 55-6, 58, 60, 65-7, 69, 70, 86, 125, 128, 139, 149, 206, 248, 268, 287
Eritrea, 41-3, 52, 276
Ethiopia, 40-3, 47, 50, 157, 159, 162, 167, 168, 182, 185, 274-5, 278, 298, 305, 320
exports, 100, 117, 210, 216-19, 242, 243, 254-5, 260, 261, 264, 266, 272, 281

Farouk, King, 22, 44, 108
First, Ruth, 254-5, 258-9
food, 191, 192-3, 203, 207, 243, 244, 289
Formosa, see Taiwan
forward defence area, 160, 255, 258, 264
France, 13, 20, 42, 74, 105, 208, 244, 250-1, 258, 260-4, 265, 274, 280, 284, 308, 312, 332
free officers, 22, 25, 61, 104-12, 121
Fulani, 76-7

Gabon, 39, 182
Gambia, 35
GDP/GNP, 174-83, 191, 198, 203-5, 219, 225, 230-3, 238-9, 240-3, 278, 286, 295-6, 314
Germany, 118, 165, 244, 258, 264, 304
Ghaddafy, Colonel, 96, 104, 126, 147, 228
Ghana, 7, 33, 45, 65, 70, 84-8, 131, 152, 159, 162, 168, 173, 180, 182, 184, 313, 320
Gowon, General, 82, 192
Greece, 11, 161, 255, 258-9
growth rate, 3, 4, 5, 175-89, 191, 192, 203, 204, 207, 219, 230-3, 234, 240-2
Guatemala, 45, 159, 179, 182, 185, 288, 316, 320
guerrillas, 10, 12, 13, 14, 18, 34, 35-6, 38, 41-2, 44, 48, 51, 61, 96, 158-9, 209, 225, 228, 246-8, 274, 335
Guinea, 26, 36, 39, 73-4, 87, 181, 316, 320
Guinea, Portuguese, 10, 274
Gulf states, 40-3, 164, 321
Gurion, David Ben, 148-9, 152-3
Guyana, 10, 36, 39, 183

Haiti, 10, 288
Hausa, 76-7
health, 156, 165-74, 205
Hindu, 32, 267
Hitler, Adolf, 86
Honduras, 10, 29, 159, 162, 166-7, 171, 179, 288, 298, 300, 316, 320
Hong Kong, 10, 216-18
Hopkins, Keith, 27-8
Hurewitz, J.C., 118
Huks, 35, 38
Hussein, King, 40-2

Ibo, 47, 49, 76-84
illiteracy, 172, 286-9
imports, 156-7, 191, 194-7, 210-11, 216-18, 220-3, 225,

242-3, 259-60, 261, 266, 273-5, 281, 290, 299, 310, 320

India, 14, 35, 36, 37, 38, 45, 89, 91, 161-2, 166-7, 173, 175, 181, 186, 217, 224, 240, 251, 254, 255, 258, 265-73, 274, 282, 288, 292, 294, 298, 300, 302-3, 305, 308, 309, 310, 312-13, 315, 316, 319, 320-4

Indonesia, 7, 32, 35, 37, 44-5, 47-9, 51, 61, 89, 94-103, 106, 112, 146, 152-8, 160, 162, 164, 180, 182, 186, 251, 254, 273, 288, 292, 294, 303, 306, 312-13, 316, 320-1

industrialisation, 9, 24, 62, 241, 260, 270, 282, 283, 289, 291, 314, 318

Ionu, President, 140

Iran, 40-3, 104, 119, 159, 162, 164, 179, 181, 255, 264, 292, 294, 298, 300, 309, 316-17, 320-1

Iraq, 7, 42, 45, 51, 78, 86, 93, 104, 113-26, 159, 162, 167, 169, 173, 181, 260-1, 265, 288, 298, 309, 313, 316, 320

Ironsi, General, 49, 80, 153

Islam, see Muslim

Israel, 7, 11, 22, 34, 35, 36, 39, 41, 47, 105, 106, 115, 121, 123, 126, 135, 146-54, 157-9, 163, 169-70, 173, 178, 179, 181, 190, 227-34, 238, 240, 245, 255, 261-5, 270, 292, 293, 294, 298, 299-300, 302-3, 305-6, 308-9, 312, 316, 320, 324

Italy, 102, 244, 275, 276, 303

Ivory Coast, 159, 162, 168, 179, 182, 316, 320

Jamaica, 10

Japan, 20, 35, 61, 216-18, 226, 244

Jinnah, Ali, 90

Jordan, 36, 40-2, 120, 152, 158-9, 162-3, 169-70, 181, 255, 261, 264, 288, 298, 305, 309, 320

Juxon-Smith, Lt. Colonel, 72

Kashmir, 32, 37, 91, 245, 268, 271

Kassem, Karim, General, 86, 121-5

Katanga, 50

Kenya, 33, 35, 57, 65, 68, 74, 159, 160, 162, 166-7, 168, 179, 182, 185, 276, 316, 320

Khan, Ayub, 90, 94, 245

Khan, Liquat, 90

Khan, Yahya, 245

Khmer Rouge, 48

Korea, 20, 44-5, 157, 159, 160, 162, 166-7, 173, 178, 179, 181, 209, 211, 212, 214, 216-17, 226, 234, 254, 258, 288, 292, 294, 298, 300, 302, 309, 313, 316, 320-1, 333, 334

Kuomintang, 17, 46

Kurds, 46, 51-2, 122-3

Kuwait, 238-9

labour party, 3, 34, 148, 152

Lansana, Brigadier, 71

Laos, 14, 35, 36, 181, 254, 320

Latin America, 11, 23, 29, 44, 59, 133, 157, 161, 163, 170, 186, 251, 255, 258-9, 310-11, 323, 334

Lebanon, 35, 39, 121, 158-9, 162-3, 169, 173, 182, 261, 309, 316, 320

legitimacy, 6, 12, 21-7, 35, 38-9, 54, 55, 67, 73, 98, 149, 154

Lenin, 17

Lesotho, 10, 28, 33

Liberia, 39, 159, 162, 168, 182

Libya, 32, 42, 45, 46, 62, 74, 96, 104, 126, 163, 182, 228, 239, 264, 265, 275, 288, 298, 309, 316-17, 320

Lon Nol, General, 48

Lumumba, President, 49

maintenance, 302-9, 314-15, 318-21

Malagasy Republic, 45, 182, 288, 316, 320

Malawi, 33, 39, 65, 68, 153, 159, 160, 168, 169, 173, 178, 180, 183, 185, 288, 298

Malaysia, 35, 37, 39, 46, 51, 100, 159, 160-1, 164, 173, 179, 181, 216-18, 226, 288, 298, 316-17, 320

Mali, 43, 45, 288, 296

management, 8, 22, 39, 55, 97, 156, 177, 200, 234-5, 246-8, 279, 284, 289, 292, 308

manufacturing, 9, 195, 198-200, 218-19, 241-3, 244, 282, 286, 289, 290-301, 302, 323

Mao Tse Tung, 12, 18, 19-20, 35, 84

Marcos, President, 38-9

Margai, Milton and Albert, 71

Marxism, see Trotsky

Mauritania, 39

Mauritius, 181, 288

Melman, Seymour, 328-9, 332

Menderes, President, 141

Mexico, 7, 39, 44, 86, 127-37, 141, 145, 172, 183, 288, 290, 294, 304, 312, 316, 320

Middle East, 7, 11, 14, 25, 46, 58, 77, 104-26, 142, 152, 162, 164, 173, 184, 198, 201, 251, 254, 258-65, 274, 333

military role, 3, 6-8, 44-52, 53, 55-68, 92-4, 95, 101-3, 108-9, 120-1, 132-3, 150-1, 163, 181, 188-9, 205-7, 238, 269, 273

Mirza, Iskander, 90-2, 94, 152

Mobutu, President, 49

Mohammed, Ghulan, 90

monarchy, 25-6, 40-3, 53-4, 114, 120, 121-2, 162-3

Morocco, 33, 40-3, 164, 182, 265, 288, 309, 316, 320

Mozambique, 10, 36, 274

Muhialdin, Khalid, 111

Muslim, 32, 33, 38, 89, 91, 96, 97-9, 100-3, 105-12, 146-7, 267

Mussolini, Benito, 86

Nagas, 161, 268

Nasser, President, 7, 8, 22, 40, 44-5, 78, 84, 104-26, 132, 235-6, 265

Nasution, General, 97, 101

nation-building, 59, 69, 82-3, 89, 90, 91, 147-50, 190, 207, 226

NATO, 142, 251, 264

Naxalites, 35, 38

Nazimudden, Khwaja, 90

Nazis, 2

Neguib, 108-12

Nehru, 84, 270

Netherlands, 10, 96, 100, 244

New Zealand, 47, 161, 164, 245

Nicaragua, 45, 179, 182, 288, 316, 320

Niger, 183

Nigeria, 7-8, 45, 47, 48-50, 61, 66, 69, 76-84, 90, 158-9, 160, 168, 173, 182, 188-9, 190-207, 245, 251, 279, 280-1, 286, 288, 292, 294, 298, 313, 316, 320

Nkrumah, Kwame, 22, 70, 84-8, 131, 152-3

Nuri, General, 121

Obote, President, 279

oil, xi, 105, 192-207, 216, 238-9, 249, 281

Ojukwu, Colonel, 82

one-party states, 7, 24, 33, 64, 65, 67, 75, 85, 153

opposition, 7, 33, 34, 63, 71, 75, 85, 99, 111, 122, 128

Ottoman Empire, 78, 138, 140, 145

Pakistan, 7, 8, 32, 37, 39, 40, 41, 44, 45, 50, 62, 89-93, 119, 152, 159, 161, 162, 173, 175, 179, 181, 185, 186, 190, 217-18, 224, 245-8, 251, 254, 255, 265-73, 274, 288, 292, 294, 298, 302, 305, 309, 313, 316-17, 320

Palestine, 32, 34, 41, 104, 333
Panama, 45, 179, 180, 183, 187
Paraguay, 29, 45, 180, 187, 288, 316
Pareto, V., 3, 13,
Park, General, 44-5
party states, 6, 19, 25, 33-9, 47-52, 53, 90-1, 98, 162, 328
Pathans, 45
per capita income, 27-30, 31, 175, 180-9, 230-3, 278, 285, 291
permanent revolution, see Trotsky
Perón, General, 322
Peru, 45, 159, 171, 179, 187, 288, 294, 298, 299, 300, 309, 313, 316, 320, 321
Philippines, 35, 38, 39, 47, 159, 173, 179, 182, 185, 186, 211, 212, 215, 217, 218, 224, 226, 288, 298, 316-17, 320
Pigou, Professor, 155
plan, 9, 175, 236-7, 243-5
police, 23, 24, 33, 73, 85, 87, 207
political machines, 62-5, 66, 78
Pompidou, President, 265
population, 76-7, 156, 176, 183-4, 186, 192, 205, 209, 260, 267, 285-7
Portugal, 13-14
potential defence capacity (PDC), 298-301, 308
Prebisch, R., 289
production functions, 4
Pueblo, USS, 215

Rhodesia, 10, 36, 66, 274
Rosen, Count Gustav, 281
Russia, 15, 17, 43, 51-2, 86, 100-3, 105, 107, 114-23, 128, 141, 145, 161, 165, 170, 178, 184, 234, 239, 250-5, 258, 260, 266, 268, 270, 272, 275, 279, 280, 284, 304, 310, 312, 329, 334
Rwanda, 45-6, 288

Sadat, President, 105, 106, 229
Sarawak, 37

Saudi Arabia, 40-3, 48, 164, 181, 251, 255, 264, 309, 316, 320
Senegal, 39, 182, 316-17, 319, 320
separatism, 8, 35-6, 37, 41, 42, 44, 46, 49-52, 69, 76-83, 90, 100, 159, 161, 185, 190-207, 240-5, 249, 251, 276
Siberia, 184
Sierra Leone, 7, 33, 39, 57, 69, 70-5, 87, 153, 179, 183, 185
Sihanouk, Prince, 48
Simatupang, General, 97
Singapore, 35, 39, 159, 161, 164, 216-17, 226, 320
Six Day War, 105, 149, 229-34, 261-5, 310
Shazli, General, 239
Smith, Adam, 1
socialism, 7, 15-17, 21, 51, 85-6, 99, 114, 117, 125, 148, 235
Somalia, 35, 43-4, 45, 181, 274, 305, 309, 316, 320
South Africa, 10, 251, 259-60, 274, 281
Sri Lanka, 18, 35, 38, 39, 159, 160, 162, 173, 179, 182, 185, 186, 288, 294, 298, 300, 312
Stalin, 18-19, 84, 86, 107
Stevens, Dr Siaka, 71-87
Strategic Arms Limitation Talks (SALT), 1, 329
Sudan, 45-7, 49-50, 61, 110, 126, 146, 159, 166-7, 180, 185, 274, 276, 288, 309, 316, 320
Suez, 104-5, 111, 120-1, 235, 238, 248, 260
Suharto, General, 45, 103
Sukarno, President, 22, 37, 49, 51, 84, 94, 97, 98, 99, 100, 112, 152
Sweden, 244, 281, 303, 305, 307, 308, 314-15
Switzerland, 245
Syria, 7, 23, 26, 42, 45, 46, 78, 104, 107, 113-26, 158-9, 161-2, 167, 169, 173, 178, 179, 181, 235, 261, 262,

264-5, 288, 305, 316, 320-1

Taher, Wasfi, Colonel, 121
Taiwan, 45-7, 178, 179, 181, 184,
  186, 211, 212, 254, 288, 294,
  298, 300, 316, 320, 334
Tanzania, 33, 35, 39, 57, 65, 68,
  74, 157, 159, 168, 173, 179,
  182, 185, 278-9, 316, 319, 320
taxation, 56, 100, 195, 243, 334
Thailand, 35, 37, 45-7, 159, 167,
  173, 179, 182, 185, 186, 211,
  212, 215-18, 219-25, 226, 254,
  288, 290, 292, 294, 309,
  312-16, 320-1
Tito, President, 18
Togo, 25, 45, 158-9, 168, 182,
  296
tribalism, 47-9, 55, 69-70, 76-84,
  89, 150, 188-9, 192
Trinidad, 10
Trotsky, Leon, 12-20, 67, 84,
  107, 147
Tsar, 15-16
Tunisia, 36, 39, 180, 182, 185,
  288, 298, 313, 316, 320
Turkey, 7, 11, 44, 46, 102, 117,
  119, 127, 137-46, 159, 160-2,
  167, 173, 245, 255, 258-9,
  264, 288, 292, 294, 298, 300,
  303, 308, 312

U Thant, 327
Uganda, 35, 45-6, 57, 65, 66, 74,
  157, 162, 173, 180, 182, 185,
  235, 274, 278-9, 288, 320
umbrella strategy, 333-5
United Nations, 1, 11, 20, 177,
  327, 330-2
Upper Volta, 45, 58, 180, 182,
  296

Uruguay, 36, 39, 180, 182, 288,
  316, 320

Vaizey, John, 5
Venezuela, 159, 171, 180, 182,
  187, 288, 316-17, 320
Vietnam, 2, 8, 14, 19, 34-5, 36,
  39, 45, 46-7, 147, 157, 181,
  184, 186, 190, 208-25, 245,
  246-7, 251, 254, 258-9, 261,
  274, 288, 292, 309, 320-1,
  333, 334
violence, 2, 3, 5, 9, 12-21, 24,
  31-5, 40-3, 53-4, 73, 75, 80-3,
  95, 103, 109, 111, 121-5, 126,
  131, 134, 138, 147, 156, 157,
  168, 192, 198, 248, 254, 268,
  289, 291, 317, 331, 335

Wafdists, 108, 111
war, 2, 7, 8, 13-14, 17, 20-2, 32,
  34-54, 76-84, 93, 105-6, 146,
  158-9, 160-2, 164, 188-9,
  190-249, 253, 257, 265, 268-9,
  271-2, 277, 333
weapons, 2, 8-9, 56-7, 101, 117,
  121, 123-4, 135-6, 141-4,
  156-7, 161, 172, 188, 215,
  250-62, 291-325

Yemen, 41-3, 45, 47-8, 163, 182,
  265
Yorubas, 76-7
Yugoslavia, 17-18, 123

Zaire, 45-7, 49, 180, 185, 274,
  288, 316, 320
Zambia, 33, 36, 39, 65, 68, 153,
  168, 179, 182, 184, 185, 288,
  320
Zionism, 146-9